RAND M^CNALLY

ATLAS OF
WORLD HISTORY

R A N D   M^cN A L L Y

ATLAS OF WORLD HISTORY

Rand McNally and Company

Chicago · New York · San Francisco

CONTENTS

Frontispiece: The western hemisphere as it was known or imagined at the end of the sixteenth century. It is flanked by figures of Columbus, Vespucci, Magellan and Pizarro

Rand McNally
Atlas of World History

Text © Reed Consumer Books Limited 1981, 1992, 1993
Maps © Reed Consumer Books Limited 1981, 1992, 1993
and Creative Cartography Limited 1981 except maps and
text appearing in the United States Historical Map Section,
pages 167 through 182, which are copyright by Rand
McNally & Company

This edition published 1992 in England
under the title of the Philip's Atlas of World History
by Philip's, an imprint of Reed Consumer Books

Revised edition 1993

Original cartography by Creative Cartography Limited:
Nicholas Skelton and Terry Allen.

Produced by Mandarin Offset
Printed and bound in Hong Kong

Library of Congress Cataloging-in-Publication Data

Atlas of world history
     p. cm.
   At head of title: Rand McNally.
   Includes index.
   ISBN 0-528-83567-X. – ISBN 0-528-83566-1(pbk.)
   1. Historical geography – Maps. I. Rand McNally
   and Company. II. Title: Rand McNally atlas of world
history.
G1030.R36 1993 <G&M>
911 – dc20   93-25999
                                                       CIP
                                                       MAP

The emergence of the modern world

United States Historical Maps

This chart shows the rough chronological span of each map, and serves as a guide to the coverage of each region's history in this atlas. As well as the maps indicated for each specific region, information about that region may also be found on the maps of the relevant continent, and on the world maps.

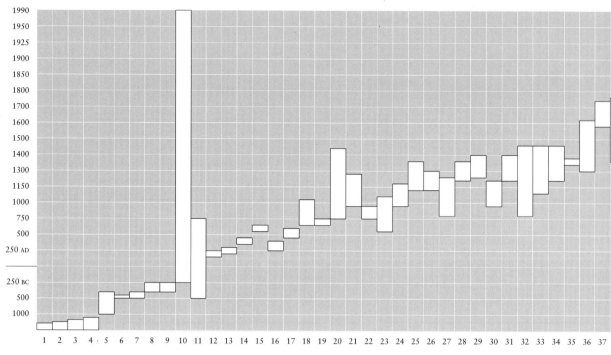

	upto1000BC	1000-460BC	460-246BC	246-1BC	AD 1-246	246-460	460-746	746-1000	1000-1146	1146-130
THE WORLD	1,2,3									
THE AMERICAS										
North America										
South America										
EUROPE				8,11	12	14	17		20	28
Scandinavia									23	
Germany and Central Europe									24	
Western Europe										25
France and the Low Countries								22		
British Isles									23	25
Spain and Portugal										
Italy										
The Mediterranean		5		8	12	14	17,19		27	
Eastern Mediterranean	4						18			26
Greece and the Balkans	4	5	7				18	21		
AFRICA				11					20	
North Africa	3						19		27	
EURASIA				11					20	
Russia								21		
Persia and Asia Minor	3	6		9		15	19		27	
INDIA	3				16					
THE FAR EAST				11					20	
China					10	13			30	
Japan										
AUSTRALASIA	1									

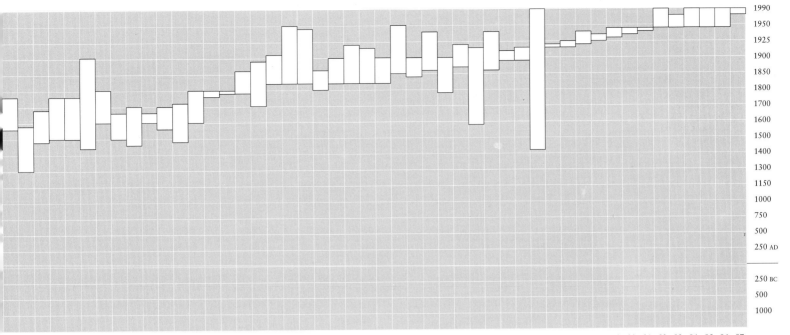

1300-1400	1400-1500	1500-1600	1600-1700	1700-1800	1800-1850	1850-1900	1900-1925	1925-1950	1950-1990	Region
	36		46			58	67		83,84,87	**THE WORLD**
				45						THE AMERICAS
			44	53	68	69		78		*North America*
			43		59					*South America*
35	48			52	55,60	57	75	78,80,81	82	**EUROPE**
			50							Scandinavia
34	42		49		61		76	77		Germany and Central Europe
		42,47								*Western Europe*
			51	54						France and the Low Countries
				56						British Isles
32										Spain and Portugal
33						62				Italy
								81		*The Mediterranean*
	39								86	Eastern Mediterranean
						63				Greece and the Balkans
			46		66		74			**AFRICA**
								81	86	*North Africa*
31										**EURASIA**
	41				70		71,76			Russia
									86	Persia and Asia Minor
29			40			65			85	**INDIA**
			37			64	73	79	85	The Far East
			38							China
						72				Japan
			46			67			87	**AUSTRALASIA**

'Show me the map of a region,' a great French geographer used to say, 'and I will tell you its history'. The greatest historians, from Herodotus in the fifth century BC to Idn Khaldun in the fourteenth century AD and Fernand Braudel in the twentieth, have emphasized the interaction of environment and human development. Enduring characteristics of states and societies have been shaped by their climate and natural resources, their topography and communications. We could no more attempt to understand the past without maps than without records.

The first business of any historical atlas is to show the development of human society in its physical setting. Ideally it should contain, in addition to historical information, much of the material of a geographical atlas, which is also indispensable for every student of history. It might show, for example, the relief, climate, soils and vegetation of the world in detail not only as they are today, but at appropriate moments in the past. But although historians, geographers and (especially) archaeologists have made great strides in these directions even since the first edition of this Atlas appeared in 1981, it is not possible to do that job systematically. The history of climate is only now taking shape. Some of the changes in the world's coastlines over the centuries, or in the courses and deltas of its rivers, have been studied in very great detail; others hardly at all. Still more distant, though by no means unattainable, are comprehensive accounts of the changes in vegetation, natural and cultivated; in the animal populations from which humans have taken food, clothing, labor and transport; in the insect ones which have ravaged them with disease, and prevented or limited their access to many areas of the globe right up to the present. All of these things are represented in this Atlas, but we are still far from the day looked forward to by the great English historian F W Maitland, when we will know enough about our ancestors to make their 'common thoughts of common things become thinkable once more'.

Nevertheless, while the maps in this volume are intended to be informative to the experienced as well as accessible to the beginner, they unhesitatingly give priority to clarity. They are meant to be attractive, to encourage the reader to linger, pondering the connections between, say, access to precious metals and the rise of the Abbasid empire, or between the aggrandisement of the French monarchy in the eighteenth century and the dissemination of French ideas. They are meant to stir the imagination as well as inform, and to provide a constant reminder of the real world in which the conflicts and controversies of the history books have taken place. Full-page or double-page maps of as many areas as possible show one or two points in the history of those areas in depth rather than many superficially; multiple insets crowded with valuable but invisible detail have been avoided wherever possible.

The selection of maps is designed to illustrate subjects which are of particular interest and importance in themselves, but also to assist the reader to form a general view of human history as a whole. Accordingly, the text offers neither detailed commentary on particular maps and the subjects which they illustrate nor a compendium of facts and dates, but a series of essays on some of the larger themes and questions, which individually may provide a historical context for a particular group of maps. Together, the text and maps present a scaffolding upon which the reader may begin to construct her or his own understanding of world history. Both maps and text are therefore selective. In principle the problems of selecting and defining subjects for treatment, of soundness of evidence, permissibility of inference and objectivity of judgement, are exactly the same in presenting world history through maps as through a written narrative. In practice they are often starker. It may be impossible to explain that two sets of apparently comparable data are of quite different orders of reliability. The fortifications of Justinian's Africa or Norman Wales, the shrines of classical Greece or Gupta India, the linguistic minorities or mining areas of nineteenth-century Europe - the members of almost any set of information - are far too numerous to be shown in full. Selection cannot be evaded: a decision to show some of the places which were bombed during the Second World War, or whose bombing had a particular tactical or strategic significance, is equally a decision not to show the bombing of many other places which might quite reasonably be held to have been equally significant or horrific. One must, therefore, approach these (or any other) maps at least as critically as one would a textbook, remembering that more exact truth about any subject than can be contained in the limits of plain statement is to be found only by consulting the specialist works devoted to them.

The theme which has guided our selection of subjects is a very simple one. At most periods of history scores, even hundreds of human societies have lived on this planet quite oblivious of one another's existence and quite unaffected by one another's doings. Today we live in a world which is inescapably, however unhappily, a single community. Its peoples increasingly tend towards uniformity in their culture and ways of life, and are inextricably bound together in their political destinies. The maps have been chosen with this inter-relationship in view, and concentrate on the forces which have contributed most directly to it. The distances between peoples have been bridged by the expansion of communities, by exploration and trade, by the search for land or precious metals. The differences between them have been broken down, often with the utmost brutality, by the imposition of domination, by conquest and the construction of systems of government, as well as by the simple necessity of cooperation; by the promulgation of religious and political ideologies which have absorbed or eliminated innumerable cults and regimes; and by the creation of literate cultures which have expressed and perpetuated the values, ideas and common bonds of ruling groups.

Concentration upon such themes inevitably seems to produce another version of the old story that history is about winners. Among the omissions, those of the many societies, especially of the ancient world, of Afria, the Americas, central and southeast Asia and Oceania, which have been the victims rather than the beneficiaries of these unifying processes, are most conspicuous, and very much to be regretted. Yet however regrettably, any view of the development of human society is inescapably dominated by the evolution, the achievements, and simply the presence of the great civilizations. It is not so easy to strike a balance between them. Europeans no longer claim the lion's share of world history as confidently as they did even a generation ago. Yet it remains true, for better or worse, that the impact of Europe on the rest of the world has been great. The formation of the world community is very largely the consequence of European expansion, imperialism, technical inventiveness and industrialization, products of the conditions and internal development of European societies. Consequently most readers will have a greater need for maps illustrating the domestic history of Europe than of other regions. Nevertheless, we no longer inhabit a world which wishes, or dares, to understand its history in terms of only one of its parts. That too is reflected in the contents and design of the volume.

The 23 contributors to this Atlas have benefited from the help and advice of several times that number of friends and colleagues in many academic fields, including the staffs of many libraries, and they have relied on the tolerance and encouragement of many wives and families, whom it is impossible to list by name.

The editor's debts are enormous; foremost to the contributors, whose willingness to undertake a novel and difficult task in a short time, many of them at the request of a stranger, has been equalled by the patience with which they have dealt with his questions and quibbles since. To say that responsibility for all errors rests with the editor alone is no mere formality, for among his many debts to the contributors not the least is for the forebearance with which they have accepted his suggestions and submitted to his judgements.

The associate editors have performed a thankless task with inexhaustible grace and good humor. Without their knowledge and judgement and their readiness to undertake the execution of a very large proportion of the maps and text, the editor's task would have been quite impossible; they are responsible for many of the Atlas's virtues and none of its defects.

I cannot sufficiently express my personal gratitude to all those who have made it possible for me to complete it, and especially, for everything they have put up with, to my wife and daughter.

Preface to the revised edition

For the 1992 edition the bibliographies were reused throughout. Map 82, *Europe since the Second World War*, was recast and redrawn, and other maps relating to the period since 1945 were revised to take account of the events of the 1980s, especially in the USSR, Eastern Europe, and the Middle East. For this edition the latter sections have been revised to take account of events up to 1993, and a new map, *The disintegration of the Soviet Union*, has been drawn. Sadly, war in the former Yugoslavia continues, and we have been unable to cover this in detail.

GENERAL EDITOR

RI Moore   *University of Newcastle upon Tyne*

ASSOCIATE EDITORS

Mark Greengrass   *University of Sheffield*
Bernard Wasserstein   *Brandeis University*

CONTRIBUTORS

Graeme Barker   *University of Leicester*
Julian Birch   *University of Sheffield*
Keith Branigan   *University of Sheffield*
JG de Casparis   *University of Leiden*
Gordon Daniels   *University of Sheffield*
JF Drinkwater   *University of Nottingham*
Mark Elvin   *St Antony's College, Oxford*
Richard Fletcher   *University of York*
Bernard Hamilton   *University of Nottingham*
Peter Hardy   *SOAS, University of London*
Robert Irwin
Colin Jones   *University of Exeter*
Edmund King   *University of Sheffield*
DO Morgan   *SOAS, University of London*
TA Reuter   *University of Southampton*
Francis Robinson   *Royal Holloway and Bedford New College, University of London*
J Roy   *University of Nottingham*
John Stevenson   *Worcester College, Oxford*
David Turley   *University of Kent*
A Wasserstein   *The Hebrew University of Jerusalem*
Henry S Wilson   *University of York*
John Woodward   *University of Sheffield*

The ancient world 1

THE BEGINNINGS OF CIVILIZATION

1 The human revolution
The earliest members of our *genus* were confined to Africa and the frost-free zones of Europe and Asia. About 40,000 years ago they were succeeded in Europe by *homo sapiens sapiens*, who spread across the world.

Fossil remains of primitive forms of man have been discovered from sites in Africa dating to the beginnings of the Pleistocene Era (the first Ice Age), at least two or three million years ago, such as Lake Turkhana and Olduvai Gorge (see Map 1), but the process of anatomical development leading up to these 'hominids' can be traced back much further, to at least fifteen million years ago.

The earliest true member of our genus, called *homo erectus*, belongs to the Middle Pleistocene period, roughly half a million years ago. Like the ancestral hominids, *homo erectus* was confined to Africa and the frost-free zones of Europe and Asia.

From about 100,000 years ago Neanderthal Man (now commonly regarded as a member of the species *homo sapiens* rather than as a divergent species) occupied much the same area of world. He was replaced in Europe about 40,000 years ago by fully modern man, *homo sapiens sapiens*. Like the earlier forms of man *homo sapiens sapiens* was a hunter-gatherer, but culturally he was more advanced – at what is termed the Upper Palaeolithic stage. He was equipped with a stone and bone technology much more sophisticated than those of earlier hunters, as well as a conceptual repertoire that included systematic burial of the dead and adornment of the living, and a fertility ideology best known from the so-called 'Venus figurines' and painted caves such as Lascaux in France and Altamira in Spain.

Modern man spread rapidly over the globe. He probably reached North America about 20,000 years ago, by means of a land bridge that existed then between Siberia and Alaska (the plain of Beringia, where the Bering Straits are now) and a corridor between the northern ice sheets of Canada and Alaska. To reach Australia by about 35,000 years ago he must have used sea-going craft of some sophistication, for no land bridge existed across the Wallace Line. All the more remarkable, the rapid expansion of modern man over the world took place at the climax of the Ice Age, when many parts of the world were ice-covered and when the temperate regions of today were extremely inhospitable. Yet, well-adapted to these severe conditions, man the hunter had colonized nearly all the ice-free parts of the globe by the end of the Ice Age, 12,000 years ago.

Gordon Childe's use of the term revolution to describe the beginnings of agriculture has been criticized because we now know that agriculture took many thousands of years to evolve in different parts of the world. Nevertheless the development

of food production remains the most revolutionary advance in prehistoric subsistence technique. The origins of agriculture probably lie in the highly specialized forms of hunting and plant collecting that had developed amongst many Palaeolithic societies by the end of the Ice Age 12,000 years ago. Three or four thousand years later there is clear evidence for farming communities in the hills of Palestine, Turkey, Iraq and Iran and in surrounding areas such as Greece and Crete, perhaps in Egypt, and in Turkmenia (*Map 2*). These regions are thought to have been the natural habitats of the wild ancestors of domesticated wheat, barley, sheep and goats – the staple crops and stock of the first farmers here. Although research has tended to concentrate in the Near East (because very early farming was expected here, given the development of the Sumerian and Egyptian civilizations by 3000 BC), current work in the Americas, the Far East and South-East Asia indicates that agricultural systems using different crops and animals may well have developed at similarly early dates, within three or four millennia of the end of the Pleistocene Era.

In the Americas, domesticated animals were by and large unimportant. Instead a wide range of plants was taken into cultivation in different areas, including avocado pears, beans, peppers, pumpkins, squashes, and maize which eventually became the major staple. In China pigs and millet were the staple resources of the first farmers, and people in New Guinea kept domesticated pigs, grew yams and taro. Later on rice became the staple crop in the Far East, and the first agriculture in sub-Saharan Africa was based mainly on cattle and millet.

Between 3000 BC, when urban life was beginning in Mesopotamia and Egypt, and the time of Christ, farming spread over the most accessible parts of the world. Many regions beyond these areas of early farming were still occupied by hunting and gathering societies, some of which have survived to modern times, such as the Aborigines of Australia and Bushmen of southern Africa. Within the farming world, also, some societies continued with the hunting and gathering way of life and others practised both types of subsistence. On the fringes of the farming world there have always been other societies practising 'intermediate' economies like the reindeer herders of Lapland and Siberia, or the Bedouin camel herders of the Arabian and Saharan deserts.

In Europe the spread of agriculture from the south-east to the north-west between 6000 and 3000 BC has long been regarded as accompanying the movement of new people – the first farmers – into a sparsely inhabited environment. In recent years, however, it has become increasingly clear that a vigorous hunter-gatherer population was living in most parts of Europe, and that the development of prehistoric agriculture in Europe has to be understood as much in terms of the adaptation of existing people to new resources (for cereals and sheep and goats must have been introduced to temperate Europe from the eastern Mediterranean) as in terms of the arrival of colonist farmers. Similarly, the beginnings of farming in other parts of the Eurasian and African continents used to be regarded as the result of the diffusion of ideas or people or both from the 'hearth area' of early agriculture in the Near East, but the variation we now see between early farming peoples across the world – different crops and animals, different farming techniques, different timescales of development – makes it clear that many prehistoric societies in different parts of the world developed agricultural systems in the millennia following the end of the Ice Age without any major stimulus from each other.

Dry farming (that is, farming without irrigation) had developed in the hills of Mesopotamia by 6000 BC. In the next two thousand years, population pressure in these hills seems to have forced the colonization of the Tigris and Euphrates plains below, where rainfall was insufficient for dry farm-

MAP 1 THE HUMAN REVOLUTION

▨	Extent of settlement by early man (Homo erectus) about half a million years ago
○	Early man sites
▨	Extent of settlement by modern man (Homo sapiens) at the end of the Pleistocene Era c.10,000 BC
◉	Modern man sites
⟶	Migration routes
▨	Extended land mass during the Pleistocene Era
▨	Areas covered by ice in the late Pleistocene Era

ing (*Map 3*). To survive, the new villages had to develop simple irrigation systems to farm the land of the Twin Rivers. The new technology both demanded higher levels of social and economic complexity and in turn allowed much higher levels of population than were possible in the hills. By 3500 BC the Sumerian civilization had evolved in lower Mesopotamia: it consisted of a collection of a dozen or so cities and their territories. The cities were dominated by temple complexes housing priestly élites who controlled a large part of the social, economic and ritual life of the city state. Writing systems were developed for accounting purposes, and craft technology attained a very high level of sophistication.

By 3000 BC a very different civilization was established in Egypt. There was a single state rather than a series of small city states, geared to the exploitation of the Nile valley by highly organized irrigation systems, controlled by a single ruler (the pharaoh) and his regional governors. By 2500 BC a third – as different – civilization emerged in the Indus valley, the Harappan. The nature of the leadership is not clear, but the cities were carefully planned on a grid system (quite unlike the Sumerian and Egyptian cities) with artisans' quarters and residential areas, well provided with drains and fresh water supplies, and with massively defended citadels containing public buildings.

These civilizations are so different from each other that the Egyptian and Indus cities must almost certainly be thought of as independent in origin rather than as the result of diffusion from Sumeria, although there is considerable evidence for systematic trade between Sumeria and both Egypt and the Indus valley. Civilization continued virtually uninterrupted in Mesopotamia and Egypt for thousands of years, up to the classical period, but the Indus state collapsed after only a few centuries, in about 1700 BC. The state system here depended on intensive irrigation agriculture, and over-exploitation of the valley may have led to soil deterioration, erosion and flooding, until the weakened state fell prey to outside attack.

The second millennium BC saw the emergence and florescence of complex state societies in Crete, mainland Greece and central Turkey (*Map 4*). In China, proto-urban societies may have developed by c.2500 BC, but the first dynasty recorded in the Chinese annals to be identified by archaeology is that of the Shang (traditionally dated 1523-1027 BC). Shang society, according to both documentary records and excavation, was extremely hierarchical and warlike. Subsistence was still based on millet and pigs rather than rice (irrigation was very limited), but craft techniques were highly sophisticated, particularly bronze casting, jade carving, pottery and silk weaving.

In the New World, complex societies emerged in Mesoamerica and Peru at the end of the first millennium BC. The Maya civilization in Mesoamerica (Guatemala, Yucatan and Belize) achieved its climax between AD 300 and 900. Massive ceremonial centres were constructed in the rain forests by a stoneage society for a priestly élite which seems to have owed much of its power to its control of the ceremonial calendar and its ability to predict astronomical events. The centres were not cities, for the ordinary people were dispersed throughout the countryside. In Peru the ceremonial centres began in the first millennium BC, but the

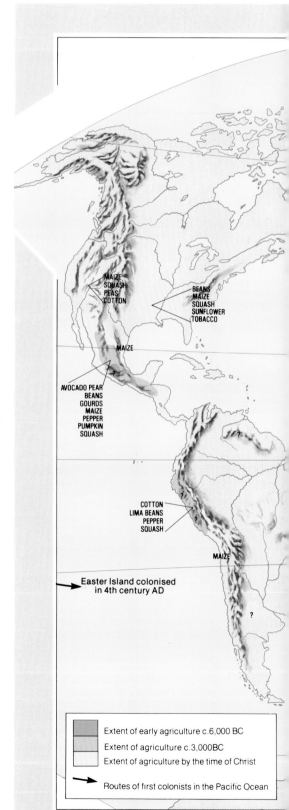

Left: The Black Obelisk. Obelisk of Shalmaneser III. King of Assyria 859-824 BC. The inscriptions record annals of the reign and show tribute being brought to the king by those he conquered.

2 The Neolithic revolution
The great prehistorian Gordon Childe coined the term 'Neolithic revolution' to describe the transformation in prehistoric society represented by the beginning of agriculture: it was to be the springboard for early civilizations in several parts of the world.

MAIZE
SQUASH
PEAS
COTTON

BEANS
MAIZE
SQUASH
SUNFLOWER
TOBACCO

MAIZE

AVOCADO PEAR
BEANS
GOURDS
MAIZE
PEPPER
PUMPKIN
SQUASH

COTTON
LIMA BEANS
PEPPER
SQUASH

MAIZE

Easter Island colonised
in 4th century AD

Extent of early agriculture c.6,000 BC

Extent of agriculture c.3,000BC

Extent of agriculture by the time of Christ

Routes of first colonists in the Pacific Ocean

Moche and Nazca states flourished at the same time as the Maya. Like the Maya they were founded on maize cultivation and were dominated by huge ceremonial centres, but on the other hand the Andean cultures were technologically more advanced, practising irrigation and bronze smithing.

By the beginning of the second millennium AD these early states had been replaced by the major imperial civilizations, the Aztecs in Mesoamerica and the Incas in Peru (see also Map 36). The fundamentals of these civilizations were much as before – monumental centres, obsessive and savage

religions, all-powerful élite groups and relatively primitive technologies. Unlike the Maya, the Aztecs built true residential cities and intensive irrigation systems in the arid highlands of Mexico. Both Aztecs and Incas controlled large imperial domains, exacting tribute from subject states, but neither was able to organize effective resistance when the Spaniards invaded and their empires were swiftly dismembered, the Aztec in 1519-1521 and the Inca in 1527-1532.

In sub-Saharan Africa, two notable prehistoric states flourished between about AD 1000 and 1500, roughly contemporary with the Aztec and

Inca civilizations. In Nigeria, stimulated by Arab caravan trade across the Sahara for gold, ivory and slaves (Map 27), complex hierarchial societies (like the Yoruba) developed in the savannah zone between the desert and coastal west Africa, best known today from the fine bronze heads of Ife made by the cire perdue technique of casting, a skill acquired from the Arab traders. In central southern Africa, the zimbabwe states developed c. AD1200-1600 out of the preceding simple agricultural societies of the African Early Iron Age, in Rhodesia and in Mozambique. Cattle were a major source of wealth for the zimbabwe rulers, who traded with

MAP 2   THE NEOLITHIC REVOLUTION

MAP 3 THE URBAN REVOLUTION

The Major Early States

EGYPTIAN OLD KINGDOM

Co

Memphis · A

Co
T

Co
A

Abydos

Thebes

Di M

Nile

0 I

	BC 3500	3000	2500	2000	1500	1000	500	0	500	1000	1500	AD
MESOPOTAMIA	1 SUMERIA											
EGYPT	2 EGYPTIAN OLD KINGDOM											
INDUS	3 HARAPPA											
CRETE	4 MINOAN											
GREECE	5 MYCENAE											
TURKEY	6 HITTITE											
CHINA	7 SHANG											
MESO AMERICA								8 MAYA		AZTEC 11		
ANDES								9 MOCHE / 10 NAZCA		INCA 12		
WEST AFRICA										YORUBA 13		
SOUTH AFRICA										ZIMBABWE 14		
	BC 3500	3000	2500	2000	1500	1000	500	0	500	1000	1500	AD

Below: More captives and spoil being brought to Ninevah (Kuyunjik), probably after the Assyrian conquest of tribes inhabiting Chaldaea or southern Babylonia.

M	Marble	**O**	Obsidian	**L**	Lapis Lazuli
A	Alabaster	**T**	Turquoise	**Tb**	Timber
C	Carnelian	**Co**	Copper	**Ld**	Lead
S	Steatite	**Si**	Silver	**Bi**	Bitumen
D	Dentalium (Mother of Pearl)	**Go**	Gold	**Di**	Diorite
		Ti	Tin	**I**	Ivory

EARLY DYNASTIC SUMERIA

INDUS VALLEY OR HARAPPAN CIVILISATION

Centre of civilisation
Extent of trading contacts

Arab and then Portuguese communities on the east coast for Arabian, Persian and Indian glass beads (and occasionally even Chinese porcelain) in exchange for gold, iron and ivory. Like the American civilizations the African states were unable to withstand European technology and military organization, although their destruction was less cataclysmic.

3 The urban revolution
Childe described the next major stage in the evolution of prehistoric societies as the 'urban revolution'. He referred mainly to the earliest civilizations of Mesopotamia, Egypt and the Indus valley, but the same revolutionary process also took place in other parts of the world.

Below: The ziggurat of the moon-god Nonna, built by Ur-Nommu (2250-2233 BC) at Ur.

Further reading: P. Mellars and C. Stringer, *The Human Revolution* (Edinburgh U. P. 1989); G. Barker, *Prehistoric Farming in Europe* (Cambridge U. P. 1985); J. Gowlett, *Ascent to Civilization* (Collins 1984); Charles L. Redman, *The Rise of Civilization* (Freeman 1978); J. G. D. Clarke, *World Prehistory in New Perspective* (Cambridge U. P., 1977); G. Daniel, *The First Civilizations* (Thames & Hudson, 1968).

The ancient world 2

THE ANCIENT MEDITERRANEAN

A fter some three thousand years of prehistoric settlement the Minoan civilization emerged in Crete around 2000 BC.

4 Minoans, Mycenaeans and Hittites; and
5 Phoenicians and Greeks
After about 2000 BC the shores and islands of the Mediterranean were gradually colonized by a succession of enterprising peoples who laid the foundations of the cultural and commercial unity upon which classical civilization was based.

The island was controlled by a series of palaces, of which the best known are Knossos, Phaistos and Mallia (*see Map 4*). Each palace, which was undefended, had a large courtyard at its focus, surrounded by elegant monumental buildings, often decorated with highly coloured frescoes. The palaces also housed workshops for craftsmen, who were especially skilled in the working of precious metals and stones, and substantial storerooms. The palaces were primarily administrative centres. Their officials organized agricultural production in the surrounding countryside, (particularly of sheep for wool, and cereals, olives and vines), the collection and storage of foodstuffs, the distribution of rations to craftsmen and agricultural workers, and trade with the outside world. The Minoan script, 'Linear A', still undeciphered, was presumably developed for the complex accounting which this 'palace economy' required.

In about 1450 BC, perhaps in the wake of a volcanic eruption on Santorini (Thera), Crete seems to have fallen under the control of the Mycenaeans, who had established themselves in mainland Greece at about 1700. Their palace architecture, craft skills and decorative arts were very similar to those of Minoan Crete. The Mycenaean script, 'Linear B', is an early form of Greek. It was also primarily an accounting device, for the administrative centres of Greece operated much the same sort of economy as those of Crete. However the Mycenaean centres were usually much smaller and closer together than the Minoan and had massive defences.

In their heyday the Mycenaeans not only controlled Crete and the Cyclades, but traded throughout the eastern Mediterranean, mainly in wine and olive oil. They set up colonies in Italy, Cyprus and the Levant. Some of the most remarkable evidence for their trade comes from a Mycenaean shipwreck with 'ox-hide ingots' (copper weights of a standard measure) discovered off Cape Gelidonya in southern Turkey. The wealth and power of the Mycenaean lords in life are spectacularly illustrated by the fabulous metalwork placed with them in death in the Shaft Graves of Mycenae.

Urban life in Anatolia began on a significant scale with the emergence of the Hittite state after 2000 BC. There had probably been petty chiefdoms in the area before that, for the treasures of the 'royal tombs' of Alaca Hüyük and Troy, dating from about 2500 BC, provide clear evidence of concentrated wealth, advanced craft skills and social hierarchy. However the process of social stratification in Anatolia was apparently accelerated by contact with the established civilization of Mesopotamia. The region was drawn into the trading networks of the higher cultures to the south-east. Shortly after 2000 BC an Assyrian colony was established outside the town of Kültepe (Hittite Kadesh) to organize the export of metal, particularly copper, back to Mesopotamia. The Hittites built a great capital city at Bogazköy (Hattusha), with massive defensive walls four miles in circumference. Perhaps their most significant achievement was their mastery of iron production, which gave them military supremacy in their time. They were far more warlike and expansionist than the Minoans and Mycenaeans, and at the height of their power sacked Babylon (destroying the Babylonian first dynasty) and defeated an Egyptian army near Kadesh.

The Minoan, Mycenaean and Hittite civilizations all collapsed in about 1200 BC, and in Egypt the system of government of the Pharaohs crumbled temporarily. The immediate cause in every region seems to have been military attack, but such raids should be regarded more as symptoms of internal disintegration than as a fundamental cause of collapse. Social and economic failure, compounded by natural disasters such as drought and disease, opened the way for the invaders. In addition, the fact that iron making had become very widely diffused in Anatolia and Asia Minor by 1000 BC not only contributed to the confusion of the following centuries, as one people after another bid for supremacy, but suggests that the loss of the Hittite monopoly of ironworking was one reason for their decline. Advanced civilization had lost its technological lead over its barbarian neighbours.

Whatever its cause, the collapse of 1200 BC inaugurated a long period of obscurity and confusion from whose debris the continuous history of Western civilization begins to emerge. By around 500 BC, the Eurasian landbridge of the Middle East and Anatolia had been subjected to a unified political domination which stretched to the edges of desert, sea and steppe, while the shores of the Mediterranean had been settled by colonists from the Levant and the Aegean (*Maps 5 and 6*). This contrast between the two great homes of classical civilization was not only geographical: the words 'Persian' and 'Greek' already stood, as they would continue to do, for 'despotism' and 'democracy'.

The Assyrian empire, which controlled the trade

Left: Phoenician ivory furniture panel depicting a lion attacking a slave, gilded and decorated with carnelians and blue enamel. The Assyrians collected Phoenician ivories. This one was thrown into a well during the sack of the Assyrian city of Nimrud in 700 BC and found 1951.

MAP 4 MINOANS, MYCENAEANS AND HITTITES

Major Minoan settlements
Major Mycenaean settlements
Possible Mycenaean colonies
Major Hittite settlements
Other Aegean and Levantine towns

0   300 km
0   200 miles

Castiglione   Scoglio del   Punta delle
               Tonno   Terrare
                    Torre Castelluccia

Thapsos

Aegean Sea

Troy
Mytilene
Thebes
Corinth   Athens
Olympia   Mycenae
Argos   Tiryns   Delos
MYCENAEANS
Pylos   Sparta
Phylakopi
Santorini

Smyrna
Sardis
Ephesus
Miletus
Trianda

HITTITES
Gordion   Bogazkoy   Alaca Hüyük
                        Alisar Hüyük
                        Kültepe
Karahüyük-   Tyana   Arslantepe
Konya   Karahüyük-
                       Elbistan
Tarsus   Adana   Carcemish
Mersin
Aleppo
Ras Shamra
Kadesh

H. Iakovos   Enkomi
Kourion

Cape Gelidonya
shipwreck

Byblos
Tell Ramad
Sidon
Tyre
Tell Abu   Megiddo
Hawan   Tell el-Farah
           Jericho
Gezer   Ghassul

MINOANS   Knossos
           Mallia
Phaistos

Mediterranean Sea

MAP 5 PHOENICIANS AND GREEKS

Phoenician colonies   Carthaginian expansion
Greek colonies   Greek colonisation
Mother cities   Greek trade
Phoenician routes   Points of conflict
Phoenician trade   Etruscan expansion

0   600 kms
0   300 miles

Atlantic
Ocean

CELTS

TIMBER
Spina
?TIN
Nicaea
Massilia
Emporiae

IBERIANS

ETRUSCANS
Alalia

COPPER
IRON
Kyme   Neapolis
Posidonia   Elea
             Metapontum
Pyxus   Laos   Sybaris
Caligari

IRON
SILVER
COPPER
GRAIN
Tartessus
Gades
Tingis   Malaca
Lixus

Ebusos

Mediterranean Sea

Drepane
Himera   Panormus
480
Utica   Selinus   Naxos
Hippo
Carthage   Gela
Hadrumetum   Syracuse
Thapsus   Malta

NUMIDIANS

SLAVES
IVORY
GOLD

Sabratha
Lepcis Magna

SCYTHIANS
Olbia
Tyras   Panticapaeum
         Phanagoria
GRAIN   Theodosia   GRAIN
TIMBER   Chersonesus
SLAVES
Istria
Tomis   Black Sea   IRON
Odessus   GOLD
Mesembria   COPPER
Apollonia
Byzantium   Sinope   Amisus
Chalcedon   Cerasus
Heracleia   Trapez
Pontica

SILVER
TIMBER
Epidamnus
Apollonia
Tarentum

Abdera   Cyzicus   PHRYGIANS
Sestus   Lampsacus
Olynthus   Abydus
Chalcis   Phocaea   LYDIANS
Megara   Eretria   Miletus   Aspendus
          Samos   Chios   GOLD   Side
Corcyra   Lesbos   METALWORK
Leucas   POTS   Samos   SLAVES
          OIL   Phaselis
GRAIN   WINE
Locri   SILVER
Rhegium   Corinth   Rhodes   IRON
Zacynthus   COPPER
          Sparta   POTS OIL   Posideum
                    WINE   (Al Mina)
GRAIN
PERFUME   TEXTILES
                                      METALWORK
                                      DYE
                                      GLASS
                                      Sidon
                                      Tyre

Apollonia
Barca   Cyrene   Naucratis
         GRAIN   GRAIN
                   Memphis
                   EGYPT
SLAVES
GOLD

17

routes between Mesopotamia and the Mediterranean from the time of Ashur-narsi-Pal (r.883-859 BC) and conquered Egypt in that of Essarhaddon (r.680-669), provided the most centralized and the most brutal government that man had yet seen. Its populations were subjugated by mass murder, deportation and enslavement on a huge scale. Assyrian governors, supported by a professional and internationally recruited army, imposed a single code of law and administration. Even more than the Medes who overthrew them, destroying their capital of Ninevah in 612, the Assyrians were the precursors of the more enduring despotism of the Persian empire.

The Achaemenids had ruled Persia as tributaries since about 700 BC. Cyrus I (r.559-29) rebelled against the Medes, capturing their capital at Ecbatana in 550. He extended his rule to the banks of the Jaxartes and, with the seizure of the Lydian kingdom and the exaction of tribute from the Greek cities of the Ionian coast, to the shores of the Aegean. The conquests of Darius I (r.521-486) completed the empire (Map 6). He established a system of imperial government which gave a common institutional and cultural heritage to the whole region. Both from the administrative districts (satrapies) of the directly ruled empire and from his subject kings he demanded a fixed annual tax. A complex bureaucracy maintained a standing army and labour forces to construct vast temples and cities, extensive irrigation works, a common coinage and the system of royal roads – the most famous running from Sardis to Susa – which both symbolized and permitted a new degree of unity and coherence. The wealth and power of the king of kings were reflected in the magnificence of his palace, the elaboration of his court ceremonials, his proclamation as immortal by his subjects, (who prostrated themselves before him in the gesture which the Greeks would long regard with contempt as the supreme expression of oriental servility), and the proliferation of harems and later of the palace eunuchs whose sinister influence would play behind the thrones of this region for the next two thousand years and more.

Oriental despotism was founded upon the physical domination of those who cultivated the land through the ruthless and large-scale centralization which was necessary to create and maintain the vital irrigation systems. The bare, steep and deeply indented shores of the Mediterranean did not require irrigation on so large a scale nor did they permit the easy expansion of communities across large areas of land. The peoples who lodged around it were compelled to independence by their isolation from each other, and to inter-dependence by the constant need to exchange men and goods across the sea.

By comparison with these fundamental bonds, the larger political structures which the wealth of the Mediterranean basin periodically called into being were ephemeral. When the Roman Empire collapsed it became apparent that, among the components into which it crumbled, those which had been created by Greek colonization between c.750 and 550 BC (Map 5) still remained distinct. They persisted, politically and culturally vital, for another thousand years (see Maps 17 and 21).

The Greeks believed that the maritime expansion of the Phoenician cities – Aradus, Byblus, Berytus, Sidon and, greatest of all, Tyre (Maps 5 and 9) – preceded their own. In fact there is no evidence that anyone traded between Greece and the Phoenician coast until the Greeks themselves founded a colony at Al Minah in the eighth century BC, or that the Greek colonies in Sicily displaced Phoenician ones. The early Phoenicians seem to have been content to trade where 'civilized' peoples had already settled, for example at Cyprus, Rhodes and Crete. The first proven colonies appeared after about 750 BC (probably following Assyrian attacks on the mother cities) in Sardinia, Sicily, Africa and Spain; those at Leptis Magna, Utica, Hadrumetum and Gades were among the first. And Gades, with its proximity to the Guadalquivir river and the metal deposits of Spain, suggests the motive. In a pattern that would appear again (compare Map 27) the Phoenicians exchanged for raw materials – slaves, ivory and above all metals – the fripperies of civilization such as metal ornaments, glassware, and the legendary purple cloth of Tyre. Phoenician colonization, in short, began at much the same time as Greek, and in much the same way, developing in response to pressures on the mother cities some time after a pattern of irregular trading had been established. Phoenician colonies, unlike those of the Greeks, were tied to their founders by an obligation to pay tribute. Carthage (traditionally founded in 814) became the effective leader of the western colonies when Tyre fell to the Assyrians in the eighth century; it then founded an empire of its own with the planting of a colony at Ibiza in 654-53 (see Map 8).

The extension of the Hellenic world to Sicily and the shores of the Black Sea was intimately bound up with the evolution of cultural unity and a measure of political co-operation among the Greeks. During the dark age around 1200, when the Dorian Greeks apparently moved southwards into Thessaly, Boeotia, Achaea, the Peloponnese and some of the islands, settlement apparently continued at some Mycenaean centres, including Crete and Athens (Map 7). According to tradition the re-occupation of the Ionian coast and islands was organized from Athens around 1000. The story may reflect a preponderance which Athens had already attained, for it was the first centre of iron-age culture in Greece.

Expansion beyond the Aegean basin followed in Mycenaean footsteps. From about 700 BC eastern goods, designs and ideas were brought from the Levant by the Euboeans. A little later they planted the first western colony at Cumae (Kyme). Others followed rapidly; the fact that Reggio and Messina were among the earliest, though not the most fertile or convenient spots available, suggests that securing supplies of metal from Etruria was an immediate objective. The unending search for metal took the Greeks to the Rhône delta, the Spanish coast and the shores of the Black Sea in the next century. Nevertheless trade was not the most important reason for their expansion. If there was a prime cause, over-population is the most likely. The severe limit which the poor soils, narrow plains and inhospitable hills of the Aegean basin set upon natural increase was perfectly clear to its inhabitants, and simple overcrowding as well as political dispute compelled many of the early colonists to leave their native cities.

Emigration produced a measure of co-operation among the Aegean communities. The colonies were founded by a relatively small number of cities. Samos, Phocaea and Miletus founded many settlements along the Black Sea and in the west, as did Chalcis and Eretria of Euboea, and Megara on the mainland. Corinth and Achaea contributed most of the colonies in Sicily and the toe and instep of Italy. Since it would be absurd to suppose that all the colonists came from these few places, they must be regarded as organizers and initiators of colonising activity on the part of others.

Westward expansion was checked by an alliance of the Etruscans and Carthaginians at Alalia, c. 540, a battle which marks the appearance of new powers in the western Mediterranean. Both would be succeeded in their turn by the Romans (Map 8). Commerce continued, however, and in return for their metals the Etruscans had already acquired, though they had not absorbed, a substantial inheritance of Greek culture in the form of metalwork, pottery and fresco painting far more advanced than they could have attempted themselves. This was what the Greeks had to exchange (in addition to their wine and olive oil, which were highly valued) for the extensive variety of goods which they imported.

The colonies not only provided the cities of Aegean Greece with an outlet for their surplus population but enabled them to support a greater one themselves, particularly as the great granaries of Sicily and Southern Italy, Egypt (through Naucratis) and the northern shores of the Black Sea were opened up. Rapidly increasing population provided the foundation for the achievements which ensured that the cultural influence of the Greeks would always surpass the limits of their political power.

6 The Achaemenid empire in Persia
The Achaemenids set up the Persian empire, established common legal and administrative arrangements and a common currency and built a system of royal roads linking the earliest centres of civilization.

7 The Greeks in the Aegean
'We sit around our sea like frogs around their pond', Socrates said of the Greeks. The people of the cities of island and mainland Greece began to come together for games and religious worship, united by a common culture and institutions rather than by political union.

Further reading P. Levi, Atlas of the Greek World (Phaidon 1970); J. Boardman etc., The Oxford History of the Classical World (Oxford U. P. 1986); M. I. Finley, The World of Odysseus (second ed. Viking Penguin 1978); J. Boardman, The Greeks Overseas (second. ed. Thames & Hudson, 1980.); N. Spivey and S. Stoddart, Etruscan Italy (Batsford 1990).

MAP 6 THE ACHAEMENID EMPIRE IN PERSIA

SCYTHIANS

Macedonia
Thrace
Darius I

IONIA
Athens
Sardis
LYDIA II
Cyrus II
PHRYGIA III
Ancyra
Royal Road
Xerxes I

ALARODIA XVIII
TIBARENE XIX
Caucasus
SAKA XV

CILICIA IV
ARMENIA XIII
Oxus
Jaxartes

CASPIA XI
PARTHIA XVI
BACTRIA XII
Bactra
Hindu-Kush

SYRIA V
Cambyses II
Euphrates
Tigris
Assyria-Babylonia IX
Rhagae
Hecatompylos
Cyrus II
GANDARA VII

Jerusalem
Arbela
Bisitun
Babylon
ELAM VIII
Ecbatana (Summer capital)
Cyrus II
MEDIA X
Zagros Mts
Cyrus II
DRANGIANA XIV
Helmand
INDIA XX
Indus

EGYPT VI
Memphis
Nile
Susa (Winter capital)
Pasargadae (Cyrus's capital)
Persepolis (Ceremonial capital)
PERSIS (Achaemenid homeland)
PARIKANIA XVII

Thebes

⊙ Achaemenid capitals	→ Achaemenid campaigns
XVI The twenty Achaemenid Satrapies according to Herodotus	Empire under Darius 1

0 600 km
0 300 miles

MAP 7 THE GREEKS IN THE AEGEAN

THRACE
Byzantium
Bosporus
Chalcedon
Propontis

Tarentum
MAGNA GRAECIA
Gulf of Tarentum
Sybaris
Croton

MACEDONIA
Pella
Amphipolis
Abdera
Thasos
CHALCIDICE
Stageiros
Olynthus
Samothrace
Imbros
Aegospotami 405 BC
Sestos
Lampsacus
Cyzicus
Abydos

Methone
Mount Olympus
Potidaea
Lemnos
Hellespont
Tenedos
PHRYGIA

Ionian Sea
Corcyra
Dodona
EPIRUS
THESSALY
Larissa
Aegean Sea
Assos

Leukas
AETOLIA
Thermopylae
Thermopylae 480 BC
Artemisium 480 BC
Skyros
Lesbos
Mytilene
MYSIA
Pergamon

Ithaca
Delphi
Chaeronea
BOEOTIA
Thebes
EUBOEA
Chalcis
Eretria
Leuktra 371 BC
Marathon
Marathon 490 BC
Chios
Phocaea
Kyme
LYDIA
Sardis
Royal Road (length 1500 miles, journey on foot between Sardis and Susa about three months)

Kephallenia
Gulf of Corinth
Plataea 479 BC
Plataea
338 BC
ATTICA
Megara
Athens
Piraeus
Andros
Samos
Clazomenae
Clarus
Ephesus

Zakynthos
ELIS
Corinth
Nemea
Salamis
Aegina
Salamis 480 BC
Tenos
Ikaria
Mycale 479 BC
Miletus
Didyma
CARIA

Olympia
ARCADIA
Mantinea
Tegea
Mycenae
Epidaurus
Troizen
ARGOLIS
Argos
Keos
Delos
Paros
Naxos
Halicarnassus
Cos
Knidos
Astypalaea

Messina
Straits of Messina
Locri
Rhegium
PELOPONNESE
MESSENIA
Sparta
LACONIA
Amorgos
Melos
Rhodos

Syracuse
Kythera

Mediterranean Sea

CRETE
Knossos
Gortyn

✕ Major battles of the Persian Wars	
✕ Other battles	
○ Pan-Hellenic Games	
⊙ Shrines and oracles	

0 200 km
0 100 miles

19

The ancient world 3

8 The rise of Rome
Three centuries of almost continuous warfare made Rome the first and last power to unite the shores of the Mediterranean under a single regime, overthrowing the empires of Carthage (destroyed 146 BC), the Seleucids (64 BC) and the Ptolemies (30 BC) and, especially in the west, garrisoning the conquered territories with colonies of Roman citizens.

The belief of the Greeks that they inhabited an island of freedom in a sea of despotism was well founded. By 500 BC the monarchies and aristocracies of heroic Greece had mostly gone, to leave a world comparatively little marked by variations of wealth and privilege.

Its free citizens were accustomed to ruling their own lives, and, except in Sparta, many slaves differed little from them in the pattern of their everyday lives, the structure of their families and the range of their occupations. The Greeks began to express a sense of community when they came together for festivals of games and music – the Olympiads were reckoned from 776 BC – and at the shrines of the most famous oracles (*Map 7*); and many of them joined together, under the leadership of Sparta and Athens, to reject Persia's demand for a general submission after the brutal suppression of the revolt of the Ionian cities (499-94), and to win the ensuing war.

The plays, the histories, the philosophy of the golden age which followed are marked by an intense curiosity about the nature of man as a social animal, possessed of the power to shape his destiny and thereby obliged to define and seek 'the good'. 'We Athenians, in our own persons, take our decisions on policy and submit them to proper discussion', Pericles, the greatest of their leaders, told his fellow citizens. 'We give our obedience to those whom we ourselves put in positions of authority.' The quest for the highest good, to which the actions of free men should be directed, is ideally depicted in the dialogues of Plato (428-347), while the results of calm enquiry into the nature of the visible world are triumphantly set out in the writings of his pupil Aristotle of Stagira (384-22). Aristotle's works, surviving in effect as lecture notes collected by his pupils, lack the charm and grace of Plato's, but they cover every branch of the knowledge of his time, from aesthetics and politics to botany and physics. Their conclusions dominated western thought for more than 2000 years and their method still does. If we fail to be startled by Aristotle's close and dispassionate observations of diligently collected facts, from which conclusions are drawn with scrupulous attention to the soundness of argument and the legitimacy of

MAP 8   THE RISE OF ROME

Roman possessions by	300BC		Imperial frontier 27BC
"	"	" 270BC	**AEGY** Roman provinces 27BC
"	"	" 200BC	Provincial boundaries and boundaries between client states
"	"	" 133BC	
"	"	" 44BC	▼ Transmarine colony founded by 27BC
"	"	" 27BC	■ Transmarine colony founded under Augustus
Client states within the Roman Empire			Extent of the Carthaginian Empire at its height
			QUADI Barbarian peoples

0 ——— 750 km
0 ——— 500 miles

deduction, or to be astounded by the absence of any appeal to the supernatural to resolve the mysteries of nature, it is because the 'father of reason' has taught us to take reason for granted. Nor did this reason defeat itself by resting on instinct. Its basis in the nature of language and knowledge themselves was examined and set forth in the logical works which remain the foundation of all rational thought.

The conquests of Aristotle's pupil Alexander of Macedon (*Map 9*) constitute another remarkable monument to the curiosity of the Greeks. Beyond destroying a Persian empire already in decay they had little political purpose or importance. After Alexander's death in 322 his empire fragmented into a shifting assortment of successor (*diadochi*) states ruled by his generals and their descendants, of which the most important were those of Egypt under the Ptolemies and Syria-Iran under the Seleucids. But Alexander's journey represented an extension of Greek civilization from the Nile to the Indus. The Achaemenids had already done much to unite this area (*Map 6*). Although the Ptolemies adopted a lighter coinage which ran through the Nile valley and the southern and western Mediterranean – the Phoenician world – there was a great expansion in the volume and regularity of the exchange of goods across this great common market, now settled by Greek communities linked to one another by the ties of language and culture (*see Map 9*).

Some of the new cities were only glorified fortresses. In many others the Greeks (who, despite some intermarriage with the existing populations, remained socially and culturally dominant) built temples, gymnasia and theatres, educated their children in Greek schools and settled disputes before Greek judges according to Greek law. The universality of their influence is attested by the foundation of the two greatest libraries of antiquity, at (Egyptian) Alexandria and Pergamum, or by the inscription which records the arrival at the frontier city of Ai Khanum, in modern Afghanistan, of a visiting lecturer from mainland Greece.

The wealth and sophistication of the Hellenistic world are most familiar today through its dynamic and often tortuous sculpture, the Venus of Milo or the Laocoön, and its mechanical ingenuities such as the lighthouse at Alexandria, the screw of Archimedes, the steam engine invented by Hero of Syracuse or the water organs and animated dolls which amused the court of the Ptolemies. But failure to develop equal skill in metallurgy prevented most of these devices from becoming more than playthings, and the lasting achievements were still in the area of theory, especially in mathematics and physics. The work of Euclid (*c*.300 BC) and Archimedes (*c*.287-212 BC) in these fields was not surpassed until the age of Descartes and Newton.

The diffusion of Greek culture in the Hellenistic age multiplied the manuscripts in which it was preserved. Many of them were copied by the technique invented at Pergamum of writing on animal skins – parchment, much more durable than papyrus – which made it possible for their contents to survive the vicissitudes of a thousand years and be taken up again by the Arabs.

The Jews, whose kingdom had been founded about 1000 BC under David, split by rival claimants, crushed by the Babylonian captivity (586-538 BC) and revived under the protection of the Achaemenids, flourished in this age of cultural exchange. The destruction of Jerusalem by Nebuchadnezzar in 587 began the dispersal (*diaspora*) which became the continuous experience of the Jews (*see Map 11*). It also gave rise to the practice of regular collective reading of the scriptures and insistence upon close observance of the Law – for the Destruction was interpreted as divine punishment for its neglect – which have con-

9 The Hellenistic world
In the footsteps of Alexander the Great, the Greeks founded scores of cities in the old Persian empire, and absorbed others at economically and strategically vital points. They created a network which connected all the known civilizations of the world, and which was completed when the Chinese opened the silk route *c*. 112 BC.

MAP 9 THE HELLENISTIC WORLD

Olbia
Tyras
Istrus
Tomi
Callatis
Odessus
Mesembria
Apollonia
Chersonesus
Panticapaeum
Phanagoria
Theodosia

ILLYRIA
THRACE
MACEDONIA
Pella
Cassandreia
Thessalonica
Lysimacheia
Larisa
Demetrias
Byzantium
Chalcedon
Heraclea
Amastris
Tius
Sinope
PAPHLA-
GONIA
Amisus
Trapezus
Eupatoria
Pharnaceia
PONTUS
Amaseia
Artaxata
ARMENIA
Caucasus

Sestus
Abydus
Lampsacus
Alexandria Troas
Ilium
Philtaereia
Mytilene
Lysimacheia
Pergamum
Cyme
Clazomenae
Delphi
Chalcis
Thebes
Athens
Corinth
Megalopolis
Argos
Messene
Sparta
Delos
Samos
Priene
Miletus
Cos
Halicarnassus
Rhodes
Crete

Nicomedia
Prusias (Cierus)
Cyzicus
Myrleia
Cius
Prusa
Nicaea
BITHYNIA
Poemanenum
Apollonia
Stratoniceia
Cadi
Nacrasa
Attaleia
Hyrcanis
Apollonis
Sardes
Eumeneia
Seleuceia-Tralles
Ephesus
Hierapolis
Stratoniceia
Laodiceia
Seleuceia
Themisonium
Attaleia
PISIDIA
Seleuceia
Ptolemais
Antiocheia
Arsinoe
Antiocheia
CILICIA
Patara
Telmessus
LYCIA
Calynda
Aspendus
Apamea (Celaenae)
Peltae
Blaundus

Ancyra
Pessinus
Docimeium
Synnada
Lysias
Antiocheia
Philomelium
PHRYGIA
Dorylaeum
Apollonia
Cecaumene
Laodiceia
Eusebeia
(Tyana)
CAPPADOCIA
Ariarathea
Eusebeia (Mazaca)
Hierapolis
(Castabala)
Antiocheia
Seleuceia
(Mopsuestia)
Antiocheia
(Adana)
Antiocheia
(Tarsus)
Antiocheia
(Mallus)
Alexandria
Issus
Nicopolis
Cyrrhus
Antiocheia
Europus
Seleuceia
Zeugma
Samosata
Apamea
Antiocheia-Edessa
(Orrhoe)
Carrhae
Antiocheia
(Nisibis)
Singara
Gaugamela
Alexandria
(Arbela)
Seleuceia

MEDIA

Haleb
Chalcis
Bambyce
Ichnae
Nicephorium
MESOPOTAMIA
Apollonia
Artemita
Chala
Epiphaneia
(Ecbatana)
Laodiceia
Heraclea
Zagros

Cyprus
Salamis
Balanea
Apamea
Lysias
Larisa (Sizara)
Epiphaneia
Arethusa
Laodiceia
Palmyra
Dura-Europus
Euphrates

Aradus
Orthosia
Tripolis
Byblus
Laodiceia (Berytus)
Sidon
Tyre
Chalcis
Arsinoe
Damascus
Seleucia
Antiocheia
Seleuceia (Abila)
Dium
Antiocheia (Gerasa)
Philadelphia
Gadara
Berenice
Samaria

Philoteria
Scythopolis
Ptolemais (Acre)
Dora
Apollonia
Joppa
Azotus (Ashdod)
Ascalon
Anthedon
Raphia
Marisa
Jerusalem
Gaza

Cyrene
CYRENAICA
Paraetonium
Alexandria
Naucratis
Siwah
Memphis

Neapolis
Seleuceia
Babylon
BABYLONIA
Tigris
Orchoe
(Uruk)
Seleuceia
(Susa)
SUSIANA
Alexandria-
Antiocheia

EGYPT
Nile
Petra
Arsinoe
Ptolemais
Thebes
ARABIA

Legend

- ● Greek cities founded before 336
- ● Greek cities founded 336-c.1BC
- ○ Non-Greek cities Hellenised 336-c.1BC
- ○ Other non-Greek sites
- ✕ Battles of Alexander
- → Alexander's route
- –·→ Return of Craterus
- – –→ Return of Nearchus
- Main routes in Asia
- Desert

500 km
300 miles

60°

70°

80°

40°

Jaxartes

Tien Shan

○ Alexandria Eschate

S O G D I A N A

Oxus

Pamirs

○ Ai Khanum

○ Antiocheia
(Merv)

○ Bactra-
Zariaspa

B A C T R I A *Kush*

Khawak
Pass

Indus

A R I A

Hindu Alexandria-ad-
Caucasum

Elburz Mts.

○ Hecatompylus

P A R T H I A

Taxila ○

Himalayas

Euopus
Rhagae)

D R A N G I A N A

○ Alexandria
(Herat)

Nicaea ○ Bucephala
○ Euthydemeia
(Sagala)

*Caspian
Gates*

Apamea ●

○ Alexandria
(Ghazni)

Hydaspes *Acesines*

*Hyphasis)
(Beas)*

I A

P E R S I S

● Demetrias

Hydraotes

40°

30°

Zaradrus

Mts.

C A R M A N I A

○ Prophtasia

Helmund

● Alexandria in Arachosia
(Kandahar)

A R A C H O S I A

30°

Methone ●

● Pasargadae

Bolan
Pass

○ Alexandria

● Persepolis

Mulla
Pass

● Alexandria

Indus

G E D R O S I A

Patala ●

I N D I A

Gerrha ●

60°

70°

20°

50°

23

MAP 10   THE EXPANSION OF THE HAN CHINESE SETTLEMENT

Areas of dense Han settlement c.2 AD

Areas of rapidly increasing Han settlement c.1000 AD

Limits of dense Han settlement at the present day

Areas of dense mixed Han and non-Han settlement at the present day

○ Capitals of the Early Empire and Early Middle Empire

○ Capitals of the Late Middle Empire

◯ Capital of the Late Empire

3000m contour line

400m contour line

Grand canal of the T'ang dynasty (7th century AD)

Grand canal of the Late Empire (15th century AD)

Great Wall of the Chin dynasty (3rd century BC)

Extension of the Han dynasty 2nd century BC)

Great Wall of the Ming dynasty (14th-16th cents. AD)

Old silk routes

Coniferous forest

Steppe

Desert

Mountain vegetation

Forest and meadow

Rain forest

0   500 km

0   300 miles

Semi-oases

Nan Shan

Kunlun Shan

Huang Ho

Northern limit of wheat cultivation

Peking

Hsien-yang
Ch'ang-an

Lo-yang K'ai-feng

Huang Ho

Northern limit of rice cultivation

Nanking

Hang-chou

Yangtze

Yangtze

Nan Ling

Si Kiang

Mekong

Sungari

Amur

Overseas migration during the second millennium AD

tributed so much to Jewish survival. In the Hellenistic age, according to the Jewish historian Josephus, 'countless myriads whose numbers cannot be ascertained' spread through Syria and Asia Minor to Armenia and the Crimea, and around the Mediterranean. The great Jewish community at Alexandria produced many distinguished philosophers and the first Greek translation of the Old Testament. This meeting of Jewish and Greek culture created the essential context, socially and intellectually, for the appearance and early development of Christianity.

Some time before the rise of the Achaemenids a new religion appeared among the peoples of the Iranian plateau. Its prophet, Zoroaster, is one of the most shadowy of religious leaders, every detail of his life and teaching being open to radically differing interpretations. Probably he preached in eastern Iran in the first half of the sixth century BC. His principal innovations were the monotheism which denounced the many gods of Iranian paganism in favour of Ahuru-Mazda, the creator, and the stark and uncompromising confrontation which he proclaimed between those who followed his teaching – the Truth – and adherents of the old cults – the Lie, perhaps reflecting the bitter hostility in eastern Iran in his time between the settled farmers of the plateau and the nomads of the steppes to whose depredations they were constantly exposed.

Zoroaster preached a universal faith commending 'good thoughts, good words, good deeds' (including either opposition to or great moderation of animal sacrifice) and offering eternal peace to the blessed and the torments of the damned to the wicked. There is little doubt that the Achaemenid kings from Darius I onwards accepted it as a religion of state, though its hostility to the older cults was considerably softened by the readmission of the worship of gods other than Ahuru-Mazda, in a subordinate position. Other religions were still tolerated, and this, together with the great extent of the Achaemenid empire, gave Zoroastrianism an influence on many other faiths, including both Judaism and Hinduism, and later Christianity and Buddhism (*see Map 11*). Its close association with the Persian empire persisted, and during the Sassanid revival (*Map 15*) it flourished again, championed from the time of Bahram I (*c.* AD 273-6) by savage persecution of the religious minorities which abounded in the Persian world. It was apparently during this second period of prosperity that Zoroastrianism, in common with Manicheeism (which under Shapur I [*d.* 273] had almost supplanted it as the official religion and spread widely through the late antique world in spite of universal persecution) developed its prophet's delineation of the war between good and evil into a theological dualism which divided creation between the realms of Light and Dark, Spirit and Flesh, inspiring a radical asceticism which left its mark on most of the world religions.

The origins of Hinduism are lost in obscurity. It grew slowly from the Vedic religions of the Aryan peoples who conquered the Indus valley about 1000 BC, and did not attain a generally accepted theology until, perhaps, about AD 500, but hints of its unique institution, the system of caste, have been found in the Harappan as well as the Aryan civilization. As Hinduism expanded it absorbed the cults of many gods and many styles of religious life. But its essential character derived from caste, the belief that people are divided into self-contained and sealed groups, or castes. Into one of them each person is born, and will marry and die within it, living scrupulously in accordance with its particular rules, prohibitions and customs, to be rewarded if merit and fortune permit by reincarnation in a higher caste. The original groups were occupational – warriors (*kshatriyas*), priests (*brahmans*), cultivators (*vaishyas*) – and among them the brahmans quickly took over the first place by proclaiming the divine origin of kingly authority. A fourth caste, those of non-Aryan origin – *shudras* – appeared very early, and beneath these four a network of subcastes was elaborated, defined by occupation and, increasingly with time and Aryan expansion, by race. Essentially a device to preserve the racial purity of the Aryan conquerors by allowing them to absorb but not to mix with the conquered peoples, caste has remained until the present day the framework of Indian social and political life.

Resentment of brahman dominance first appeared among the *shudras* and the *vaishyas*, whose importance as landowners and as the leaders of an increasingly farflung trade conflicted with their low caste. The principles of Jainism appeared perhaps a century before the birth (*c.*540 BC) of its effective prophet, Mahavira, who won a substantial following in the Ganges valley. The core of his teaching was the renunciation of killing, upon which he insisted so absolutely that his followers not only refused to eat meat but wore muslin masks over their mouths to avoid inhaling insects. It was not a creed to appeal to farmers, but it attracted, and still retains, considerable support in the merchant community.

The teaching of Gautama Buddha (born *c.*566 BC, the son of a *kshatriya* prince) was also based on the renunciation of desire. The Buddha's path, however, was not that of bodily asceticism – which he tried and found wanting – but of meditation, directed to a balanced and moderate life, cleansed of the passions which were the cause of suffering. Salvation lay in *nirvana* (extinction), freedom from the cycle of suffering, death and rebirth. Buddhism rejected caste and the idea of a personal God. It was disseminated by monks who wandered from place to place begging for alms. The universality of its appeal was expressed in its repudiation of social and even sexual distinctions (which the brahmans were emphasising increasingly) in the egalitarian organization of Buddhist monasteries and nunneries.

The decision to undertake systematic proselytisation, which eventually made Buddhism the religion of east and south-east Asia, was taken at a great council at Pataliputra in 250 BC, shortly after the conversion of Ashoka, ruler of the Maurya

Above right: A stone-rubbing of a portrait of Confucius.

10 The expansion of the Han Chinese settlement
Beginning in the first millennium BC, the expansion of the Han Chinese people and of Chinese culture from the central river valleys has been continuous for more than two thousand years. It has been closely related to the ability of the Chinese to control and exploit an extremely varied natural environment.

11 The appearance of the world religions
Between about 1000 BC and AD 500 all the formative religions and philosophies of the world except Islam established themselves as the bases of the great civilizations. Here short-term fluctuations in their influence are ignored to show the relationship between the areas in which they began and those over which they exercised permanent influence.

MAP 11 THE APPEARANCE OF THE WORLD RELIGIONS

575

c.400

450
500

ROMAN EMPIRE

Rome

Constantinople

4th cent.

ARMENIA

Edessa

Athens

Antioch

150 - 300

PERSIAN

Ctesiphon

Jerusalem

Babylon

EMP

Alexandria

NOBATAE
c.550

380 - 500

YEMEN

Socotra

ALWAH
c.580

ETHIOPIA
c.350

The Holy Land –
David to the time
of Christ

☐ Capitals of Israel and Judah
◼ Solomonic fortifications
   (10th century BC)
▓ Herodian fortresses
   (40–4BC)
○ Cities of the Philistines
   (12th-8th century BC)

0   50km
0   30 miles

Sidon

Damascus

Zarephath

Ijon

Mt Hermon

Tyre

Caesarea Phillipi

Kadesh

Dan

Achzib

Hazor

Acco

Capernaum

Bethsaida

Gennesaret

Cana

Sea of
Galilee

Tell Abu Hawam

Tiberius

Mediterranean Sea

Nazareth

Dorsaria

Megiddo

Ramoth Gilead

Caesaria

Taanach

Beth
Shan

Narbata

Salim

Dothan

Tirzah

Samaria

Succoth

Shechem

AMMON

Antipatris

Joppa

Shilo

Alexandrium

Lod

Beth-
Horon

Bethel

Rabbah

Baalath

Gezer

Mizpah

Jericho

Ashdod

Ekron

Gibeon

Cyprus

Emmaus

Jordan

Beth Shemesh

Jerusalem

Bethany

Qumran

Ashkelon

Azekah

PHILISTINES

Achzib

Bethlehem

Hyrcania

Gaza

Lachish

Hebron

Herodium

Machaerus

Dead
Sea

City of Moab

Tell Beit Mirsim

Gath

Ziklag

Masada

MOAB

Beersheba

Malatha

Christianity in Roman Empire and later
Christianity
Taoism
Buddhist missionaries
Buddhism
Judaism
Magian Zoroastrianism
Zoroastrianism
Hinduism

500 BC | 400 | 300 | 200 | 100 | 0 | 100 | 200 | 300 | 400 | 500 | 600 AD

2nd cent. BC
3rd and 2nd cents BC
2nd-4th cents AD
KOREA
372 AD
593-621 AD
JAPAN
c.500
KASHMIR
Ch'ang-an
3rd cent. BC-1st cent. AD
CHINA
NEPAL
c.250 BC   Patan
Benares   Pataliputra
RE
INDIA
pre 500
c.300-350
PYU
c.400 AD
MONS
c.400 AD
FUNAN
c 300 AD
273-36 BC
CEYLON
3rd cent. BC

Christianity important before 312
Christianity established in Roman Empire 312-92
541 Other areas converted to Christianity after 312
Christian missions
Boundaries of Hasmonaean Kingdom
Jewish diaspora c 600 BC-AD 200
Predominantly Zoroastrian throughout period
Magian Zoroastrianism established by Sassanids (AD 226-650)
Predominantly Hindu throughout period
Hindu influences in areas of other religions
Buddhism predominant from 3rd cent BC
620 Converted to Buddhism subsequently
Buddhist missions
Confucianism established from c 200 BC
Taoism widely held popular religion

0 |———| 1000 km
0 |———| 600 miles

The Ganges valley in the time of the Buddha

KOSALA
Kapilavastu   Kusinagara
Sravasti
Ayodhya   Kasia   Mithila   VIDEHA
MALLA   Vaisali
Yamuna   Sarnath   KASI   Champa
Kaushambi   Kasi   Ganges   Pataliputra   ANGA
(Benares)   MAGADHA   Rajgir
Gaya

0 |———| 300 km
0 |———| 200 miles

27

empire from about 272 to 231. Ashoka was converted through revulsion from the bloodshed of the wars he himself had waged to gain control of the trade routes to the south. He distinguished clearly between his personal conviction and his imperial duty, as he saw it, to treat all religions with impartial respect. Nevertheless the association between the evolution of the world religions and the appearance of great political structures is more than coincidence. Between the accession of Chandragupta Maurya in 321 BC and the death of Ashoka, the Mauryan emperors used their control of the Ganges and Indus valleys to bring under their sway an area which stretched from territory beyond the Indus, recovered from the Seleucids, to the far south of the sub-continent. The rock and pillar inscriptions of Ashoka not only show the extent of his influence (*Map 16*) but illustrate the spirit in which it was exercised. In several languages, including Greek, they command religious tolerance, respect for human dignity and gratitude for the benevolence of a paternal ruler. His messages were designed to promote unity in a heterogeneous kingdom hastily assembled, but ruled with a sophistication which stretched from collecting taxes and maintaining communications to creating an imperial espionage service and planting banyan trees along the road to give shade to travellers. This degree of political evolution, common to the cradles of all the great religions, not only created conditions in which they could spread and flourish, but rested on a degree of homogeneity among those who made the systems of government work, and their ability to express and share values which were necessarily more abstract and reflective than the blood-stained cults of warrior kings.

Chinese civilization too began to assume its familiar aspect during the first millennium BC. The Chou dynasty, which replaced the Shang probably in 1027, presided over a world effectively ruled by a nobility which gave it formal allegiance. Traditionally the nobles owed their lands to the king and gave him military service in return. The very emptiness of his power in practice suggests that it was some sense of community among the Chinese that led them to acknowledge his rule. This allegiance remained a fiction until the Age of the Warring States (481-221 BC) ended when the warrior state of Ch'in swallowed all the rest, to be replaced after only fourteen years by the real founders of imperial China, the Han (*Map 13*).

Behind these events the permanent features of Chinese society were already evident. The expansion of civilization which has been the central thread of 2000 years' development (*see Map 10*) was already in progress. Increasing activity in the Huang-ho valley by the seventh century BC was quickly followed by the first stages of the conquest of the south. The wealth of this warlike and sophisticated world was produced by a vast peasant labour force – this was already the world's most

12 The Roman Empire at its height
By AD 211 the Roman Empire had expanded to fill its natural frontiers, completed where necessary by man-made barriers. Within them the whole empire was now subjected to a uniform system of administration whose important centres were connected by a network of roads radiating from Rome.

populous region – tied to the land in subjection to the nobles. To judge from the beauty of their pottery, painting and bronzes (the art of bronze-casting had been inherited from the Shang) and from the importance which they attached to literacy, this nobility was already more than a simple warrior caste. By 800 BC it had assumed the twin responsibilities of organising government and conducting the worship of its ancestors according to the traditional rites. In consequence China had no need of, and never developed, a specialized priestly class.

The preoccupations of the nobility shaped its philosophies. By around 500 BC three attitudes to the relations between the individuals and the state had become apparent: henceforth they would compete for influence over the government of China. Rejection was represented by the Taoists who, inspired by the fifth-century teacher Lao-tze, advocated complete withdrawal from worldly affairs to submit, in contemplative calm, to the Way (*Tao*), the cosmic principle that sustained the harmony of the universe. Lao-tze said that his disciple should know of the existence of villages beyond his own he would hear their cocks crow in the morning.

The Taoists in a sense sidestepped the great debate of the Age of Warring States. The Legalists sought order through a universal system of law to which all men should be held subject by the authority of a powerful, centralized state. On these principles the Ch'in dynasty (221-206 BC) made a determined assault upon the fragmentation which was blamed for the years of war. The old kingdoms were broken up and replaced by administrative districts with different boundaries; the nobles were transported and the peasants upon whom their power had rested were freed. To destroy local customs and loyalties all libraries in private hands were ordered to be destroyed. Uniform weights and measures were introduced, the script (which, by denoting ideas rather than sounds has enabled Chinese of different regions to communicate freely without being able to understand one another's dialect) was simplified and standardized, and the first Great Wall was completed to keep out barbarian horsemen (*Map 10*).

The death of Shih Huang Ti, the First Emperor – as he justly called himself – in 209 BC was followed by rebellion and the fall of his dynasty, but he had already laid the foundations of the unity which the Han achieved. They adopted the principles of Kung Fu-tzu – Confucius (551-479 BC) – who had looked not to the force of law, but to the power and example of tradition, enshrined in scrupulous adherence to precedent and diligent observance of ritual. Confucius and his followers put their trust in the disinterested skills of bureaucrats, honest and modest in their conduct, and carefully inculcated with the values of loyalty and justice through the study of the literary classics. 'Documents, conduct, loyalty, faithfulness' were their watchwords. Under the Han, classical works were recovered and recopied, and a new literature created whose leading achievement was the inauguration of the series of official dynastic histories. By recording in detail the wise acts of successful emperors and officials, and the errors of foolish ones – as the Confucian historians saw them – these embodied

the code of the official class and became the repositaries of a tradition of government which lasted until this century. Local officials were carefully trained, and though most were still appointed on the recommendation of nobles and other officials, recruitment by public examinations, perhaps China's most remarkable gift to the modern world, was begun.

The Confucian tradition, elaborated by generations of disciples (among whom Mencius, in the fourth century BC, emphasized that the welfare of all mankind must be the goal of good government) has been almost as much the formative thread of

Chinese as Hinduism has of Indian history. In sharp contrast Confucianism has no interest in the supernatural. Even the worship of the ancestors is explicitly recommended as reinforcing the values of the ruling class, and of the here and now.

Confucianism and Legalism both took for granted what was already the most remarkable thing about China, the idea that the cultural unity of this vast area, with its great variety of soils and terrains, its extremes of climate and profusion of peoples, was more important than the political powers which rose and fell upon it. The Chinese, like the Greeks, defined barbarians as those who did not speak their language. Unlike the Greeks they were isolated from other advanced peoples by distance and the immense physical barriers which surrounded them. By the time their isolation was breached they were secure in the conviction of their superiority to the rest of mankind. This belief remained unshaken by the occasional necessity to submit to barbarian power until Chinese culture could absorb it. When the Chinese entered into contact with the European powers in the nineteenth century it was to accept not diplomatic relations, but tribute.

Further reading: C. Blunden and M. Elvin, *Cultural Atlas of China* (Phaidon 1983; Facts on File); R. Dawson (ed.) *The Legacy of China* (Oxford U. P. 1964); A. L. Basham, *The Wonder that was India*, (third ed. Sidgwick and Jackson 1978); A. Andrewes, *Greek Society* (Penguin 1971; Norton); R. Lane Fox, Alexander the Great (Allen Lane, 1973); R. Ghirshman, Iran (Penguin, 1978).

MAP 12   THE ROMAN EMPIRE AT ITS HEIGHT

The ancient world 4

By the last centuries BC the political systems of the regions of the most ancient civilizations (see Map 3) had proved able to survive their creators by absorbing conquerors. Iran was ruled by Greeks (under the Seleucids) and Parthians (from 247 BC to AD 227) much as it had been by the Achaemenids, whose tax-gathering system and claim to divinity were taken over with equal nonchalance.

The shores of the Mediterranean and the banks of the Ganges and the Yellow River now became in their turn the seats of empires which future rulers in those regions would strive to imitate and aspire to restore.

From 206 BC to AD 9 and from AD 25 to 220 the Han – the longest-lived of China's dynasties and the only one to regain power – extended the reach of imperial government southward to control the coast as far as the Gulf of Tonkin, introduced Chinese civilization to Korea, and drove the nomads of the steppes back beyond the Gobi desert to take control of the caravan routes which brought China for the first time into contact with the west (*Map 13*). Political unity and improving communications – road and canal systems had been developing for centuries, more often for military and political than for commercial reasons, and had been greatly extended and systematized by the first Ch'in emperor shortly before 200 BC – stimulated trade, and created a cash economy and a wealthy merchant class. The Emperor Wu (*r*.140-86 BC) made minting and the distribution of salt state monopolies, and made part of the land tax payable in grain which could be stored for redistribution in times of famine, offsetting one of the commonest causes of revolt.

The vision of empire had been left to India by the Mauryas in the third century BC. It was most nearly realized by Candra Gupta (*c*.AD 320-35) and his successors. The Guptas ruled the densely populated Ganges valley directly, but their influence over much of the rest of the subcontinent was expressed through a network of tributaries and alliances reminiscent of the relations of the Chinese and Roman empires with the barbarian peoples beyond their boundaries (*see Map 16*). The ensuing stability contributed to a marked increase in the prosperity of the privileged classes, and with it an opulent flowering of sculpture, building and literature which made the fourth and fifth centuries AD the golden age of Hindu culture.

The drama of the rise and fall of empires tends to obscure their nature, which is more truthfully shown by their internal than by their external frontiers. *Map 10* shows how the Han Chinese

people, who carried Chinese culture with them as they spread from their homeland in the Yellow River basin, advanced gradually through the most fertile and accessible country, while above them on the mountains and beyond them in the rain forests of the tropical south lived peoples who were very slowly – or never – assimilated into Chinese civilization. In India disease exacerbated and caste acknowledged the same failure of conquest to eradicate multiplicity, and in Europe the spectacular expansion of the Roman empire along its roads and through its cities conceals the reality of peoples of mountain and forest remaining effectively untouched by the march of Roman civilization.

The great empires rested on the ability to exploit the process of colonization, the formation of settlements to become agricultural centres. The expansion of the Han Chinese is paralleled by that of the Romans, who conquered the neighbourhood of Latium in 498-93 BC. Their progress was temporarily checked when the Celts sacked the city in 387 BC, but after regrouping their allies they launched the series of wars that made them masters of Italy south of the Po by 272 BC, and then of the Mediterranean and of western Europe (*see Map 8*). At each victory the Romans annexed territory and peopled it with colonists, at first as individual settlers and later in heavily fortified self-governing towns with the right to control the land (*territorium*) around them. Thus they provided land for Roman citizens, defence of the conquered territories, and bases for further expansion.

The process of conquest transformed the conquerors. The very precariousness of Rome's early existence helped to shape a society for which warfare was not an occasional expedient but a normal, even necessary, part of its life. Expansion confirmed the pattern. There were perhaps only four or five years in which Rome was not at war between 327 and 241 BC, and perhaps ten in the next century and a half. This was too great a burden for a peasant economy to bear. In the prolonged absence of their proprietors, small farms went unworked. The ruin of many was completed by the devastation of southern Italy in the war of 218-201 BC against Hannibal and perpetuated

13 China under the Early Empire
Under its longest-lived dynasty, the Han (206 BC-AD 9, AD 25-220), the economic, administrative and cultural foundations of Chinese unity were laid securely enough for it to survive the fragmentation of the third century and re-emerge under the leadership of the highly developed north.

when expansion in the wake of that victory took Roman armies ever further from home and for ever longer periods (*see Map 8*). In the second century BC periods of conscription of ten to sixteen years were normal, to support an army which has been estimated at about one-eighth of all citizens, one of the highest proportions ever known.

The victories which ruined the peasantry brought immense gains to the generals. Vast fortunes were created by the spoils of war and the pillaging of the provinces which followed. Much of the loot was invested in land which the peasantry was being forced to abandon. lt was stocked

instead with slaves, of whom the wars created a plentiful supply; great factory farms (*latifundia*) were built up, producing specialized crops and large profits, owned by syndicates of shareholders who probably never set eyes on them. Such holdings soon dominated the agriculture of southern Italy and Sicily and became widespread throughout the western empire.

The republican constitution of early Rome could not stand the strain. The dispossessed drifted into the city to live off the public dole of corn, and provide in the mob a reservoir of discontent and instability. The professionalisation of the army

followed the destruction of its citizen base – the property qualification for military service was abolished in 107 BC – and this created an even more tempting instrument for the ambitious. The immense fortunes of the few, renewed by conquest and dissipated in display and competition for office, fuelled political jobbery on a dizzying scale. The restoration of the peasantry through redistribution of land was the only solution, as Tiberius and Gaius Gracchus saw; their deaths, in 123 and 121 BC, showed that the oligarchy would not accept it. A century of bloody warfare across the Roman world followed, as the generals bid in turn

MAP 13 CHINA UNDER THE EARLY EMPIRE

Frontiers of Western Han dynasty (late 2nd century BC)

Frontiers of Three Kingdoms, AD 220-280

Areas under Chinese control during 1st century BC

nan Non-Chinese peoples

l A l Non-Chinese states

⊙ National capital

◐ Cities: Former Han only

◑ Later Han only

?○ Location doubtful

Transport and irrigation canals

Main commercial routes

Ⓢ Centres of salt production

▮ Centres of iron production

◆ Other industries

Areas of intensive agriculture

Min River irrigation system

Areas flooded in AD 11

Delta lands built up after the Han period

500km

300 miles

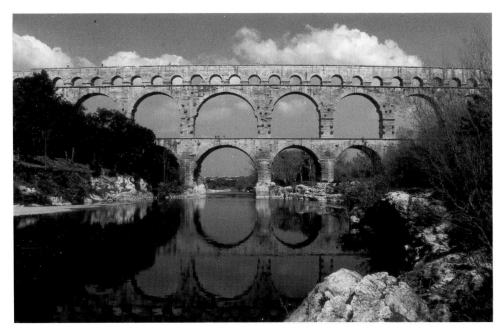

prey to the now-familiar combination of peasant revolts, ambitious princes and invading barbarians. The permanence of Rome was also illusory. Expansion of the frontiers did not end with Augustus, as he had intended. There were still client states to be reduced, restless neighbours and outsiders to be subdued. The victories of Trajan (r.98-117) were as spectacular as those of any of his predecessors, and it took his successors another century to bring the frontier to natural limits and consolidate control within them in the fortress-empire of Septimius Severus (*Map 12*).

In 212, the year after his death, all free inhabi-

for supreme power. It ended only with the overthrow of the republic, the brief dictatorship of Caesar, and the inauguration of the Empire and reorganization of its government during the long reign of Augustus (*r.*27 BC-AD 14).

The burden of military service affected the Chinese peasantry in much the same way as the Roman. The cost of raising and supplying huge armies precipitated the revolts and civil war in which the Ch'in dynasty failed. The defence of the great walls was a heavy drain on manpower, and the maintenance of the growing administration drained the taxes. The free peasant economy gave way to *latifundia* – in effect – in which merchants and officials invested their profits. The Emperor Wu, though, unlike the Gracchi, was strong enough to carry out extensive confiscations of land. These weakened the princes and created a reserve of land for granting to small proprietors, though in practice they were more often used to reward favourites and hangers-on. But Wu's northward expansion against the barbarian threat produced, as he feared, just the consequences that his land policy was designed to avert. By AD 9 famine, peasant revolt and aristocratic turbulence brought his dynasty down. It was restored, in AD 25, by a coalition of magnates, and under the Later Han the growth of great estates and the reduction of the peasantry to personal dependence on the proprietors again continued unchecked.

From the borders of Scotland to the Sinai desert, from Tangier to the Black Sea, the physical remains of the Roman Empire are more numerous, more massive and more durable by far than those of any other civilization. Their roads still carry traffic, their aqueducts water, their drains sewage. These are the visible fruits of the Augustan Peace and the end of the long struggle of the Romans to win their empire, and among them to control it. The piecemeal structure which left each province as it was won to be looted by its governor was replaced by a unitary administration (*compare Maps 8 and 12*). Cities were planted over the western Empire of a new size, with water supplies, baths, theatres and markets. Superb communications and internal order – the Mediterranean was freer of piracy in the

first two centuries AD than it would be again before the nineteenth century – permitted a wide circulation of goods within the Empire. International trade was swollen as Rome exchanged its wines and pottery, its glass and precious metals, for the furs and amber of the northern barbarians, the spices, jewels, textiles and dancing girls of India, and, at times, the silks of China.

Since their imposing and intricately decorated buildings were of wood and their finest paintings on silk the physical remains of the Han are less imposing, although nothing Roman matched the magnificence of the Han tombs and their contents. In China too restoration was immediately successful. The Later Han recovered control of the northern frontier and the central Asian territories and routes, resumed the colonization of the south, and presided over an epoch of commercial expansion and cultural brilliance. In AD 166 the Emperor received men who claimed to be envoys of the western ruler An Tun (Marcus Aurelius Antoninus), though he suspected that they were only merchants trying to smooth their path.

At that moment it seemed that both empires had attained a secure height of splendid achievement. But their problems had been evaded, not solved. The maintenance of armies, the defence of the walls and the support of the bureaucracy still, in both empires, laid an insupportable burden on the peasantry. In both, land and power accumulated in the hands of magnates increasingly able to evade imperial control and taxation, thus transferring these burdens ever more relentlessly to the shoulders of the primary producers. The pressure of barbarians on the frontiers hastened the process of internal dissolution.

By the time a real envoy from Rome reached China in AD 226 the Han empire had fallen apart,

Above: The Pont du Gard, built in 19 BC to carry water from the River Eure to Nîmes

14 The later Roman Empire
The Emperors Diocletian (*r.* 284-30s) and Constantine (*r.* 312-337) overhauled the administration, and divided the Empire between East and West, but failed to make it either strong enough to prevent entry of peoples living beyond its frontiers or flexible enough to absorb them.

Imperial frontier in AD 395
Disputed areas
Asia   Proconsular governships
∟LIA   Diocese
Boundary of diocese
Boundary of Praetorian prefecture
Praetorian prefecture of the Gauls
  "   "   " Italy and Africa
  "   "   " Illyricum
  "   "   " East
Division of Empire in AD 395
Imperial capital
Frontier "sub-capital"
Diocesan capital

0   600 km
0   400 miles

tants of the empire were granted citizenship. But in 251 the Emperor Decius was killed by Goths who had crossed the Danube, and in the next two decades every frontier collapsed, Persia under the newly established Sassanid dynasty again became a formidable threat (*see Map 15*), and raiders on sea and land penetrated the heart of the Empire. Rome was saved by military takeover. A succession of common soldiers culminating with Diocletian (*r.284-305*) seized the throne, excluded the aristocracy from military command, doubled the size of the army (to some 600,000 men), imposed a rigid and detailed direction of labour, and radically

decentralized the government of the Empire (*Map 14*). These measures gained for it another century of life, one of the most brilliant and fascinating in its history, though increasingly based on the wealthier and more populous eastern part of the Empire and its new capital at Constantinople. But the fundamental problems were aggravated, especially in the west, where population declined, land went out of cultivation, trade declined and cities shrank. The Empire had not changed its nature, or made life bearable for those who bore it on their backs, and they showed no inclination to save it by resisting new invasions. 'What are kingdoms if not great

robberies?' asked Augustine of Hippo, one of the ornaments of late antique culture. Writing a few years after the Visigoths had sacked Rome in AD 410, he knew that the answer was – nothing.

Further reading: J. Gernet, *A History of Chinese Civilization* (Cambridge U. P. 1982); A. Cotterell, *The First Emperor of China* (Macmillan 1981; Viking Penguin); R. Thapar, *A History of India*, vol. 1 (Penguin 1966); P. Garnsey and R. Saller, *The Roman Empire* (Duckworth 1987; University of California Press); K. Hopkins, *Conquerors and Slaves* (Cambridge U. P. 1978); R. N. Frye, *The Heritage of Persia* (Weidenfeld and Nicolson 1983)

MAP 14   THE LATER ROMAN EMPIRE

The ancient world 5

EMPIRES AND BARBARIANS

The Ottoman conquest of the Byzantine Empire in the fifteenth century and the Manchu of Ming China in the seventeenth (Maps 37 and 43) were the last of the barbarian invasions. Since then the backward peoples of the world have retreated before the advanced.

Formerly, though the frontiers of civilization always tended to expand in the long run, they were always liable to collapse before the invader, and known to be so by those who lived within them. The decline of the great empires of antiquity was one of the most momentous and has remained one of the most discussed of these collapses. In AD 316 northern China was overrun by the Hsiung-nu, who divided it into several kingdoms. Between 375 and about 410 several peoples crossed the Roman frontiers, this time to stay (see Maps 14 and 17). Throughout the fifth century the Hephthalites (misleadingly called White Huns) launched campaigns against Bactria which eventually forced the reorganization of the Sassanid empire on a strictly military footing under Khosrau I (Map 15) and they are often credited with the collapse of the Indian empire of the Guptas.

It is easy to exaggerate. The Gupta emperors, whose influence outside the Ganges and Indus valleys was so indeterminate that its decline hardly requires explanation (Map 16), were already facing disaffection among their underlings, and had been forced to debase their coinage before the attacks became serious in the middle of the fifth century AD. The Sassanid empire, after spectacular expansion in the two centuries after its foundation in AD 226, was riven by disputed succession, aristocratic faction, bitter social division and religious animosity (compare Map 11). The fragmentation of northern China reflected Chinese social divisions as well as the rivalries of the barbarian tribes, who were thoroughly siniticised by contact and often by inclination. When one of them, the Toba, became strong enough to reunite the region and found the Northern Wei dynasty (439-535) they adopted Chinese ways in agriculture and administration, manners and dress, made Chinese the language of their court and moved their capital to Lo-yang (see Map 13). Throughout this period traditional education, literature and the arts flourished in China, as they did in India and Persia. Only in the western Roman world did the end of a political regime threaten that of the culture which had accompanied it.

The western barbarians admired the Romans. The Goths adopted the Arian form of Christianity, for example, not because it was anti-Roman but, on the contrary, because when their apostle Ulfilas was consecrated in 341, Arian teaching was that commended by the court and bishops of Constantinople. Later the Romans used the 'heresy' of the barbarians as a rationalization of the same aloofness that made them refuse to receive ambassadors from the Visigoths before the battle of Adrianople in 379 at which the Emperor Valens was killed, or to discuss food supplies with them outside the walls of Rome in 410 before the city was sacked. The barbarians set up their own kingdoms inside the western empire during the fifth century not from choice, but because they were denied assimilation.

When Justinian became emperor in Constantinople in 527 the west was the most hopeful spot on his horizon. Theodoric the Ostrogoth had ruled Italy as an imperia nominee from 493 to 526 in the spirit of his famous saying that 'Every Goth wants to be a Roman; only a poor Roman would want to be a Goth.' Gaul was dominated by the sons of Clovis, who had accepted baptism from Catholic bishops and a consular robe from the Emperor Anastasius (see Map 17). By contrast the Danube frontier was heavily pressed by Avars and Slavs and war had just broken out with the old enemy, Persia, formidably strong again under Khosrau I. Worst of all, generations of imperial incompetence had allowed great stretches of territory to fall under the unfettered domination of noble families, and through conceding or selling to the magnates the right to make appointments (the suffragium) seen the imperial bureaucracy itself become simply an expensive extension of their privilege.

Justinian's claim to greatness is that he tried to dismantle that privilege, his misfortune that his propaganda still disguises it. His quaestor Tribonian renewed the basis of imperial authority with a new, and as it turned out definitive, codification of Roman law, the Corpus Juris Civilis. His praetorian prefect, John the Cappadocian, overhauled the administration: Justinian's enemies said that he kept a torture chamber beneath the palace, to make the rich pay their taxes. His general, Belisarius, sustained imperial prestige and won rich rewards at little cost by reconquering the provinces of Africa (533-4) and Italy (535-40). It was a bold strategy which nearly worked. But in 540 Khosrau I attacked, breaking the 'eternal peace' for which he had been handsomely paid in 532, and the Slavs took the opportunity to cross the Danube. In 542 plague killed perhaps a quarter of the population of the Empire, and, recurring every few years, left armies devastated, land uncultivated and taxes unpayable. The struggle for survival destroyed Justinian's policy. While vast sums were raised to man and fortify the Persian and Danube frontiers the reconquered provinces rebelled and Italy became the Vietnam of the age; Slav incursions became ever deeper and more frequent, the Persian threat more ominous; and to resist them posts and power were once more mortgaged to the magnates, this time irredeemably.

Like many radical reformers Justinian pretended only devotion to the past, seeking the loyalty of his subjects by proclaiming his intention to restore the Roman Empire, and that of the bishops by professing a fervent concern for Catholic unity. In fact what he conquered was the old Greek world, soon to shrink almost to its ancient extent (compare Maps 17, 5 and 20). He gave it a law, a tradition of imperial absolutism in church and state, and, through the public and religious buildings which he everywhere erected or inspired, a uniform and magnificent art. He failed to rescue it from the rapacity of its aristocracy.

15 The Sassanid empire in Persia
The Sassanid revolution against the Parthian kings in AD 224 brought to power a dynasty which, seeing itself as successor to the Achaemenids, created a powerful and highly centralized state in Persia. It expanded to take over the Kushan empire to the east and present a growing threat to Rome in the west, especially after its reorganization by Khosrau I. The Hephthalites, or White Huns, were nomad invaders from the steppes.

16 The empire of the Guptas in India
The Gupta empire was the first native state to establish itself since the fall of the Mauryas – the extent of whose empire is indicated by the inscriptions of Ashoka – in 180 BC. It based its power on the Ganges valley and at its height exercised a hegemony over much of the sub-continent through a variety of links of which few were permanent.

Background illustration: Tartars travelling on horseback. Attributed to Li Tsuan Hua, Chinese tenth century

17 The world of late antiquity
The distribution of population – though the figures given are highly conjectural – reflects a lasting division between the Greek, Roman and barbarian worlds which reappeared as the Roman Empire disintegrated and the struggle for political and cultural leadership intensified. The 'frontier of literacy' shows the northern limit in Gaul of inscriptions and other indications of secular literacy.

Further reading: Peter Brown, *The World of Late Antiquity* (second ed. Thames and Hudson, Norton 1989); Ramsey Macmullen, *Corruption and the Decline of Rome* (Yale U. P.); Patrick Geary, *Before France and Germany* (Oxford U. P. 1990); Edward Gibbon, *The Decline and Fall of the Roman Empire* (1776-88, many subsequent edns, including J. B. Bury, Macmillan 1909-13); T. Barfield, *The Perilous Frontier: Nomadic Empires and China* (Basil Blackwell 1989).

MAP 15 THE SASSANID EMPIRE IN PERSIA

SOGDIANA

Turks

Caucasus

Constantinople

620

NORTHERN
MILITARY REGION

ARMENIA

Bukhara

Samarqand

Hephthalites
crushed c.560

Hindu Kush

Nisibis

Maragheh

Ardabil

AZERBAIJAN

Takht-i-Suleyman

Qazvin

Damghan

Marv

Hecatompylos

Nishapur

Balkh

EASTERN MILITARY REGION

BACTRIA

Antioch

613

Arbil

Rhagae

Hamadan

Isfahan

Herat

KHURASAN

R O M A N   E M P I R E

E A S T E R N

GHASSANIDS

Kermanshah

Sassanid invasions

MEDIA

Euphrates

Tigris

WESTERN
MILITARY
REGION

Ctesiphon

Dezful

Jundi Shapur

Susa

Shushtar

KHUZISTAN

Yazd

SISTAN

Alexandria

Nile

619

LAKHMIDS

Ahvaz

Ram Hormuz

Istakhr

Kerman

Sirjan

Jiroft

Bishapur

Shiraz

CARMANIA

Gur

SOUTHERN
MILITARY REGION

PARS

Siraf

481 Hephthalite invasion

Sassanids

Persian-Turkish campaign

Indus

	Empire under Khosrau I, 531–579	⟶	Hephthalite invasion of Persia
⊙	Sassanid capitals	--- →	Persian-Turkish campaign against the Hephthalites
ARY	Major provinces and military districts under Khosrau I.	⟶	Campaigns of Khosrau II against Byzantium

0 ___ 600 km
0 ___ 300 miles

MAP 16 THE EMPIRE OF THE GUPTAS IN INDIA

Bactria

Hindu Kush

KUSHANS

Taxila

Kandahar

Helmand

Quetta

Jhelum

Indus

Bolan Pass

YAUDHEYAS

Suflej

Frontier Kingdoms

Himalaya

Delhi

Ahichatra

Tribal

Brahmaputra

Mathura

Yamuna

Republics

MALAVAS

Prayāga

Ganges

Varanasi

Damodarpur

Pāṭaliputra

Kauśāmbī

Bihar

Mṛgásikhāvana

Dašapura

Devnimori

Besnagar

Forest

Ujjayinī

Trade route

Kingdoms

Surashtra

Malwa

Indrapura

Sanchi

Narmada

Junagarh

VĀKĀTAKAS

Nagpur

Ajanta

Cuttack

Godavari

Deccan

Western Ghats

Southern Kingdoms

Eastern Ghats

Krishna

Irrawaddy

PALLAVAS

Kāñci

Kaveri

Anurādhapura

SINHALA

●	Inscriptions of Ashoka (c.272–231 BC)
	Limit of known Gupta influence
	Gupta Empire, 390 AD
	Conquests of Candra Gupta, c.390 AD
	Tributaries of the Guptas
	Temporary tributary
	Satellite kingdom
	Independent kingdom
⊙	Shrine

0 ___ 600 km
0 ___ 300 miles

MAP 17 THE WORLD OF LATE ANTIQUITY

Atlantic
Ocean

North Sea

Baltic

PICTS

Iona

Lindisfarne

Devenish

NORTHUMBRIANS

Armagh
Kells
Whithorn
Clonard

MERCIANS

St. Davids

EAST
ANGLIANS

Tintagel

WEST
SAXONS
KENT
Canterbury

c. 540-
560

c. 460

Rhine

Cologne

c. 511-48

Elbe

Oder

KINGDOM
OF THE FRANKS
(481)

Trier

Rouen
Soissons
Reims
486

Dol

Rennes

486

Paris

Faremoutiers

ALEMANIA

Le Mans

Sens
Auxerre

Orléans

Tours
Bourges

Bay of
Biscay

Poitiers

Vouillé
507

Nevers

Luxeuil

c. 511-48

Besançon
St. Gall

Bregenz

Danube

Chu

LOMB

Clermont

Lyons

BURGUNDIAN
KINGDOM
(443-534)

The Alps

Milano

Monza

Aquileia

568

Bordeaux

Limoges

Vienne

Verona

Grado

Parenzo

KINGDOM
OF
THE SUEVI
(464-585)

Oviedo

Leon
Palencia

Braga

Pamplona

Burgos

511

Cahors

Pyrenees

Toulouse

Narbonne

Rhône

537

Avignon
Arles

Pavia

Po

Bobbio
Parma

Genoa

Cuneo

Luna

Ravenna

Pola

Rimini

Ancona

Salona

VISIGOTHIC
KINGDOM
(455-711)

Saragossa

Ebro

Tortosa

Gerona

Marseille

Lérins

Perugia

Auximum

KINGDOM OF THE

Subiaco

Rome
OSTROGOTHS
(489-555)

Lucera

Reccopolis

Toledo

Tarragona

Corsica

Ajaccio

Monte Cassino

Capua

Merida

Valencia

Balearic Is.

Sardinia

Naples
Salerno

Brindisi

Taranto
Otranto

Seville

Cadiz
Cartagena

Ibiza

KINGDOM

Forum Trajani

Cagliari

Cosenza

Croton

Vivarium

Tingis
Septem

OF THE

Palermo

Messina

Reggio

Atlas Mts.

Pomaria

Caesarea

Sitifis

MAURETANIA

VANDALS
(442-534)

Hippo Regius

Cirta
NUMIDIA

Timgad
Thelepte

BYZACENA

Thagaste

PROCONSULARIS

Carthage

Grasse

Hadrumetum

Caput Vada

Sicily

Agrigento

Syracuse

Mediterra

Tacape

Sabrata

Leptis Magna

TRIPOLITANIA

▬▬▬	Empire at 526 A.D
▬ ▬ ▬	Conquests of Justinian c. 527-565
▬▬▬	Byzantium in Italy c. 600
▬▬▬	Germanic kingdom c. 500
▬▬▬	Visigothic kingdom after 507
♟	Fortifications of Justinian
⊞	Churches built by Justinian
⌂	Archbishoprics (western Europe only)
✚	Latin monasteries
✜	Irish monasteries
✜	British monasteries
☉	Jewish and Syrian communities in Europe
▬▬▬	Northern frontier of secular literacy
◄◄	Expansion of Avars
◄◄◄	Expansion of Lombards
◄◄	Expansion of Franks
←	Expansion of Anglo-Saxons
◄	Anglo-Saxon settlement c. 500
←	Celtic migration
◄	Slav raids
←	Berber raids

Population density c. 500:

▓	over 15 per km²
▒	5-15 per km²
░	under 5 per km²

0 _____ 400 km
0 _____ 200 miles

UTIGARS

AVARS   KUTRIGURS

561

Caucasus   Caspian Gates

Cherson   Bosporus

Black Sea   Sebastopolis   LAZICA

DS

GEPIDAE   567   Noviodunum

582

HERULI   Iron Gate   Trebizond

Sirmium   Gate   SLAVS   Tomi   Theodostopolis

gidunum   Viminacium   Danube   Durostorum   Satala

Nissus   527-30   Novae   Odessus

Sardica   581-4   Mesembria   Sebasta

Philippopolis   Martyropolis

Justiniana Prima   Adrianople   Heraclea   Ancyra   Amida

558-9   Dara   SASSANID

Dyrrachium   586   Thessalonica   Constantinople   558-9   Melitene   Edessa   Carrhae   EMPIRE

587   Nicaea   Caesarea   Beroea   Callinicium

Aulona   Berrhoia   Dorylaeum   Antioch   Circesium   Tigris

587   Mytilene   Iconium   Seleucia   Laodicea   Euphrates

Smyrna   Laodicaea   Palmyra   Ctesiphon

587   Athens   Ephesus   Emesa

Aegean Sea   LAKMIDS

Crete   Cyprus   Constantia   Damascus

rranean Sea   Tyre

Nablus   GHASSANIDS

Jerusalem   Bethlehem

Ptolemais   Gaza

Alexandria

LIBYA   EGYPT

Heliopolis

Memphis   Nile   Mt. Sinai

Taurus Mts.

Heirs to the ancient world 1

18 The making of Byzantium
After administrative and military reorganization, Constantinople (Byzantium) and its hinterland, to which the eastern Roman Empire was reduced by the invasions of Slavs and Arabs in the seventh century, became the centre of fresh expansion and a vigorous civilization in the eighth and ninth centuries.

MAP 18 THE MAKING OF BYZANTIUM

Territory which remained constantly in Byzantine control

Territory occupied by Slavs

First Bulgarian Empire at its greatest extent

Territory reconquered by Byzantium from the Arabs

Territory permanently in Arab control

The boundary of the Byzantine State in c.1050

Byzantine campaigns of re-conquest and raids into Arab territory

Great Fence of Thrace

× Arab raids into Byzantine territory

× Bulgarian raids into Byzantine territory

× Russian raids into Byzantine territory

Military road

⊙ Theme capitals, where known

SEL Themes

AVA The Empire's northern neighbours in c. 700

MAC Neighbouring states in c. 1050

0 _____ 300 km

0 _____ 150 miles

*T*he bloody rivalry between Persia and Byzantium which had continued since the end of Justinian's reign in 565 was rudely interrupted when Arab armies seized the Byzantine provinces of Syria in AD 635, Palestine in 638 and Egypt in 642, and took the Persian capital of Ctesiphon in 636. In those years the ancient world gave way to the modern.

The conquests of Islam, which continued only slightly less rapidly until its armies seized Toledo, Samarqand and Multan in 711-13 (*see Map 19*), changed the course of world history. The Mediterranean basin, upon whose commercial and cultural unity classical civilization had been built, was divided for ever. The fragmentation of the Roman world which had become increasingly obvious in the preceding centuries (*Maps 14 and 17*) now became permanent, and each part was sent on its own distinctive path (*Maps 18, 21 and 22*). The world of Islam became a vast market linking all the economies of the known world to support a civilization of opulent splendour, whose hunger for manpower and raw materials stimulated the opening up of the forests and plains of central Europe and initiated the systematic plundering of Africa that has sustained the development of advanced economies ever since (*Map 27*). The pattern of the great religions of the world, and its principal cultural and political divisions, was completed (*Maps 11 and 20*).

The Arabian peninsula in the time of Muhammad (traditionally, *b*.570) combined violence with sophistication. The endemic feuding of both the pastoral Bedouin who occupied its rugged desert terrain and the merchant dynasties of the cities, and the incessant warfare between the two represented, but dissipated, immense military potential. Muhammad's uncompromising monotheism – 'There is no God but God, and Muhammad is the messenger of God' – provided the basis for the common purpose and common allegiance that would unleash it. His power was rooted in diplomacy. The *Koran*, revealed to him in a series of visions from about 610 onwards, contained the basis upon which, as his followers said, 'Allah has sent us a prophet who will make peace between us'; the message was largely one of repudiating the network of family obligation and social custom of traditional Arab society, with its ever-violent code of manliness, honour and revenge, in favour of a stark confrontation between the believer and his God, whose inexorable judgement would ask only whether the precepts of the *Koran* had been unflinchingly observed, regardless of worldly connection and reputation. Muhammad unified the peninsula by diplomacy, aided when necessary by the doctrine of holy war – 'It was not you who slew them, but Allah who slew them', as the prophet assured his followers when the slaughter of a Meccan caravan seemed momentarily to have flouted the *Koran's* prohibition of violence. He was planning the conquest of Syria when he died in 632.

His work was continued by the Caliphs (successors) Abu Bakr (*r.*632-4) and Omar (*r.*634-44). Their decree that the land of those who surrendered would remain inviolate while that of any who had actually to be conquered would be forfeit to the state, to be merely leased again to its former owners, facilitated the advance. It was a prudent policy, for the Arab armies, with no advantages save great speed of movement, the brilliance of their generals, and remarkable confidence in their own destiny, could probably not have overcome sustained resistance, despite their spectacular victories over numerically superior forces at Yarmuk (636) and Qadesiya (637). But the Roman hold on Africa and the Middle East was tenuous in the extreme, and the Sassanid empire on the point of collapse. These two powers had recently waged savage wars in which they alternately committed the most brutal atrocities upon the subject populations of the Middle East who repeatedly passed from the control of one to the other, with religious minorities, Christian and Jewish, suffering particularly heavily, being constantly vulnerable to accusations of treason and collaboration. These wars simply emphasized the weakness and the unpopularity of both their rules. The new Islamic masters demanded more modest taxes and services, and did not even inconvenience their new subjects to the extent of living in their towns, preferring to build new ones for themselves nearby; inevitably they were readily welcomed by exhausted and long-tyrannized communities. Like the fall of the Roman Empire in the west, the collapse of so much of the eastern Roman Empire and of its Persian counterpart rid their former lands of an expensive, cumbersome and blood-stained rule that had long outlived its vitality and its usefulness.

The established world religions also underwent fundamental changes in the early centuries of the Christian era. Hinduism now assumed greater coherence by concentrating its literature and religious activity upon three of the many gods whose worship the Vedic religion had embraced, Brahma (the creator), Vishnu (the preserver) and Shiva (the destroyer of the corrupt world). The myth and ceremony associated with the last two in particular, together with the Sanskrit language, were deliberately employed by various dynasties to disseminate Aryan culture from its strongholds in the north of the subcontinent. Hinduism, however, was not a missionary religion. To an even greater extent than Judaism, which was disseminated widely in the West through the travels of the Jews, but did not usually attempt to convert outsiders (*see Map 11*), Hinduism spread with but not beyond those who were born into it. Birth was indeed the only means of entry, and the absorption of new peoples by the creation of sub-castes – a technique which could not be applied to individuals – was necessarily a slow business. The process of rapid evangelisation in India was left to the Jains and to Buddhism, which, like Christianity in the West, was a religion of personal conviction and conversion.

The teaching of the Buddha was not written down for several centuries after his time, with the result that a large number of sects offered competing versions of it. Some held, despite his warning that he was not to be deified, that the historical Buddha was only one of a series of incarnations in which the divine being appeared, sacrificing the *nirvana* which he had earned by his perfection to secure the redemption of others through his own suffering. As such he could be represented and

MAP 19 THE CONQUESTS OF ISLAM

Legend:

Asad — Arab tribes

Conquests of Islam to 632

Conquests of Islam to 634

Conquests of Islam to 644

Conquests of Islam to 661

Conquests of Islam to 750

→ Movement of Islamic armies

■ Amsar (military settlements and camps)

Eastern border of Byzantine Empire. c. 630

Sassanid Empire. c.630

Desert

0 ——— 500 kms
0 ——— 300 miles

19 The conquests of Islam

Within ten years of the death of Muhammad in 632 the armies of Islam had conquered most of the old Roman Empire and occupied the Persian capital; within 70 they commanded territories stretching over 5000 miles, of which only Spain and Portugal are no longer predominantly Muslim.

worshipped in the *bodhisattvas*, the idealized stone images which now proliferated in the great monuments of Buddhist art. Early in the second century AD, those who held this belief, together with others who wished to incorporate new practices and philosophies into their faith, separated to follow their 'Greater Vehicle' (*Mahayana*) from those who clung to the 'Lesser Vehicle' (*Hinayana*) of the teaching of the historical Buddha, literally observed. As Buddhism spread the Mahayana system became predominant in China, Japan, Korea and Vietnam, while the Hinayana prevailed in Burma, Thailand, Cambodia and Ceylon.

Buddhism probably reached China along the central Asian trade routes in the early years of the Later Han dynasty; the traditional date is AD 65. Its early development there was slow, hindered both by philosophical difficulties – such as the flat contradiction between the Chinese veneration of family and the Buddhist renunciation of all family ties – and by practical ones such as the difficulty of translating the Sanskrit scriptures – which reached China haphazardly and piecemeal. The work was done by Chinese monks who made a number of pilgrimages to India for the purpose. By the fourth century, however, China was ruled by barbarians. The foreignness of Buddhism became a positive attraction, and many of the rulers adopted Buddhist monks as political advisers to offset the influence of the Confucian Chinese around them. The favour of the courts and the lavish patronage of the powerful stimulated the spread of Buddhism in northern China in the fourth and fifth centuries, accompanied by magnificent temples and sculptures. At the same time the noble Chinese families who had migrated to the south in large numbers found the Buddhist custom of withdrawal an attractive expedient in troubled times, and chose to make the monasteries, which they founded in large numbers, centres for the preservation of their own cultural traditions. Hence Buddhism contrived to appeal both to the Taoist aspiration of withdrawal from the world, and to the Confucian veneration of tradition and scholarship, while in the north it won great influence among the non-Chinese. In consequence although it was occasionally subjected to persecution Buddhism became the third of China's religions. Conversely it is a notable proof of the essential stability and sophistication of Chinese culture that it was, until comparatively recent times, the only one in the civilized world which did not require to be underpinned by religious monopoly.

The early history of Christianity had a great deal in common with that of Buddhism. It too was founded essentially as a movement of reform within an older religion, by comparison with which it stressed personal spirituality rather than formal adherence to law, charity rather than ascetic prohibitions. It too repudiated political structures, social distinctions and, implicitly, the priority of kinship loyalties, renouncing violence and emphasising the brotherhood of mankind. Like the Buddha, Christ was regarded by his followers as a perfect being who redeemed the sins of mankind through his own suffering. In his case too the absence of a strictly contemporary record of his teaching encouraged the multiplication of sects

among his devotees, most of whom came to attribute to him a divinity which he had not explicitly claimed. They drew upon the philosophical and cultural traditions of their time to evolve a universal theology to support their cult. Particularly important was the reconciliation of Christian theology with the neoplatonist system of philos-

20 Religions of the medieval world
Between the eighth and fifteenth centuries, four universal religions (all with internal sects and divisions which are not shown here) came to dominate the civilized world, eradicating paganism from most areas. The social and cultural patterns which they created or reflected have endured.

MAP 20 RELIGIONS OF THE MEDIEVAL WORLD

ICELAND
1000

NORWAY
1020

FINNS
1220

SWEDEN
1110

DENMARK
960

LETTS
1260

LITHUANIA
1386

BULGARS
c. 900

RUSSIA

GOLDEN HORDE

1313-41

KHAZARIA
800-1242

ENGLAND

SAXONY
785

POLAND
1000

Kiev

1313-41

GHUZZ
TURKS
970

FRANCE

HUNGARY

900

PORTUGAL

CASTILE
AND
ARAGON
1000 1248

GRANADA

1350-1453

BULGARIA
870

Rome

Constantinople

TREBIZOND

1300

1071

1071

ARMENIA

BYZANTINE EMPIRE

Madeira
1418

MAGHRIB

Baghdad

Jerusalem

ABBASID EMP.

Canaries
1417

Cairo

800-1000

EGYPT

Medina

Mecca

800-1100

AIR
1350

NUBIA

1324

SENEGAL
c. 1030

GHANA
1076

MALI
c. 1250

c. 1300

ALWAH

ETHIOPIA

Aksum

Socotra

800-1000

SOMALIA
1100-1300

1250-
1450

MOGADISHU
1100-1200

	Christian in 750
785	Pagans converted to Christianity, 750-1450
→	Members of other world religions converted to Christianity
	Islamic in 750
1030	Pagans converted to Islam, 750-1450
→	Members of other world religions converted to Islam
⇢	Lands of other world religions conquered by Islam, but not converted
	Buddhist in 750
889	Pagans converted to Buddhism, 750-1450
→	Buddhists reverting to Hinduism
	Hindu in 750
	China 750-1450: Buddhism, Confucianism, Taoism
	Korea 750-1450: Buddhism, Confucianism
	Judaism established religion
	Manichaeism established religion
	Pagan areas throughout this period

0   1000 km

0   600 miles

NAIMANS
1009-c.1300
KERAITS

HOKKAIDO

800

CHAGATAI HORDE
1250-1400

UIGHURS
762-c.1300

After 1368

Peking ○

KOREA

JAPAN

1300-1400

S I N K I A N G

KASHMIR
855

950 - 1050

Hang-chou ○

C H I N A

Ise ○

832-910

T I B E T
Lhasa ○

1030

NEPAL
1300

790

c 1200

Benares ○

MAGADHA

○ Bodhgaya

SULTANATE
OF
DELHI

c. 1200

B
U
R
M
A

1300-27

VIJAYA-
NAGAR

T
H
A
I
L
A
N
D

KHMER
Angkor ● EMPIRE

CEYLON

SAMUDRA
1297

TRENG-
GANU

1300

M
A
L
A
C
C
A

1414

S
U
M
A
T
R
A

JAVA *860* BALI

43

ophy, based on the idea of the unity of creation, which also provided an idealist foundation for the pagan cults of the third and fourth centuries AD. Finally, like Buddhism, Christianity was assisted in its diffusion by the regular and far-flung communications of a great empire (*see Map 11*), but attained real social power and political influence by exploiting its decline.

The Christians of the Roman Empire were conceded freedom of worship by Constantine in 313, and the communities which were now found in most parts of the Roman world could come into the open. Christianity did not, however, immediately become the dominant religion of the Roman world. During the fourth century the legal disabilities which it had suffered were gradually transferred, by imperial decree, to the traditional pagan cults. In the east, where the cities in which Christianity flourished were most populous and the pagan aristocracy least influential, the order to close the temples and the prohibition of pagan worship in public were taken as licence for successful persecution. Monks and holy men from the deserts of Egypt and the mountains of Syria led bloodthirsty mobs in a reign of terror which destroyed the fabric of pagan life and culture. The worst excesses were the destruction of the shrine of Serapion at Alexandria, and with it the greatest library of antiquity, in 391 and in 415 the lynching of Hypatia, the virgin queen of the neoplatonist schools.

In the west, social leadership and public office remained in the hands of the Roman aristocracy. To its members paganism, which was now heavily impregnated with neoplatonist idealism, expressed the values and enshrined the traditions of their class, much as Confucianism did in China. The aristocracy did not hurry to implement the anti-pagan decrees of the upstart emperors they despised, and they were under little popular pressure to do so. A pagan attempt to recapture the Western Empire failed only through the chance of

battle (or, as the winners said, a miracle) as late as 394. Christianity triumphed only when the Roman aristocracy came to see it as the means of preserving their culture from the collapse of the empire, and the church as the vehicle through which, under traditional leadership, Rome would recover its ancient pre-eminence. As the empire dissolved, the scions of the Roman aristocracy adopted episcopal mitres to resume the leadership that their forefathers had exercised in senatorial purple. They copied the manuscripts which contained their culture and collected them in monasteries, where literacy might, however precariously, be preserved. When these men began to come to terms with the invaders the foundations of a new age were laid. In Gaul Clovis, king of the Merovingian Franks, was converted in *c.*500, and made them the guides and mentors of a dynasty which brought Gaul under a single, if rapidly enfeebled, rule and inaugurated Europe's most important Catholic regime (*see Map 17*).

Thomas Hobbes described the Roman Church as 'the ghost of the Roman Empire sitting crowned upon the grave thereof'. So it was elsewhere. The world religions neither replaced nor transformed the ancient civilizations. They were the means by which the civilizations survived the ruin of their original political structures. Even Islam, the starkest and most uncompromising of the new faiths, was no different. The Abbasid revolution began in Khorasan in 750 to restore the fundamentals of Islam. The Umayyad dynasty which it replaced had

Further reading: Diana Eck, *Banaras, City of Light* (Princeton U. P. 1982); R. Lane Fox, *Pagans and Christians* (Allen Lane, 1986; Harper); Judith Herrin, *The Formation of Christendom* (Basil Blackwell 1987, Princeton U. P.); D. Obolensky, *The Byzantine Commonwealth* (Weidenfeld and Nicolson 1971; St. Vladimir's); M. Cook, *Muhammed* (OUP 1983); Ira M. Lapidus, *A History of Islamic Societies* (Cambridge U. P. 1988); R. Dawson, *The Chinese Experience* (Weidenfeld and Nicolson 1978).

treated conquest as a means of enriching the Arab aristocracy, and was led by the very families which had once driven the Prophet from Mecca. Under their rule Christian Arabs enjoyed high office, and the capital was moved from Medina to the Roman city of Damascus, where, like the Dome of the Rock in Jerusalem, the Great Mosque was decorated by Byzantine craftsmen, in Byzantine style. The Abbasid regime turned its back on the corrupting shores of the Mediterranean, to rule from Iran a central Asian empire of great wealth and magnificence. Its caliphs claimed over their subjects absolute powers which they exercised ruthlessly with the help of Persian officials. Their splendid courts observed the etiquette and ceremonial of the Sassanids, whose literature and art now experienced a revival. Their new capital was at Baghdad, 35 miles from the ruins of Ctesiphon.

MAP 21 THE BYZANTINE COMMONWEALTH

VIATKA

L. Ladoga
Beloozero
Ladoga
1167
Khlynov

Birka
Reval
NOVGOROD
c.1000   Novgorod the Great
Yaroslavl
Volga
Nishni Novgorod

LETTS
Izborsk   Pskov
Ярославль   Rostov
c.1040   Suzdal   Great Bulgar
Bukhara
Riga
1201
Kholm
Tver
SUZDAL
Vladimir
1198

TEUTONIC ORDER
LITHUANIANS
Dmitrovo
Moscow   Murom
c.1090

Wolin
c.1140
Koenigsberg
1254
Polotsk
1105
SMOLENSK
Kolomna
Ryazan
c.1200
BULGARS
Baltic Sea
Elbing
1237
PRUSSIANS
Smolensk
c.1136
RYAZAN

WESTERN
Magdeburg
962
Gneizno
1000
Thorn
1234
Plock
1075
Cherven
Bryansk
Saracen Route

EMPIRE
Poznan
968
KINGDOM OF
POLAND
Pinsk
VOLHYNIA
CHERNIGOV
Starodub   Trubchevsk

BOHEMIA
Breslau
c.1000
Turov
c.1120
KIEV
Novogorod
Sevirsky   Kursk
Sarkel

Prague
975
1000
Cracow
c.1000
Vladimir-
in-Volhynia
1090
Chernigov
c.1066
Donets
Volga

Olmutz
1063
MORAVIA
Przemysl
Galich
c.1160
Belgorod
c.989
Kiev
989
PEREJASLAV
c.1040
Itil
Bukhara
Baghdad

Salzburg
KINGDOM OF
HUNGARY
GALICIA
Perejaslav
c.1000
989
Dnieper

The Alps
Danube
Esztergom
Carpathians
Варяжский
C U M A N S
1091-1240
Don

Aquileia
Venice
11th-12th
centuries
Kalocsa
c.1000
P A T Z I N A K S
895-1091
KHAZARS

STATES OF
Ancona
Pazin
Rijeka
Seni
Zagreb
1093
Alba Julia
c.1106
Belgorod
Sea of Azov
Bosporos
Sarkel
ALANIA
Alania

THE CHURCH
Zadar
Sibenik
Spalato
CROATIA
Sirmium
c.1252
Singidunum
Danube
Cherven
Pliska
CHERSON
Cherson
c.900
KINGDOM OF
GEORGIA
Tiflis

Rome
Grottaferrata
Hvar
Ragusa
Milisevo
1230
Studenica
1200
Sopocani
1263
Turnovo
Preslav
Black Sea

Monte Cassino
1057-86
Capua
Naples
Amalfi
Melfi
Bari
Dyrrachium
Pec
c.1200
SERBIA
Neziri
1164
Sardica   BULGARIA
Rila
Philippopolis
Mesembria
870
Trebizond
c.1250
Echmiadzin
ARMENIA

Salerno
Brindisi
Taranto
Veles
Ochrida
1037-56
Prespa
Adrianople
Claudiopolis
Neocaesarea
Colonela
Camacha

NORMAN KINGDOM
OF SICILY
Rossano
Kurbinovo
1150
Thessalonica
Trajanopolis
Constantinople
Nicaea
11th cent
Ankara
Sebastea
Caesarea
Melitene

Palermo
1132-43
Lecce
1282-9
Arta
Larissa
Mt. Athos
Cotyaeum
Rock monasteries
of Cappadocia
c.850-1200

Cefalù
1148
Mileto
Messina
Hosios
Lucas
c.1000
Nea Moni
Chios
1042-54
Mitylene
Lesbos
Smyrna
Antioch
Iconium
Caesarea

Monreale
1184-92
Troina
Syracuse
Daphne
11th cent
Patras
Aegean
Sea
Ephesus
Laodicea

Malta
Athens
11th cent
Patmos
Side
Seleucia
Black
Mountain
Antioch

Myra
Taurus Mts.
Euphrates
Tigris

Rhodes
Koutzivendi
1164
Constantia

Candia
Crete
Cyprus
ABBASID
CALIPHATE

Tyre

Jerusalem
1048, 1170
Bethlehem
c.1167
St.Saba

Alexandria
Nile

Sinai

Mount Sinai

Orthodox Christendom (Greek rite)
Orthodox Christendom (Slavonic rite)
Orthodox Christendom (Georgian rite)
Latin Christendom
Patriarchal sees
Metropolitan sees and archbishoprics*
Bishoprics*
Latin archdioceses and dioceses in which Glagolitic rite was used
Orthodox monasteries (Greek rite)
Orthodox monasteries (Slavonic rite)
Orthodox monasteries (Georgian rite)
Greek monasteries of the Latin obedience
Strongholds of the Teutonic Knights
187   Centres of Byzantine artistic activity with dates of prominence
Boundary of Byzantine Empire at its greatest extent c.1045
Boundary of the Norman Kingdom of Sicily
Creation of new provinces in the Orthodox Church
Creation of new provinces in the Latin Church
R E J   Principalities of Kievan Russia on the eve of the Mongol invasions
Main Viking routes
*Where appropriate, approximate dates of foundation are given

0   500 km
0   300 miles

45

Heirs to the ancient world 2

LAND AND POWER

The differences between the eastern and western parts of the Roman Empire, still clearly visible in the modern world (compare Maps 14 and 84), were greatly accentuated when the Roman state itself, having disappeared from the west, emerged from its difficulties in the east with even more comprehensive pretensions than it had had before.

The Byzantine Empire came very close to destruction at the beginning of the seventh century. Persian armies reached the Nile and the Bosphorus for the first time since the Achaemenids (*Map 15*). The Slavs overran the Balkan peninsula and laid siege to Constantinople. When Heraklius became emperor in 610, he considered abandoning the city and setting up his capital at Carthage. Yet by 629 his armies had recaptured Jerusalem, and their approach to Ctesiphon had provoked a coup d'état there. The conquests of Heraklius were immediately nullified by those of Islam, which threw Byzantium desperately on the defensive again. In preparing for them, however, he renewed the foundations of a Byzantine state which re-established itself as the dominant power in the Balkans, the bulwark of Christendom against Islam and the peoples of Asia (*see Map 18*), and the evangelist of the Slavonic peoples (*Maps 20 and 21*).

Heraklius broke the sequence which led from military expansion to swollen bureaucracy and heavy taxation, the ruin of the peasantry and reliance on mercenary armies, and which had brought down the great empires of antiquity. Ordinary soldiers were given land in frontier regions in return for military service; otherwise they were exempt from taxation. Their sons inherited the obligation. The provinces were reorganized into *themes (see Map 18)* under the command of generals to whom the civilian administration was subordinated. Thus a cheap and effective defence force was created, needing neither complex administration nor long lines of supply, and the peasant class, the source of future recruitment, was strengthened. And these soldiers were not only less expensive than mercenaries but could be better trained, enabling the empire to recover military superiority over its barbarian neighbours. In the long run the

22 The empire of Charlemagne
The exploitation of land between the Seine and the Rhine brought power to the Carolingian family, enabling it to unite much of western Europe and create a common institutional and cultural heritage. But there was no apparatus of the state: the personal movements of the kings provide the best indication of their real power and their priorities.

MAP 22 THE EMPIRE OF CHARLEMAGNE

Legend:
The Kingdom of the Franks, 768
Charlemagne's empire at its greatest extent
Partition of Verdun, 843
Lands of St. Peter
Archbishopric — with scriptorium
Bishopric — with scriptorium
Monastery — with scriptorium
Royal palace
Trading centre
835 Main routes of Viking raids with dates
Main routes of Saracen raids
300 km
200 miles

Map labels: FRISIA, MERCIA, EAST ANGLIA, North Sea, WESSEX, KENT, Utrecht, Durstedt, Nijmegen, Xanten, Maastricht, Thérouanne, Arras, Amiens, Péronne, Liège, AUS..., St. Wandrille, St. Ouen, Beauvais, Laon, Soissons, Thionville, Bayeux, Lisieux, Rouen, Reims, Verdun, Metz, Coutances, Evreux, St. Denis, Senlis, Châlons-sur-Marne, NEUSTRIA, Avranches, Sées, Paris, Ponthion, Toul, Mont St. Michel, Chartres, Sens, Troyes, BRITTANY, Rennes, Le Mans, Orléans, Ferrières, Germigny-des-Prés, Fleury, Langres, Luxeuil, Vannes, BRETON MARCH, Nantes, Tours, Auxerre, Flavigny, Dijon, Besançon, Bourges, Nevers, Autun, Chalon-sur-Saône, Noirmoutier, St. Maixent, Poitiers, Macon, AQUITAINE, Saintes, Limoges, Menat, BURGUNDY, Clermont, Lyon, Bay of Biscay, Angoulême, Brioude, Périgueux, Le Puy, PROVENCE, Bordeaux, Aurillac, Valence, Gap, Cahors, Rodez, Agen, Moissac, GASCONY, Auch, Bayonne, Toulouse, Albane, Arles, Aix, Oloron, Carcassonne, Marseilles, KINGDOM OF THE GALICIANS AND ASTURIANS, Roncesvalles, Comminges, Pamplona, MARCH OF SEPTIMANIA, Narbonne, Elne, Ripoll, SPANISH MARCH, Saragossa, Urgel, Gerona, EMIRATE OF CORDOBA, Barcelona, Mediterranean Sea, To Seville, Cadiz, Murcia, Valencia, Balearic Is. and Mediterranean coast creation of provincial strongholds for military dynasties would inevitably cause trouble, but, until that happened, after the death of Basil II in 1025, the system of Heraklius sustained the most successful and creative period of Byzantium's history.

The Byzantine theme system has been compared with that which enabled the Sui (589-617) and T'ang (618-906) dynasties to reunify China and carry out governmental reform and territorial expansion. In 590 Emperor Wu of the Sui dynasty decreed that old soldiers were to be given land; it was distributed both to veterans and to those who remained as guards in frontier regions. As in Byzantium this created a trained peasant militia and strengthened the class from which soldiers were recruited, permitting significant advances in training and technique. At the same time a network of canals was built, using forced labour on a huge scale. Its masterpiece, the Grand Canal – forty paces wide – joined the north of China to the Yangtze basin, the most productive agricultural region (*Map 10*). This facilitated the supply of the armies, and permitted taxes in grain to be collected and redistributed more efficiently, an important insurance against famine and rebellion. The principle of recruitment to the imperial bureaucracy by examination was revived, and gradually became the sole means of entry. In these respects the reunified China repeated, more systematically and on a larger scale, the policies of the early emperors.

In the seventh and eighth centuries the T'ang emperors presided over one of the greatest periods of Chinese civilization. It was exceptionally open to contact with the west, welcoming missionaries of the Nestorians and the Manichees (*Map 20*), and giving refuge to the last Sassanid emperor, who died an exile in Chang-an. But the immense extension of the empire which stimulated these contacts required the creation of professional armies which, operating on distant frontiers, became effectively independent powers and the source of the revolts in which the dynasty failed.

Byzantine influence was extended in a different way. The churches of Rome and Constantinople, already growing apart in doctrinal emphases, were further separated by the Lombard invasion of Italy in 568 (*Map 17*). Islam engulfed the patriarchal sees of Jerusalem, Antioch and Alexandria. Constantinople remained as the unchallenged arbiter of eastern Christendom. As its missionaries spread their faith in Asia Minor and among the Slavs (*see Map 20*) they disseminated the influence of the Byzantine state of which their church was, in effect, an arm, for it was under direct imperial control. Monks, scholars and artists carried Byzantine civilization in the wake of the missionaries, to form the culture and shape the destinies of the Slavonic peoples (*see Map 21*).

The Byzantine and Chinese empires were revived by vigorous assertion of the power of the state. The Carolingian empire was the product of its decay. As the Roman world declined its trade diminished, its cities shrank, its roads fell out of use and its institutions ceased to operate. Power resided exclusively in the possession of land. This meant that sooner or later power in Europe would move to the north, whose deep and rich soils were potentially far more fertile than those of the Mediterranean regions. The revolution began in the eighth century. With the assistance of the 'heavy' plough, whose mould-board turned the soil over instead of simply scratching its surface, land in the middle Rhine region, where it seems to have been introduced, began to be cleared and population to grow. The Carolingian family which controlled Austrasia seized the opportunity to endow an army of mounted warriors. Charles Martel conquered northern Gaul, vindicating his claim to supremacy by defeating an Arab army at Poitiers in 732. His son Pepin III overthrew the last Merovingian in 751, and got the Pope to legitimize his coup in return for support against the Lombards. Pepin's son Charlemagne (r.768-814) brought the emerging society of western Europe under a single rule for the first time (*Map 22*), and entered legend when Pope Leo III crowned him emperor at St Peter's in Rome on 25th December 800.

The coronation of Charlemagne was an echo of the past. In reality he was already spending most of his winters at his 'new Rome', Aachen, in the region which had already become, as it remains, the cockpit of Europe (*Map 22 inset; compare Map 57 and Map 75 inset*). The shift of wealth and power

Encloses itinerary of:
— — — Charles the Bald
········· Lothar I
———— Louis the German
———— Louis II
—··— Charlemagne, 1-4 stays
Charlemagne, 5-7 stays
Charlemagne, more than 12 stays
Towns most frequently visited by:
Charles the Bald
Louis the German
Louis II

there was no way to reward them except by granting them benefices (presents) of land. This equation of landholding with service, the classic definition of feudalism, became effectively, though not yet legally, universal in Charlemagne's reign. It wrote the death warrant of his empire. Land was power; once transferred it might not easily be recovered. For a time the system had worked well. Charles Martel and Pepin III entrusted the government of their growing kingdom to fellow-members of the Austrasian nobility from which they sprang. Charlemagne tried to maintain the coherence of this ruling group by bringing up their sons at his court.

But by the end of his reign corruption and rebellion already made it plain that control was gone. The feudatories took advantage of the rivalries of his successors to tear the empire apart, and the Vikings – though not strong enough to destroy well-governed kingdoms, as the Muslims in Spain and Alfred in Wessex (d.899) showed – took advantage of the disorder to plunder the towns and monasteries, spreading terror wherever they appeared.

The Merovingian kings had regarded public rights and duties as private property which might be given to favoured subjects, and especially to the Church. A grant of 'immunity' from taxation to a

was clearly displayed by the appearance of new centres of population (*portus*) where merchants stopped along the Rhine and its tributaries, while the Roman cities of the Mediterranean languished, and by the establishment of most of the *scriptoria* (writing offices) on what in the sixth century had been the barbarian side of the northern limit of surviving indications of literacy (*compare Maps 17 and 22*). By the middle of the ninth century the growing importance of the strongholds on the eastern frontier foreshadowed the rise of the Saxon empire when Otto I in his turn inaugurated a dynasty, secured a papal coronation at Rome in 962, and, succeeding where the Carolingians had failed, founded an enduring empire (*Map 24*).

The Carolingians conceived the responsibilities of kingship more broadly than their predecessors had. Charlemagne attempted, persistently and often successfully, to provide protection through his courts for *miserabiles personae* – the weak – against the tyrannies of the powerful, and, in a measure which led directly to the appearance of universities in the twelfth century, he commanded every bishop to provide elementary education in his diocese for those who could benefit from it. His enthusiasm for learning and patronage of scholars stimulated a renaissance in art and literature. So many of the earliest surviving manuscripts of classical works are written in the script invented by Carolingian scribes that Italian Renaissance scholars mistakenly dubbed it 'Roman', as we still do.

The Carolingian Empire was ruined by the force which raised it. Charlemagne's government barely extended beyond his personal presence, except so far as his will was understood and respected by the counts and bishops who governed the empire in his name. As a result, on *Maps 22 and 24*, his itinerary and those of his successors display the extent of their power more truthfully than largely notional boundaries. But just as, with literacy confined to a very few, there was no way to govern the empire except through the nobility, in a natural economy

MAP 23 THE WORLD OF THE VIKINGS

landlord entitled him to raise the taxes from the land involved for his own benefit, and by extension to demand the services which had formerly gone to the state, to do justice and keep for himself its considerable profits. As the Carolingian Empire disintegrated, the counts, most of whom already had immunities of this kind, kept for themselves the public rights which their office had conferred on them. Collectively referred to as the *ban* – the right to compel – these rights were exercised over all free men, and were therefore much more extensive, and potentially more lucrative, than those of landlordship. But by about 1001 the counts had

suffered at the hands of their own retainers the usurpation which they had inflicted on the kings. Effective power was exercised from the castles which had appeared everywhere, over such an area as one man and his retinue could control by direct force. And over that area the castellan, unchecked by any superior power, claimed the *ban* for himself, and with it whatever 'customary' rights and payments he chose to demand. The powers that had once been the state's were now indistinguishable from those conferred by the ownership of private property.

This ruthless consolidation of seigneurial power

was one consequence of the impoverishment suffered by the nobility in the tenth century. Another was the rush to bring new land into cultivation during the eleventh, increasing the revenues of its owners as well as supporting a rapid growth of population. It was caused not only by the extravagant lifestyle, but especially by the custom of dividing land between all the children of each generation. To preserve the integrity of the inheritance, male primogeniture was now introduced in northern France. This change produced the most characteristic figure of European medieval society, the younger son who, as the mounted knight bound to his aristocratic relations by a common code of chivalry, was condemned to wander far and wide until by his wits and his sword he could win a rich wife, or her price in combat. Political power would lie with whoever could assert control over his feudatories and attract these adventurers to his banner. The Duchy of Normandy, probably founded by some such process (although the Normans told a splendid tale that they were descended from Viking pirates who had been confirmed in the duchy by a Carolingian king), showed the way. Its younger sons and dispossessed wandered over Europe to play prominent parts in the reconquest of Spain, the foundation of the Kingdom of Sicily and the crusades (*Maps 21, 26 and 32*). Meanwhile its Duke William I (*r.*1033-87) subdued his inheritance and won himself a kingdom in England, which his successors plundered with ruthless brilliance to create an empire which dominated western Europe in the twelfth century (*see Map 25*). It was broken only by even greater exponents of feudal power, their rivals of the French royal house of Capet.

Opposite July from Les Tres Riches Heures Duc de Berry

23 The world of the Vikings
Settlement was a major objective of Viking activity, and by the tenth and eleventh centuries created a distinctive northern community, based on maritime communications, whose legacy is still apparent. The Vikings were quickly converted to Christianity in England, but elsewhere their pagan burial places provide abundant evidence of their presence.

24 Germans and Slavs 900-1200
The expansion of Christianity in Germany and central Europe encouraged the extension of agriculture and assisted the formation of territorial entities, both German and Slav, linked with varying degrees of intimacy in a common allegiance to the Empire of Otto I and his successors. This development brought the region increasingly into the mainstream of European affairs.

25 Normans, Angevins and Capetians
The Norman kingdom and then the Angevin empire dominated western Europe in the twelfth century, to be ousted by Capetian France in the thirteenth. The power of both monarchies rested on their control of castles, towns and the church, and on the exploitation and extension of their rights of justice over subjects.

Further reading: H. Pirenne, *Mahomet and Charlemagne* (Allen and Unwin 1937; Barnes and Noble); Richard Hodges and David Whitehouse, *Mohammed, Charlemagne and the Origins of Europe*, (Duckworth 1983; Cornell U. P.); Georges Duby, *The Early Growth of the European Economy* (Weidenfeld & Nicolson 1974; Cornell U. P.); Marc Bloch, *Feudal Society* (Routledge 1961; University of Chicago Press); Cyril Mango, *Byzantium* (Weidenfeld and Nicolson 1980); Ray Huang, *China: A Macro History*, (East Gate 1988); David Ludden, *Peasant History in South India* (Princeton U.P. 1985; OUP India 1989).

Legend:
- ←c.800 Routes of Viking colonisation
- ⊙ Main towns in British Isles under Viking lordship
- Archdioceses with date of foundation
- Dioceses with date of foundation
- × Battles
- ○ Principal English mint towns
- ○ Scandinavian mints
- ◡ Military camps
- ▲ Viking graves in the British Isles : one grave
- ▲ Viking graves in the British Isles : more than one grave
- Southern limit of the Danelaw in England
- Areas in England most heavily settled from Denmark
- Areas in England most heavily settled from Norway

0 300 km
0 200 miles

49

MAP 24 GERMANS AND SLAVS 900-1200

Boundaries of Empire, c. 1050

Other boundaries

Frontier between Romance and Germanic languages

Uncertain or disputed frontier

Lands lost to Empire after 983

Concentrations of royal lands in early eleventh century

Concentrations of royal lands in late twelfth century

□ Palace ◆ Fortification

Archbishopric with date of foundation

Bishopric with date of foundation, date from which permanently established

Monastery with date of foundation

Centre of monastic reform with date of foundation

I T C Country or German duchy

H E S Main new territorial centre in late twelfth century

M E I Lesser territorial division

O B O Slav and Magyar peoples

M a g Slav and Magyar tribes

Surrounds places visited more than four times by Otto I, 936-973

Surrounds places visited more than four times by Henry IV

Surrounds places visited more than four times by Frederick I, 1152-90

0 ___ 150 km
0 ___ 100 miles

Baltic Sea

DENMARK
HOLSTEIN
Schleswig 948
BILLUNG MARCH
BRUNSWICK
Lübeck 968, 1149
Ratzeburg 1149
Schwerin 1052, 1167
OBODRITES
NORTH MARCH
WILZI
Havelberg 948, 1149
BRANDENBURG
Hevelli
Brandenburg 948, 1157
Kolberg c 1000
Kammin 1140, 1176
POMERANIANS
PRUSSIANS
CUJAVIA
Włocławek c 1000
Płock c 1000
Gniezno c 1000
Poznán 968
GREAT POLAND
POLES
POLAND
SILESIA
Breslau 966
SILESIANS
Crakow c 1000

FRISIA
Bremen 848
Verden
SAXONY
Osnabrück
Minden
Hildesheim
Münster
Corvey
Goslar
Gandersheim
Halberstadt
Magdeburg 968
SORBS
LAUSITZ MARCH
MERSEBURG MARCH
Merseburg 968, 1004
MEISSEN MARCH
Meissen 968
Naumburg 968, 1029
ZEITZ MARCH
Milzeni

Utrecht
Nijmegen
Werden
Paderborn
WESTFALIA
HESSE
Fritzlar
Hersfeld
Erfurt
THURINGIA

BRABANT
Aachen
Liège
Gembloux
Stavelot
(LOWER)
LOTHARINGIA
Cologne
Siegburg 1068
Fulda
FRANCONIA
Prague 973
Sázawa 1035
Olomouc 960, 1063
BOHEMIA
CZECHS
MORAVIA
MORAVIANS
Kabars
Nitra 1034
MAGYARS
Vác

Prémontré 1120
Reims
Verdun
Metz
Gorze
Toul
(UPPER)
LUXEMBURG
Trier
Prüm
Frankfurt
Mainz
Ingelheim
Trebur
Bamberg 1007
Würzburg
NORDGAU
WÜRZBURG
Nuremberg
Regensburg
Windberg 1125
Niederalteich
EAST MARCH
Melk
Heiligenkreuz 1136
AUSTRIA
Győr 1009
Esztergom 1000
HUNGARY
Veszprém 1009

Worms
Lorsch
Speyer
PALATINATE
Eichstätt
Passau
Freising
BAVARIA
Salzburg
Rottenbuch 1074
Tegernsee
Admont 1074
CARINTHIAN MARCH
STYRIA
Gurk 1072
CARINTHIANS
Veszprém
Horka
Botond

Citeaux 1098
Gorze
SUABIA
Augsburg
Reichenau
Constance
St. Gallen
Hirsau
WELFS
CARINTHIA
Kalocsa 1000

FRANCHE-COMTÉ
Cluny 909
Besançon
St.Blasien 1065
Basel
ZÄHRINGER
Chur
Brenner Pass
TIROL
Brixen 967
CARINTHIA
KRAIN MARCH
Pécs 1009

DUCHY OF BURGUNDY
Dijon
Payerne 961
Lausanne
L. Geneva
Genève
The Alps
TRENTO
Trent
AQUILEIA
Aquileia
Grado
Trieste
Zagreb 1093
CROATS
CROATIA

Lyon
Vienne
SAVOY
Great St.Bernard Pass
Little St.Bernard Pass
Mont Cenis Pass
Fruttuaria 1092
TURIN
Turin
Simplon Pass
Sion
ITALY
Bergamo
Brescia
Milan
Lodi
Cremona
Vercelli
Pavia
Piacenza
Mantua
Padua
VERONA
Verona
Venice
Adriatic Sea

MAP 25 NORMANS, ANGEVINS AND CAPETIANS

North
Sea

Atlantic
Ocean

Legend

- ⌂ Archdioceses
- ⌂ Dioceses (selected)
- ✥ Centres of monastic reform
- ✚ Cathedral and monastic schools
- ◆ Universities
- ✚ Outbreaks of popular heresy in the eleventh and twelfth centuries
- **1022**
- ⬛ Scottish burhs and castles
- ⬛ Castles
- ✚ Monasteries
- ● Pilgrimage centres
- ——— Itinerary of Richard of Anstey, 1158-1163
- – – – Pilgrimage routes to Rome
- ——— Pilgrimage routes to Compostela

Expansion of Capetian lordship:

- Royal demesne in 1180
- Additions of the period 1180 to 1223
- Further additions of the period 1223 to 1285
- Further additions of the period 1285 to 1328
- Irish dioceses to which English bishops were appointed in the 13th century
- Welsh marcher lordship in the early 14th century
- Earl David's lordship c. 1114-1124
- ● Towns given the customes of the Norman town of Breteuil
- Greatest extent of Angevin Empire in France

0   200 km
0   150 miles

Mediterranean Sea

51

Heirs to the ancient world 3

26 The world of the Crusaders
Between the invasions of the Seljuk Turks in the eleventh century and the Mongols in the thirteenth the Byzantine and Arab worlds were subjected to successive attacks from both western Europe and central Asia. The Latins lost Constantinople in 1261 and Acre in 1291, but the empire of the Turkish Mamluks, like that of Byzantium, survived until the Ottoman conquests.

The politics and culture of the medieval civilizations deliberately imitated or unconsciously perpetuated those of the ancient world.

It was not in the first instance their achievements in those fields, impressive as they were, that enabled these civilizations to break out of the rhythms which had governed the rise and fall of civilizations for millennia. The crucial achievement both of China and western Europe was to transform economic life sufficiently to produce a sustained population growth which, although it was liable to prolonged recession such as that associated with the epidemics of the later middle ages (*see Map 35*) was, in the long run, irreversible. Recent estimates put the population of Europe at about 36 million in AD 1000, 79 million in 1300, and 81 million in 1500; of China at 66 million, 86 million and 110 million at the same dates; and of the Indian sub-continent at 79 million, 91 million, and 105 million. By contrast such evidence as there is – usually very little – suggests that the population of most other parts of the world remained stagnant. That of the world of Islam reached a peak during its golden age, between about 800 and 1000, and was generally somewhat in decline thereafter.

The agricultural advances of the early middle ages which sustained this growth were very similar in China and in Europe. The heavy plough was widely used in both regions by about 1000, and was increasingly assisted by other technical advances. In Europe there were iron tools, efficient harnessing for animals and wind- and water-mills, and similarly in China dams, dykes, waterwheels and other aids to irrigation. As Europe had an eastward frontier region, in addition to its great expanses of forest and marsh, so China had the ricegrowing region of the south to invite steady expansion and continuous growth over a very long period (*Maps 10, 23 and 34*). Finally, in large parts of both regions the partial freeing of slaves since ancient times combined with the widespread enserfment of free men by coercion had produced a manorial organization which could permit the direction of labour and the investment of capital in such land and tools as large projects might require. To sustain their growth, however, agricultural

MAP 26 THE WORLD OF THE CRUSADERS

Legend:
- Land lost by Crusaders in or before 1187
- Land held or gained by Crusaders after 1187
- Land held by Byzantines after 1204
- Land acquired by Venice in 1204
- Muslim land
- Ayubbid Empire, 1170-1250
- M E N Muslim powers in 1096
- 1 E L Muslim powers in 1291
- Crusader attacks on Moslem territory
- Reconquests by Byzantines of Nicaea
- Mongol attacks
- Haj route from Damascus
- Syrian campaigns of John II and Manuel I Comnenus
- Crusader castles
- Assassin castles
- Latin metropolitan sees
- Centres of Italian trade in Crusader States
- Ports held by Venice after 1204
- Battles
- Boundary of Byzantine Empire in 1180

0 _____ 300 km
0 _____ 200 miles

communities needed markets to reward them for producing beyond their immediate needs, and cities to drain off their surplus population and encourage its rapid replacement. The second part of the medieval economic revolution was the creation of world-wide markets, exchanging goods and services more regularly and in greater volume, across greater distances, and in particular providing a growing demand for manufactured goods.

The conquests of Islam united the economies of the Persian and much of the Roman worlds, between which there had previously been little exchange. They also implanted a way of life which demanded the creation of a massive international trade. The conquerors did not expect to demean their hands with labour, and were inhibited in the exploitation of their new subjects by the readiness of most of them to convert to Islam. They expected to live in cities – Baghdad was the largest city in the world, two million in population, within half a century of its foundation in 762 – and to enjoy the enormous variety of goods which could be collected from across their vast territories. Yet those territories, the home of the most ancient civilizations, were near exhaustion, their soils poor, their forests stripped bare, their population very low. So the world of Islam became a trading empire on a scale never seen before (see Map 27). At first the imports were paid for largely with the silver of the fabled mines of the Hindu Kush, inherited from the Sassanids, but after the Abbasid revolution the migration of Arabs and other dissidents from Persia began to open up the Islamic west. North Africa was brought more firmly under control, and ports were established on the Nile and new towns on the desert caravan routes to bring gold and ivory, as well as slaves, from the Africa interior, both east and west.

The needs of Islam had momentous consequences for Europe. In Carolingian times Metz and Verdun, junction between the German interior and the routes to Spain and Africa (via Marseilles), were important slave markets and Muslim wealth was a major, if distant, stimulus of the traffic along the Rhine and its tributaries (Map 22). Later the riches of the forests beyond the Elbe and in Bohemia and Carinthia made the more easterly route down the Adriatic the main thoroughfare to the Mediterranean leading to the rise of Venice, its mistress, and the Po valley, its link with western Europe. The revenue gained from those flows of Muslim wealth not only gave Otto the basis of an empire in the north, but drew him and his successors continually both eastwards and southwards (Maps 24 and 33).

The great pioneers of trade between the north and the advanced world were the Vikings. By the ninth century they were in touch with Muslim traders along the Volga, whose upper waters were easily accessible from the Baltic (see Map 21). For a century Persian silver poured into Scandinavian hoards (Map 23): more than sixty thousand Muslim coins have been found there, and as many more in northern Russia, Poland and Pomerania. By the end of the tenth century, when trade with Islam began to fall away, the Vikings – known as Varangians to the Greeks – had also reached the Black Sea by way of the Dnieper, down which the Rus people of Kiev had long brought their furs, honey and wax to Byzantium.

Along the rivers of Russia the Vikings forged permanent links between northern and eastern Europe (compare Map 28). Their voyages into the Atlantic, leading to the colonization of Iceland and settlement in Greenland and somewhere on the North American coast at Vinland, constituted the first extension of the known world since ancient times and, after their own conversion, a major expansion of Christendom (see Map 20).

Within the huge area which their ships and nautical talents opened to them the Vikings settled in many places, though seldom (most scholars now think) in large numbers. Colonies appeared in the ninth century at the mouths of many of the rivers along which they raided, including the Elbe and the Weser, the Rhine, the Seine and the Loire, but the most important were on the islands of the North Sea and around the British Isles, the nucleus of a great seaborne empire in the time of Cnut (r.1014-35), and still a region of distinctive cultural and political traditions (Map 23).

The history of the Vikings is a reminder that piracy is never far from trade, or trade from colonization. The raids on the accumulated treasures of the monasteries of Francia and England – almost

MAP 27 THE GOLDEN AGE OF ISLAM

27 The golden age of Islam

The conquests of Islam joined the markets and trade routes of the known world. The wealth of its aristocracy stimulated a vast and varied trade which supported a brilliant civilization, although political fragmentation had already begun by the ninth century.

the only respect in which their activity differed from that of the warring nobles of Christian Europe – have given them the fearsome reputation of legend and exaggerated the importance of their destructive activity. Their voyages mark the beginning of the maritime unity of Europe, joining the coastal traffic of the Channel and the North Sea to that of the Atlantic and Mediterranean seaboards for the first time. Little of the tribute which they

collected from the Franks and English found its way back to the Scandinavian hoards. It was most probably used to buy land for settlement, or to be recirculated as part of the trade which in their hands so clearly foreshadowed the medieval economy at its height (*see Map 28*).

Rather as the Vikings benefited from the disintegration of the Carolingian empire Europe as a whole profitted from the decline of Islam and Byzantium. The political unity of the Caliphate ended after the Abbasid revolution, when the leaders of provincial armies – emirs – became increasingly inclined to declare themselves independent of Baghdad. The process was accelerated by the growing habit of granting them the farm of

taxes and revenues of the state in place of payment for their troops, and completed when Baghdad itself was seized by a Persian prince in 945, leaving the Caliph as a spiritual figurehead, bereft of real power. In the eleventh century the precipitous decline of its external trade, a series of rebellions and civil wars among the Muslim peoples, which saw the creation of a Berber empire in Africa and Spain, and the devastation of Libya and Tunisia by Bedouin tribesmen (it was now that the ancient agricultural prosperity of the region was destroyed), and, most important, the advance of the Seljuk Turks from central Asia (*Map 26*), – all laid the Muslim world open to Christian attack.

The dissolution of the Caliphate of Cordoba in

WAX FURS HORSES
HONEY SLAVES

WAX FURS HORSES
HONEY SLAVES

GOLD

GOLD
UTENSILS

GOLD
JEWELLERY

GOLD
JEWELLERY

SLAVES
FURS
WAX
LEATHER
WEAPONS

Aral Sea

GHUZZ TURKS

GOLD
SILK

SLAVES
IRON
WEAPONS
COPPER

SILK
LUXURY GOODS

Tashkent

Syr Darya

Kokand

TEXTILES

Kashgar

KHAZARS

Caucasus

SHIRVAN

Derbent

Caspian Sea

KHWARIZM

Oxus

Samarqand

SUGHD

Volga

Don

ack Sea

Tiflis

Bardaa

Qaliqala

Trebizond

Bukhara

Balkh

Hindu Kush

SLAVES
TEXTILES
PERFU...

RUM

ARMENIA

ARRAN

Ardabil

Tabriz

Maragheh

Rasht

JURJAN

Merv

KHORASAN

Kabul

Konya

Taurus Mts

Marash

AWASIM

Amid

Akhlat

AZERBAIJAN

GILAN

TABARISTAN

Jurjan

Tus

Mayafariqin

Nishapur

Herat

Kandahar

Multan

Tarsus

Edessa

Mardin

Qazwin

Rayy

KUMIS

Kayin

KUHISTAN

Aleppo

Nisibis

Mosul

JAZIRA

Hamadan

JIBAL

Zagros Mts

Qom

Isfahan

Yazd

Zaranj

SEISTAN

GO
SILK

Antioch

Harran

Ar Raqqah

Nahrawan

Samarra
836

Nahavand

Istakhr

Kirman

Helmand

Tripoli

Homs

SYRIA

Euphrates

Canal

Baghdad

Dizful

Wasit

Istakhr

KIRMAN

Beirut

Damascus

Ukhaidir

Kufa

Tigris

Ahwaz

KHUZISTAN

FARS

MAKRAN

Tyre

Acre

PALESTINE

IRAQ

Shiraz

Qalat
Mans...

Gaza

Jerusalem

Basra

Al-Ubulla

Siraf

Hormuz

Tiz

Daybul

SIN

HEJAZ

BAHRAYN

Al-Hasa
894

YAMAMA

As Sohar

Muscat

OMAN

SPICES
TIN
WEAPONS
TIMBER

Aswan

Red Sea

Medina

IRON
GRAIN
CORAL
TRINKETS

SLAVES
GOLD

Aydhab

SALT
TRINKETS
JEWELLERY

Mecca

Jidda

Spain in 1010 provided the Christian kings of León and Castile with an opportunity to enlarge their territories and to launch the reconquista which was to be the theme of Spanish medieval history (*see Map 32*). It rapidly became a European enterprise as the prospect of land and booty attracted knights from far and wide, and the monastic orders came behind them to bring spiritual comforts and Christian services in return for a handsome share of the spoils. Still richer pickings in southern Italy were available to the followers of the Norman adventurers who by 1048 had conquered most of Apulia and Calabria from the Byzantine Empire (*see Map 21*). They forced the Pope to recognize their conquests in 1059, and turned against Islam in 1072

when they captured Palermo, which their descendants would make the capital of the wealthiest and most sophisticated kingdom in the twelfth-century West.

The death of the Byzantine emperor Basil II in 1025 was followed by a period of prolonged conflict between the military dynasties of the provinces and the civilian aristocracy of Constantinople, during which the state was permanently weakened by the farming out of revenues and offices in bids for political support. Basil's annexation of Bulgaria and Armenia (which was implemented after his death, in 1043) removed what had been in effect buffer states against the Asiatic nomads. In 1065 Armenia fell to the Seljuk Turks and in 1071 they

defeated the Emperor at Manzikert to take Anatolia, as the Arabs never had. In the same year Bari, his last stronghold in Italy, fell to the Normans.

The assault of Christian Europe on the Middle East and the Balkans (*Map 26*) was conducted, in principle, not by wandering adventurers but by its anointed leaders. The Pope issued the summons to

---

28 The medieval economy at its height
By the thirteenth century the traders and trade routes of Europe were well enough established to encourage increasing economic specialization, and the growing cities – though still very small by world standards – provided markets for luxuries from far afield as well as for the products of their own hinterlands.

MAP 28 THE MEDIEVAL ECONOMY AT ITS HEIGHT

Bergen

COPPER

Fulun

IRON

Stockholm

Visby

North
Sea

Baltic

COAL

Dublin

Chester

WOOL

Hull

Boston

Norwich

Ipswich

Danzig

Rostock

Lübeck

Thorn

WOOL

London

Bristol

TIN

Southampton

Utrecht

Brunswick

Frankfurt
an der Oder

Magdeburg

Bruges

Antwerp

Ghent

Louvain

Duisberg

COPPER

IRON

SILVER

Ypres

St Omer

Lille

Brussels

Liège

COAL

IRON

Harz Mts

Wrocław

Arras

Tournai

Douai

Cologne

Erfurt

TIN

WOAD

Péronne

Rouen

IRON

Frankfurt am Main

IRON

Erzberg Mts

Seine

Reims

Mainz

Prague

Paris

Lagny

Worms

Nuremberg

Provins

Metz

Regensburg

Troyes

Strasbourg

Rhine

Danube

Tours

Bar-sur-Aube

Augsburg

Vienna

Atlantic
Ocean

Loire

Bourges

Dijon

Besançon

Inn

Bay of
Biscay

Poitiers

La Rochelle

Lyon

St Gotthard

Brenner

The Alps

Pontebba

Drava

Bordeaux

St. Bernard

Milan

Brescia

Verona

Padua

Garonne

Mt Cenis

Pavia

Mantua

Venice

Bayonne

Albi

Rhone

Piacenza

Po

WOAD

IRON

Toulouse

Nimes

Avignon

Genoa

Parma

Modena

Bologna

Zara

Pyrénées

Montpellier

Arles

Pistoia

Forli

Béziers

Aigues
Mortes

Marseilles

Lucca

Florence

Ancona

Valladolid

Pisa

Siena

Volterra

Adriatic
Sea

Saragossa

Perpignan

Orvieto

Dubrovnik

Douro

Medina del
Campo

Ebro

Barcelona

Viterbo

Lisbon

Tagus

Toledo

Rome

Setúbal

Guadiana

Badajoz

Valencia

Gaeta

Barletta

Cordoba

Seville

Guadalquivir

Jaén

Palma

Ibiza

Naples

Salerno

Cádiz

Jerez

Granada

Múrcia

Cagliari

Málaga

Almería

Salé

Trapani

Palermo

Messina

Casablanca

Honein

Bougie

Bône

Tunis

Catania

Syracuse

Atlas Mts.

Mediterranean

Djerba I.

Tripoli

Genoan trade routes
Genoan trading posts and colonies
Venetian trade routes
Venetian trading posts and colonies
The Gascon wine trade
Main routes of Hanseatic trade
The main routes of north-south and of east-west
communications
O Towns with over 10,000 inhabitants in A.D. 1300
o Other towns
Champagne Fairs
Tunis Towns mentioned by the Florentine merchant,
Francesco Pegolotti c.1340
Main areas of cloth production for export
Granaries
Main centres of wine production for export
S Salt

POPULATION DENSITY IN A.D. 1300
Inhabitants per km²

31 or more
21 to 30
11 to 20
10 or less

0   400 kms
0   300 miles

Reval
Novgorod
WAX
FURS
Pskov
Riga
W. Dvina
FURS
Niemen
TIMBER
Smolensk
Vistula
Pripet
Dnieper
Volga
Oka
Kiev
Volga Astrakhan
acow
L'vov
Don
PPER
Dniester
Tane
Carpathians
Caspian
Sea
Dnieper
Moncastro
Caffa
Soldaia
Tisza
Caucasus
Danube
Black Sea
Varna
Trebizond
Tabriz
Stip
Pera
Constantinople
Taurus Mts.
Aegean
Sea
Phocaea
ALUM
Negroponte
Ephesus
Aleppo
Killini
Antalya
Antioch
Modon
Ayas
Euphrates
Cyprus Famagusta
Tigris
Candia
Beirut Damascus
Crete
an
S   e   a
Acre
Jerusalem
Damietta
Alexandria
Cairo
Nile

the First Crusade at the Council of Clermont in 1095, and his successors always took the lead in marshalling the resources of the feudal west for future crusades. The Second Crusade (1147-49), preached by the spiritual leader of Christendom in his time, St Bernard of Clairvaux, was led by the Holy Roman Emperor and the King of France; the Third (1189-92) by the Kings of France and England. The ostensible origin of the crusading movement was the request of the Byzantine Emperor Alexius I for western mercenaries to help against the Turks; its ostensible goal the defence of the Holy Places against the infidel. Jerusalem was taken in 1099 and held until 1187, and western feudal kingdoms constructed in the Holy Land. But its most important consequence was the sack of Constantinople by crusaders in 1204 and the dismemberment of the Byzantine Empire.

The crusades are often described as part of the expansion of feudal Europe. But the fleets of the First Crusade were provided by the Genoans and the Pisans, and the Fourth Crusade was directed to Constantinople by its Venetian paymasters, whose interests in the Balkans had expanded rapidly since Alexius I had bought naval assistance from them in return for extensive trading privileges throughout his Empire. Genoa and Pisa had begun their rise to power late in the tenth century, on the profits of piracy upon Muslim vessels in the Mediterranean; Venice by exporting slaves to Egypt. Throughout the period of the crusades the Italian cities were the main paymasters and the chief beneficiaries. The fortunes of the crusading states fluctuated far more according to the extent to which Italian trading interests were threatened than with the attitudes of the feudal monarchs. Unlike the knights and their clerical brothers who devoted much energy (and much sincerity) to convincing themselves of the

righteousness of the holy war, the cities felt no need to disguise their interest, and no ideology inhibited their pursuit of profit. 'The Venetians, the Genoese and the Pisans bring into Egypt choice products of the West, especially arms and war materials' wrote Saladin, the greatest of the Muslim leaders. 'This constitutes an advantage for Islam and an injury to Christianity.' In return for those goods, they brought to the West, which now offered a rapidly expanding market for luxuries, the spices, silks and perfumes of the Orient. Networks of trading posts were established and continued to flourish long after the crusading kingdoms had died (*Maps 26 and 28*) – as they did after the Mongol conquests diverted the Far Eastern trade routes towards the Black Sea ports (*see Map 31*), so that there was no longer any need for the Venetians and their compatriots to maintain outposts in the Holy Land.

The clash of values between the merchants and the knights which the crusades revealed so clearly was already transforming European society. Around 1000 society could be described as consisting of 'those who fight, those who pray and those who work (*agricultores*)'. The growth of population and diversification of economic activity brought new classes into being. Cities grew rapidly in what had been a wholly rural world (*see Map 28*). Their inhabitants clashed bitterly with each other as sharp divisions of wealth and power appeared between the weavers or seamen, often wretchedly poor, and the patricians, rapidly forming their own dynasties, who employed them; the cities themselves clashed with the secular and ecclesiastical aristocracy as they sought freedom to conduct their own affairs, protect their own interests, and eventually dominate the countryside around them (*see Map 33*). New tensions produced new institutions, new mentalities and a new cul-

ture, often sharply opposed to the chivalrous code of the aristocracy and the hierarchical conservatism of the church. The contrast was observed with distaste, but not with contempt, by Otto of Freising when he described the expedition of his nephew the Emperor Frederick Barbarossa to Italy in 1154. 'That they may not lack the means of subduing their neighbours' he wrote of the Milanese, 'they do not disdain to give the girdle of knighthood to young men of inferior status, and even some workers of the vile mechanical arts whom other peoples bar like the plague from respected and honourable pursuits. From this it has resulted that they surpass all other states of the world in wealth and power.'

Above: A street market at Soochow by Chang Tse-tuan, early twelfth century.

29 India under Muslim domination
The Sultanate of Delhi, founded in 1211 by Turks from Afghanistan, was the principal centre of Muslim power in India; but the fortunes of both Muslim and Hindu kingdoms fluctuated with the loyalties of the chiefs and officials commanding the military strongpoints which controlled the trade routes and the countryside. The invasions of Timur destroyed the hegemony of Delhi, and independent sultanates emerged in several regions.

Further reading: Janet Abu Lughod, *Before European Hegemony: The World System, AD 1250-1350* (OUP New York 1989): P. H. Sawyer, *Kings and Vikings* (Methuen 1982); Jacques le Goff, *Medieval Civilization* (Basil Blackwell 1988); J. R. S. Phillips, *The Medieval Expansion of Europe* (Oxford U.P. 1988); K. N. Chauduri, *Asia before Europe* (Cambridge U.P. 1990); Mark Elvin, *Patterns of the Chinese Past* (Methuen 1973; Stanford U.P.); R. Latham (trans.), *The Travels of Marco Polo* (Penguin 1958).

MAP 29 INDIA UNDER MUSLIM DOMINATION

Banu

Kabul

Kurram
Pass

Ghazni

Khyber
Pass

Batai
Pass

Gumal
Pass

Bolan
Pass

Karakoram

Himalayas

Jammu

Bhera   Sialkot   Nagarkot and Kangra
Jawalamukhi
1305
1322

Lahore   Pakpattan   Dipalpur
1241
1297-8

Talamba

Multan
1245

Sunam   Samana *1305*
1292   *1322*
Bhatinda
Sirsa   Thanesar

Uchch
1245

Bhatnair

Hansi   Tirawari
Kalanaur   Panipat
Meerut
Delhi   *1329*
Rewari   *1303*
Narnol   Baran   Amroha *1305*
Sambhal
Koil   Aonla
Bada'un
1305

*Thar
Desert*

Nagor

Jaisalmer

Mathura   Mainpuri   Bahraich
Bayana   Bhongaon
Chandwar   Etawah
Mandor   Ajmer   Gwalior
Siwana   Ranthambhor   Kalpi
Jalor   Banda
Mahoba

Sihwan
1299
1303

Thatta

Indus

Sutlej

TIRHUT

Gorakhpur   Darbhanga

Brahmaputra

JAUNPUR
Dalmau
Awadh
Jaunpur
Kara   Maner
Benares   Bihar   Pandua   Gaur   Sylhet
Kalinjar   Nadia
Rewa

Chanderi   Khujuraho

Idar   Dungarpur   Mandasaur   Bhilsa   Sanchi   *BENGAL*
Patan   Sarangpur   Raisen
Chittor   Ujjain   *MALWA*
Champaner   Dhar
GUJARAT   Baroda   Mandu   Hoshangabad
Ahmadabad   Cambay   *Narmada*   Kherla
Dwarka   Broach   Sultanpur   Asirgarh   Ratanpur
Thalner   Burhanpur   Raipur   *ORISSA*
Junagadh   Surat   Chittagong
Mangrol   Daman   Wairagarh   Bhubaneswar
Somnath   Daulatabad   Mahur   Puri
Paithan   Konarak

*Arabian
Sea*

Kalyan   Sirpur
Chaul   *Deccan   Ghats*
Godavari
Dabhol   Bidar   Warangal
Sangameshwar   Gulbarga   Golconda
Khelna   Bijapur   Rajmundry
Mudhol   Raichur
Belgaum   Mudgal   *Bay of Bengal*
Goa   Kampili   Kondavidu
Vijayanagar   Gooty   Udayagiri
Chataldrug   Nellore
Penukonda
Araga   Chandragiri
Mangalore   Kanchipuram
Dorasamudra   Mulbagal   **Mamallapuram**
Srirangapatna
Sarangam   Chidambaram
Calicut   Kannanur   Tanjore
Tirumangalam   Madurai

Quilon

Strongpoints and headquarters:

Delhi Sultanate c.1300
Delhi Sultanate after 1300
Independent sultanates c.1400
Bahmani Sultanate from 1347
Vijayanagar Empire from the 1340's
Areas contested by Bahmani and Vijayanagar
Rajput
Temporarily held by forces of Delhi
Areas controlled by Hindu Rajas
Areas dominated by Hindu chiefs
Expeditions of Khaljis
1296
1307
1309
1310
1311
Muslim shrine
Hindu shrine
1303   Dates of Mongol attacks before 1398
Invasion of Timur, 1398-99
Trading ports

500 km
0
0   300 miles

59

Heirs to the ancient world 4

TRADITION AND INNOVATION

The conquests of Islam which had halted at the Indus in the eighth century (see Map 19) were carried into India by Mahmud of Ghazni (r. 999-1030), whose West Asian empire was based on Afghanistan, and more permanently by Muhammed Ghuri, who conquered the kingdom of Delhi in 1192. His successors failed to create an Indian empire but the Sultanate of Delhi became the dominant political power of northern and central India, and the principal force in the establishment of Islam and its culture in the sub-continent (see Map 29).

Throughout the Islamic world conquest made a clear break with the past. The adoption of a new religion which accompanied it involved the explicit repudiation of the old cultures and traditions, even if in practice they remained deeply influential, and their literature and thought provided the foundation for the brilliant civilization of Islam's golden age. In Christendom and in China, on the other hand, the classical past and its traditions and values were cherished, and played a formative role in the civilizations' development. In both civilizations respect for tradition, as might be expected, acted as an inhibiting force, but by the end of the fifteenth century it was clear that the difference in the ways in which it had done so was to have momentous consequences.

By about 1100 the economic revolution had produced in China many of the features of an industrial society (*see Map 30*). Coal and iron were mined on a large scale, and the iron put to a great variety of uses for nails and chains and currency, in bridges and in buildings, for machinery, for the textile industries and agricultural tools, which were probably more widely available to the peasantry at this time than in the early twentieth century. Most of it, however, went to the state armaments factories, which every year turned out arrowheads by the million, swords and suits of armour by the tens of thousands, even armoured vehicles for use against cavalry. Other major industries included salt-processing, ship-building and printing, for a population in which both literacy and numeracy were widely diffused. Networks of roads and canals built and maintained by the state and elaborate arrangements for credit, including a paper currency, sustained a thriving internal trade. Ships with watertight bulkheads – unknown to Europeans until the nineteenth century – exchanged silk and porcelain for the luxuries of the civilized world in the Pacific, the Indian Ocean and the Persian Gulf.

If the wealth of the Northern Sung period (960-1126) enabled China to sustain tremendous military strength it also made it an ever more tempting prey to its barbarian neighbours. The Liao and the Hsi-Hsia were relatively civilized states with which the Chinese had regular if not invariably cordial diplomatic and trading relations. But in 1125 the Liao fell to invaders, the Chin Tartars from Mongolia who went on to occupy much of northern China, including the capital Kai-feng. The immediate consequences were not catastrophic. The industrial north was lost but the Southern Sung dynasty retained the regions where agricultural wealth had been increasing rapidly and overseas trade was most naturally based. The new capital at Hangchou soon became the largest city in the world, the centre of a wealthy, sophisticated, more urban, and in many ways more ostentatious society than its predecessor.

In the long run the fall of Liao had graver consequences. The Chin state became a conduit through which Chinese iron weapons passed to the Mongols beyond, to provide – quite literally – the sharp edge of the most horrific and most dramatically successful of all the barbarian invasions. Temujin was declared Supreme Monarch – Chingiz Khan – of the Mongol tribes in 1206 after he had unified them in years of bitter warfare. By simple military superiority – they were usually greatly outnumbered by their civilized opponents – and unexampled ferocity, his armies conquered the greatest empire in history. *Map 31* suggests that their raids were designed to prepare the way, by systematically eliminating every possibility of rivalry elsewhere, for the invasion of China, the traditional objective of the inhabitants of the Mongolian steppes. Chingiz died in 1227, while completing his second and permanent occupation

30 The China of the Northern Sung
About 1100 China probably excelled the rest of the world in economic development, literacy and numeracy. A far-flung trade and the presence on its boundaries of the relatively settled and civilized states of the Hsi-Hsia and the Liao made it more nearly part of a system of international relations than was the case under the Han or the Manchu.

Below: Merton College, Oxford, founded 1264 by Walter de Merton, Chancellor to Henry III.

31 The Mongols
The unification of the Mongol tribes under Chingiz Khan paved the way for the destruction of states and kingdoms throughout central Asia and eastern Europe, culminating in the conquest of China and the creation of the greatest land empire in history. It disintegrated rapidly, but Timur (*r.* 1360-1405), a descendant of Chingiz, threatened to renew it, and was planning to attack China at the time of his death.

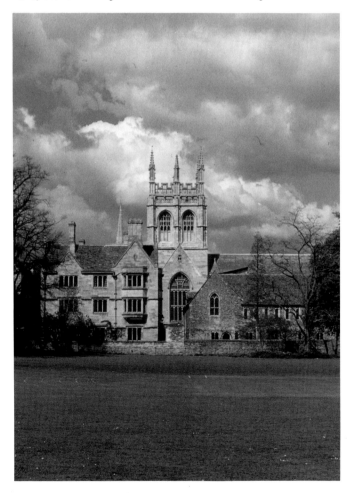

MAP 30 THE CHINA OF THE NORTHERN SUNG

Frontier of Northern Sung c.1100
Territory of Hsi-hsia at maximum extent
Territory of Liao
Major trading centre
Intermediate trading centre
Minor trading centre
Other cities
Main trade routes
Canals
Major navigable waterways

T'ang capital
Northern Sung capital
Southern Sung capital
Hsi-hsia military centres
Hsi-hsia capital
Liao chief residency
Liao residencies
HSI   Administrative circuits c.1100

0   400 km
0   200 miles

Gobi

CH'I-TAN
(LIAO)
(937-1125)

HSI-HSIA
(990-1227)

Huang-ho
(Yellow R.)

Northern course
of Huang-ho

Eastern course
of Huang-ho

T'U-FAN

TA-LI

TA-YUEH

G   Gold   P   Porcelain
S   Silver   C   Coal
I   Iron   Tea-growing
Cu Copper   regions
L   Lead   Salt-producing
T   Tin   regions

MAP 31 THE MONGOLS

Cologne
Breslau
Prague
Cracow
Venice
Kiev
Invasion of eastern Europe 1240-42
RUSSIAN PRINCIPALITIES
GOLDEN HORDE
Danube
CUMANS
Don
Volga
New Sarai
Tana
Old Sarai
Ural
1240
1224
1236
CHAGATAI
Constantinople
Black Sea
Caspian Sea
Aral Sea
L. Balkhash
1223
1219
Mediterranean Sea
SELJUKS OF RUM
TREBIZOND
Caucasus
Tiflis
KHWARAZM
Urgenj
Otrar
Balasaghun
QARA KHITAI
Tien
Konya
LESSER ARMENIA
1221
Maragheh
Tabriz
Oxus
1220
Bukhara
Samarqand (Timur's capital)
Kashgar
Aleppo
AYYUBIDS
Damascus
Sultaniyeh
1220
Alamut
Rayy
KHWARAZM-SHAH'S EMPIRE
Marv
Nishapur
Balkh
Hindu Kush
Acre
Jerusalem
1260
CALIPH DOMINIONS
Euphrates
1258
Baghdad
Hamadan
Isfahan
Herat
MAMLUK EMPIRE (from 1250)
Nile
Tigris
Kerman
ILKHANATE
Indus
Delhi
Shiraz
Ural Mts.
Ob
Himalaya
DELHI SU

Legend:

⊕ Pre-Mongol conquest capitals
⊙ Capitals of Mongol Khanates
RDE Mongol Khanates within the Empire
IRE Pre-Mongol states
Approximate boundary of empire at death of Chingiz Khan 1227
Approximate boundary of Empire c.1280
Boundaries of Mongol Khanates
Campaigns under Chingiz Khan 1206-27
Later major Mongol campaigns
Route of Marco Polo
Route of the elder Polos
Route of John of Plano Carpini, 1245-7
Route of William of Rubruck, 1253-7
Empire of Timur (Tamberlane), c.1405
Principal directions of Timur's invasions outside his empire

0   1000 km
0   750 miles

KHANATE

1218

Beshbalik

h'an

UIGHURS

Shachou

Kun'un Shan

TIBET

Tsangpo

TANATE

Ganges

Brahmaputra

Tagaung

Salween

BURMA

KHMER
EMPIRE

Mekong

Yenisey

L. Baikal

**MONGOL
TRIBES**
(unified 1206)

Qaraqorum

G o b i

1211

Shang-tu

1209

1226-7

HSI-HSIA

1215

Ta-tu

Ning-hsia

GREAT

Hwang-Ho

CHIN
EMPIRE

K'ai-feng

Feng-yüan

Conquest of Sung
1252-79

Ch'eng-tu

Yangtze

SUNG
EMPIRE

Hang-chou

Ch'üan-chou

Kuang-
chou

Amur

Yangtze

ANNAM

CHAMPA

to Singapore

63

of the Hsi-Hsia. The subjugation of China (which required the Mongols to learn new techniques of waterborne and siege warfare), as well as that of Russia and parts of the Middle East, was completed by his successors. They divided his empire between them, but always recognized the ruler of China as the Great Khan to whom the others remained subordinate in theory, and for some time in practice.

The Mongols drew a line across the history of Asia. Their savagery, no doubt exaggerated by legend, was quickly moderated as they realized the value of prosperous subjects. The Mongols lived on tribute and quickly saw how they could profit from trade, which they always encouraged. Italian merchants were prominent beneficiaries. Their bases in the Crimea and on the Black Sea became the great terminals of the overland trade which flourished as the routes to China and Qaraqorum became safer, and busier, than ever before. Correspondingly, the one successful defence against the Mongols, that of Egypt by its Mamluk rulers, severed Africa once again from the Middle East and made Mesopotamia a southern backwater of the empire of the steppes (*compare Maps 31 and 27*).

The political consequences of the Mongol conquests were less beneficial. Unlike most previous conquerors they did not govern their empire through existing administrations. They appointed in each region governors from some other part of the empire, or outside it altogether, whose sole function was to see that their tribute was paid and their dictates respected. Nothing less than total compliance was accepted from these officials, and no constraint was placed on the means by which they secured it. This system not only made Mongol rule detested but left a brutal and absolutist legacy. The Russian principalities, for example, which had emerged from the disintegration of the Kievan state (*Map 21*), had retained from their Byzantine inheritance a tradition that the ruler should consult the interests of his subjects and respect the restraints of Christian conduct. Their successor when the Mongol empire began to disintegrate was the Duchy of Moscow, whose effective founder Ivan I (*r. 1328-40*) secured his position by receiving from the Khan, for himself and his descendants, the right to collect the tribute in return for guaranteeing its payment (*see Map 43*). He got with it the right to exercise the Khan's absolute power over his new subjects. It was the beginning of a very different political tradition.

The Mongol conquest of north China was carried out with appalling ferocity. When it was completed the Chinese were treated as a subject people for the first time in their history. This followed the fall of a dynasty which had presided over unequalled peace and prosperity. The lesson was not lost. Chu Yuan-chang, the founder of Ming dynasty (1368-1644) left on his grave the words 'Rule like the T'ang and the Sung'. Action

32 Spain in the middle ages
The gradual 'reconquest' of Spain by Christians – by no means an exclusively military process – left Muslim and Jewish communities in the Christian kingdoms. Their co-existence produced the most distinctive characteristics of Iberian history, providing the main channel through which Greek and Arabic philosophy and science reached the West in the twelfth century, and, later, a bitter legacy of intolerance and persecution.

was suited to the words with a devotion that was, in the long run, self-defeating. The examination for the imperial bureaucracy, brought to a peak of scrupulous impartiality by the Sung (under whom scripts were recopied to protect the anonymity of the candidates) was restored. But its syllabus now demanded not only a minute knowledge of the great commentators on Confucius of the Sung period, but unquestioning adherence to their precepts. Even the form in which essays were to be written was soon exactly prescribed. The Sung had fallen not through any difficulty in maintaining their armies and military expenditures, such as had brought down their predecessors, but because Chinese weapons, knowledge and materials had been exported to the barbarians. The conquest had been assisted, perhaps decisively, by Chinese advisers. The Ming regime drew itself apart from the outer world. In spite of some notable achievements like the voyages of Cheng Ho to the African coast and East Indies between 1405 and 1433 the navy was run down, and trade and cultural contacts with outsiders increasingly discouraged. The accumulated wisdom and governmental expertise of the Chinese past was applied with devoted skill to the maintenance of the agricultural wealth of the interior and the development of internal trade and communications to produce a self-sufficient economy, maintaining relative prosperity and an advanced culture, without resort to the world beyond. It did so at the price of stagnation.

Compared with the territories which the Mongols ruled, western Europe was remarkably diverse in its economy and culture. This was due partly to its range of climate and terrain, and partly to the variety of influences to which it had been subjected. That it exhibited, nevertheless, a common culture and common attitudes and assumptions was the work of the Catholic Church. Ever since Pope Gregory I had organized the conversion of England just before 600, it had assumed responsibility for bringing new peoples within the orbit of civilization – with which indeed Christianity was synonymous among the western as it was among the eastern successors of the Roman Empire (*see Map 20*). In the middle of the eleventh century the Papacy began to shake the Church away from lay control, beginning a conflict with the German emperors which dominated European politics for centuries. The church gradually secured its freedom to elect its own popes, appoint its own bishops and other officers, and subject its clergy to its own (canon) law and machinery of government, centred on Rome, rather than those of the secular powers. In 1215 the Fourth Lateran Council, attended by more than 400 bishops from all over Europe, endorsed a programme of doctrinal, ritual and moral precepts to be observed by the faithful and administered and enforced by a clergy which was now clearly distinguished from the laity in dress, conduct (quite often in practice as well as in theory) and allegiance.

The clergy was Europe's equivalent to China's mandarins. No prince or magnate was without his clerical advisers, who often had very great influence. Since the clergy had a monopoly of literacy, except perhaps in Italy, from the ninth to the thirteenth centuries, the operations of government were necessarily in their hands. Great advances in

administration were made in the twelfth century, through written instruments, the keeping of records and accounts, the making of surveys of land and resources (of which the English Domesday in 1087 was the most remarkable example); these were carried out by clerks (*clerici*) under the supervision of the bishops and abbots who were the monarch's closest advisers. While the clerks contributed indispensably to the development of royal power they also strove, with a good measure of success, to set limits to its use. Charlemagne had been encouraged, as a Christian prince, to conquer Saxony, but his clerical adviser Alcuin rebuked him for massacring its pagan inhabitants. The men who staffed the Treasury and Chancery which gave Angevin England the most powerful grip over its subjects of any government in the Latin world (*see Map 25*) wrote 'mirrors for princes' which portrayed royal virtue as lying in moderation, compassion for the weak and respect for the rights and interests of their subjects. And when the barons of England decided, in 1215, to protect their rights and interests by rebellion, the archbishop of Canterbury helped them to write their manifesto, which became Magna Carta.

Like the mandarins, the European clergy derived their own common standards and culture from the intensive study of a body of venerated writings and commentaries on them. Like the mandarins they strove in their best moments to preserve their caste from becoming a closed one, notably (from the eleventh century) by insisting on celibacy, so that it could not be hereditary. But here the analogy, however loose, breaks down. The clerks were too various a class, serving too many masters with an insufficiently sophisticated bureaucratic apparatus either to maintain the same degree of conformity among themselves as the mandarins could, or the same degree of control over the world around

33 Italy in the middle ages
The cities of northern Italy used their early prosperity to establish independence as self-governing communes and their control over the countryside around them. By the end of the thirteenth century they were beginning to surrender to despotism. Their population is shown here on the eve of the Black Death, *c.* 1340.

34 Germany and Central Europe in the later middle ages
The expansion of German settlement in central Europe continued until the fourteenth century. It provided the chief stimulus to economic and commercial development and assisted the continuing consolidation of the territorial principalities in the Empire and in the kingdoms of Poland, Bohemia and Hungary.

MAP 32 SPAIN IN THE MIDDLE AGES

Legend:

1147	Areas and cities reconquered by Christians from Muslims
	Archbishoprics
	Monasteries influenced by Cluniac observance
	Monasteries influenced by southern French monastic observance
	Cistercian monasteries
	Principal royal residences and centres of government, shown for León-Castile and Aragon only
	Principal establishments of the Military Orders
	Principal Jewish communities on the eve of the pogroms of 1391
	Places at which translators are known to have worked in the 12th and 13th centuries
	Principal ports of the later middle ages
	Principal centres of banking in the later middle ages
	Genoese establishments in the 15th century
	Pilgrimage roads to Santiago de Compostela
	Sheepwalks (cañadas), approximate course

0   200 km
0   150 miles

MAP 33 ITALY IN THE MIDDLE AGES

St Gotthard
Septimer
St Bernard
Mt Cenis
Turin
Asti
Alessándria
Vercelli
Novara
Como
Bergamo
Brescia
Villach
Pontebba
Aquilèia
Grado
Brenner
REPUBLIC OF VENICE
Treviso
Vicenza
Verona
Padua
Venice
Chioggia 1381
DUCHY OF MILAN
Legnano 1167
Milan
Lodi
Pavia
Crema
Cremona
Mantua
Piacenza
Parma
Bobbio
Reggio nel'Emilia
Modená
Ferrara
X 1244
Po
Cisa
Bocchetta
Genoa
Via Aemilia
Bologna
Ravenna
Faenza
Forlì
Rimini
Futa
Pistoia
Camáldoli
San Godenzo
Mandrioli
Lucca
Pisa
Arno
REP. OF FLORENCE
Vallombrosa
Meloria 1284
Arezzo
Ancona
Siena
Via Francigena
PAPAL
Fonte Avellana
Perugia
STATES
Orvieto
Viterbo
Via Flaminia
Tiber
Farfa
Via Latina
Tagliacozzo 1267
Subiaco
Rome
Via Latina
Monte Cassino
Civitate 1061
Manfredonia
Capua
Aversa
1265 X
Benevento
Barletta
Trani
Bari 1071
KINGDOM
Naples
Conza di Campania
Via Appia
Acerenza
Monopoli
1293
Sorrento
Salerno
Bríndisi
Amalfi
OF NAPLES
Táranto
Corsica
Elba
Ligurian Sea
Adriatic Sea
Tyrrhenian Sea
Rossano
Cosenza
Santa Severina
Sardinia
Cágliari
Lipari Is.
Straits of Messina
Messina
Réggio Calabria
Trápani
Palermo 1090
KINGDOM OF SICILY
Catania
Mediterranean Sea
Tunis
Pantelleria
Malta
Drava
Sava

Legend:

- ░ Roads
- X Battles
- ⌂ Archdioceses
- ✛ Principal monasteries
- ◆ Principal universities
- ⋯⋯ Guelf alliance in Tuscany
- —— Ghibelline alliance in Tuscany
- ● Early communes
- ⊙ Town/city population over 50,000
- ○ "   "   "   "   c.50,000
- ⊙ "   "   "   20,000-40,000
- ○ "   "   "   c.10,000
- ▓ Areas dominated by Rome, Milan, Genoa, Florence and Venice c.1100
- —— Boundary of lordship 1450
- **Milan** Centre of lordship 1450

0 _____ 200 km
0 _____ 150 miles

MAP 34 GERMANY AND CENTRAL EUROPE IN THE LATER MIDDLE AGES

Legend:

- □ Town of over 20,000 population
- △ Town of 10-20,000 population
- ○ Town of under 10,000 population
- Archbishopric/bishopric with important territory
- Archbishopric (with date of foundation)
- Bishopric (with date of foundation)
- ◆ University
- ■ Member of Hanseatic League
- **MAI** Electoral territory
- GELD Important territory
- Boundaries of Empire in 1378
- Boundaries of lands of Teutonic Order in 1378
- Other boundaries
- Important trade routes
- Alpine passes
- Hapsburg lands in 1378
- Wittelsbach lands in 1378
- Luxemburg lands in 1378
- Lands of Swiss Confederation in 1378
- Areas of German settlement
- Areas of extensive use of German town law

Scale: 0 — 150 km / 0 — 100 miles

Baltic Sea

North Sea

DENMARK
Schleswig
HOLSTEIN
Stralsund
Greifswald
Kammin
Rostock
MECKLENBURG
POMERANIA
Lübeck
Ratzeburg
Schwerin
Stettin
Hamburg
Lüneburg
BREMEN
BRAUNSCHWEIG
Havelberg
BRANDENBURG
Verden
Berlin
Lebus
Brandenburg
Magdeburg
Minden
Braunschweig
Halberstadt
SAXONY
LAUSITZ
Osnabrück
Hildesheim
Goslar
MÜNSTER
PADERBORN
Merseburg
Meissen
Bautzen
BRESLAU
Deventer
Naumburg
Breslau
Soest
WESTFALIA
HESSE
Dortmund
BERG
Cologne
Erfurt
THURINGIA
Königgratz
Leitomischl
Olmütz
FULDA
Aachen
Königsberg
Frombork 1243
Elbing
Marienwerder
Danzig
TEUTONIC ORDER
Kulm
Thorn
DOBRZYN
Wfockfawek
Pfock
Warsaw
Lowicz
Gniezno
Poznan
Kaliszo
(GREAT) POLAND
(LITTLE)
Glogau
Cracow
GALICIA

Maastricht
COLOGNE
JÜLICH
NASSAU
Frankfurt
TRIER
Mainz
MAINZ
WÜRZBURG
BAMBERG
Cheb (Eger)
Prague 1348
Pilsen
BOHEMIA
Brno
MORAVIA
Nitra
Trier
LUXEMBURG
Worms
PALATINATE
Speyer
Heidelberg
UPPER PALATINATE
Nuremberg
Regensburg
Eichstätt
Esztergom
Vác
Reims
Verdun
METZ
LOTHARINGIA
Toul
Strasbourg
Nördlingen
WÜRTTEMBERG
Tübingen
Ulm
Augsburg
Freising
Munich
BAVARIA
Chiemsee 1216
Passau
AUSTRIA
Vienna 1468
Wiener Neustadt 1468
Bratislava
Gyor
Pest
HUNGARY
Veszprém
Kalocsa
Pécs

HOLLAND
Haarlem
Kampen
Amsterdam
Deventer
Leiden
GELDERN
Hague
Delft
ZEELAND
BRABANT
Antwerp
Melines
Brussels
LIÈGE
Namur
HAINAULT
Tournai
Cambrai

BURGUNDY
FRANCHE-COMTÉ
Basel 1460
Zürich
Solothurn
Lucerne
Zug
SWISS CONFEDERATION
Chur
Constance
Lausanne
L. Geneva
Sion
Geneva
Dijon
SAVOY
Lyon
DAUPHINÉ
Grenoble
Great St. Bernard
Little St. Bernard Pass
Mont Cenis Pass
Turin
Pavia 1367
Vercelli
MILAN
Milan
Bergamo
Brescia
Cremona
Mantua
Piacenza
Po
VERONA
Verona
Vicenza
Padua
Venice
Treviso
Aquileia
Trieste
KRAIN
Lubliana 1462
Zagreb
Dakovo 1229
Drava
Sava
Adriatic Sea

TIROL
Brenner Pass
St. Gotthard
Lukmanier Pass
Septimer Pass
Splugen Pass
The Alps
Brixen
Trent
CARINTHIA
Lavant 1228
Seckau 1218
STYRIA
Gurk
SALZBURG

67

them. On the contrary, the relative autonomy of the European intelligentsia from the structures of both church and state was its most distinctive characteristic. It stemmed directly from the collapse of the Roman state in the west, which compelled the guardians of learning and culture to develop their own institutions (at first in the monasteries), find patrons and protectors wherever they could, and in doing so acquire a measure of independence which they never entirely lost.

The tremendous advance of thought and learning in the twelfth-century West both owed and contributed much to this independence. It was largely a by-product of the assault on Islam, and in the first place of the Spanish reconquest. Islamic civilization far excelled that of Europe; when the largest libraries of the West contained four or five hundred volumes that at Cordoba had four hundred thousand. Among them were the works of the Greek and Hellenistic philosophers and scientists, translated into Arabic after the conquests of Syria and Egypt, but for the most part unknown to readers of Latin. Now they were translated with the help of Christian Arabs and of the Jews who were well established all over Spain (see Map 33). Later Norman Sicily, the crusading kingdoms and Constantinople became centres of translation directly from Greek. The flood of new material, rising fast from about 1140 onwards, transformed every branch of knowledge and teaching. At the same time the transformation of Europe into an urban and bureaucratic society was creating an immense demand for education. In consequence the teachers in the great cities were able to establish their right to decide who should be of their number, and who and what they should teach. From the thirteenth century the universities of Europe, led by Paris and Bologna (see Maps 25, 33 and 34) were legally self-governing corporations, effectively independent of both Church and state.

Like the universities, the towns of Europe won their freedom in the high Middle Ages, successfully demanding from the end of the eleventh century charters which granted them exemption from the taxes and jurisdiction of their feudal lords. Northern Italy, its cities more numerous and much more populous than those of any other region, was Europe's urban region par excellence (compare Maps 28 and 33). To the profits of their far-flung trading colonies (see also Map 26) they were now adding those of the banking and insurance services, which they provided all over Europe, often playing a critical role in political events in consequence. The Bardi and Peruzzi banks had more branches and more capital at the beginning of the fourteenth century than the Medici bank (see Map 35) had a hundred years later, and had far more liquid wealth at their disposal than any monarch. In such a world the skills of literacy and numeracy were necessarily widely distributed. The intense competitiveness and rich opportunities of city life produced on the one hand continuous, often bitter and eventually self-destructive conflict both within and between the cities, and on the other a secular culture of immense vitality, the greatest masterpieces of European building, painting and literature, and a tradition of political and intellectual independence which survived the efforts of German emperors and papal agents alike to subdue it.

The agricultural expansion upon which economic growth and political development rested reached its limit in most places in the late thirteenth century. Falling crop yields and more frequent famine produced the Black Death which between 1347 and 1352 killed up to a third of the population in the worst affected regions (see Map 35). Recurrent epidemics delayed recovery until the end of the century and beyond. Prolonged and savage wars over much of Europe increased the consequent miseries, and swelled the taxes which monarchs extorted from their subjects. The peasant revolts which followed, severely frightening the governors of France and England in particular, were paralleled by the growing bitterness of civil conflict in the towns, and rising signs of popular discontent with the privileges and exactions of the clergy. All these elements were involved in the devastating and fateful wars which originated in criticism of clerical corruption by a distinguished scholar and teacher, John Hus (who died at the stake in 1415) and became a popular rebellion with aristocratic support, against the imperial domination of Bohemia (1419-36; see Map 35). This war foreshadowed the wars of the Reformation era in bloodiness and bitterness as well as in the issues involved.

The growth of government in the twelfth and thirteenth centuries and the miseries of the fourteenth contributed to the creation of a less open and less pluralistic society. The Church vindicated its claim to spiritual leadership by persecuting as heretics those who resisted it. They were especially numerous in the Low Countries, Lombardy and the Languedoc, where their presence provided the Capetian kings with an excuse for the brutal conquest of the County of Toulouse (1209-29; see Map 25) and the Pope for the creation of the Inquisition. The Church's demand for Christians to conform now also encouraged a rising tide of popular hostility towards the Jews, who were ordered to wear distinctive clothing by the Fourth Lateran Council. The withdrawal of royal protection (which was largely responsible for their unpopularity in the first place) as the rise of the Italian banks made their financial services superfluous and the debts owed to them an embarrassment led to their expulsion from England in 1290 and France in 1306; and they were driven from western Germany towards the new lands in the east when a succession of pogroms made them scapegoats for the Black Death. In Spain too, where three cultures had coexisted fruitfully for so long, tolerance broke down, and persecution of the Jews started in earnest in 1391; the Inquisition made up for its late arrival there, in 1480, by pursuing their descendants – particularly those who had converted to Christianity – with special ferocity. Secular monarchs did not hang back. In 1307 the king of France seized the lands of the Knights Templar in his dominion, justifying the action by torturing them

until they confessed that they were part of an international satanist conspiracy. A century later the technique was being widely imitated by those who had grudges against their neighbours: accusations of witchcraft were pursued by inquisitors and magistrates with an enthusiasm which would bring scores of thousands to the stake all over early modern Europe.

Nevertheless these reverses did not undo the achievements of the twelfth and thirteenth centuries. Economic failure in some areas was offset by rapid development in others. The Hansa towns of northern Europe formed a political and trading

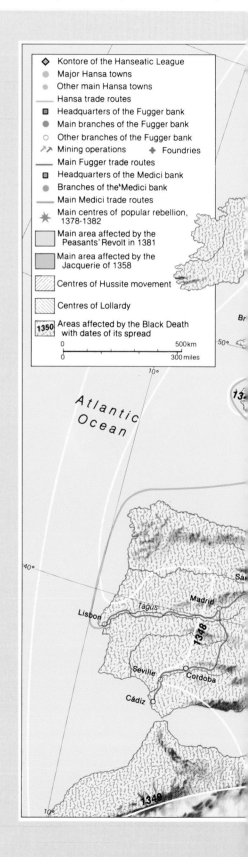

35 The economy of the later middle ages
In the fourteenth century Europe was seized by disease, famine and revolt. Nevertheless new trade routes were established and new centres of production and exchange opened up, especially in central and eastern Europe, to create a larger, more varied economy: compare with *Map 28* which this map complements, but does not supersede.

monopoly which dominated their area, and contributed greatly in the thirteenth and fourteenth centuries to the development of the Baltic and the eastern expansion of the Germans (*see Maps 34 and 35*); the extension of their routes through southern Germany to the Mediterranean and along the Atlantic coast helped to create a larger and more varied European trading community. If the Flemish cloth industry declined, Dutch shipping grew vigorous on the Baltic trade; and wars in the Iberian peninsula hastened the maritime expansion of Portugal. The tyrannical ambitions of the European rulers were also a sign of the limitations on

their power, and of how little they controlled the vital forces of European society; the peasant revolts attacked political weakness as well as financial exaction, and the Inquisition could prevent neither the dissemination of religious disaffection among the people nor the increasing boldness of speculation among the intellectuals both inside and outside the Church. For many Europeans the fifteenth century was not a happy time or, as they saw themselves become the last heirs of antiquity when Constantinople fell to the Ottoman Turks in 1453, a secure one. Nevertheless, theirs was a fortunate inheritance.

Further reading: D. O. Morgan, *The Mongols* (Basil Blackwell, 1987); Morris Rossabi, *Khubilai Khan, His Life and Times* (University of California Press 1988); Joseph Needham, *The Grand Titration* (Allen and Unwin 1969; Books Demand UMI); R. Mottahedeh, *The Mantle of The Prophet: Religion and Politics in Iran* (Chatto and Windus 1985; Simon & Schuster Trade); R. I. Moore, *The Formation of a Persecuting Society: Power and Deviance in Western Europe, 950-1250* (Basil Blackwell 1987); George Holmes, *Europe: Hierarchy and Revolt, 1320-1450* (Collins 1975); Lauro Martines, *Power and Imagination* (Allen Lane 1980; Random House).

MAP 35 THE ECONOMY OF THE LATER MIDDLE AGES

The age of European supremacy 1

EUROPE AND A WIDER WORLD

Opposite page above: Columbus landing at San Salvador in the Bahamas, October 12 1492.

36 The European discovery of the world
Late in the fifteenth century the Europeans began to discover the oceans and the other advanced people of the world. The Portuguese established a maritime empire in the Far East from the base provided by their earlier exploration of the African coast, while the Spanish conquered a land empire in America from their base in the Caribbean.

Further reading: G. V. Scammell, *The World Encompassed* (Methuen, 1981; University of California Press); Eric Wolff, *Europe and the People Without History* (University of California Press, 1982); Philip D. Curtin, *Cross-cultural Trade in World History* (Cambridge U.P. 1984); C. R. Boxer, *The Portuguese Seaborne Empire* (Hutchinson 1969); J. H. Elliott, *The Old World and the New* (Cambridge U.P. 1970); J. Burckhardt, *The Civilization of the Renaissance in Italy* (1 ed., Penguin, 1860).

At the end of the fifteenth century Europe was not evidently the most advanced civilization. Those of India, the Islamic world and, especially, China were richer and more sophisticated. Yet within three hundred years Europe had seized control of the oceans, destroyed the Aztecs, Incas and Mayas of South America (Map 36), conquered vast territories throughout the Americas and in India and Siberia, and organized a complex and immensely profitable worldwide commercial system (see Map 46).

It seems surprising that China, with its huge land mass, large population and stable political organization under the Ming dynasty (1368-1644) did not 'discover' Europe. After 1400, sturdy Chinese junks traded extensively in the Pacific and Chinese paper currency circulated widely. In seven expeditions between 1405 and 1433 the Grand Eunuch Cheng Ho sailed to Borneo, the Philippines, Ceylon, Malacca and East Africa. The conservatism of China's governors stifled the initiative. The mandarins disliked Muslims, eunuchs and favourites – Cheng was all three – and regarded trade as exploitation, and the outside world with suspicion. Official records of Cheng's expeditions were destroyed within 30 years, monopolies discouraged commerce, the paper currency collapsed, and external influences were discouraged. The Ottoman Turks, who presented such a desperate threat to Europe (*see Map 39*) had similar inhibitions. The rich bankers of Constantinople in 1500 were foreigners, Greek Christians or (like the 'Fugger of the Orient', Joseph Nasi) Portuguese Jews, and the Ottomans dispatched no ambassadors to the west, translated none of its literature – much of it by now available in print – and relied on slaves in their army to provide new military technology.

The 'age of reconnaissance' was launched from the smallest and least-endowed of European principalities, Portugal. The capture of the North African Moorish city of Ceuta in 1415 was followed by nearly a century of patient exploration of the West African coast, frequently interrupted by war in the Iberian peninsula, and by Portugal's domestic concerns (*see Map 36*). At last Bartholomeu Diaz triumphantly rounded the Cape of Good Hope in 1487, and in 1498 Vasco da Gama reached India. Within a decade and a half the Portuguese, using Asian pilots, bribery, and extensive naval bombardment, established fortresses and trading sta-

tions at Goa, which became the spiritual, administrative, and commercial centre of the Portuguese empire, Malacca, the centre of the spice trade in the Orient, and the Moluccas. The port of Mozambique was founded in 1507, and Ormuz, the guardian port of the Persian Gulf, in 1515. In 1557 they made a base on the China coast at Macao. For a few years nearly all the spices for Europe were carried by the Portuguese, but they never established a monopoly of the trade. They were dependent upon a delicate commercial system, always subject to disruption, in which the gold from the Zambeze area bought spices in the Indies, which paid for the expedition on its return.

Discovery begat imitation. The rivalry between Portugal and Castile spread down the West African coast with Castile's capture of the Canary Islands in the 1470s. Portugal (like the crusading powers of the thirteenth and fourteenth centuries) appealed in vain to the Pope to protect the monopoly granted in Papal Bulls of 1454 and 1456. In 1493, five years after Diaz returned from the Cape of Good Hope, Christopher Columbus' ship the *Nina* put into Lisbon, having returned across the Atlantic in a Spanish-sponsored expedition which claimed that it had discovered Cathay (Asia). Columbus, descended from a family of Genoese cartographers, was a careful and accurate navigator. The route of his first voyage to the 'West Indies' became that used by Spanish shipping to and from the New World, and his speed of crossing was rarely beaten in the sixteenth century. Castile claimed, and received, Papal protection for this new route to 'Asia', and an important line of demarcation between Portuguese and Castilian 'Asia' was achieved in the Treaty of Tordesillas (1494), although its precise geographical position was still disputed.

The purpose of Columbus' three subsequent

voyages was rather different from that of the Portuguese explorers. He took with him not trading goods, but farmers, artisans, priests, tools, seeds and animals, to establish a new community across the Atlantic. Colonies were established at Española, and Santo Domingo (*see Map 43*). Increasingly, after 1500, as explorers' reports were digested, the suspicion hardened that this was not Asia but a new world. The conviction was strengthened by John Cabot, Amérigo Vespucci and others and confirmed in 1519, when Ferñao Magalhaes (Magellan) sailed round the tip of southern America. His captain, del Cano, became the first man to sail round the world (*Map 36*). In less than 30 years the map of the main islands of the Caribbean was established, but that was twice as long as it had taken the Portuguese, with the aid of their Asian pilots, to chart the East Indies.

The early settlements in the Caribbean proved disappointing. They were vulnerable, quarrelsome and economically insecure. European diseases and ill-treatment cut down the native Carib population. Partly to escape the quarrels, various expeditions were sent through the Gulf of Mexico. On the basis of their intelligence a new colony was established in Panama in 1519 and a larger expedition set out for Mexico under the command of the first and greatest of the *conquistadores*, Hernan Cortès (*Map 44*). His letters and four other eyewitness reports of his conquest of Mexico give a uniquely detailed account of their aims and methods. They reveal Cortès trying to prevent unnecessary bloodshed amongst the Aztecs he was conquering, aware of his difficulties in controlling the ill-disciplined forces under him, fascinated by the new culture before his eyes, constantly alive to the classical precedents for the conquest of primitive peoples (such as Julius Caesar's), and persistent in his attempts to maintain the chivalric and knightly values of his native southern Spain. But Cortès could not prevent the destruction of the capital of the Aztecs, Tenochtitlán, (where, subsequently, he founded Mexico City), and to reward the extravagant aspirations of his followers he distributed Aztec villages amongst them in *encomienda*, a system of quasi-manorial tribute.

With the Mexican example before them, other *conquistadores*, with less sympathy and more greed, carved out similar empires for themselves. Guatemala (1523-42), New Granada (1536-9), and central Chile (1540-58) were all conquered, but they never rivalled Mexico and Cuba. *Conquistadores* like Francisco de Pizarro and Nuño de Guzmán bloodily subdued the Incas and Mayas. Wherever there were Indians, the *encomienda* system was established, and the parasitic Spaniards lived off the tribute in the cities which they founded in the New World – Panama, Darien, Santiago, Lima, Santa Fé de Bogotá. The finest fruits of conquest, the first productive silver mines, were discovered at Potosí in central Peru in 1545, which remained the biggest single source of silver in the world for a hundred years (*see Map 43*).

The age of the *conquistadores* was troublesome and brief. They had undertaken great hardships and risked their lives and fortunes, and some had great rewards. Others were overwhelmed by the unexploitable, untapped reserves of space in America. Hernando de Soto, whose expedition reached the Appalachians and the Mississippi, or Coronado who crossed the Rio Grande and reached the Prairies, could make nothing of the vast expanse of lands, nomadic peoples and roving herds of cattle (*see Map 36*). Francisco de Orellana, who sailed down the Amazon after crossing the Andes, despaired of the dense tropical forests of the Amazon basin. Even those who were successful attracted the suspicions of the Crown, and if they escaped the knives of their rivals were soon replaced by an effective royal administration. Some settled as ranchers and miners. Others, like Cortès, returned to Spain to a bored and litigious retirement.

The motives of the Portuguese seamen and the Castilian *conquistadores* were mixed, powerful and long-established. Memories of crusade were still powerful in the Iberian peninsula. The last province of Castile was captured from the Moors in the same year that Columbus set out for America (*see Map 32*). None of the early explorers would have repudiated the motive which was attributed to Prince Henry the Navigator (master-mind of the Portuguese explorations in the middle of the fifteenth century) by his contemporary biographer: the conversion of the natives to Christianity and the defeat of the Infidel. But Prince Henry was also interested ('as was natural') in profit. The pace of Portuguese discoveries increased once they had reached the gold, slaves, and spices along the Guinea coast. More gold was discovered in the kingdoms of East Africa, and with the spices of the East Indies provided the basic staples of the Portuguese empire. Two powerful legends symbolized the motives of the early explorers: that there was a powerful Christian ruler somewhere to the East (*Prester John*), and a powerful and rich city of gold somewhere in the Orient (*Cathay*).

The first thing that distinguished Europe from

other civilizations and enabled it to discover the world was its ability to imitate, especially in technical developments. The fifteenth century saw, for instance, a fruitful combination of the Arabic type of Mediterranean ship with Atlantic vessels, to produce a craft which could go anywhere and get back again. The combination of lateen and square-rigged sails, developed by Portuguese shipbuilders in the caravel, could be worked by a small crew (shortage of water and food was the main hazard of long voyages) and could sail closely to the wind. Other advances in hull design produced ships which could sail their course more accurately. Few expeditions were mounted in first-class ships, but even fewer suffered from defects in their sailing craft. Mounted with guns, they proved capable of protecting oceans as well as discovering them. The other tradition alive in the Spanish peninsula was that of mathematics and astronomy, in the hands of Jews. Jewish mathematicians produced traverse tables to indicate approximate journey times and Jewish astronomers produced manuals for the declination of the sun at various latitudes. In Portugal, unlike Spain, Jews were tolerated.

Secondly, Europe did not despise merchants and mercantile wealth. The towns of northern Italy had grown rich upon the trade of the Mediterranean; Italian merchants traded in the bulk-cargoes of grain, salt and fish and, more importantly, with the Arabs in silks, spices and precious metals (*see Maps 28 and 35*). In their manner of conducting their business, sharing their risks, accounting for their profits, and facilitating credit, they were admired and copied in the cities of the southern Netherlands and southern Germany. The Portuguese crown, after initial reluctance, encouraged the participation of merchants in its ventures, and the great fleet which sailed from Lisbon in 1505 was largely financed by foreigners – Genoese, Florentine and German. In later expeditions the Crown undertook the voyages, but sold the entire cargoes, frequently in advance, to merchant syndicates. Once the colonies

of the New World were established, it was the merchants of Antwerp who provided the colonists with the goods of the Old World, and the bankers of the Spanish crown in Genoa and Augsburg (like the Fuggers) who distributed the silver from the mines of Potosí across Europe.

Above all, the 'age of reconnaissance' was also the 'age of renaissance'. One of the most brilliant chapters of Jacob Burckhardt's famous book, *The Civilization of the Renaissance*, was entitled 'The Discovery of the World and of Men'. In it he discussed the delicate relationship between two forms of exploration, that of the inner world and the senses, and that of the physical world. He compared the accounts of medieval travellers outside Europe with those of the Renaissance explorers and concluded that the medieval travellers took what they found for granted, neither criticising it nor comparing it with their own experiences. The Renaissance explorer was different. Having gained a sense of historical perspective from the rediscovery of the different culture and civilization of the ancient world, he was more receptive, intellectually readier to appreciate, without rejecting, the different cultures and civilizations around him. Yet this is difficult to apply to most of the *conquistadores*. And it took two centuries for Europe to absorb the impact of the initial discoveries of the sixteenth century. Only by 1600 were the flora and fauna of the New World adequately described and categorized; it took longer for its carbohydrates (potato, sugar and maize) and vitamins to change the European diet. Only by 1700 was the New World in North America and Brazil beginning to be settled (*Map 44*). Only in the seventeenth century did the Dutch and English develop effective commercial and colonial empires along the lines of the Portuguese or Castilian. When the fruits of discovery had been absorbed, the process could begin again – this time in Siberia, India, Australia and on the margins of America.

MAP 36 THE EUROPEAN DISCOVERY OF THE WORLD

Arc

Spitzbergen

Bylot-Baffin
1616

Baffin
Island
Davis
1585/87

Eskimos

North-West Indians

Eskimos

Hudson
Straits

Frobisher
1576

Hudson
Bay

Hudson 1610

Algonquins

Button
1612

S. Cabot
1517

Davis 1587

Cabot 1497

Bristol

Eur

Drake
1579

Cabrillo
1542

Cartier
1534

John Cabot
1497

Cabot 1498

Drake

California

John Cabot
1498

American Indians

Verrazano
1523-4

Atlantic Ocean

Lisbon

Cadiz

John Cabot
1498

Westerlies

Azores

de Soto
1539

Gomez
1524

Diego de Sevilla
1432

Ulloa
1539

Texans

Ponce de Leon
1515

Bahamas Is.

Columbus 1492

Canary
Islanders
1312?/1336

Gonçalo Velho
1416

Nomads of
the Sahara

Becerra
1533

Cortes
1519

Urdaneta 1565

Mexico City
(Tenochtitlan)

Caribs

Cuba

Española

N.E. Trades

Nuno de Tristão
1441/43

Cordoba
1517

Columbus
1502-4

Columbus
1493-4

Spanish Main

Cape Verde Is.
Cadamosto de Noli.
1456/8

Diniz Diaz
1443-4

West
Sudanese

Timbuctoo

SONGHAI

East
Sudanes

Aztecs

Mayas

Montejo
1527-8

Columbus
1502-4

Nuno de Tristão
1446

Niani

MOSSI

HAUSA

Pedro de Evora
1482

Saavedra 1527

N.E. Trades

Dávila
1514

Balboa
1513

Ehinger
1529

Vespucci 1499

Columbus
1498

A. Fernandez
1446

Guinea coast
peoples

S. da Costa
1461/70

BENIN

Peop
Afri

Bastidas
1500

Caribs

A. de Hojeda
1498-9

Magellan 1519

João de Santarem 1471
Fernando Po
1472 Sequeira
1472

Pacific
Ocean

Isthmus of
Panama

Pizarro and Almagro
1524/26

Ruiz de Estrada
1526

S.E. Trades

KONG

Diego Cão
1485-6

Equator

Mendaña and Quiros 1595-6

Pizarro
1528

Brazilian
Indians

Pinzon
1499-1500

Fernão Noronha
1501/2

João da Nova
1501

Mendaña 1567-69

Incas

Terra de
Vera Cruz

America
(name first used in 1507)

João da Nova
1502

Bantu

Gê.
Botecudos

Treaty of Tordesillas 1494

Drake 1577/80

Saint Helena
Bay

Chilean
Indians

Chaco
Indians

Brazilian
Indians

Walfish Bay

Bartholemeu Dia
1486-88

Drake

PORTUGAL
SPAIN

Magellan 1519-20

Dias de Solis
1516

Patagonians

Valdivia
1540

Vasco da Gama 1497

Tristan da Cunha
c. 1510

Westerlies

Cabral 1500

Roaring Forties

Port Saint Julian
1520

Falkland Is.
Hawkins
1594

Magellan's Straits

Tierra del Fuego
F. de Hocues
1526

Legend

	Hunter-gathering cultures
	Nomads and stock-raisers
	Primitive cultures
	Advanced cultures
	Literate civilisations
	Routes for voyages of discovery

Drake Explorers

- □ Spanish expeditions
- □ Portuguese ··
- ■ French
- ■ English
- □ Dutch

- – – – Political lines of demarcation between Spanish and Portuguese exploration
- ▬▬▬ The world known to Europeans, c. 1450
- ▬▬▬ The world known of by Europeans, c. 1450

Mayas Peoples

← Approximate prevailing winds (shown for the first quarter of the year)

c Ocean

Barents 1596-7

Novaya Zemya

Willoughby-
Chancellor 1553

Barents
1594

Borough
1556

Willoughby
1553

Archangel

Arctic Circle

Reindeer Hunters

Hünos
Ghiliaks
Goldes

Mongols

eans

Kazak
Kirghiz

East
Mediterranean
Europeans

Koreans

Japanese

Pinto
1549-51

Francis Xavier
1549-51

Tokyo

Muslims

Tibetan
shepherds
and nomads

Near east
shepherd
peoples

Chinese

Pinto
1543

Mascarenhas 1517

Hawaiian
Islanders

Arab
nomads

Covilha

Ormuz (Dubaiji)
1507

Hindu and
Muslim Indian

Macão

Tropic of Cancer

de la Torre
1544-5

Aden
1524

Covilha
1488-90

Malabar
Coast

Goa
1510

Calicut

1498

Perestrello
1514-16

Philippines
Negritos

Drake

Pacific
Ocean

ETHIOPIA

Nile
peoples

ADAL

S.W.
Monsoon
July

Cochin

Colombo
1510

Végas

1516

Magellan

Somalis

Da Gama 1498

Diego Lopez de
Sequeira 1509-10

Sakais
Semangs

Simao d'Abreu
1523

Serrano 1511
Francis Xavier 1546

of the
Congo

East
African
Lake
peoples

Covilha
1488-90

N.E.
Monsoon
January

Indian Ocean

Malacca
1511

Peoples of
Indonesia

Melanesian
Papous

Equator

BURUNDI

Malindi

Sumatra

Antonio d'Abreu 1511

Ortiz de Retes
1545

LUBA

Zanzibar
Da Gama
1498

Seychelles

Koubous

Java

NDA

S.E. Trades

East
African
nomads

Mozambique

MWENEMUTAPA

Melgachians

Zimbabwe

Sofala

ROZWI

Diego Diaz
1500

Pedro
Mascarenhas
1507

Drake 1577-80

del Cano (after Magellan) 1521-22

Treaty of Saragossa
1527

Australians

Tropic of Capricorn

ttentots

oisan

Cape of
od Hope

Cabral 1500

PORTUGAL
SPAIN

Polynesians

Southern Ocean

The age of European supremacy 2

THE EURASIAN LAND EMPIRES

Above: The Taj Mahal.

37 The Far East in the seventeenth century
The Manchu occupation of China after the fall of the Ming dynasty in 1644, and the establishment of the Tokugawa shogunate in Japan in 1603, installed strong regimes. Both now achieved internal order and prosperity though with social rigidity and deep suspicion of the westerners who were now beginning to appear in the Far East.

38 The Manchu empire at its height
The enormous extension of the Chinese empire under the Manchu dynasty brought an end to the millennial conflict between urban and agrarian China proper and the peoples of the steppes, mountains and forests beyond. A dual political entity came into being: the older (Ming) empire remained under bureaucratic rule while most of the new acquisitions were ruled by the Court of Colonial Affairs (Li-fan-yuan) working through local rulers and chiefs.

Both China and Japan looked back to the philosophy of Confucius and developed it in different ways into a powerful ideology serving the practical needs of empire.

In China, Confucianism stood for benevolent and patriarchal bureaucracy with a mildly conservative, conformist and inward-looking stamp. In Japan, by contrast, it was a newer ideology, only officially adopted by the Tokugawa dynasty in the early seventeenth century, expressly imported upon a Chinese model to uphold a warrior aristocracy (turned bureaucracy) and an autocratic emperor (*see Maps 37 and 38*).

Ming China was an impersonal empire. An ambitious, forceful emperor could act decisively but the weight of tradition guarded by the mandarins of the largest and most impressive bureaucracy of the early modern world limited his power. Central government was located in the planned capital of Peking after 1421, and its six ministries supervised major areas of imperial life through a carefully organized provincial administration which extended to the borders of old Han China. Mandarins were recruited nationally through rigorous examinations. Incompetence and corruption were checked by the Office of Censors, to which young bureaucrats were seconded to censure their elders and advance themselves through their zeal and integrity.

The military power of the empire (by contrast) was separate and subordinate. Positions in the army were hereditary, and the quality of the armed forces gradually deteriorated. Troops were stationed defensively along the (partially) reconstructed Great Wall. Although the Tartars advanced to the gates of Peking in 1556, the Ming dynasty was largely spared heavy pressure on its landward frontiers.

The prosperity of the Chinese empire in the sixteenth century reflected its political stability. It was first disrupted by the Japanese invasion of Korea in 1592 and 1597 (*Map 37*). The Japanese were repulsed, but the economic stagnation of many regions in the next century increased the relative cost of the administration, and peasant rebellions enfeebled the central government. The emperor, surrounded by up to 10,000 eunuchs, withdrew to the seclusion of his court, and left power entirely in the hands of a divided bureaucracy. These weaknesses were exploited by the

Manchu, militarily formidable neighbours on the north-east border who, partly under Mongol influence, rejected Chinese overlordship about 1609. They took Peking in 1644 and in another four decades had firm control over the whole of China and Taiwan. Whereas the Mongol Yuan dynasty had ruled China through foreigners, the Manchu relied on the established machinery of imperial government to control the former empire, while their vast new territories were ruled by a newly-created Court of Colonial Affairs that worked through local rulers and chiefs (*see Map 38*).

Sixteenth-century Japan was an island kingdom, with no real central government, political stability or civilian rule. In theory sovereignty resided in the emperor, in the court at Kyoto, but in practice power had passed through civil war from the hands of his hereditary military commander (the *shogun*) to local overlords (*daimyos*) who commanded a hereditary caste of warriors (the *samurai*). Under the *daimyos* Japan suffered a century of fierce warfare and shifting allegiances. Powerful Buddhist monasteries and merchant guilds added to the forces of fragmentation, while self-governing leagues of farmers and landowners were formed to resist the *daimyos*.

From this confusion a series of military leaders emerged to attempt, often with great cruelty, to impose their authority upon Japan. Odo Nobunaga took Kyoto in 1568 and destroyed the Buddhist temples, massacring 20,000 monks. His lieutenant and successor Hideyoshi eliminated the remaining opposition, appointed himself chief minister and legalised the position of the *samurai* as an exclusive nobility of the sword. Hideyoshi's ambitious and unsuccessful invasions of Korea failed to consolidate his rule and it was left to his former councillor, Tokugawa Ieyasu (appointed *shogun* in 1603) to complete the work of his predecessors by imitating rather than irritating the Chinese empire. He founded a bureaucracy, imported Confucianism, established a new imperial capital at Edo (Tokyo) and provided the basis for the *Pax Tokugawa* that lasted for two hundred years.

The *Pax Tokugawa* was, like the Manchu dynasty in China, an oriental *ancien regime*. The rigid

caste system exploited the peasantry and allowed no social mobility. 'The offspring of a toad is a toad; the offspring of a merchant is a merchant' was the saying in Japan. Japanese towns and merchants benefited particularly from peace. By 1691 Edo, with its population of over half a million, became one of the largest cities in the world. Here, as in other Japanese cities, the wealth of merchant townsmen supported a refined patrician culture, similar to that in the towns of China.

In both China and Japan, the Confucian *ancien regime* excluded Europeans. Portuguese overtures at Canton were rebuffed and only allowed to return to China at Macao in 1557 (*see Maps 36 and 46*). The Dutch operated from Taiwan from 1626 until they were expelled in 1662. Only the Spanish maintained a regular presence for trade at four open coastal ports, and only the Jesuits were allowed into Peking, where they accepted Chinese customs and dressed their Christianity in Confucian disguise until they too were expelled, in the eighteenth century. But their missionary efforts (like Europe's trading ventures) remained superficial. In Japan, the Europeans were initially more successful. From 1540 the Portuguese (exploiting political uncertainty and the dislike of Buddhist monks) established a lucrative trade monopoly based on Nagasaki, and fostered Christian churches and seminaries. Under Tokugawa rule official tolerance quickly diminished; persecution began in 1629. By 1650 some 2000 Christians (including 70 European priests) had been killed. From 1639 trade with outsiders was forbidden except that Chinese and Dutch traders were allowed to call at Nagasaki once a year. China and Japan remained almost closed to the wider world until the nineteenth century, when the impetus of western imperialism destroyed their isolation (*see Map 64*).

The great Islamic powers in the sixteenth and

MAP 37 THE FAR EAST IN THE SEVENTEENTH CENTURY

RUSSIA

OUTER MONGOLIA

Gobi

MANCHURIA

Sakhalin

Amur

SINKIANG

INNER MONGOLIA

Willow Palisade

Mukden

40°

Sea of Japan

Great Wall

Peking

Pao-ting

Pyongyang

KOREA

Seoul

Taegu

Pusan

TIBET

C H I N A

Lan-chou

Hsi-an

T'ai-yuan

Huang-ho

Chi-nan

East China Sea

Fukuoka
Hirado
Nagasaki

J A P A N

Osaka

Kagoshima

Kai-feng

Nanking

Ch'eng-tu

An-ch'ing

Yangtze

Su-chou

Hang-chou

Wu-ch'ang

Nan-ch'ang

Ch'ang-sha

Kuei-yang

Fu-chou

Ryukyu Is.

Yün-nan-fu

Kuei-lin

Ch'üan-chou

T'an-sui

T'ai-wan

Anpeijo

BURMA

Hsi-chiang

Canton

Pescadores Is.

Takao

Hanoi

Haiphong

Macao

Pegu

Rangoon

Vinh

SIAM

Hue
Suran

Faifo

Paknam

Bangkok

Kachao

GREAT VIETNAM

CAMBODIA

Phnom Penh

Saigon

Kagayan

Manila
San Miguel

PHILIPPINES

South China Sea

Ringoru

Singora
Pattan

Kotabaru

MALAYA

Brunei

Pacific Ocean

Malacca
Johore

SUMATRA

BORNEO

Ternate
Halmahera
Chidor

Moluccas
Bacan

Jambi

Kotawarinki

CELEBES

Seram

Ambon
Banda

NEW GUINEA

Makassar

Bantam
Batavia

Surabaya

JAVA

Indian Ocean

(Port.)
TIMOR

Arafura Sea

Legend

▨	Manchu homeland
↖	Route of Manchu entry into China
	Territories under Manchu control by 1640
	Territories under Manchu control by 1645
	Territories under Manchu control by 1650
	Territories under Manchu control by 1660
	Territories under Manchu control by 1685
	Territories under Manchu control 1690-1730
◉	Imperial capital
○	Seats of governors of Manchu Empire
⊕	Seats of Governors-General of Manchu Empire
◆	Manchu Banner garrisons
— —	Japanese trading routes until 1633
– – –	Japanese official 'red seal ships' trading routes
⊞	Harbours used by Japanese trading vessels
⊙	Places with Japanese townships
○	Places where Japanese resided
—·—·—	Main routes of Japanese armies. 1592-6
·········	Main routes of Japanese armies. 1597-8
	Netherlands territory
	Spanish territory

0 ————— 1000 km

0 ————— 600 miles

SINO-RUSSIAN TRADE
(TEA COTTON CLOTH ETC.
FOR FURS ETC.)

L. Balkhash

○ Tarbagatai

Kobdo ○   Uliassutai ○

ZUNGHARIA
(1757)
(MILITARY ADMINISTRATION)

MONGOLIA
(FEUDAL)

⑥
Ili
(Hui-yuan)
(Kulja)

Urumchi ○   ⑤

Tien Shan

○ Aqsu
Kashgar

Tarim

Turfan ○

Hami ○

EASTERN
TURKESTAN
(1759)
(MILITARY ADMINISTRATION)

Yarkand ○

Kunlun Shan

Khotan ○

An-hsi ○

Tsaidam

Su-chou ○   ③

Kan-chou ○

LADAKH

Leh ○

Indus

Ch'ing-Hai
(Koko Nor)

Hsi-ning ○

Lan-chou ○

TIBET
(1720 to 1751)
(PROTECTORATE)

③

Yalung

Chamdo ○

Himalayas

NEPAL

Shigatse ○

Lhasa ○

Ta-chien-lu ○   ④

5

Ch'eng-tu ○

Katmandu ○

SIKKIM

BHUTAN

Darjeeling ○

⑤

Lu-chou ○

Ganges

Brahmaputra

7

Ta-li ○

Teng-yueh ○

MIEN-TIEN
(BURMA)

K'un-ming ○
⑥

Salween

Mekong

Red

Ava ○

HSIEN-LO
(SIAM)

Chiao-chou ○

YUEH-NAN
(ANNAM)

Provinces included in main economic regions

1 CHIH-LI, SHAN-TUNG, HO-NAN, AN-HUI (partly), CHIANG-SU (partly)

2 SHAN-HSI, SHAAN-HSI (SHENSI), KAN-SU

3 CHIANG-SU (partly), CHE-CHIANG (partly), AN-HUI (partly)

4 CHIANG-HSI, HU-PEI, HU-NAN

5 SSU-CH'UAN

6 CHE'CHIANG (partly), FU-CHIEN, KUANG-TUNG (partly)

7 KUEI-CHOU, YUN-NAN

8 KUANG-TUNG (partly) KUANG-HSI

MAP 38 THE MANCHU EMPIRE AT ITS HEIGHT

Nerchinsk

Aigun

Amur

akhta

ai-mai-ch'eng

Urga

MANCHURIA

Sungari

Tsitsihar

③

Liao

Chi-lin

②

o b i

Mukden
(Sheng-ching)

Nui-chuang
Yalu

CHAO-HSIEN
(KOREA)

①

Sui-yuan
Kuei-hua

Kalgan

Je-ho

P'ing-jang

PEKING

T'ien-chin

Ching-ch'eng

Ördös

Pao-ting

Mouth of Huang-ho
after 1853

Teng-chou

ing-hsia

T'ai-yuan

Cheng-ting

Te-chou

JAPAN

Lin-ch'ing

Chi-nan

①

Huang-ho

1

Mouth of Huang-ho
before 1853

YANGTZE-MANCHURIA
TRADE
(COTTON CLOTH AND TEA
FOR SOYA BEANS ETC.)

Nagasaki

Wei

Hsi-an

2

K'ai-feng

Hsu-chou

Huai-an

Yang-chou

②

Han

Hsiang-yang

Nanking

Chen-chiang

Shang-hai

an-hsien

Yangtze

Chiang-ling

Han-k'ou

An-ch'ing

Ho-fei

3

Su-chou SC

Sung-chiang

T'ai

Hu-chou

S

C

SINO-JAPANESE TRADE
(SILKS, SUGAR, DRUGS ETC.,
FOR COPPER ETC.)

hung-ch'ing

Han-yang Wu-ch'ang

Chiu-chiang

Hang-chou

Shao-hsing W

Ning-po

4

Yo-chou

L. Tung-ting

Ching-te-chen

P

L. Po-yang

Ch'ang-te

Nan-ch'ang

Wen-chou

Heng-yang

Kan

Ch'ang-sha

Hsiang-t'an

③

T'AI-WAN – MAINLAND
COAL EXPORT TRADE

L'IU-CH'IU ISLANDS

Kuei-yang

Fu-chou

T'an-sui

Kan-chou

Ting-chou

Ch'üan-chou

6

Kuei-lin

Chang-chou

Amoy

Ch'ao-chou

Swatow

T'AI-WAN
(1683)
(Civil administration)

Hsi-chiang

Wu-chou

Canton

Hui-chou

⑤

Nan-ning

Fo-shan I

8

Macao
(Portuguese)

SINO-S.E. ASIAN TRADE
(FABRICS, METAL GOODS, PORCELAIN ETC.,
FOR WOODS, RICE, RAW COTTON ETC.)

SINO-WESTERN TRADE
(SILVER OPIUM (ILLEGALLY) ETC.,
FOR TEAS, SILKS, PORCELAIN)

Chiung-chou

HAI-NAN

Legend

	The Ming Empire c.1600
	Regions of the Manchu Empire administered by the Court of Colonial Affairs
	Regions acquired by the Manchu, administered by imperial bureaucracy
(1683)	Date of establishment of Manchu rule
	Tributary states of Manchu Empire
	Tributary states of Lhasa
——	Wall rebuilt late 14th century
– – –	Wall rebuilt 15th-16th centuries
- - -	Wall rebuilt 16th century
	Major imperial courier routes
②	Maximum time in weeks permitted for mounted courier from Peking
	Other courier and trading routes
•••••	Willow Palisades (northern limit of legal migration by Han Chinese)
	Economic regions: core areas
	Economic regions: peripheral areas
⊙	Major trading centre
◉	Port open to western trade after 1757
	Grand Canal
	Desert

0 _____ 500 km
0 _____ 300 miles

I	Ironware exporting centre
W	Wine exporting centre
P	Porcelain exporting centre
S	Silk exporting centre
C	Cotton exporting centre
SC	Silk and cotton exporting centre

seventeenth centuries were Ottoman Turkey, Safavid Persia and Mughal India (*see Maps 39 and 40*). They had much in common. Each was centred about a great capital city: Istanbul, Isfahan and Delhi. For each, Islam was not only a religion but a social and political code, essentially urban, worn lightly by some of its adherents and subject to some internal dissension, but still a common bond. Each city throughout the Islamic world had its mosque, built on an axis oriented on the heavenly city, Mecca, to which all Muslims turn in prayer. Arabic was a *lingua franca* for religion, government and law.

For all three empires, the sixteenth century was one of creation, growth and consolidation. The Mughal dynasty was founded by Babur (*d*.1530), a military adventurer who saw himself as the heir to the Mongol empire of Chingiz Khan. In 1522, he seized Qandahar, the key to northern India, and took Lahore. Mughal authority was established throughout northern India within four years (*see Map 40*), and reached its height under Akbar (*r*.1556-1605). Similarly, the Ottoman Turks had established themselves in Anatolia, captured Constantinople in 1453 and continued to expand their empire, until it reached its height under Süley-

man the Magnificent (*r*.1520-66) (*see Map 39*). He alarmed Christian Europe by capturing Belgrade in 1521 and the island of Rhodes in 1522, arriving at the gates of Vienna in 1529 and 1532. Persia, too, had its Akbar or Süleyman, in Shah Abbas I, known as the Great (*r*.1587-1629), whose reign dominated the memory of Persia through the seventeenth century.

In each case, the easy talent for the absorption of different cultures and racial and ethnic groups characterized these regimes in their early period of expansion (*Map 40*). Akbar I declared himself, in 1572, sole arbiter of religious matters in his realms

MAP 39 THE OTTOMAN TURKS

and repealed all discriminatory taxes on racial and religious minorities within the empire. Avowing a policy of toleration, he embarked upon discussions with various religions, including the Portuguese Jesuits, and finally devised a new universal faith. Ottoman Turkey gave the Catholic peasantry of Hungary and the orthodox inhabitants of Greece a welcome release from the seigneurial burdens and intolerance of Reformation Europe. Christians, Muslims and Jews served in the famous slave-based Janissary *corps* of the Ottomans.

Their achievements brought the Muslim powers wealth and sophistication, but also created a burden of empire which could not be indefinitely sustained. Each, in turn, ended its expansion in the seventeenth century with enormous internal problems. Feeding and fuelling their inflated capitals became a major problem in itself when the decline in economic activity in the seventeenth century affected the Islamic empires, as it had done, to a lesser extent, the Oriental ones. Frontiers and the long lines of communication with them were an enduring problem. The Mughal Jahangir sent his armies into the Deccan, which all Mughal emperors aspired to conquer, and which became the obsession of his successor in the decade 1670-80 (*see Map 40*). The Mughals also struggled with military potentates in irrepressible Bengal and worried over the frontier city of Qandahar. In Persia Shah Abbas was forced into offensive war in Khorasan. Even Süleyman the Magnificent admitted defeat outside Vienna and for the most part in the western Mediterranean. His Ottoman successors were forced to loosen their grip on Algiers and Tunis, suffered rebuffs from the Muscovites on the Steppes, saw Cossack oarsmen in the Bosphorus and were troubled by insubordinate tributary princes in Transylvania.

In the face of these problems, each empire in its turn looked to autocracy, centralization and militarism as the immediate solution. But structural change did not come easily. In the Ottoman empire, the Janissaries rebelled frequently (the outbursts were customarily announced by the overturning of the barrack-room soup-cauldron). In Persia, Shah Abbas' standing army of Christians from Georgia and the Caucasus also rebelled. Centralization caused provincial rebellions, such as those in Wallachia, Moldavia and Turkestan in the Ottoman empire and Bengal in the Mughal empire. These revolts were serious because provincial governors exploited them to influence the imperial succession. Across the Islamic world, court intrigue surrounding the succession of the shah, sultan or emperor was a constant danger. There was no formal law of succession in any of the empires. Emperors existed by right of conquest and survived by their ability to eliminate rivals. The harems of the ruler ensured a regular supply of pretenders, and brutal practices were adopted to limit them. The Ottomans had law which allowed successful

Above right: The Khân of Khurâsân on his return to Persia after being defeated by Shah Jehan, whose Taj Mahal at Agra (completed in 1648) can be seen in the background.

39 The Ottoman Turks
The Ottoman challenge to Christendom began in the early fourteenth century. The capture of Constantinople in 1553 was followed by increasingly rapid expansion until the empire reached its strategic limits under Süleyman the Magnificent (*r.* 1520-66).

40 The India of the Mughals
Between 1526 and 1636 the Mughals, from a base in Afghanistan, acquired control over most of the Indian subcontinent by seizing military and administrative centres along the main trade routes. Until the reign of Aurangzeb (*r.* 1668-1707) a balance between its various peoples was maintained in their administration; thereafter growing disunity and disaffection among the ruling élites undermined Mughal control, to the benefit of the intruding European powers.

41 The rise of Muscovy
Moscow's position at the intersection of the great trade routes and the ruthless determination of its Grand Dukes to subordinate every resource and institution to their power, suppress their fellow princes and shake off the rule of the Mongols (to whom Ivan III stopped paying tribute in 1480) made Moscow the unchallenged centre of the emergent Russian empire.

MAP 40 THE INDIA OF THE MUGHALS

MAP 41 THE RISE OF MUSCOVY

Lake Onega

Lake Ladoga

Lake Onega

Gulf of Finland

Ladoga

Oreshek

Narva

Olvangorod

Novgorod

Pskov

Polotsk

Vitebsk

W. Dvina

Dnieper

Smolensk

Vyazma

Volokolamsk

Mozhaisk

Borovsk

Starodub

Novgorod Severskiy

Chernigov

Rylsk

Putivl

Kursk

Kiev

Pereyaslav

Pripet Marshes

Belgorod

COSSACKS

CRIMEAN TATARS

Crimea

Kerch

Black Sea

Sea of Azov

Azov

Don

Donets

Don

Khoper

Volga

TATARS

Kazan

Nizhnii Novgorod

Gorodets

Murom

Volga

Makarev

Galich

Ustiug

Sukhona

N. Dvina

Onega

Beloozero

Vologda

Kostroma

Yaroslavl

Rostov

Uglich

Volga

Tver

Pereyaslavl-Zalesski

Alexandrovskaya Sloboda

Yuriev Polski

Zagorsk

Suzdal

Vladimir

Moscow

Kolomna

Oka

Solotcha

Ryazan

Oka

Msta

Volkov

Desna

Bug

Dnieper

Dniester

Kremlin or fortress

Major monastery

Porterage ℗

Territory of Muscovy in 1300

" " " 1340

" " " 1389

" " " 1425

" " " 1462

" " " 1505

" " " 1533

" " " 1584

Marshes

0   200 km

0   150 miles

emperors to put their rival to death by strangulation with a silken bow-string. The Mughals tried to ensure a clear succession by nomination, but their efforts were ruined by ambition or bad blood. In Persia the practice of blinding royal princes who were potential contenders grew up from the end of the sixteenth century, and later both Persia and Turkey adopted the formal imprisonment of every heir to the throne. Enforced seclusion and incarceration led to a observable decline in the quality of their rulers.

The Islamic empires began to quarrel amongst themselves. War between Persia and the Ottomans,

intermittent from 1502 onwards, became more violent in the seventeenth century. In the process the Islamic state adopted more exclusive ideologies; the Sunnite faith was preferred by the Ottomans and Shi'ite orthodoxy by the Persians. Both became less inclined to tolerate Christian and Jewish minorities. A rebellion among the Christians of Greece brought the European fleet (against orders) to Lepanto, where it won the sixteenth century's greatest offensive victory against the Ottomans. European merchants could not be excluded from the Islamic capitals, whose lavish tastes demanded fine cloth and precious metals. In their wake, later

in the seventeenth century, came the rising military and naval power of Europe, whose colonial expansion the Islamic powers would find difficult to resist.

Despite the absorption of many Slavs into the Ottoman and Hapsburg empires, and the subjection of others to the Tartars, two separate Slav empires existed in the early modern world. On the borders of Europe Poland stretched from the Baltic to the Black Sea, while under Ivan III (r. 1462-1505) the Grand Duchy of Muscovy threw off the Tartar yoke and made Moscow the centre of a Russian empire (see Maps 41 and 50). Both states

MAP 42   THE HAPSBURG EMPIRE

expanded during the sixteenth century. In 1569 the kingdom of Poland, endowed with strong representative institutions, a vigorous aristocracy and (until 1572) a hereditary monarchy of the European kind, joined in a condominium with the Grand Duchy of Lithuania, to which it had been driven closer by the common threat from Muscovy. The expansion of Muscovy was far more remarkable. The whole area around the independent city of Novgorod was subjugated in 1478, the Kazan Khanate in 1552, and Astrakhan in 1556. From the accession of Ivan IV in 1553 the realm of Muscovy expanded in each year by an area equal to the size of Holland until, by 1600, it was as large as the whole of Europe.

Prosperity encouraged expansion. Russia gained the route across the Urals to Siberia and control of the Volga and the routes to the Caspian Sea, and would have liked a port on the Baltic. Russian fur-trappers moved easily across Siberia and by the middle of the seventeenth century reached the Pacific Coast and the borders of China (*see Map 70*). New towns were established on the Volga and Belaya as visible signs of the wealth of the silk, rug and precious metals trade with Persia. Meanwhile Poland extended its authority over the old Hanseatic ports of the Baltic, Danzig and Riga, (*Map 50*) and the resulting prosperity was demonstrated in newly founded universities, churches and printing presses.

The foundations of Russia were entirely different from those of Poland. The essence of the Russian state lay in its patrimonialism. The tsars (as the grand dukes styled themselves officially from 1547, to emphasize their legendary descent from a brother of the Emperor Augustus) stressed that, on their hereditary lands, they were *gosudar*, supreme lord, ruler, autocrat. The land stewards of the patrimony (the *votchina*) provided the basis for the expanded and from the 1550s reorganized state officialdom (the *prikazi*). Trade in the Duchy had always been the private possession of the grand dukes and the tsars extended this monopoly over wholesale commerce and the manufacturing and mining industries of Russia at large.

Outside the domain of the grand dukes of Muscovy were the lands of the *boyars* (the aristocracy) and the Church. Since feudalism had never been established in Russia there was no vassalage or conditional land tenure to provide a law common to the aristocracy and the tsar. As Moscow extended its influence the *boyars* were gradually subjected to the will of the tsar, beginning in the 1470s when Ivan III denied their freedom to serve another prince. In the sixteenth century the tsars created new nobles and rewarded loyal service. In 1564 Ivan IV (the 'Terrible') divided the country clearly between his domain (*oprichnina*) and the rest (*zenichina*) so that in the former he could enforce his authority more vigorously. *Oprichniki*, a group of tsar's bailiffs, were permitted to abuse or kill the *boyars* in the domain with impunity, and to loot their properties. Although the *oprichniki* were withdrawn in 1572 the power of the *boyars* was destroyed and private land in secular hands no longer played a significant role in Muscovite Russia. The Church retained its wealth, and the monasteries and kremlins (some of which were designed by German military engineers) of the duchy of Moscow provided a solid base for the government and internal security of the tsars. The Russian Orthodox church, with its own patriarchal structure, fitted well with the tsars' pretensions, and each reinforced the authority of the other.

Conquered territories were treated as the tsar's patrimony. Independent cities such as Novgorod lost their privileges, and mass deportations, which became common in the expansion of Russia, emphasized that, as a German traveller remarked in the middle of the sixteenth century, 'All the people consider themselves *kholops*, that is slaves of their Prince'. Serfdom also spread outwards from the patrimony of the tsar, where no peasant considered himself the owner of land or property. As peasants seized the opportunities which expansion offered to abandon the domain and colonize the new territories of the Kazan and Astrakhan the tsars abandoned the custom which had given peasants freedom to leave their masters on one day in each year, began to keep a close watch on their debts and dues, made systematic enquiries of their own rights and finally, in 1592, introduced serfdom. Most Russian peasants had become serfs by 1650.

By prodigious efforts and at great cost the tsars transformed Russia into a gigantic royal domain. The costs were highest in the seventeenth century. Dynastic uncertainties, peasant rebellions, revolts of the Cossacks to the south and of Lithuanians to the west, produced civil disturbance beside which that of Europe at the same time pales into insignificance. In the long run the autocratic system of the tsars emerged victorious, and under Peter 'the Great' (*r.*1682-1725) the Russian *ancien regime* began.

Not so in Poland. The Lithuanian-Polish condominium collapsed three years after it was established. With the extinction of the Jagiellonian dynasty, Poland adopted an elective kingship (in form rather like that of the neighbouring Holy Roman Empire) but without a strong, well-endowed dynasty like the Hapsburgs to give it direction and muscle (*compare Map 42*). In the elections of the following centuries members of the European ruling dynasties were chosen as kings and pursued their own dynastic interests to the detriment of Polish peace and security. Poland's magnates (unlike the *boyars*) successfully defended their individual patrimonies and held the great offices of state. In a state racially, culturally, religiously, ethnically and politically divided, the monarch's authority rapidly gave way to the creeping political paralysis (disguised by the weaknesses common to all states in the seventeenth century and by a certain tolerance born of potential anarchy) which became evident in the eighteenth century and would make Poland the despair of the *philosophes* and the prey of the autocrats.

42 The Hapsburg empire
The devolution of the succession to four royal houses on Charles of Hapsburg between 1515 and 1519 and his election as Holy Roman Emperor in 1519 created a unique empire. Its territorial extent, claim to absolute rulership and championship of Catholicism threatened almost every interest and made it the focus of European politics for the next two hundred years.

Further reading: Jonathan Spence, *Emperor of China* (Cape, 1974; Random House); Susan Naquin and Evelyn S. Rawski, *Chinese Society in the Eighteenth Century* (Yale U.P. 1987); Conrad Totman, *Japan Before Perry* (University of California Press 1981); Francis S. Robinson, *Atlas of the Islamic World since 1500* (Phaidon 1982; Facts on File); Richard E. Pipes, *Russia under the Old Regime* (Weidenfeld and Nicolson 1974; Scribner); F. Braudel, *The Mediterranean and the Mediterranean World in the Age of Phillip II* (2 vols, Collins 1972-3; Harper Collins).

**Map labels:**

D. OF PRUSSIA (to Brandenburg 1618)

Vistula

KINGDOM OF POLAND

Oder

Breslau

SILESIA

Carpathians

MORAVIA

Brünn

KINGDOM OF HUNGARY

Pressburg

Vienna

D. STYRIA

Graz

D. STYRIA

Buda

Mohacs

Danube

1683 Frontier

1547 Frontier

OTTOMAN EMPIRE

Adriatic Sea

KINGDOM OF NAPLES

47

40°

20°

50°

Palermo 1647

Messina

Sicily

Malta

The age of European supremacy 3

COLONIES AND COMMERCE

The first European colonial empire was that of Spain. By 1600 it was the largest and the most populous and productive.

Theoretically, the Spanish crown claimed sovereignty over the Americas west of the line laid down by the treaty of Tordesillas in 1494 (*see Map 36*). In practice, wealth was concentrated in the fertile areas in central and southern America where the ranching of cattle and the cutting of woodland provided the basic necessities for the colonies. Except by the Jesuits, there was little settlement northwards from Mexico or eastwards from Peru. The ranch (or *hacienda*) became the chief productive unit. The other industry was silver, mined by Spaniards and Indians and requiring extensive initial investment. Neither *hacienda* nor mine employed Indians as slaves. A debate amongst theologians at Salamanca in 1550 had decreed that American Indians were not (the term was borrowed from Aristotle's *Politics*) 'slaves', although African natives were.

By 1700, the Spanish empire had suffered infringements. Portuguese smugglers had established themselves at the mouth of the Río de la Plata, a vital trade route through southern America to upper Peru. With Spanish encouragement the Jesuits colonized the wild Indian country in central southern America and reduced Uruguay to an ordered buffer-state. In the Caribbean, Dutch, English and French buccaneers plundered Spanish trade from Curaçao (which itself became Dutch from 1634), Jamaica (English from 1655) and Santo Domingo (French from 1665). But territorial losses were trifling and the Spanish remained the masters of the trade in the Pacific throughout the eighteenth century (*see Map 46*).

The problems of Spain's colonies were not territorial but structural and economic. Spanish trade across the Atlantic became depressed in the decade 1610 to 1620, and remained acutely so for the rest of the century. The interlocking economy of ranches, mines and plantations went into a severe recession, partly as a result of the depletion of the Indian population through plagues and a resulting acute shortage of labour (*Map 43*). The cost of mining and transporting silver outweighed the profit, so that the volume of silver produced reached its peak in the 1580s and dropped to its lowest point for a century in the 1650s. The colonies imported less from the Old World as they became self-sufficient. What trade there was ceased to benefit the merchants of Seville, who found themselves paying heavily for protection against piracy, attacked by the Inquisition for their suspect religious (or racial) background, and required to advance large sums of money to a rapacious Spanish monarchy, to keep its Catholic court solvent and its wars with the heretics active. The profits of the Spanish empire passed to smugglers who paid no duties and who were not obsessed by bullion, being prepared to take their returns in bulk cargoes such as sugar, hides and tallow.

The Portuguese overseas empire suffered the territorial depredations that the Spanish empire largely escaped. From 1580 to 1640, Portugal was politically united with Spain and, under the union, Portugal gained little and lost much (*Map 42*). Her colonies were able to trade only to a limited extent with those of Spain. Portuguese merchants found themselves harassed by the Inquisition, and taxed to pay for the Hapsburg's dynastic ambitions while her colonies, fair game to Spain's enemies, enjoyed no effective protection. Ceylon and Malacca were captured by the Dutch (*Map 37*); Goa declined to insignificance; African Guinea and Angola were conquered and a profitable strip of northern Brazil was also annexed by the Dutch.

But, unlike those of the Spanish empire, the merchants of Lisbon (in collaboration with the new, independent House of Braganza) adapted, developed and strengthened what was left to them after 1640. They quickly regained Angola and expelled the Dutch from Brazil (*Map 43*). There, in the northern captaincies of Bahía and Pernambuco, João IV, the first Braganza king, established sugar cane. Northern Europe in particular was sugar-starved and in the seventeenth century the plantations of Brazil, equipped with elaborate mechanical gins and refineries, supplied Europe with enough sugar to turn the product from an aristocratic delicacy into something of popular consumption. Sugar became the first trans-oceanic bulk cargo.

To operate the mills and tend and cut the cane required slave-labour. Sugar and slavery were, from the beginning, intimately associated (*Map*

Left: A plan for a slave ship (*c.*1790). A well-designed slaver could carry as many as six hundred people, with virtually every inch of the hold filled with the living cargo.

MAP 43 COLONIZATION AND SETTLEMENT IN SOUTH AMERICA

Santiago
(1514)

SUGAR
Española

Virgin Is.
(1648-)

Anguilla (1650-)
St Martin (1648-)

Santiago
(Jamaica)
(1509)

Santo
Domingo
(1496)

Guadeloupe
(1635-)

Caribbean Sea

Martinique
(1635-)

Curaçao
(1634-)

(1627-)

*Atlantic
Ocean*

PEARLS

(1635-)

Quesada
(1536-38)

COCOA

Tobago (1632-54)

Maracaibo

Caracas
(1567)

*Gulf of
Darien*

Cartagena
(1532)

De Herrera
(1533-4)

Trinidad
(1498)

Panama
(1519)

TOBACCO
HIDES

GOLD

Stabrok (Georgetown)

Santa Fé de Bogotá
(1538)

Orinoco

New Amsterdam

Paramaribo

Surinam
(1667)

Cayenne
(1674)

GUIANA

DRUGS

Equator

Quito
(1534)

G. Pizarro (1539, 1542)
De Orellana (1541)

Negro

Manáus
(1674)

Amazon

Belém do Pará
(1616)

Maranhao

(1526)
Tumbes

(1638)

Madeira

Xingu

Olinda

Recife

São Francisco

Lima
(1535)

(1684)

MERCURY

Cuzco

Ica
Nazca

Titicaca

La Paz

Matto Grosso

Minas Geraes

TOBACCO
SUGAR
COTTON

Bahia

Tiahuanaco

GOLD

Coramba

La Plata
(1538)

(1691)

Porto Seguro

SILVER

Potosí
(1545)

The 'Paulistas'

COPPER

Atacama Desert

(1609)

Concepción

São Paulo
(1532)

Santos
(1545)

Rio de Janeiro

Santiago
del Estero

Asunción
(1537)

La Serena
(1544)

Córdoba
(1573)

Santa Fé

Valparaiso
(1541)

Santiago
(1542)

San Luis

De Irala (1543-48)

Rio Grande

Buenos Aires
(1536)

Montevideo

Rio de la Plata

HIDES

Parana

Valdivia
(1552)
Osorno

Valdivia
(1540, 1553)

Legend

Spanish · Portuguese

- Areas colonised by 1640
- Areas colonised by 1750
- Frontier lands in 1750
- Jesuit mission states
- Principal routes of colonial trade
- ⊙ Spanish audiencia
- ● Portuguese captaincies
- — — Extent of the Inca empire in 1525
- ■ Inca temples
- → Principal colonising routes (with names of explorers)
- Dutch colonies
- French colonies
- English colonies

0 ——— 1000 km
0 ——— 600 miles

Population chart

	1520	1650	1750
Estimated world population (in millions)	480	550	700
Estimated American Indian population (in millions)	78	10	6·5
Estimated European population (in millions)		3·5	11
Head of cattle in America (estimated in thousands)	10	100	130

F. Pizarro (1524-27)

Spanish transcontinental route c.1600

85

MAP 44 COLONIZATION AND SETTLEMENT IN NORTH AMERICA

Legend

Spanish | French | English

Areas colonised by 1640
Areas colonised by 1750
Frontier lands in 1750

Dutch colonies
Jesuit mission states

Principal colonising routes
Aztec empire in 1519
▲ Aztec and Maya temples
■ Forts and fortified trading posts
---- Fur-trade routes
UTE Indian tribes in frontier regions
⊙ Spanish audiencia
Principal routes of colonial trade

0 _____ 1000 km
0 _____ 600 miles

Hudson Bay

FISH

Rupert's Land
(Hudson Bay Co. Ltd.)
SKINS

Newfoundland
St John's

Ft la Tourette
(1684)

Ft St Charles   Ft. St. Pierre   NIPISSING

Québec
(1608)

Tadoussac
(1600)

Île St. Jean   Île Royale

OTTOWANS   Trois Rivières (1634)   MAHIGANS   Nova Scotia   FISH

Sault Ste Marie
(1668)   Montréal
St. Lawrence

HURONS   New Hampshire (1629)
NEW FRANCE   Salem (1628)
Fort Orange   Boston   New Plymouth (1620)
(Albany)   Rhode Island (1623)
Fort Nassau (1614)   New Haven   New Amsterdam (New York)   40°
(1636)   Breuckelen (Brooklyn) (1646)
MOHAWA   NEW NETHERLANDS
Philadelphia   (1616; English occ. 1664)
GRAIN
Maryland (1632)

Rocky Mts

SERRANO

HUPI   UTE

ZUNI   Santa Fé
(1609)

WICHITA

TAWAKONI   Fort Necessity
(1754)

Jamestown (1607)
THE THIRTEEN COLONIES
Virginia (1624)
TOBACCO
RICE
INDIGO

El Paso
(1659)

KICHA

Coronado
(1540-3)   APACHE

Fort Prudhomme
(1682)

30°

OPATA   Mississippi   Missouri

San Antonio
(1718)   SKINS   New Orleans
(1718)   APALACHE

Pensacola
(1696)   Ft. Caroline
(1562)

St Augustine
(1565)   *Atlantic Ocean*

De Alarcon
(1540)   Florida
(1513)

Rio Grande

Culiacán
(1531)   Monterrey
(1596)

The Bahamas
(1646-)

SILVER   Zacatecas   *Gulf of Mexico*   Havana
(1515)

20°   TOBACCO
SUGAR
Española (1492)
Santiago   Santo
(1514)   Domingo
(1496)

Guadalajara
(1531)   LEATHER   ▲   ▲ Chichen Itza
Mexico City
(Tenochtitlan)   ▲   MAYAS
Cuextatlan   ▲
▲   ▲

Santiago
(Jamaica)
(1509)   *Caribbean Sea*

AZTECS

Acapulco   ▲
Antigua
(1542)   Old Providence I.
(1631-41)

to Manila   *GUATEMALA* (1635)   Mosquito Coast

León
Granada
(1522)   Gulf of Darien

Nombre de Dios

Pacific Ocean

MAP 45 SLAVE ECONOMIES OF THE WESTERN HEMISPHERE

Coffee
Cotton
Mining
Mixed agriculture
Rice
Sugar
Tobacco

1820's   Period of most extensive cultivation
         or intense activity
★ 1831   Site of slave revolts with date
◆   Significant maroon (organised runaway
         slave) activity
CUBA   Date of final emancipation enactment
1886

1500 km
1000 miles

Atlantic Ocean

Pacific Ocean

1712
1800 1800
1800
1831
U.S.A.
1865
1739
1822 1800
1811
1860
French planters
1790's
1860

1545-1600
MEXICO
1829
Various
18th c.
Mexico City
1725-1735

16th c.
17th c.
16th c.
17th c.
1548

CENTRAL
AMERICA
1824
Cartagena
1619
Antioquia
1598
Choco
1820's
16th c.
Popayan
1540s-50s
1820's
16th c.
ECUADOR
1854
18th c.

1533
18th c.
1726
c.1850
1805
1812
Jamaica
17th c.1734 1760
1795 1831
c.1750
BRITISH WEST INDIES
1834
16th c.
1791
c.1780
1522
1527
19th c.

CUBA 1886
ST. DOMINGUE 1794
SANTO DOMINGO 1822
PUERTO RICO 1873
DANISH ANTILLES 1848
SWEDISH ANTILLES 1846
FRENCH ANTILLES 1848

Guadeloupe
1833
Martinique
Barbados
1816
17th c.

Dutch sugar planters 1650's

1530
1550
1532
1795
1730's
Buria
1552
Yaracuy
VENEZUELA 1854
16th c.
18th c.
COLOMBIA
1852
Orinoco
c.1770
1823
1763
1731
19th c.
DUTCH
ANTILLES
1863

Amazon

PERU
1854
16th c. +
1848
Lima
1578

BRAZIL 1888
Palmares
17th c.
1807-1835
Bahia

Gois
c.1730

BOLIVIA 1861

1700-1750
Minas Gerais
1820
19th c.
1850s
19th c.

PARAGUAY
1869

CHILE 1825

Copinpo
17th c.

URUGUAY
1853

ARGENTINA
1853

Tropic of Cancer
Equator
Tropic of Capricorn

Mississippi
São Francisco
Parana

Estimated slave
imports

5mm = 150,000

British North America
and United States
Spanish America
including Cuba
British West Indies
French West Indies
Other West Indies
Brazil

1451-1600
1601-1700
1701-1810
1811-1870

87

MAP 46 TRADE AND DOMINION

Arctic

GREENLAND
(Denmark)

Iceland
(Denmark)

RUPERT'S
LAND

SWEDE

DENMARK

GREAT
BRITAIN

Bristol

St. Malo

FRANCE (Emancipated 1789) AUSTRIA

Bordeaux

PORTUGAL SPAIN

Lisbon Seville

Cadiz

Canary Is.

Azores

| TOBACCO |
| RICE |
| FURS |
| INDIGO |
| MEAT |
| TIMBER |
| GRAIN |

Canada £·12m

Newfoundland £2·6m

Bahamas £2·6m

£2·9m

American Colonies (29)

| SUGAR |
| COFFEE |

£5m

| SUGAR |
| GOLD |
| HIDES |
| COFFEE |
| DIAMONDS |
| CALICO |
| TAXES |

| SUGAR |
| COFFEE |
| INDIGO |
| COTTON |

Antilles (85)

French Antilles and St. Domingo

Brazil (42) £1·8m

New Spain (65) £4·5m

| SUGAR |
| COCHINEAL |
| INDIGO |
| HIDES |
| TAXES |

Quebec
Montreal
St. Pierre & Miquelon
Boston
Nova Scotia
New York
Philadelphia
Jamestown
THIRTEEN COLONIES
GEORGIA
Indian Reserve
LOUISIANA
CANADA
New Orleans
FLORIDA (Br. 1763-83)
Bermuda
VICE-ROYALTY OF NEW SPAIN
Vera Cruz
Cuba
Santiago
Bahama Is.
Haiti
Santo Domingo
St. Thomas (Denmark)
St. Croix (Denmark)
Leeward Is. (Br. and Dutch)
Guadaloupe (Fr.)
Lesser Antilles (Fr. and Br.)
(75)

Jamaica
Belize
Mosquito Coast
Porto Bello
Curaçao
Trinidad
Middle Passage

Spanish South America

Cape Verde Is.

St. Louis
Gorée
Fort James

SEGU

ASHANTI
Accra
DAHOMEY
OYO NUPA
Lagos BENIN

Atlantic

| SILK |
| SPICES |

Acapulco
To Manila

Pacific Ocean

VICE-ROYALTY OF NEW GRANADA
ESSEQUIBO
SURINAM
Cayenne

VICE-ROYALTY OF BRAZIL

VICE-ROYALTY OF PERU

Spanish transcontinental route

VICE-ROYALTY OF RIO DE LA PLATA

Buenos Aires

Rio de Janeiro

Bahia

Recife

DUTCH BRAZIL (1630-54)

(30)

| SLAVES |

| SLAVES |

Fernando Poó

São Paulo de Loanda ANGOLA

St. Helena

Ocean

| PEPPER |
| SPICES |
| SILK |
| COFFEE |

| SPICES |

| SILK |
| CALICO |

| SILK |
| CALICO |
| COFFEE |
| PEPPER |
| INDIGO |
| DRUGS |

£2m

£1·5m

£1·5m

£1·4m

(165-215)

(170-225)

Capetown

Indonesia a
Malaysia G

China

Ind

Falkland Is.
(Fr. 1763-5, Br. 1765-70, Sp. 1770)

Southern

(1741)

Legend:

	British c.1770
	French ,,
	Dutch ,,
	Portuguese ,,
	Spanish ,,

▬▬▶ Outward trade

◀━━━ Homeward trade

○▶ Indications of colonial rivalry

⚓ Trading factories in the Far East

▨ Russian Empire in 1763

┄┄ Boundaries of French Louisiana before 1763

(22) Average number of days in sea-crossing

£1·8m Value of trade in decade 1760-1770

▨ Areas of Europe with free peasantry

▨ Areas of Europe where peasantry were subjected to very light seigneurial dues

▥ Areas of Europe whose emancipation was undertaken, or commenced in the late eighteenth century

▤ Areas of unfree peasantry

Ocean

RUSSIAN EMPIRE

POLAND

OTTOMAN
EMPIRE

Arctic Circle

Aleutian Is
(to Russia, 1745)

JAPAN

Pacific
Ocean

MANCHU CHINA

SILVER

Delhi

Tropic of Cancer

Patna

Canton

Formosa

BENGAL

Macao

Port Zeelandia

Diu   INDIA   Calcutta

Mariana
Islands

Daman

NORTHERN
CIRCARS
(1752, Fr.; 1766, Br.)

ANNAM

Bombay

1780

Manila

Philippines
(1762-4 to Br.)

FUNJ

Masulipatam

Tourane

ETHIOPIA

Goa   Rangoon

Bhatkal

To Acapulco

Mangalore

1762-4

Madras

Caroline
Islands

Ceylon

Mogadishu

Brunei

BUNYORO

Malacca

Equator

Malindi   Sumatra   Singapore   Borneo

Mombasa   Sukadana   Moluccas

LUBA

Zanzibar   Palembang   Banjarmasin   Amboina

Indian Ocean

Benkulen   Macassar   New Guinea

UNDA

MARAVI   Batavia   INDONESIA

Mozambique   Java   Timor

BUTUA   Beira

Madagascar

Mauritius

Réunion

Fort Dauphin

NEW HOLLAND

Tropic of Capricorn

Capetown

165-
195

Ocean

45). In Brazil the natives were nomadic, shy and primitive and their enslavement was forbidden. There were no such problems with African negroes, and the inland slave markets in the Black Monarchies of Angola provided a suitable source (*Map 46*). Boats on an outward voyage from Lisbon shipped slaves at Louanda, sailed to Bahía on the trade winds, and returned to Portugal, again with the wind behind them, filled with refined sugar. It was an ideal navigational and trading pattern.

The Dutch copied the Portuguese with larger mercantile resources, and with speed and success. The Portuguese eastern empire had been gained quickly by piracy and force. It was equally quickly dismembered by the Dutch in the early seventeenth century, using the same methods (*Map 46*). Muslim traders – even Portuguese trading stations – did not hesitate to trade with the new rivals. In some respects, though, the Dutch were different. Their merchants operated as a single trading company. A national charter of privileges guaranteed their monopoly status, organized such administration, jurisdiction and defence as were necessary, and enabled their risks to be shared. As a result, the Dutch operation in the East Indies never suffered from a shortage of capital and it was able to expand the range of goods shipped from the east. Not content with spices, peppers, tea, chinaware and gruffgoods (saltpetre and cottons), the Dutch governor-general introduced coffee-beans into Java and the first small shipment of Javanese coffee reached Amsterdam in 1712. It was a marketing triumph and soon coffee was one of the most profitable items of Dutch trade.

Secondly, the Dutch used the active bullion market in Amsterdam – developed during the days of shipments of Spanish silver to the Netherlands (*Map 42*) – to buy precious metals with which to pay cash for the goods of the East. Because there was no commodity that Europe could readily sell to the Orient the commerce of the East Indies remained, even for the Dutch, vulnerable to changes in the price of bullion in Europe.

Thirdly, the Dutch exploited the 'country' trades, the port-to-port conveyance through the Indian Ocean and towards the China Sea, of pilgrims to Jidda, of piecegoods to the Red Sea and the Persian Gulf from Surat and Bombay; from Madras to the many ports of the Moluccas. Other European nations established rival East India Companies. The English Company prospered during the seventeenth and eighteenth centuries and a French *Compagnie des Indes orientales* was founded by Colbert in 1664. But they suffered from government interference, interloping, and the indolence and petty corruption natural to great corporations. None had such a wide basis for the barter of spices and such a well-established mercantile position in the east as the Dutch (*Map 37*).

The Dutch also attempted to establish a commercial presence in the West Indies from the middle of the seventeenth century. But they never secured a firm footing against the English and the French, who were vigorously backed by their respective governments. By 1713 the days of the pirates were over and the pattern of control of the Caribbean islands was clear, governed by a treaty (the Peace of Utrecht in 1713), fully recognized and guarded by

naval forces. The West Indies became part of the regular pattern of European diplomacy, and in particular of the rivalry between England and France, both of whom became accustomed to send fleets to the Caribbean at the beginning of any European war. All the colonies of English North America put together were still of less value in 1750 than a dozen sugar islands. The West Indies supplied more English imports and accounted for more English exports both in value and quantity than the American colonies (*Map 46*).

By 1700 the eleven English colonies of the North American mainland occupied a continuous strip of coastal territory (*Map 44*). Two days' travel inland brought one to untouched Indian country. Boston, the largest town, had only 7000-8000 inhabitants. Economic activity was on a small scale. The largest enterprises were those of the tobacco planters of Virginia and Maryland (*Map 45*). If their winters had been warmer they would have grown sugar. As it was they were tied to a product that exhausted the land quickly, required heavy labour, and declined steadily in price throughout the eighteenth century. Only the enormous size of their holdings and their slave labour enabled the Virginian planters to maintain their position. The other colonies were, from a commercial point of view, thoroughly unsatisfactory. Pennsylvania, Delaware, and Philadelphia were modest *émigré*-settled states of self-sufficient farming communities. New York traded with pirates and privateers and was a constant nuisance to the English government. The New England farmers worked small estates and frustrated the English government's attempts to monopolize the area's wood for ships.

The English colonists of the mainland did not only fail to live up to expectations. They also broke laws. In 1651 and again in 1667, the English Navigation Acts had established the basis of a network of rules designed artificially to direct the flow of English colonial commerce. Colonists were to trade only with their mother country. They were encouraged (by bounties) to produce the goods which England lacked and discouraged (by duties) from rivalling home industries. Goods were to be transported, in English ships, direct to the 'mother' country. In practice the legislation was regularly ignored. New England colonists exploited the country trades with both French and English islands of the Caribbean. They sold provisions to the French sugar-islands in time of war and traded directly with continental Europe.

The burden of defending the colonies grew greater in the eighteenth century. French colonization reflected the absolutism of its founders. From the beginning it was regimented by the state, with the result that the French settled far more of northern America than the British and began to constitute a threat both to the fur trade in the north and to English settlements along the Mississippi. The European war of 1756 to 1763 was also fought in America, between Britain and France. It was natural that the English government should wish to tax its colonists to defray the cost of defence. But by their charters the colonies possessed elected assemblies which, in practice, could neither be dislodged nor ignored. When pressed by the English government, they revolted and won their independence from the Crown in 1776 (*Map 53*).

The success of the rebellion appeared to be a disaster for British colonial expectations. But subsequent developments emphasized what liberal economists like Adam Smith were already preaching – that trade did not depend upon colonial dominion but upon economic power. The Industrial Revolution in Britain, founded in part on the wealth generated by the old colonies, provided the dynamic for a new imperialism. England's reaction to the disaster was to explore new areas for dominion. James Cook explored the remainder of the oceans, discovering Australia in 1775, Mungo Park set off from the Gambia in search of the Niger twenty years later, and the British East India Company expanded its territorial hold on mainland India.

Another form of liberalism also changed the nature of colonialism at the end of the eighteenth century. During four centuries of the European slave trade, ten million Africans were exported to slavery, of whom some 60% were transported between 1720 and 1820. At this time, the English, French and Portuguese handled 90% of the trade and the English share in most years was equal to the combined total of the others. Public opinion among the educated in Europe had never accepted slavery entirely, but moral unease and rational disquiet had stopped well short of wholesale condemnation. From the late eighteenth century abolitionists in America and England rejected all distinctions. The Quakers in America and the Evangelicals (known as the 'Saints') in England mounted an unprecedented campaign as a result of which slavery was abolished in most of the states of North America north of Pennsylvania (1780) and England abolished the slave trade in its own commerce (1807) – *see Map 45*. By 1824, slaving was declared piracy on the high seas and the efforts of the British navy to enforce the legislation were a tribute to its pre-eminence in the oceans. By 1820 Britain, alone of the colonists of Europe, possessed the self-confidence, righteous arrogance and naval force to infuse its commercial dominance with a sense of didactic responsibility which disguised its imperialism as the establishment of a guardianship over the less-developed world.

47 The rise of the Atlantic economies
In 1500 the Mediterranean was still the commercial, industrial and financial heart of Europe. In the years of economic crisis which began about 1610 the 'Atlantic economies' of England and Holland advanced at the expense of Spain and Italy through technical innovation, colonial expansion and the exploitation of the resources of the Baltic.

Further reading: F. Braudel, *Civilization and Capitalism* (3 vols. Collins 1981-4; Harper Collins); G. V. Scammell, *The First Imperial Age* (Unwin Hyman 1989); E. L. Jones *The European Miracle* (2 ed., Cambridge U.P. 1988); Philip D. Curtin, *The Rise and Fall of the Plantation Complex* (Cambridge U.P. 1990); Edmund S. Morgan, *American Slavery, American Freedom* (Norton 1975).

MAP 47 THE RISE OF THE ATLANTIC ECONOMIES

Atlantic
Ocean

FISH

FISH

FISH

Edinburgh

Whitby

York

FISH
Hatfield Chase
Holland Fen

North
Sea

SWEDEN

Stockholm

Copenhagen

DENMARK

Lübeck

Hamburg

Berlin

Magdeburg

Baltic Sea

POLAND

Danzig
(Guilders)

Oder

Vistula

Breslau

Cracow

Malvern Close

Norwich
Great
Yarmouth
Leiden

UNITED
PROVINCES
Haarlem
Amsterdam
(Guilders)

Antwerp
Bruges   Cologne
Ghent   Louvain
Dunkirk

HOLY ROMAN
EMPIRE

Bristol

London

Southampton

Plymouth

(Pound Sterling)

Canvey Is
Romney
Marsh

Dieppe

Amiens

Rouen

Paris

Weser

Rhine

Prague

Tatra
Mts.

Nuremberg
(Florins)

Strasbourg

Augsburg

Vienna

Danube

FRANCE
(Ecus)

Graz

Loire

Tours

Bay of
Biscay

Lyon

Geneva

The Alps

Udine

Drava

Trieste

OTTOMAN
EMPIRE

Bordeaux

Garonne

Toulouse

Rhône

Nîmes

Avignon

Milan   Brescia Verona
Turin   Padua Venice
Cremona
Po
Genoa   Bologna
Florence
(Ducats)

Leghorn

Ancona

Adriatic
Sea

Valladolid

SPAIN

Madrid

Ebro

Barcelona

Marseilles

Pyrenees

Rome

Naples

Lisbon
(Cruzados)

Toledo

Valencia

Cordoba

Seville

Granada

Alicante

Mediterranean Sea

GRAIN

Palermo

Messina

Syracuse

Cadiz

Algiers

Tunis

To and from
the New World

POPULATION OF SELECTED TOWNS 1600	POPULATION DENSITIES c.1620 (per sq. km.)	

POPULATION OF
SELECTED TOWNS 1600

⊚ over 250,000

◉ 80-120,000

◉ 50-70,000

○ 30-40.000

• other towns

0 _____ 400 km
0 _____ 200 miles

POPULATION DENSITIES c.1620
(per sq. km.)

rising
population   static
population   declining
population

Over 40 inhabitants

20-40 "

5-20 "

Under 5 "

Areas of cloth production

Areas of metal production

◆ Areas drained by Dutch engineers
in the seventeenth century

☐ Trade routes

Movement of exchange rates of major European
currencies against the Dutch guilders on the
Amsterdam market across the century, 1609-1700/9.
For France and Portugal, the base year is 1619.

◐ devaluation   ◔ evaluation

The age of European supremacy 4

EUROPE DIVIDED

T*he decisive event of the early sixteenth century was the Protestant Reformation. It split Europe into two camps. Like all powerful ideologies, Protestantism had a distinct message which divided families, cities and states.*

48 Reformation and Counter-Reformation in Europe
The spread of Protestantism and the development of a variety of sects within it provided Europe with a range of ideologies to match the profusion of its courts and the increasing complexity of its social structure. The Catholic Reformation assisted the traditional powers to counter it with new vigour.

49 The Thirty Years War
The 'Thirty Years War' was in reality a series of conflicts between a succession of contenders for supremacy in post-Reformation Europe, among which France emerged victorious. The scale, duration and bitterness of warfare led to a degree of depopulation which crippled the empire for generations, although its extent cannot be measured with precision.

50 The Baltic under Swedish hegemony
In 1523 Sweden declared itself independent of the Union of Kalmar (Denmark, Norway and Sweden), adopted Lutheranism and developed its army, navy and economy. Its Baltic empire reached its height under Gustavus Adolphus (*r.* 1611-32) and was confirmed by the Peace of Roskilde in 1660. The erosion of the Polish-Lithuanian state culminated in successive partitions and its dissolution (1772-95).

At first it was fostered in the fast-expanding universities. Later, Protestants would establish their own academies in Strasbourg, Geneva and elsewhere to teach their vigorous analysis, refine their own theology, and attack that of their opponents. The cities of Europe were also growing rapidly (*Map 47*), and in them the new ideology found an interested literate laity. Persuasive Protestant preachers and theologians – Martin Luther in Wittenberg, Ulrich Zwingli in Zurich, Jean Calvin in Geneva, Jacob Sturm in Strasbourg – aided by the enormous diffusive power of the new printing press, could compel attention, create controversy and capture converts.

Ideologies are seldom fully developed in their first generation. Lutheranism spread from Wittenberg in Germany from 1517. During its first decade it had a liberating effect in much of western Europe, but it became the official religion only in German-influenced areas, spreading with the support of princes and their courts (*Map 48*). It offered no new view of society; when groups of Anabaptists, who did so, emerged in Lutheran areas preaching indifference towards constituted authority, and even sometimes a sharing of worldly possessions, they were always as firmly repressed as they were by the Catholic Charles V at Munster in 1535.

The second generation reform – Calvinism – spread from Geneva from 1536. It was ideologically more compelling. It offered a new model for society without the inherent anarchy of Anabaptism. Calvin created a new model Church with committees of pastors and elders to enforce its hard, clear, effective moral discipline. Refugees from Catholic persecution throughout Europe came to Geneva. They were sent out again as an élite – the Saints – to conquer, destroy and replace the 'great worldly Babylon'.

The seed of the Calvinist Church was found in the blood of martyrs. Initially, official persecution created refugees. Later, in the second half of the sixteenth century, sectarian conflict dominated the politics of Europe. Calvinists held up to ridicule, menace and abuse the Catholic images, crosses, shrines, feast-day processions, burials and marriage services. The Dutch religious wars started in this way with the 'iconoclastic' riots of 1566. Catholics retaliated against the defiling of their sacred things by taking the blood of Protestants. The massacre of St Bartholomew in France in 1572 began as a government-inspired attempt to eliminate Protestants but became, under popular Catholic enthusiasm, a season of pogroms in major French cities, and a climax to the forty years of religious wars.

At first, Calvin had tried to convert peacefully; but under the pressure of persecution, his successor in Geneva, Beza, openly advocated the deposition of the persecutors. And faced with persecution, Calvinism was forced back on to a narrow social base. It became the religion of urban republics, sometimes reaching out for support from other social groups – lesser princes, turbulent magnates, backwoods gentry or the urban poor – but always retaining its urban and semi-republican ethos.

By the 1560s, the Roman Church seemed everywhere on the defensive. All Europe north of the Alps and the Pyrenees was lost or endangered; the princes were uncertain, the nobility heavily Protestant, the clergy converting. But Roman Catholicism developed a powerful authoritarian counter-ideology. The formal statement of this came in the decrees of the Council of Trent, which concluded its sessions in 1563. When it had first met, summoned by the Emperor in 1545, its purpose had been to reunite and purify the Church and to reverse the 'Monarchical' tendencies of the Papacy. Its effect was otherwise; instead of restoring authority to the bishops, it confirmed their subjection to the Papacy, and presented in hardened form the doctrine of the absolute obedience of both laity and clergy to the Papal See.

Thenceforth Rome became like one of the courts of the great European princes. The Hapsburgs – whose own swelling courts were the envy of the rest of Europe – fought their wars, centralized their government, increased taxes, sold offices, sent out permanent ambassadors to Europe and elsewhere and planned their capitals (*Map 42*). The popes did likewise, and with Spanish-Hapsburg strength behind them, Catholicism triumphed in Europe and America (*Map 43*). Spanish power even protected Italy against the Turks (*Map 39*).

The Catholicism of the Counter-Reformation became the religion of princely courts and bureaucratic and hierarchical societies. Its spiritual force cãme with the Jesuits. Their powerful casuistry was disseminated through educational institutions in Europe and in the New World. Their political influence grew, and gradually they became linked to the Spanish court. Thanks to the Portuguese Jesuits, Philip II gained the crown in Portugal in 1580. The Jesuits promised him the crowns of England and France too. Spanish interests lurked behind the Jesuits who penetrated Lutheran Sweden and Orthodox Russia. It was as Spanish agents that they were expelled from Japan in 1640.

The Catholic Counter-Reformation reached its climax in 1630. Bavaria, Poland, Austria, France and the southern half of the Netherlands had been recovered by preaching and by force. In 1621 Rome had celebrated the destruction of Protestantism in Bohemia. In 1629, La Rochelle, the last Huguenot citadel of France, had been reduced (*Map 51*). In the same year, the Jesuits were advancing northwards to the Baltic. To the east they attached a part of the Greek Orthodox church to their cause, and Catholic missionaries counted the Red Indians of Canada, the war-like *daimyos* of Japan and even they liked to think the Confucian Mandarins of China among the souls they had saved. But in one major respect, Catholic victories were pyrrhic ones. In the decades of persecution the Catholic princes of Europe expelled the Calvinists and with them their financial reserves and mercantile and manufacturing skills. The industrial heart of Europe was displaced. After the iconoclastic riots the Protestants persecuted in the Spanish Netherlands moved north and east across the Rhine. The massacre of Saint Bartholomew sent French silk workers from Lyons across the Jura. In the seventeenth century, the Catholic reconquests scattered Calvinists from Bohemia, the Palatinate and the Baltic to Protestant regions. As a result, the towns of Holland and Zealand – Amsterdam,

Right: Huguenots massacred on St Bartholomew's day.

Haarlem, Delft – inherited the prosperity of Catholic Antwerp, and the cloth industry of Hondschoote (*Map 47*). The North Sea cities – Bremen, Hamburg and Emden – were enriched from the shattered urban life of the Catholic southern Netherlands. The cities of the Rhineland – the Palatinate and Alsace – benefited from the Calvinists expelled from France and from the prince-bishoprics of the Empire. France, Germany and Italy drained its refugees into Switzerland. On the Atlantic coast, tolerant, Anglican England was a refuge for Huguenot weavers.

The economic consequences would have been less serious if Europe's economy had continued to expand. In the sixteenth century – particularly in the first 50 years – the population of Europe was growing, its cities were more wealthy, its economic activity increasing. The merchants of Antwerp, Venice and Seville traded further and deeper across the Baltic, through Germany, into the Levant, into Brazil and across to America (*Maps 35 and 46*). But this pace and confidence could not be sustained at an even rate. Shortly after 1600 it halted or slowed down. First here, then there, the economy of the European states trembled mysteriously. What was the cause of this 'decay of trade'? Was it purely economic? There certainly were weaknesses in the economic system of Europe: it was vulnerable to plagues and disease; its transport remained cripplingly limited; technological change was slow; markets for manufactured goods were relatively small. Was it purely financial? Certainly the decline in the amount of silver imported from the New World (and still the main material for coinage) went hand in hand with the general contraction. Was it the climate? Europe was indeed colder and wetter in this century than in the sixteenth and some historians have spoken of a 'mini ice-age'. Or was it the result of the growing burden of administrative centralization, particularly in Catholic states? We do not know precisely. What is clear is that the effects of stagnation were felt unevenly in Europe.

Spain, despite its overseas wealth and its military power, felt the European-wide dearth of resources most keenly. It had ceased to be able to feed itself. Disastrous plagues in the 1590s decimated its inland population; its coins depreciated to become shadows of their former sovereign glory (*Map 47*). Italy and the Mediterranean felt the same process less severely. Further north, Holland escaped these ravages. Financial constriction was avoided and capital introduced by *emigrés* was put to good use in modest technological endeavours. The Dutch became drainage engineers across the whole of northern Europe, thus releasing new land for cultivation. Their famous fly-boats brought a revolution in bulk-carrying cargoes at sea. Their industries produced products which were saleable across a broad European market – cheap, durable cloth, mass-produced Delft tiles, sugar-enriched wines, salted fish. In the wake of the Dutch Wars, which reached a truce in 1609, Amsterdam became the successor of Antwerp as Europe's mercantile centre. Its Protestant neighbours also found their currencies and their economies more stable, their cities growing. This new strength enabled the Dutch to break into the oceans of the world and establish themselves at the centre of an East Asiatic empire which lasted until the twentieth century (*Maps 46 and 67*).

Economic crisis and European war came together. From 1618, the energies of Europe were turned inwards to be consumed in the long, destructive contest of the Thirty Years War (*Map 49*). This was a complex of wars, a pattern of rival imperialism amongst the European land empires. Spanish ambitions in the Netherlands and the Baltic, Saxon ambitions in Germany, Swedish ambitions in the Baltic, all encouraged the fears and hopes of their various satellite powers. At the beginning, it was also a war of ideologies, of the Counter-Reformation against Calvinism. As such it flowed across boundaries and was never a purely German affair. The war began in Bohemia with the mobilization by the Elector Palatine of his Protestant allies in England, Holland, and other minorities elsewhere to support his election as King of Bohemia. It could have started earlier, perhaps when the conversion to Protestantism of the elector of Cologne had caused the Cologne war in 1583, or when the death of the duke of Cleves in 1609 could have plunged Europe into war but for the timely assassination of King Henry IV of France. Ranged against the Elector Palatine was the Hapsburg empire. For the Hapsburgs it was a parasitic war. Economically bankrupt (as they admitted) after expelling their productive subjects, war seemed the only way of nourishing their court and the privileged society which regularly consumed more than it generated. It enabled them to suck from the heretics the sustenance they could not create themselves. The Austrian Hapsburgs devoured Bohemia, Bavaria, the Upper Palatinate, just as the Lutheran princes – Denmark, Sweden and Saxony – absorbed Lusatia and the German coastal littoral as the reward of supporting fellow Protestants.

But the Thirty Years War marked the end of religious ideology. In their imperialism, the European monarchs took up strange alliances across the ideological divide. Protestant Sweden intervened in Germany in 1631, funded by Catholic France. Catholic Bavaria joined the Protestant princes in Europe against the Hapsburgs. Albrecht von Wallenstein, of doubtful personal religious conviction, fought the Emperor's wars for him as a mercenary and used Protestant bankers. The material destruction which caused the depopulation of swathes of Germany (especially the Elbe and lower Rhine regions) and the devastation of its cities, discredited the ideologies that had permitted such savagery. The peace of Westphalia, which ended the wars in 1648, was not attended by a representative of the Papacy or ratified by the Pope.

When all was over, who had gained and who lost? Politically, it is clear. The Spanish empire in Europe was broken, the Hapsburg empire was shaken. Saxony and Bavaria had demonstrated their independence; Brandenburg followed where they led (*Map 52*). Above all France had a firm government, clearly defined boundaries, and boundless influence in Germany (*Map 51*). But the Thirty Years War destroyed far more than Spanish hegemony. It destroyed a whole system. In the cataclysm, the hierarchical courts of the Counter-Reformation, with their patronage, their swollen officialdom, and parasitic economies, were broken. Even some Protestant countries with courts – such as England – suffered the same fate. The international churches were broken too; the Roman Catholic church destroyed the international effectiveness of the Calvinists only to weaken itself fatally in facing the challenge of scepticism in the next century. The new forms of government – sober republics and mercantilist minded absolutist states based on rationalized privileges – which had recently germinated, began to show themselves after 1660. The European *ancien régime* was beginning.

Further reading: John Bossy, *Christianity in the West 1400-1700*, (Oxford U.P. 1985); Euan Cameron, *The European Reformation* (Oxford U.P. 1991); Mark Greengrass, *France in the Age of Henri IV: The Struggle for Stability* (Longman 1984); Simon Schama, *The Embarrassment of Riches* (Collins 1987; University of California Press); Geoffrey Parker, *The Military Revolution* (Cambridge U.P. 1988).

MAP 48 REFORMATION AND COUNTER-REFORMATION IN EUROPE

FINLAND (1528)

ESTONIA (1542)

LIVONIA (1542)

COURLAND (1561)

Riga

TEUTONIC ORDER PRUSSIA (1530) (under Polish Suzerainty from 1466)

Königsberg

Danzig

Vistula

KINGDOM

Warsaw (-1572)

OF POLAND

Confessio Poloniae, Consensus Poloniae 1570/1595

Danube

Confessio Pentapolitana, 1545

MORAVIA Confessio Hungarica, 1562

SILESIA

Breslau

Vienna (1524)

Graz (1581-1621)

Baltic Sea

(Northern Mission) (1673/78/88)

Uppsala

SWEDEN (1527)

Confessio Augustana, 1593

POMERANIA (1534)

Stettin

Oder

BRANDENBURG (1539)

Berlin

Wittenberg (1524)

(ELECTORATE.) SAXONY (1539)

Dresden

Prague (1576-1612)

BOHEMIA

Confessio Bohemica, 1575

Confessio Augustana, 1530

MECKLENBURG (1548-9)

Lübeck

Hamburg

Leipzig

Zwickau

Salzburg

Regensburg

BAVARIA (1581)

Munich (1573/83)

Innsbruck

NORWAY (1539)

Confessio Augustana, 1536/1607

Skagerrak

DENMARK

Confessio Hafnica, 1530

Lund

SCHLESWIG (1542)

HOLSTEIN (1542)

Elbe

BREMEN

EMDEN (1526) (1542)

Bremen

Confessio Augustana, 1530

Magdeburg (1525)

Mühlhausen

(DUCHY.) (1526)

HESSE-KASSEL

FULDA

Nuremberg

ANSBACH (1528)

WÜRTTEM-BERG (1534)

Ulm

Hall

Augsburg (1573/83)

Donauwörth

UPPER PALATINATE

B. BAMBERG

B. WÜRZ-BURG

Heilbronn

Basel (1529)

Zurich

North Sea

Münster

Groningen

Utrecht

Amsterdam

Leiden

Dortmund

Cologne

Rhine

MÜNSTER Bc.

Ac. TRIER

MAINZ

NASSAU (1528)

RHINE P.-PALATINATE (1546) (1559)

Frankfurt (1530)

Worms

Wetzlar

Maastricht

Breda

Ghent Antwerp

Confessio Belgica, 1559/61 (1594/97)

Middelburg

Lille Tournai

Strasbourg

Münster

Meaux

Troyes

Paris (1500)

Rouen

Confessio Gallicana, 1559 FRANCE

Alençon

Angers Saumur

Loire

Marmoutiers (French Mission)

English Channel

Norwich

Canterbury

York

ENGLAND

English Mission (1623/88)

Act of Supremacy, 1534
Act of Uniformity, 1549
Act of Uniformity, 1552
Recatholicisation, 1554
Act of Uniformity, 1559

SCOTLAND

Scottish Mission (1653/94)

Confessio Scotica, 1560

Saint Andrews

Glasgow

IRELAND (1536)

Dublin

Confessio Belgica,

Confessio Helvetica, 1536/62

GRAUBÜNDEN (1525)

VAL TELLINA

1 Dalmatian Congregation

Adriatic Sea

Venice (1500)

Ravenna
Ferrara
Fathers of the Good Jesus, 1526)

Verona
Mantua
Bologna

Trent

Brescia (Ursulines, 1535)
Milan (Barnabites, 1530)

Turin

Geneva (1536)

Lyon

Genoa

187

Florence (1560)

Camerino (Capucins 1525/8)

Rome (Theatines, 1524)
(Jesuits, 1540)

Naples (-1511)

Tyrrhenian Sea

CORSICA

SARDINIA

Mediterranean Sea

SICILY

Messina

Valetta (Knights of Malta, 1523)

6 Greek Islands

Limoges
Périgueux
Bergerac
Bordeaux
La Rochelle

Rodez
Millau
Albi
Gaillac
Toulouse
Montauban

(Pères doctrinaires, 1592/1597)

Orange
Nîmes
Avignon
Montpellier

FOIX
ROUSSILLON
CATALONIA
Manresa

NAVARRE
Pamplona
Ebro

31

Madrid (1505)
Toledo

Legend

- Reformed faith dominant, c. 1560-70
- Reformed faith growing, c. 1560-70
- Considerable local reformed faith, c. 1560-70
- Some penetration of reform, c. 1560-70
- Catholic areas
- Predominantly Lutheran confessions
- Predominantly Calvinist & Zwinglian confessions
- Areas of anabaptist communities 1529-1618
- 'Eclectic' confessions (Anglican, Polish, Bohemian)
- ✚ Catholic missions and reform endeavours (with dates)
- ⊙ Reformed communities discovered by the inquisition in Italy
- ✚ Papal nunciatures (with dates)
- 6 Number of legates sent to the last session of the Council of Trent (by country or region)
- ● Imperial cities
- ✦ Sectarian riots following the massacre of Saint Bartholomew in Paris, (1572)
- ✧ Iconoclastic riots in Netherlands towns, (1566)
- △ Catholic archbishoprics lost to the Protestants
- Seigneurial lands of the king of Navarre in France

0   150 miles
0   300 kms

Printing centres for Incunabula books (those printed before 1500) in Europe
Sources of surviving incunabula

Key:
- Holy Roman Empire and Switzerland
- Italy
- France
- Spain and Portugal
- England and Scandinavia
- E. Europe (Poland, Bohemia, Hungary, Yugoslavia)

Period	Main centres		Total
1460-70	Augsburg, Nuremberg	9 4 1	14
1471-80	Augsburg, Nuremberg, Venice, Milan	41 41 9 7 4 2	104
1481-90	Augsburg, Nuremberg, Venice, Milan, Paris	63 57 23 13 7 4	167
1491-1500	Augsburg, Nuremberg, Paris, Venice, Milan, Lyon, Florence, Leipzig, Deventer	76 62 36 23 9 7	213

MAP 49 THE THIRTY YEARS WAR

Boundary of the Holy
Roman Empire in 1648

Electors of the emperor, 1618

1620 Areas of peasant unrest (with dates)

MAIN Members of the Evangelical
Union, 1609 (protestant)

Military interventions

Towns that were subject to
army plunder or sacked

Main line of march of Gustavus Adolphus

0   400 km
0   200 miles

Theatres of war:

The Bohemian War, 1618-20 and 1621-23

The Lower Saxon-Danish and
Polish-Swedish War, 1625-9

The Swedish War, 1630-34

The Franco-Swedish War, 1635-48

Population, 1618-1648:

Population decrease, 0-15%

Population decrease, 15-33%

Population decrease, 33-66%

Population decrease, over 66%

MAP 50 THE BALTIC UNDER SWEDISH HEGEMONY

Norwegian Sea

Arctic Circle

White Sea

LAPLAND

KINGDOM OF SWEDEN

Västerbotten

Gulf of Bothnia

Österbotten

Vasa

CARELIA (1617)

Archangel

L. Onega

TRONDHEIM (1658-60 to Sweden)

JÄMTLAND (1645)

HÄRJEDALEN

FINLAND

Lake Ladoga

Bergen

COPPER

Falun

Viborg

KINGDOM OF DENMARK AND NORWAY

IRON

Christiania

Uppsala

Åland Islands

Helsingfors

Gulf of Finland

INGRIA (1583-95, 1617)

RUSSIAN EMPIRE

Västeras

Reval

Narva

Novgorod

HEMP

ESTONIA (1561)

(1581)

L. Vänern

Stockholm

Dagö (1582)

Skagerrak

(1658)

L. Vättern

Linköping

(1582)

Ösel (1645)

LIVONIA (1621/29-1721)

Jonkoping

GOTLAND (1645)

Gulf of Riga

HALLAND

Baltic Sea

Riga (1621/29)

Jutland

Calmar

DUCHY OF COURLAND

Frederiksodde

Copenhagen

Helsingborg

Brömsebro

Dvina

Smolensk

Schleswig

Funen

Zealand

SKANE (1658)

Bornholm (1658-60 Sweden)

Memel

Lübeck

Hamburg (1648-1715)

Bremen

POMERANIA

FURTHER POMERANIA

(Swedish occupation 1629-35)

Königsberg

PRUSSIA under Polish suzerainty to 1657

GRAIN

Minsk

Danzig

Wismar

MECKLEN-BURG

Stettin

Elbing

GRAIN

LITHUANIA

Elbe

BRANDENBURG

Berlin

Vistula

Warsaw

Pripet

RUSSIANS

KINGDOM OF POLAND

Breslau

SILESIA

Prague

Cracow

Kiev

Dnieper

Carpathians

PODOLIA (Turkish 1672-99)

COSSACKS

Vienna

Danube

Dniester

TURKISH EMPIRE

97

Legend:

Sweden in 1560

(1561) Acquistions by Sweden 1560-1660

Swedish colonisation in Finland

Denmark and Norway

Poland in 1569 (maximum extent)

Poland in 1700

Northern limit of oak-trees (for Norway and Sweden)

Seas and lakes frozen in winter

0 400 km

0 200 miles

The age of European supremacy 5

THE ANCIEN RÉGIME

In 1660, Europe emerged from a half-century of violent convulsions. The whole continent was at peace for the first time in over a generation.

51 The *ancien régime* in France
The gradual absorption of the great fiefs by the French crown and the decay of regional institutions permitted the creation of a centralized bureaucratic government which, despite widespread and often prolonged local resistance, laid the foundations of absolute monarchy and territorial expansion.

The last 'great rebellion' ended with the restoration of Charles II in England. Descartes' logical philosophical method enthroned human reason and seemed capable of resolving every intellectual problem. Demographic stagnation and areas of economic depression would persist into the eighteenth century, but this in its way was a facet of the social and political stability which was not radically disturbed for more than a century.

The basis of this stability was the pre-eminence of rich, hereditary landed oligarchies, most of which enjoyed nobility. Every state in Europe (except certain Swiss cantons) recognized the existence of a nobility. The French revolutionaries identified the principle of noble privilege as the essential component of the *'ancien régime'* to whose destruction they were committed.

The doomed nobility of France was the prime example of European nobility. France was held to comprise three orders or estates – clergy, nobility and the third estate. This originated in the medieval division of society into those who prayed, those who fought, and those who worked. The noble order had a complex hierarchy of titles and enjoyed substantial precedence and privileges, notably personal exemption from taxation. By 1660, it not only fought but prayed (the overwhelming proportion of Louis XIV's bishops were old nobles) and worked for the state (his ministers were also old nobles). It enjoyed a certain lifestyle in which manual work, which included the retail trades, was forbidden and which, in practice, required the possession and cultivation of land. Perhaps a third of France was owned by the nobility, and this proportion was about average for Europe. In Denmark, by comparison, 85% of the land was owned by the nobility. In England, four hundred noble families owned a quarter of the soil.

The attributes of the nobleman were universally agreed upon. 'Persons of Quality' (like the Englishman, Dr Burney) roamed across Europe, armed with a sheaf of letters of recommendation which opened up the polite society of metropolis and court along their route (*see Map 52*). The allurements of town and court life were irresistible and European nobles were divided between those who

could afford them and the 'mere' squires who could not. In France, where residence in the royal palace of Versailles was the ultimate privilege, establishments had to be maintained in Paris, at court and in the country. Most ostentatious of all were the magnates of the Hapsburg empire, who not only resided at court in their Viennese palaces, but also built impressive country seats, of which the Esterhaz ('the Hungarian Versailles') was the most famous. With the European nobility went a European language (French), a cosmopolitan entertainment (music) and a common cultural attitude subsequently called 'Enlightenment'.

The central political problem for the nobility was to obtain a stable, firm government to maintain their privileges without at the same time encouraging despotism, or breeding democracy. In his *Leviathan* (1651), Thomas Hobbes, defending all forms of strong government, had argued that a sovereign power was the only source of authority, law and morality. 'The sovereign power . . . is as great as men can be imagined to make it. And although of so unlimited a power, men may fancy many evil consequences, yet the consequences of the want of it, which is perpetual war of every man against his neighbour, are much worse'. Tyranny, he said, was only a pejorative term for monarchy.

Hobbes' justification for the absolute power of the prince was used in France by Louis XIV's apologist, Bishop Bossuet, to construct a coherent theory of absolutism. The activity of Louis XIV enthralled Europe for fifty years and the memory of it haunted the eighteenth century (*see Map 51*). In many respects Louis XIV built upon the achievements of the Cardinal ministers Richelieu and Mazarin, who had introduced the bureaucratic mechanism of provincial government in the *intendants*, initiated an expansionist foreign policy, chastened the rebellious nobles in the *Frondes* (1648-53) and increased taxation. In other ways, Louis XIV's baroque taste for glory and sense of theatre led contemporaries to overestimate his absolutism. Nonetheless, he did dramatically expand the borders of France at the expense of the Hapsburgs, expel the Huguenots from his realm in 1685, and maintain a huge standing army and a

developed navy. As a result, there was a reaction after his death since he had seriously undermined the privileges of the nobility, encountered peasant uprisings and resistance within the Catholic establishment, and built up a colossal debt which was stabilized only by multiple bankruptcies in the succeeding reign.

Nevertheless, others in eighteenth-century Europe followed Louis XIV's taste for glory. Prussia became a kingdom when the Elector Frederick III of Brandenburg was given a royal dignity in 1701 and crowned 'King in Prussia'. His military reforms created a standing army which his son used to make Prussia one of the leading powers in Europe (*see Map 52*). In Austria, Maria Theresa (*r.* 1740-80) compensated for the loss of Silesia by imitating Louis XIV in her hereditary lands of Austria, Bohemia and Hungary. Even countries with a strong tradition of representative institutions established painfully in the wars of the seventeenth century, such as Sweden and the Netherlands, faced autocratic monarchs like Gustavus III (*r.*1772-92) and Wilhelm V (*r.*1766-1806). They constructed their pastiche Versailles, where royal, imperial, or ducal courts could enjoy the delicate interplay between ruler, minister, courtier, mistress and financier. Imitations stretched from Naples to Madrid, from Vienna to St Petersburg. But, significantly, the only miniature Versailles on English soil – Blenheim Palace – was constructed not for a monarch but for a general in retirement from the last of Louis XIV's wars.

As armies grew, the profession of arms took on a new meaning. Higher standards of discipline were exacted from officers. For the rank and file, developments included impressment, parade-ground drill and execution by firing squad. Other continental autocrats undertook expansionist wars with the same thread-bare justifications as Louis XIV's mixture of strategic, commercial and dynastic motives, but they added a pseudo-scientific jargon of the 'balance of power' to justify the Peace of Utrecht in 1713 or the first partition of Poland in 1773. Some have spoken of a century of limited warfare, but when reason of state demanded it there was brutality and extensive war.

MAP 51 THE ANCIEN RÉGIME IN FRANCE

**Legend (top left):**

Royal domain in 1477

Fiefs which fell to the Crown in 1477-1527

Patrimony of Charles, Duke of Bourbon, escheating to the crown in 1527

Other fiefs still outstanding in 1550

Ven Region with estates (provincial assemblies) in the sixteenth century

Art Region with estates surviving to 1661

⊙ *Siège* of a *parlement*

1643 Intendency centres in c. 1716 (with dates of first permanent *intendants*)

Généralités in c 1716

Certain peasant revolts and town revolts

**Legend (bottom right):**

Acquisitions in 1552, confirmed in 1648 (Metz, Toul and Verdun)

Acquisitions 1643-1661

Acquisitions 1662-1715

Areas "reunited" with the French Crown by Louis XIV 1684-1697

Duchy of Lorraine (occupied by France 1634-59 and 1670-1697)

Ten Imperial cities in Alsace over which France acquired jurisdiction in 1648 and which were annexed in 1672·

**Legend (bottom left):**

◆ Fortresses constructed or strengthened by Vauban

Linguistic eastern frontier of France

French border in 1715

0   200 km
0   100 miles

**Map labels:**

SPANISH NETHERLANDS
HOLY ROMAN EMPIRE
DUCHY OF SAVOY
SWISS CONFEDERATION

C. of Flanders
C. of Eu
Artois
Picardy
Normandy
Ile de France
Champagne
D. of Bar
Lorraine
Alsace
Brittany
Maine
Perche
Alençon
Orléanais
D. of Nemours
D. of Valois
Nivernais
D. of Burgundy
C. of Charolais
Franche-Comté
Anjou
Touraine
Vendôme
Bourbonnais
Bresse
Lyonnais
Poitou
La Marche
Forez
Auvergne
Dauphiné
Aunis
Saintonge
Angoumois
Limousin
Périgord
Guyenne
Massif Central
C. of Rouergue
Provence
Albret
Armagnac
Navarre
V.C. of Béarn
Languedoc
C. of Venaissin
Commines
C. of Foix
Pyrenees

Brest, St Malo, Rennes 1634 1636, 1639, Nantes, Belle Isle, Cherbourg, Le Havre 1630, Caen 1630 1631, 1639, Rouen 1630 1631, 1634, 1636, 1639, Alençon 1525 1638, Le Mans 1489, Angers 1525 1556, Tours 1630, Poitiers 1633 1631-2, 1639, 1641, Ile de Ré, La Rochelle, Angoulême, Blaye, Bordeaux 1630 1631, 1635, 1649, 1651-3, 1675, Bayonne, Pau, Tarbes, Auch, Toulouse 1613 1635, Montauban 1643, Montpellier 1639, 1644-5 1613, Narbonne 1635, Nîmes, Aix 1630, 1649, 1659, Marseille 1631, 1649, 1650, 1658, Toulon, Orange 1713, Avignon, Grenoble 1638, Lyon 1632, 1641-2, Clermont Ferrand 1636-7, 1640, 1641-3, Riom 1625, Limoges 1632, Périgueux 1637, Moulin 1633, 1636, 1640 1634 1684, Nevers 1639, Bourges 1641 1639, Dijon 1630 1635 1674, Besançon, Dôle 1678/9, Châlons, Auxerre, Orléans 638, Troyes 1630, 1641, 1642, Paris 1634 1631, 1648-9, 1653, Vertûs 1636, Reims, Soissons 1634, La Fère, Guise, St Quentin 1477, Mézières, Sedan 1678, Réthel, Montmédy, Verdun, Metz, Toul, Strasbourg 1643, Kehl, Haguenau 1681/4, Wissembourg, Landau, Freiburg 1643, Breisach 1643, Colmar, Schlettstadt, Münster, Belfort 1648, Honingen, Mont Royal, Longwy, Luxemburg, Thionville, Sarrelouis, Bonn, Arenberg, Oberstein, Lautrecken, Phillippsburg, Maubeuge 1675, Charleroi, Avesnes, Rocroi, Landrécies, Bouchain, Condé, Tournai, Lille, Aire 1678, Doullens, Cambrai, Amiens 1633 1628, 1638, 1642, Arras 1659, St Omer 1678, Gravelines, Ardres, Calais, Dunkirk

Revolts:

LUSTUCRU 1662
NU-PIEDS 1639
TORRÉBEN 1675
SABOTIERS 1658
TARD-AVISES; CROQUANTS 1593-4, 1636, 1637
TARDANIZATS 1655-6
CROQUANTS 1593-4, 1637
TARD-AVISES 1707
CROQUANTS 1643
CROQUANTS 1642
AUDIJOS 1663
CROQUANTS 1594
CROQUANTS 1635
CAMISARDS 1702-7
ROURE 1670

Acquisition dates:
Nevers 1477/82
Burgundy 1477/82
Brittany 1491
Valois 1515
Eu 1477
St Quentin 1477
Provence 1481
Foix 1589
Béarn 1620
Bar 1634

Louis XIV's armies devastated the Palatinate. Frederick II's laid waste Silesia. To pay for the wars, the autocrats established bureaucracies and increased indirect taxation on goods, windows, documents and stamps.

Like Louis XIV the eighteenth-century autocrats encountered opposition from philosophers, provincial nobles, peasants and the bourgeoisie. The philosophic Enlightenment is not easy to dissect. Philosophers, moralists, historians and political thinkers in eighteenth-century France, England and Germany gradually developed an optimistic faith in the power of human reason to reach a composite truth encompassing man and nature. They saw themselves engaged in a common battle against tyranny in politics, dogma in religion, superstition in science, prejudice in morals and hypocrisy in manners. The movement spread from England, where opposition to Louis XIV's absolutism was articulated in the works of John Locke, who set out to prove that absolutism was inconvenient, dangerous, unnatural and a threat to property. But Voltaire was, through his long life and prodigious output, the most formidable-*philosophe*. His greatest works were composed during the last years of his life at his Swiss retreat,

les Délices. His wit made the *ancien régime* ridiculous; his moral fervour made it hateful throughout the courts and salons of Europe. The philosophers created a climate of opinion in which change was seen as necessary and good. In their stress upon Truth, Equality and Liberty they laid the foundations for the ideology of the revolutions.

The most divisive issues were the position of established religion and tolerance for minorities. Everywhere the established Church was closely interlocked with the state and the aristocracy. Initially autocrats supported the Church and repressed religious extremists, whether Huguenots,

Jansenists or Quakers. But increasingly the 'enlightened' despots sought approval from the *philosophe*-inspired aristocrats and began to tolerate minorities. The expulsion of the Jesuits (who had once been the confessors and advisers of the princes) proved universally popular. Their wealth and power had made them envied, particularly for their trading companies to the New World. They were expelled from Portugal in 1759 and the order was dissolved twenty-five years later. Austria tolerated Jews from 1781; the Huguenots were officially tolerated in France from 1787. Everywhere the exclusive religion of freemasonry appealed to

aristocrats for whom an embattled and obscurantist church held no attractions. Under the influence of the *philosophes* the monarchs and aristocrats of Europe rendered the established churches vulnerable in the coming revolutions. The opposition of provincial nobilities to the autocrats was patchy and sporadic. In Prussia the nobility was so involved with the army and administration that it obediently followed where the kings led. In Russia, Catherine the Great (*r.*1762-46) took care not to offend the nobility. But elsewhere in Europe, the provincial nobilities – in Ireland, Belgium, Hungary – felt that the powers of government should be reduced (*see Maps 53 and 54*).

Peasant revolts were, likewise, sporadic. These were serious in Hungary in 1678-81, 1703-11, 1735, 1751, 1755, 1763-4, 1765-6 and 1784. They were provoked by increases in seigneurial dues but extended to complaints about taxes and tithes. Twenty thousand peasants were involved in the revolt of 1755, and in the Transylvanian rising of 1784, 30,000 rebels butchered hundreds of nobles and their families. Similar revolts occurred in Russia. Further west, there was no serious peasant uprising after those at the end of Louis XIV's reign until the *Grande Peur* (Great Fear) of July 1789 (*Map 54*). The reasons lie in agricultural prosperity and the diminishing frequency of crisis years in which famine, plague, war and heavier taxation struck simultaneously and left the peasant with nothing to lose but his life.

The cornerstones of this economic growth, particularly towards the middle of the eighteenth century, were the towns, and a non-noble élite – the bourgeoisie – dominated the towns as the nobles dominated the countryside. Many continental towns had a legally defined group of burghers (bourgeois), enjoying privileges and qualifying for the status through heredity, favouritism and great wealth. They were not a new group in the eighteenth century, but they grew both in numbers and wealth. By 1800, they easily outnumbered the titled nobility in western Europe, being about 10% of the population, though no more than 3% in Hungary or Russia. Their wealth rapidly increased through trade, the professions, government investment and contracts, and prudent industrial ventures. Merchants in Marseilles, Bristol, Nantes, Cadiz, Cork, Hamburg; manufacturers in Manchester, Lyons and Barcelona; lawyers in the capital cities and judicial centres of Europe – all contributed to the expanding bourgeoisie.

It would be premature to speak of a bourgeois 'class-consciousness' anywhere before 1815 in sufficient strength to threaten the nobility or the autocrats. Only in particular circumstances did the

Voltaire

bourgeois make use of their increased preponderance. When the forces of order failed to repress sedition, riots were sparked off by strikes, fears of bread shortage, taxation and religion. Riots in Geneva in 1781, in the towns of Holland in 1787, and in Paris in 1789 heightened the political awareness of the bourgeoisie. Religious dissent also separated some bourgeois from the common assumptions of their age sufficiently to articulate alternative ones. Baptist, Congregationalist, and Quaker merchants in England, Presbyterian manufacturers in Cork, Protestant financiers in Nîmes, Montpellier and Montauban, Jewish bankers in Berlin, Frankfurt or Hamburg were all apart from or opposed to the values of the *ancien régime* despite its palsied attempts at toleration towards the end of the eighteenth century. It is not a coincidence that the most outspoken leaders in England, America and France in the age of revolutions came from religious minorities.

In the hands of far-sighted autocrats structural change in the *ancien régime* would not have been impossible. But here lay the congenital weakness of absolutism. The painters of the eighteenth century leave nothing to the imagination. From their canvases rulers and their consorts stare out, pop-eyed and pompous, their bewigged vacuous expressions revealing the emptiness of their minds. By the end of the eighteenth century western Europe lay in the hands of mad old George III in England, booby Wilhelm V in the Netherlands, erratic Joseph II in Austria and inadequate Louis XVI in France. Dominated by their diseases, their wives and their families, they present a picture not of individual misfortune, but of the generic and ineradicable disease of the *ancien régime*.

---

52 The Enlightenment in Europe
The Europe of the *ancien regime* was an agglomerate of vested interests – churches, guilds, corporations, aristocrats – whose members shared a cosmopolitan culture, increasing luxury and the excitement of the philosophical Enlightenment in their courts and salons. Some monarchs imitated the absolutism of Louis XIV, their ambitions demonstrated in their new palaces.

Further reading: Ernest Gellner, *Reason and Culture* (Basil Blackwell 1991); Pierre Goubert, *Louis XIV and Twenty Million Frenchmen* (Viking 1970); Norbert Elias, *The Court Society* (Basil Blackwell 1983); Marc Raeff, *The Well-Ordered Police State* (Yale U.P. 1983); James Casey, *The History of the Family* (Basil Blackwell 1989); Henry S. Commager, *The Empire of Reason* (Weidenfeld and Nicolson 1978; OUP New York).

**Map labels (left column):**
St. Petersburg · Peterhof · Königsberg · PRUSSIA (1657/60, Kingdom 1701) · Lazienki · union with Saxony 4/6, 1709-33, 1735-63) · acow · Lemberg · GALICIA · Carpathians · Czernowitz · BUKOWINA · HUNGARY · Debreczin · Budapest · TRANSYLVANIA · Hermannstedt · Kronstadt · Szegedin · Tisza · LESSER WALLACHIA (1718-39) · (1718-39) · Danube · SERBIA · TURKISH EMPIRE · 300 km · 200 miles

The age of European supremacy 6

THE AGE OF REVOLUTIONS

When Alexis de Tocqueville published his work, The Ancien Régime and the Revolution *in 1856, he showed how much of the French Revolution was foreshadowed in the* ancien régime *(see Map 51).*

53 The American Revolution
Much of the thirteen colonies area remained unaffected by the war, but the concentration of British power along the coast hampered attempts to suppress the revolution. As it gained ground the predominantly bourgeois leadership showed preference for 'Whiggish' rather than 'democratic' principles – for example, for appointive rather than elective office, and a narrow, property-based franchise – in the forms of government which were adopted.

Below: Congress approves the Declaration of Independence, July 4 1776.

Its revolutionary principles were born of the *philosophes*; centralization of power in the state had already been achieved by the Bourbons; the peasantry was already emancipated; the process of reducing society to an aggregate of individuals, each purged of the bonds of blood, guild or corporation, had already begun. Above all, the French Revolution had been anticipated elsewhere, once with success (in the American War of Independence, 1775-83) and elsewhere in Europe with failure (notably in Geneva, 1780-82; the Netherlands, 1787-9; and Belgium, 1789).

These revolutions have been called 'democratic'. Some turned out that way, but they were not begun by democrats, and were not the result of a revolutionary movement. The collapse of the *ancien régime* came from conflicts between the ruling nobilities and autocrats. Leadership came, initially, not from the street, but from the provincial nobility – the outraged, but sober and conservative gentry. Among their leaders were George Washington, a successful soldier, a landowner, and a conscientious representative of the House of Burgesses in

his state, Jan van der Capellen, the radical noble who urged the Dutch to resist their prince and govern the state themselves, and a clutch of noble radicals in the French estates general, such as the vicomte de Noailles or the affable marquis de Condorcet.

The nobility allowed the revolts to happen, but the bourgeoisie rapidly became the standard-bearers. Outraged lawyers and notables organized themselves across the east coast of America, following the example of Boston, into Sons of Liberty from 1763 (*see Map 53*). In Holland, the Patriot party grew up among the regent patricians (who ruled the towns) and their supporters so that, by 1784, they numbered 28,000 volunteers and held their first national convention. In Belgium, urban oligarchs who opposed the absolutism of Joseph II joined the clergy in a revolutionary society 'for altar and hearth' in June 1789. In France the resistance of the law-courts (the issue, as in America, was a stamp duty) encouraged the calling of an estates general in May 1789. Amongst the delegates, two-thirds were from the 'third estate',

which was dominated by royal officials and lawyers from the professional bourgeoisie. Their self-confidence and their involvement in the machinery of state encouraged them to undertake a structural reform unparalleled in any other European state.

The successful revolutions reveal their ideology clearly. In the ringing terms of the American *Declaration of Independence* (1776) or the French *Declaration of the Rights of Man and Citizens* (1789) lie the manifestoes against privilege and for liberty and nationhood, blueprints for every nineteenth-century liberation movement. Liberty was a marvellous battle-cry, corrosive of all frontiers, classes, governments, boundless in its application. In the glorious dawn of 1789, when trees of liberty were being planted in France, some even dreamt of 'the possibility of a single Nation and the facility with which the Universal Assembly sitting in Paris will conduct the whole human race'. Subsequently, the National Assembly in France would grant citizenship to the great champions of liberty, Washington, Wilberforce, Schiller and Pestalozzi.

Nationalism was as corrosive as liberty but more exclusive in its impact. In August 1789, the Estates General in France transformed themselves into the National Assembly. They destroyed privilege because it damaged national integrity. A new mythology of patriotism was hastily fostered, to encourage a sense of invincible unity. Stones from the demolished Bastille were carried as souvenirs to all corners of France. In July 1793, the new nation's apparatus of flags, anthems, and identity cards was completed by an order to erect an altar of the fatherland, on which would be engraved the *Declaration of Rights* with the inscription 'The citizen is born, lives and dies for the Fatherland'.

When the Estates General referred to 'the people' in, for instance, the French *Declaration*, they meant 'the nation', sounding more democratic than, in practice, they intended to be. This impression was reinforced because their first sessions were accompanied by the enormous popular unrest in Paris which led to the fall of the Bastille on July 4 1789 and the *Grande Peur* (Great Fear) of the peasantry which destroyed seigneurial charters

MAP 53 THE AMERICAN REVOLUTION

Legend

- British Proclamation line of 1763
- Movement of British forces
- Movement of American forces
- ⊗ American victories
- ⊗ British victories
- ○ Places occupied by British forces
- ◆ Areas with substantial Loyalist/Tory sentiment
- ✳ Areas of discontent in late colonial period
- ⚓ British naval presence
- ⚓ French naval presence
- Significant proportions of non-English population:
  - Scots-Irish
  - German
  - Dutch

0   200 km
0   150 miles

Map labels

Quebec
Montreal
St. Lawrence
Burgoyne (1777)
Lake Ontario
Lake Erie
1775-76
1775-76
Fort Ticonderoga (1775)
Saratoga (1777)
Portsmouth
Lexington (1775)
Bunker Hill (1775)
Boston
Evacuation of Boston (1776)
Newport
New Haven
New York
Long Island
Hudson
INDIAN
Ohio
Victories on the Ohio
TERRITORY
Trenton (1776)
Valley Forge (1777-78)
Brandywine Creek (1777)
Philadelphia
1781
Appalachian Mts.
Chesapeake Bay
Cornwallis (1781)
Yorktown (1781)
Norfolk
French blockade of Yorktown (1781)
King's Mountain (1780)
Moores Creek Bridge (1776)
Charleston
Savannah
Savannah
Atlantic Ocean

Democratic tendencies of state constitutions, 1775-1790

Democratic	Moderate	Whiggish

State	No.	Date
Vermont	1	1777 / 1786
New Hampshire	2	1775 / 1784
Massachusetts	3	1780
Rhode Island	4	Colonial charter retained
Connecticut	5	Charter retained
New York	6	1777
New Jersey	7	1776
Pennsylvania	8	1776 / 1790
FEDERAL	9	1787
Delaware	10	1776
Maryland	11	1776
Virginia	12	1776
North Carolina	13	1776
South Carolina	14	1777
Georgia	15	1776 / 1789

and documents and lent a mobbish atmosphere to their opening deliberations.

Since their independence could only be achieved through armed rebellion the American revolutionaries had no opportunity to put their ideology into practice in normal conditions. In France, on the contrary, the National (or 'Constituent') Assembly had three years to reconstruct every aspect of French life until, exploited by revolutionary exiles from England, Holland and Belgium, enthusiasm for attacking the *ancien régime* in all its manifestations caused France to declare war on Austria in 1792. The principles of this reconstruction were legal equality, representative government (with wide, but not universal, suffrage), the complete sovereignty of the state and a centralized administration. They were expressed by the reorganization of local government into eighty-three departments established on rational lines; a national system of weights and measures (in metric units) and a national system of education. Torture was abolished; privileged guilds were dismantled; the Jews were emancipated; customs dues abandoned; seigneurial obligations suppressed. The property of the French Church was nationalized and assigned to repay government debts. In a proposed constitution for the clergy, all clerics were to be chosen on democratic principles, the religious orders dissolved and the papacy excluded from influence in the French national Church. By the outbreak of war, old France had been destroyed and the most lasting institutional achievements of the age of revolutions established.

Changes on this scale bred reaction, and this changed the nature of the revolution. Louis XVI, encouraged by *emigré* royalists and the indignation of crowned heads across Europe, took flight to the frontier, only to be stopped at La Varenne. His trial and execution excited republican fervour in the National Assembly, Paris and elsewhere, and confirmed counter-revolutionary fears. Clerical opposition to the civil constitution of the clergy also divided France bitterly. Militant revolutionaries in the cities (which were already anti-clerical) became open enemies of the Church and religion, and made the priests the scapegoats for the revolution's own shortcomings. Rural France remained stubbornly Catholic and rural insurrection after 1790 in the Vende and the south of France was uniformly against the revolution. The old army and navy did not remain loyal to the new regime; its senior officers provided the bulk of the *emigrés*. From the barracks in the cities, the new National Guard, with its distinctive *sans-culottes* trousers spread the openly democratic force of Jacobinism throughout France.

Republicanism, atheism and Jacobinism inspired the language and euphoria of the revolution after 1792. They also excited streetfighters, spies, police and the dictatorial zealots of the committees of Public Safety. At the heart of 'the Terror' (as contemporaries referred to it) lay Paris itself. The way to securing the loyalty of Paris lay in the provision of its food supplies and in winning the confidence of the street-revolutionaries. The Directory (the effective successor of the National Assembly) which ruled France after 1795, failed in both tasks. Food supplies were consistently scarce and the Paris revolutionaries (like the Jacobins in the

army) were bitterly divided between factions supporting various politicians of the Terror – Robespierristes, Dantonistes, etc. Nationally, the Directory became increasingly troubled both by those who feared reaction and by those who feared fresh popular violence. It depended increasingly upon force. Generals began to loom larger in its affairs and one of them, Napoleon Bonaparte, accepted the role offered him by some of the disenchanted. A *coup d'état* in November 1799 (Brumaire, year VIII, in the new calendar) made him First Consul of the Republic. Five years later, he inaugurated a hereditary empire, completing the transformation from revolution to dictatorship.

Napoleon was, in many ways, the incarnation of an eighteenth-century enlightened despot (*see Map 55*). Like his hero, Frederick the Great, he codified, rationalized, centralized, and militarized, without an *ancien regime* to cramp his style either at home or abroad. Napoleon's achievement was to define how much of the revolution should survive. In France, his *Code Napoléon* distilled the decisions of the Constituent Assembly into a readily understood and easily imposed constitutional settlement administered through departmental prefects. But he anaesthetized France against the republicanism, atheism and democratic Jacobinism of the Terror. His police harried one-time liberals and Jacobins in cities and in the army. The empire proclaimed the death of republicanism. His concordat with the Papacy in 1801 added to the widespread reaction against the excesses of the previous decade. Napoleon was so successful in reconciling the former nobles and oligarchs to his empire that there was little obstacle to the revival of traditional titles and the reintegration of the old French ruling-class and its monarchy in 1815. If the French Revolution had been a 'democratic' revolution, then Napoleon ensured its failure .

Napoleon's greatest achievement was outside France in the wider empire (*Map 55*). Here, too, he built upon revolutionary antecedents. The ideology of the French Revolution had crossed national frontiers in the 1790s, particularly affecting the areas where revolts had previously failed. Groups of social and political dissenters – 'Jacobins' – appeared in clubs and taverns in every city in Europe. They prepared the way for the French revolutionary armies which established themselves in the 1790s in Holland, Belgium, Switzerland and most of Italy.

Initially, France respected the self-determination of these 'allies' in revolution. Subsequently the Directory was less tolerant. In Belgium (which, as the Republic of the United Belgian Provinces, had seceded from the Hapsburg empire in 1790) a rigged plebiscite was held; property belonging to the 'accomplices' of tyranny was confiscated and an enfeebled French currency introduced. By 1795 Belgium had become once more a mere geographical expression, having been divided into nine French departments ruled from Paris. The Rhineland and north-western Italy were similarly treated, without the tiresome pretence of a plebiscite. The Dutch Provinces, Switzerland, Lombardy and Dalmatia were permitted the semblance of separate identity as the Batavian, Helvetian, Cisalpine and Illyrian republics. The inner collapse of the Directory and the European reaction against

domination dressed as liberation left only Belgium secure in French hands by 1799.

Napoleon could rebuild the French continental empire because the memory of the revolutionary wars was still green in Europe. This time, the armies exported the code, the prefects, police, and conscription (over half the army at Moscow in 1812 was non-French) and imported the treasures of Florence, Venice and the Near East. Even countries like Prussia, which remained independent, could not avoid the influence of Bonapartism. Prussian reformers began to look to the destruction of serfdom, to open the army (cautiously) to non-nobles, and to preach a distinctive nationalism.

There was remarkably little popular resistance within the Napoleonic empire to this extension of French power. Where popular risings did occur, they were the product of traditional rivalries (the Tyrolese in 1808 against the Bavarians) or religious affiliations (in Spain in 1808 and Russia in 1812). In Italy, apart from the extreme Francophobe *Carbonari*, who pledged themselves to counter-revolution after 1809 (*see Map 60*), the French constructed national institutions which would form the basis of Italian movements for unification in the nineteenth century. In Germany too, Napoleon's rationalization of frontiers, emancipation of serfs and Jews, and abolition of restrictions on commerce, earned him support from men including Metternich, Hegel, Goethe and Beethoven.

Only in the great land empires of Ottoman Turkey and tsarist Russia, and the maritime empire of England, did Napoleon fail to leave any lasting monument. When these powers were finally victorious after the battle of Waterloo (1815) against Bonaparte, it was believed that the subsequent Congress of Vienna would recreate the *ancien regime*. In fact in France as throughout most of continental Europe this proved impossible. Boundaries, administrations, armies, laws and patterns of thought had all been irreversibly changed by the revolutionary experience. And one of the guarantors of the Congress of Vienna was England which, following its own distinctive path, undertook by peaceful means the changes that the men of 1789 had accomplished by force and emerged as the champion in nineteenth-century Europe of their liberal and nationalist principles.

54 The French Revolution
Under the pressure of internal opposition and external attack (which by autumn 1793 threatened to extinguish the revolution) the National Assembly, which had dismantled the *ancien regime* in France, gave way to the growing chaos of the Terror and the Directorate. But its main achievement was permanent. As Goethe said, 'Here begins a new age in the history of the world.'

Further reading: Alexis de Tocqueville, *The Old Regime and the French Revolution* tr. S. Gilbert (Anchor 1955); Edward Countryman, *The American Revolution* (I. B. Tauris 1986; Hill & Wang); T. C. Blanning, *The Origins of the French Revolutionary Wars* (Longman 1986); D. M. G. Sutherland, *France 1789-1815: Revolution and Counterrevolution* (Collins 1985; OUP. New York); C. A. Bayly, *Imperial Meridian: The British Empire and the World, 1780-1830* (Longman 1989).

MAP 54 THE FRENCH REVOLUTION

Regions with agrarian revolts before the Great Fear

Regions affected by the Great Fear, July/August 1789

Major towns in which revolutionary committees shared power with town councils in 1789

Major towns in which revolutionary committees replaced the town councils in 1789

Major towns largely unaffected by revolutionary committees

Channel Is.

Dunkirk

Hondeschoote
Sept. 1793
Sept. 1793
July 1793
Brussels
Neerwinden
March 1793
Lille
Condé
Sept.
1793
Jemappes
Nov.
1793
Mons
Fleurus
June 1794
AUSTRIAN
NETHERLANDS
Cologne
Valenciennes
Maubeuge
Arras
le Quesnoy
Wattignies
Oct. 1793
Coblenz
Amiens

Mainz
Worms
Mannheim
Rouen
Caen
NORMANDY
Seine
Evreux
Reims
Marne
Valmy
Sept. 1792
Varennes
Meuse
Metz
Moselle
Landau
Sept.
1793
Wissembourg
Dec. 1793
Granville
BRITTANY
Brest
Paris
Nancy
Strasbourg

Rennes
Le Mans

Savenay
Dec. 1793
Angers
Nantes
Loire
Tours
Cher
VENDÉE
(Royalist resistance from 1793)
Cholet
Oct. 1793
Poitiers
Bourges
Dijon
Besançon
Saône
Rhine

St. Domingo and other West Indian colonies lost from 1793

Limoges
Clermont-Ferrand
SAVOY
Lyon
Rhône
Chambéry
Aug.
1793
Grenoble
Turin
Bordeaux
GIRONDE
Dordogne
Garonne
Massif
Central
Mende
Durance
Sept. 1793
Bayonne
Montauban
Avignon
Nîmes
St. Jean de Luz
April 1793
Toulouse
Montpellier
Marseille
Toulon
Royalist
1793
Corsica
lost 1793
Pyrenees
Vernet X Sept. 1793
Trouilles
Sept. 1793
Perpignan
April 1793
Mediterranean Sea

Occupied by France 1792-3

Sustained Federalist resistance in 1793

Federalist and other civil unrest in 1793

Major Federalist strongholds

Major émigré centres

Advance of European powers

Naval blockade and harassment, 1793

Loss of overseas possessions

0   200 km
0   100 miles

The age of European supremacy 7

THE INDUSTRIAL REVOLUTION

55 The Europe of Napoleon
The conquests of the French revolutionary armies were accompanied everywhere by the collapse of the *ancien régime*, to be replaced by the prefectoral system of government and the legal code which Napoleon had devised for France; despite the victory of 'legitimacy' in 1815 the *Code civil* continued to provide a basis for liberal regimes in Europe throughout the nineteenth century.

As France was the progenitor of political revolution in the nineteenth century, England was the home of the industrial revolution. Industrial innovation was not new in itself, but the series of self-perpetuating and apparently unstoppable developments which were set in motion by the advances made in eighteenth-century Britain transformed the life of man and the nature of human society more profoundly and more rapidly than anything that had happened since the appearance of agriculture (see Map 2).

The industrial revolution originated in new methods for the exploitation of coal, iron and steam-power, which complemented and stimulated one another to create a massive increase in production, wealth and population. 'Carboniferous capitalism' (as it has been christened) had advanced far enough in Britain by 1815 to enable her to take a decisive lead in post-Napoleonic Europe (*Map 56*). Belgium followed the same course (under British influence) after its independence in 1830, and parts of Germany and France had experienced the same changes by 1870 (*see Map 57*).

Coal, already mined on an unprecedented scale in England in the seventeenth century, was transported from the coalfields of Northumberland and Durham by sea to provide the capital with domestic fuel. In the eighteenth century, it provided a source of energy which ended the domination of wind and water. By 1800, Britain was using 11 million tons of coal a year; by 1870, 100 million tons. The mines of the Newcastle area attracted civil and mechanical engineers as well as surveyors and managers of a higher calibre than anywhere else in Europe.

By the end of the seventeenth century iron too was worked on a large scale in England. But the vital process of producing pig iron by using coal (reduced to the form of smelting coke) established by Abraham Darby at Coalbrookdale in 1709

MAP 55 THE EUROPE OF NAPOLEON

Main campaigns of revolutionary and Napoleonic armies

Frontiers after 1815

German Confederation, 1815

Areas under direct French rule during revolutionary and Napoleonic periods:

for more than 10 years

5-10 years

less than 5 years

Main satellite regimes with date of establishment

Departmental administration introduced

Code civil remained in force after 1815

Later adoption of a legal code based on *Code civil*

(1873) Date of adoption of code

Departmental boundaries

0   300 km
0   200 miles

increased the supply and reduced the cost. Iron freed the engineer from dependence upon wood and expensive soft metals. Its uses seemed endless. Pig iron output in Britain rose from about 20,000 tons in 1720 to 250,000 tons in 1806. By 1830 Britain produced more iron than continental Europe and America combined.

The steam engine used the new source of energy and the new material. Atmospheric engines were already used in England in the early eighteenth century to drain water from mines. In the 1760s, James Watt (1736-1819) produced a genuine steam engine. In the 1770s, he went into partner-ship with a metal manufacturer from Birmingham, Matthew Boulton, and their manufactory mar-keted a stationary steam engine which could force draught to blast furnaces, drain mines and power factories. As Boulton wrote in 1781, 'The people in London, Manchester and Birmingham are steam-mill mad'.

The application of steam-power to transport followed. Eighteenth-century turnpike trusts had improved English roads but the canal boom of the 1780s, which completed the improvement of river navigation undertaken since the seventeenth cen-tury, was vital for the transporting of bulk cargo such as iron ore and coal in the early industrial revolution (*Map 56*). While there were some steam-powered barges in the early nineteenth cen-tury, railways united the forces of iron, coal and steam-power. The first regular working railway – from Stockton to Darlington – was completed in 1825. By 1840, there were 1500 miles of trunk route in operation and many more under construc-tion. By 1870 the English network was complete with over 15,000 miles of 'iron road'.

Britain also developed the first sizeable factory industry in cotton products, which were soon being exported throughout the world. The cloth industry in England flourished in the eighteenth century, producing woollens and worsteds, linens and, on a smaller scale, cottons. Everywhere in Europe the fabrication of these cloths was farmed out to rural spinners and weavers and finishing undertaken in the towns by the merchant entrepreneurs. Capacity was low and price was high because up to eight spinners were required to keep one weaver at work. The famous spinning jenny which was invented in 1770 by James Hargreaves replaced the old spin-ning wheel in the hands of rural workers. Cheaper cloth and the delays and expense of transport made industrial concentration an attractive prospect. Samuel Crompton (1753-1817) produced a hybrid jenny which could easily be steampowered and arranged in factories. Cartwright's powered loom, introduced after 1800, offered the same advan-tages. By the turn of the century, there were cotton mills on the Lancashire Plain. Less than two million pounds weight was imported through Liverpool in 1700; over fifty million pounds by 1800.

The industrial revolution wrought enormous changes. The construction of the railways, for instance, brought work to armies of navvies, trans-formed the value of land and stimulated unpre-cedented financial speculation. Their operation changed the meaning of time and distance. Lon-don, a capital city which (like every capital in Europe) had grown prodigiously in the eighteenth century, was the focus for many of these changes. But it was the new industrial towns of the Black Country and Lancashire Plain, mushrooming out to meet each other in conurbations, which experi-enced most keenly the first industrial revolution. Manchester, its population rising from 75,000 in 1800 to 400,000 in 1850, was surrounded by industrial towns expanding around their factories, workshops, blast furnaces and coke ovens. In them, change was untrammeled by institutions. Plans and regulations came too late. Streets of terraced houses were thrown up cheaply, often without sewerage and water. Poverty and insani-tary conditions had been dispersed in the country-side, but concentrated in towns they reached horrifying proportions. Typhoid and cholera epidemics broke out throughout Europe in 1832 and again in 1848 and 1849 (*Map 58*). Because of the inadequate sewers, the water-borne germ was spread by polluted rivers. Many other diseases – notably scarlet fever and small-pox – were endemic and dangerous killers. The problem was an intense-ly serious one in England because by 1851 more than half the population was living in cities.

Migration to, and mobility within, these new industrial cities emphasized the chasm between rich and poor. Housing, income, living standards, life-expectancy, education, geography, all reinforced the distinction. Every nineteenth-century industrial city had its West End and its East End, later its inner-city slum and its outer-city suburb. Amongst some contemporaries, it aroused guilty feelings which spilled over into early socialism. Others turned sour and escapist, reacting (like Wordsworth) to 'Industry's command' by retreating to a romantic nature and idealized past. Friedrich Engels was inspired to radical politics after seeing the industrial unrest around Manchester; his friend, Karl Marx, an exile from the European Revolutions of 1848, used the industrial cities of England as his model for a class struggle in which the industrial proletariat would shortly triumph.

Marx was proved wrong in Europe in the generation after 1848, partly because prosperity increased and was not confined to a narrow oligarchy. Real income per head rose substantially in Britain after 1850, for this was a century of falling prices in food as well as clothing and housing. Agricultural changes enabled England to meet the increased demand for food for its rapidly expanding population until the 1870s. These changes had already made the English countryside physically, economically and socially different from the rest of Europe by 1800. Open fields, where the absence of hedges between neighbouring plots preserved customary agricultural techniques, stretched across all the plains of Europe with the exception of the Po Valley, Flanders and England. There in the course of the seventeenth and eighteenth centuries, enclosed fields, farmed with all the intensity of a cottage garden, dramatically broke with traditional communal practices and made innovation possible in crops and methods. Economically, the English countryside was less isolated from its markets than that of the rest of Europe. Socially, no other country had such a large class of tenant farmers, capable of investing so much in agricultural expansion, new machinery, stock and seed. As a result, Britain avoided T. R. Malthus' law of population, that in history population always expanded beyond the means to sustain it.

Marx was also proved wrong because state legislation and new technology alleviated the problems of the industrial city. The state intervened in factory safety, public health and education in Bri-

tain in the later nineteenth century. The technology of conveying fresh water in iron pipes and sewerage in glazed pottery pipes reduced the dangers of water-borne infection; western Europe was clear of cholera by 1911. Cleaner gas heating, electric lighting, electric trams and underground railways all improved urban life dramatically by 1900. Co-operative shops and chain stores improved marketing and distribution in towns. As a result, it was the philosophy of infinite material progress rather than Marxism which appeared to be confirmed at every turn to urban man in the late nineteenth century.

The benefits and wealth generated by the industrial revolution were not confined to Britain. In 1850, Britain was the manufacturer, clothier, banker, shipper, insurer and transporter to the world, a pre-eminence demonstrated at the Great Exhibition of 1851. London invited the whole world to its shop-window, confident that its wares would outstrip all comers. But the pre-eminence did not last for long. Flanders began its industrial revolution in the 1830s; the Rhur in the 1850s and 1860s imitated British technology, frequently used British capital and engineers and sometimes avoided British mistakes. By the 1870s, the second phase of the industrial revolution (as it is now commonly called) had begun in Germany and the United States (see Maps 57 and 69). In this second phase, a new trinity of steel, electricity and petro-chemicals dominated the industrial world. By 1900, Germany and the United States produced more steel than Britain. The United States developed – with its natural resources and tycoons – the technology of the internal combustion engine. Germany, with the help of state intervention and adventurous bankers, exploited electrical technology for power, transport and communications. After the turn of the century, the exploitation of hydro-electric power in the Alps helped France and Italy at last to increase the pace of their progress towards industrialization. English manufacturers, secure in their belief in progress, the continued primacy of coal and their imperial self-sufficiency, fitted snugly into a liberal society where tradition and innovation had been reconciled, and met competition with complacency. They were inevitably less conspicuous in the Great Exhibitions in Paris in 1867, Chicago in 1880 and Melbourne in 1891

than they had been in 1851. In Europe, as in Britain, food prices fell, spreading the benefits of industrial change amongst the citizens of the new industrial towns and compelling change amongst the peasantry of Europe which felt the demands from the new markets.

In another important respect, the industrial revolution was a 'Prometheus Unbound'. In 1846 the abolition of tariffs on corn imported into England was, in retrospect, a sign that the days of British self-sufficiency were numbered. The opening-up of the prairies in the 1870s and 1880s in America (Map 68), the application of mechanized farming methods there, and the impact of railways and steamships on transport, resulted in the large-scale importation of American wheat to Europe. A similar pattern was established with the imports of butter, cheese and Canterbury lamb from New Zealand (using refrigerated shipping) in the 1880s. The canned meat trade also developed from South America to Europe. The export of European capital across the world and the migration of Europeans which followed it, emphasized European predominance in the nineteenth century (see Map 67). But it also, with the development of world communications by telegraph and telephone, and the new patterns of trade established in the wake of the industrial revolutions, created the basis for a world community in the twentieth century.

Above left: The first large Iron Bridge, built across the River Severn at Colebrookdale, England, in 1777.

56 The Industrial Revolution in Great Britain
The complementary exploitation of coal, iron and steam power produced the rapid diversification of economic activity and huge increases in production which made Britain the first industrial society, rapidly becoming wealthier, more populous and more urban, in the first half of the nineteenth century.

---

57 The Industrial Revolution in Europe
Except in Belgium, industrialization did not gather pace in continental Europe until the second half of the nineteenth century. Its 'second phase', dominated by steel, chemicals and electricity, was led by Germany. In the most backward regions industrialization was far too late to absorb an explosion of rural population which created acute social tensions and rising emigration.

58 Cholera 1817-1952
The growth of world-wide communications with colonialism and of concentrated urban populations with industrialization made western man terrifyingly vulnerable to infectious diseases until they could be checked by the advances in medical knowledge, sanitation and public health.

Further reading: E. A. Wrigley, *Continuity, Chance and Change* (Cambridge U.P. 1988); David S. Landes, *The Unbound Prometheus* (Cambridge U.P. 1969); E. L. Jones, *Growth Recurring* (Oxford U.P. 1989); Eric Hobsbawm, *The Age of Capital* (Weidenfeld & Nicolson 1975; Scribner); Richard J. Evans, *Death in Hamburg: Society and Politics in the Cholera Years, 1830-1910* (Oxford U.P. 1987).

MAP 56 THE INDUSTRIAL REVOLUTION IN GREAT BRITAIN

Percentage area of each county enclosed
by Act of Parliament, 1700-1845

over 30% enclosed

10% – 30% enclosed

under 10% enclosed

Major trunk canals

Navigable rivers, 1850

Principal railways completed by 1850

● Main railway junctions and depots

Shire boundaries

Major economic activities by 1870

W   Woollen manufacturing

C   Cotton textile manufacturing

H   Hosiery manufacturing

S   Silkworking

J   Jute manufacturing

Cu   Copper mining and smelting

T   Tin mining and smelting

L   Lead mining and smelting

I   Iron mining and smelting

M   Metalware and cutlery

SB   Shipbuilding

B   Brewing

FP   Food processing and refining

CG   Salt, soap, chemicals and glass

Sh   Shoes and leather

P   Pottery

SL   Slate quarrying

Coalfields known in 1881

Selected urban populations in 1801 and 1851
vertical scale : 2mm=15,000 persons

0   150 km

0   100 miles

Outer
Hebrides

Inner
Hebrides

North West Highlands

Grampian Mts.

Southern Uplands

Pennines

Cambrian Mts.

Irish Sea

North
Sea

English Channel

Inverness

Aberdeen

Fort William

Dundee

Perth

Stirling

Dunfermline

Greenock

Glasgow

Paisley

Edinburgh

Newcastle-on-Tyne

Sunderland

Durham

Carlisle

Workington

Middlesbrough

Darlington

Barrow in Furness

Lancaster

York

Blackpool

Preston

Bradford

Leeds

Hull

Blackburn

Halifax

Wakefield

Barnsley

Huddersfield

Bolton

Oldham

Wigan

Grimsby

Liverpool

Salford

Manchester

Sheffield

Doncaster

Holyhead

Birkenhead

Warrington

Lincoln

Bangor

Chester

Crewe

Stoke-on-Trent

Nottingham

Derby

Burton on Trent

Leicester

Wolverhampton

Ironbridge

Newtown

Birmingham

Coventry

Rugby

Northampton

Peterborough

Norwich

Worcester

Bedford

Cambridge

Ipswich

Hereford

Brecon

Colchester

Merthyr

Swansea

Newport

Gloucester

Oxford

Didcot

Cardiff

Bristol

Swindon

Reading

London

Chatham

Bath

Salisbury

Dover

Folkestone

Southampton

Portsmouth

Brighton

Dorchester

Bournemouth

Exeter

Plymouth

Torbay

Redruth

Camborne

Penzance

Caledonian Canal

Forth-Clyde Canal

Leeds and Liverpool Canal

Aire-Calder Nav.

Derwent

Trent Nav.

Chesterfield Canal

Trent and Mersey Canal

Nene Nav.

Great Ouse

Grand Junc. Canal

Oxford Canal

Severn

Wye

Thames and Severn Canal

Thames

Kennet and Avon Canal

Royal Military Canal

1801

1851

MAP 57 THE INDUSTRIAL REVOLUTION IN EUROPE

Population, 1850-1910:

Declining

Stable

Increase up to 50%

Increase 50% - 100%

Increase more than 100%

Selected urban populations
in 1850 and 1910:

under 100,000

100,000 - 500,000

500,000 - 1,000,000

over 1,000,000

Emigrants from Europe, 1881-1910,
with principal destinations

Alsace-Lorraine, ceded to Germany, 1870

Area within which the main rail network
was complete by 1870

Lines constructed by 1848

Other major lines constructed, 1848-1870

Other major lines constructed, 1870-1914

Industry, c.1870:

Areas of coal mining, c.1870

Areas of iron working, c.1870

Areas of textile production, c.1870

Industry, c.1914:

S Steel

E Engineering

Sb Shipbuilding

C Chemicals

El Electrical industry

O Oil production

0   500 kms
0   300 miles

North Sea

Mediterranean Sea

to N. America
from Scandinavia
1,535,000

to N. and S. America
from Germany
2,143,000

to N. America
from Germany
2,143,000

to U.S.A. from Ireland
1,414,000

to N. America, S. Africa and
Australasia from Great Britain
7,144,000

to U.S.A. from Low Countries
171,000

to Central and S. America
from France 223,000

to S. America
from Portugal 775,000

to Central and S. America
and N. Africa from Spain
1,472,000

to N. and S. America from Austria-Hungary 1,799,000

to U.S.A. and N. Africa
from Italy 6,187,000

Helsinki E

Gulf of Finland

St Petersburg □ S

Sb E □ S

to U.S.A. from Russia 1,680,000

Stockholm
E S Sb

Baltic Sea

Riga

Dvina

Königsberg
Danzig Sb
Sb

Vilna E

Minsk

Dnieper

C

Posen

Vistula

Warsaw E S C
Łódz
E

E

Breslau E

C Cracow

E Kladno

E

enna

E I S
C Budapest
C E

Diosgyor

Szeged

Belgrade

Lemberg

O O
O

O

Czernowitz

Kiev

Krivoy Rog
S E
E

Dnieper

Dniester
E C Odessa

Kharkov

Donets

S E
E

Yuzovka
Rostov
O

Don

E O

Black Sea

O

O Ploesti
O Bucharest
Danube

Sofia

to U.S.A. and S. America from Turkey in Europe c.160,000

S Constantinople

to U.S.A. from Rumania c.75,000

O Ankara

40°

50°

Bari
Brindisi O

to U.S.A. from Bulgaria, Serbia and Montenegro c.40,000

Salonica

essina

c.190,000

to U.S.A. from Greece

Athens

Smyrna O S

O Adana

S Aleppo

Beirut O
S Damascus

20°

40°

MAP 58 CHOLERA, 1817-1952

Historical and present day base of Indian cholera

Areas affected 1879-1911

1830 Date of first occurrence

1923 Date of last outbreak

1850

Clear to west of this line after 1923

Clear to west of this line after 1911

1831 1946 1822
1946
1948
1821
1948
1817
1817

1850

1833

1831 1829
1830

1952
1948 1952
1941

1837

1831
1848
1831
1833

1833

1837

1820

1820

1820

1857

1867
1866
1867

1862

111

The age of European supremacy 8

LIBERALISM AND NATIONALISM

Although reaction appeared triumphant in the aftermath of 1815, as conservative rule was restored to most of Europe (Map 60), the twin forces of liberalism and nationalism which had been unleashed by the French revolution continued their volcanic rumblings beneath the surface of international politics.

Liberalism stressed freedom of internal and international trade, the removal of traditional constraints on the free operation of the market (including the abolition of institutions such as slavery and serfdom, the stripping of monopolistic corporate privileges and the emancipation of religious minorities), minimal governmental interference in the economy or society, liberty of the individual, and responsible representative government through parliaments as against arbitrary, hereditary rule. Drawing on the thought of the Scottish economist Adam Smith, the English political theorists Locke, Jeremy Bentham and James Mill and the French *philosophes*, liberalism was the ideological expression of the interests of the rising middle classes in industrial societies. It was natural, therefore, that it should find its political home in this period in the world's foremost industrial society, Britain. Measures such as the emancipation of Catholics (1828), the first parliamentary reform act (1832), and the abolition of slavery in the British empire (1833) were typical liberal achievements. With the abolition of the Corn Laws (the tariff on imported corn) in 1846, Britain moved into the era of free trade from which, because of her industrial and commercial dominance in the world's markets, she continued to prosper for several decades. Although it was not until about 1858 that a Liberal Party coalesced in Parliament, liberal principles dominated English politics at home and abroad for much of the earlier period, and it was to England that liberals elsewhere tended to look for inspiration and support.

A striking example was the liberation of Latin America from Spanish and Portuguese colonial rule (*Map 59*). The leaders of the liberation movement, Francisco de Miranda, Simón Bolívar, and José de San Martín, were much influenced by the ideas of English liberalism, and by the American and French revolutions. After the collapse of the short-lived first Venezuelan republic, proclaimed in 1811, Miranda was imprisoned in Spain (dying in gaol in 1816), while Bolívar fled to neighbouring

New Granada, and thence after 1814 to Jamaica and Haiti. During the next three years he organized his army anew, and in 1817 he returned to Venezuela, landing at Angostura. From there he led his troops (among whom were several thousand European, particularly British, volunteers) in a series of epic campaigns through difficult country, capturing Bogotá in 1819, and Quito in 1822. Meanwhile in the south of the continent San Martín had formed his 'Army of the Andes' in Argentina. In one of the most remarkable campaigns in military history, San Martín led his forces across the Andes and into Chile, fewer than half surviving the journey. After inflicting defeat on the Spaniards at the battle of Chacabuco, he was able to proclaim the independence of Chile in 1818. By 1821 he had made a triumphal entry into Lima after a thousand-mile sea voyage with his men in a fleet commanded by the British admiral, Lord Cochrane. The two liberators met at Guayaquil in 1822, but they fell out, and Bolívar wrested leadership of the movement from his rival. After 1825, with the liberation of the sub-continent virtually complete, Bolívar devoted his energies to preserving the unity of 'Gran Colombia' – but in vain. By the time of his death in 1830 the former Spanish empire had fragmented into small units. By contrast the former Portuguese territory of Brazil remained united after its bloodless separation from Portugal in 1822 under the Emperor Pedro I. The liberation process had received strong support from the USA, whose President, James Monroe, in 1823 enunciated his celebrated 'doctrine' prohibiting European intervention against the nascent republics, and from Britain, whose Foreign Secretary, Canning, in 1826 declared that he had 'called the New World into being to redress the balance of the Old'.

In the Old World, however, liberals faced more formidable opposition as conservative governments concerted their defensive measures in the 'congress system'. This was the term applied to the four-power alliance of Britain, Russia, Prussia, and Austria, in November 1815, whereby the signatories agreed to meet periodically in congress to discuss common measures to preserve the *status quo* as enshrined in the Treaty of Vienna (*Map 60*). However, as the system, masterminded by the Austrian statesman Metternich, was rapidly revealed to be a 'Holy Alliance' of conservative forces determined to crush liberal tendencies throughout Europe, Britain gradually dissociated herself from the arrangement. Britain objected to the French military intervention in Spain in 1822, conducted with the blessing of the Holy Alliance, which repressed a liberal revolt there. Austrian intervention in Italy to crush liberal rebellions, particularly those of the secret nationalist society, the *Carbonari*, further aroused British indignation. The marriage of liberalism and nationalism found its ultimate consummation in the Greek War of Liberation between 1821 and 1829 (*Map 63*). Romantic revolutionaries from all over Europe, among them Lord Byron, flocked to the Greek cause and sang its praises. Russia, stealing a further march on the Turks, supported the Greeks. In the naval battle of Navarino (1827) British, French, and Russian forces defeated the Turks. With conservatism now in some disarray, the liberals took an important stride forward in 1830, when the last

Above: Simon Bolívar (1783-1830).

59 Independent Latin America
Protected from hostile European intervention by Britain and America (the Monroe doctrine was proclaimed in 1823), the liberation movements ended the Spanish American empire, but failed to create a united republic – Bolívar's Gran Colombia – in its place. Disputes over land, minerals and access to the coast continued to weaken and divide the new states.

60 Reaction and revolution in Europe
The revolutions of 1848, though directly responsible for a change of regime only in France, marked a decisive stage in the progress of liberal ideas and the aspirations of national minorities. These had presented a growing and increasingly successful challenge to the *status quo* imposed by the Congress of Vienna of 1815.

MAP 59 INDEPENDENT LATIN AMERICA

Atlantic
Ocean

Pacific
Ocean

To Brazil: 3m. 1835-1913 from Portugal, Spain, Italy

To Uruguay from Italy, Spain

To Argentine: 4.5m. 1857-1913 from Italy, Spain

Canal Zone
(U.S. occ. 1903)

Curaçao

Cartagena
Maracaibo
Margarita
Caracas
Trinidad
Panama
PANAMA
1903
Coffee
× Carabobo 1821
San Carlos
Mompós
COLOMBIA
1819
VENEZUELA
1830
Georgetown
Paramaribo
Cattle
Cattle
Orinoco
DUTCH
GUIANA
Cayenne
Bogotá
× Boyacá
1819
Coffee
Angostura
BRITISH
GUIANA
FRENCH
GUIANA
Sheep
Sugar
7
8
9

GREATER COLOMBIA
1819-30

× Bombóná
1822
1
Negro
TIMBER
Gurupá
Belém

Equator
× Pichincha
1822
Bananas
Quito
3
2
Manaus
Amazon
PARÁ
Equator

ECUADOR
1830
Cattle
5
4
RUBBER
RUBBER
Maranhão
Cotton
Coffee
Ceará
Guayaquil
6
RUBBER
RUBBER
MARANHÃO
CEARÁ
RIO GRANDE
DO NORTE

Sugar
TIMBER
RIO NEGRO
RUBBER
RUBBER
Cocoa
Sugar
PARAIBA
Pernambuco

FEDERATION
COPPER
PERU
1821
RUBBER
ACRE
RUBBER
BRAZIL
1822
PERNAMBUCO
Coffee
ALAGÔAS
Tobacco

Trujillo
10
S. Francisco
BAHIA
Bahia
SILVER
× Junín
1824
11
13
12
OF PERU AND BOLIVIA
1836-39
GOIÁS

Callao
× Ayacucho
1824
14
RUBBER
MATO GROSSO
Lima
Cuzco
15
Pisco

La Paz
BOLIVIA
1825
SILVER
TIN
COPPER
Minas Novas
Coffee

NITRATES
Tacna
Chuquisaca
Corumbá
MINAS
GERAIS
Diamantina

Arica
18
GUANO
Potosí
CHACO
16
17
19
SÃO PAULO
ESPIRITO
SANTO

Iquique
PARAGUAY
1811
20
Coffee
Sao Paulo
Rio de Janeiro

Antofagasta
23
Jujuy
24
TIMBER
Asunción
21
22
SANTA
CATARINA
Cattle
Santos

Copiapó
× 1812
Salta
Cattle

COPPER
MANGANESE
TIN
SILVER
× 1812
Tucumán
ARGENTINA
1810
RIO GRANDE
DO SUL
Cattle
Porto Alegre

La Serena
Santa Fé
URUGUAY
1828

Valparaíso
× Chacabuco
1817
Córdoba
Rosario
Cattle
Montevideo

Santiago
× Maipú
1818
Mendoza
San Luis
Cattle

CHILE
1818
San Luis
Cereals

Concepción
Cattle
River Plate
Buenos
Aires
Sheep

Valdivia
Cattle

Patagonia
Sheep

25

26

Falkland Islands
(Br. 1833)

27
Tierra del
Fuego

1	to Brazil 1905
2	to Brazil 1904
3	to Ecuador 1880-1922
4	to Ecuador 1880-1942
5	
6	to Peru 1942
7	to Brazil 1904-5
8	to Brit. Guiana 1899
9	to Brazil 1900
10	
11	to Bolivia 1867-1903
12	to Bolivia 1867
13	to Bolivia 1867-1909
14	to Bolivia 1867-1902
15	to Brazil 1927
16	to Paraguay 1935
17	to Bolivia 1880-1935
18	to Chile 1883
19	to Brazil 1870
20	
21	to Argentina 1874
22	to Brazil 1895
23	to Chile 1884
24	to Argentina 1874
25	to Argentina 1881
26	to Chile 1902
27	to Argentina 1881

Mountain
Desert and semi-desert
Temperate forest and scrub
Tropical forest and scrub
Grasslands

Population:
c.1880 c.1910
● ○ 100,000 and over
● ○ 200,000 and over
□ 1,000,000 and over
○ Other towns under 100,000
— Main railways c.1910
--- Bolívar's route 1817-24
--- San Martín's route 1817-22
— Borders c.1830
--- Subsequent border changes
Border of Greater Colombia,1819-30 and
border of Federation of Bolivia and Peru,1835-39
→ European immigration (showing country of origin)

0   1000 km
0   600 miles

113

MAP 60 REACTION AND REVOLUTION IN EUROPE

Atlantic Ocean

Key

	State borders after 1815
G	Predominant linguistic groups (see key opposite)
g	Linguistic minorities (see key opposite)
	Boundary of Jewish 'Pale of Settlement' in 1835
	Border of German Confederation 1815
	Belgian frontier after 1830
→	Route of Russian forces in Poland, 1831
■	Quadrilateral fortresses in northern Italy
⚑	Congresses
✳	Centres of popular unrest in Britain, 1815-48
✳	1820 centres of revolt in Spain
✳	Centres of Carbonarist activity in Italy, 1815-30
	Areas of Carlist strength in first Carlist War. (1833-40)
⇢	Route of main column on Garibaldi's retreat from Rome (July 1849)
✳	1830 revolutions
✳	Centres of revolutionary activity 1848

Population of major cities:
c.1800   c.1850
○ ●   under 100,000
○ ●   100,000 – 200,000
◇ ◆   200,000 – 500,000
□ ■   over 500,000

500 km
300 miles

United Kingdom — Glasgow, Edinburgh, Belfast, Dublin, Huddersfield, Manchester, Liverpool, Stockport, Bradford, Wakefield, Barnsley, Sheffield, Nottingham, Birmingham, Leicester, Norwich, Isle of Ely, Newport, Bristol, London, Calais

SGe, IGe, ig, IG, e, We, E

France — Le Havre, Rouen, Paris, Reims, Metz, Nancy, Orleans, Nantes, Limoges, Lyons, Geneva, Grenoble, Bordeaux, Toulouse, Marseilles, Brest, Rennes, Channel Is., Le Mans

Fe, BR, BRf, br, Gf, PRf

Portugal — Lisbon, Oporto(?), Madrid

PO, PO, po

Spain — La Coruña, Oviedo, Burgos, Saragossa, Pamplona, Barcelona, Madrid, Valencia, Cordoba, Seville, Cadiz, Tangier, Gibraltar (Br.), Ceuta (Sp.), Melilla (Sp.)

S, B, CAs, S, S, S, S, S

Pyrenees, Andorra, Ebro, Douro, Tagus, Guadiana, Guadalquivir

Balearic Is.

Corsica (Fr.) — Ajaccio, CO, fi

Sardinia (K. OF SARDINIA) — Cagliari

Mediterranean Sea

MOROCCO   ALGIERS   TUNIS

Sweden & Norway — Christiania, Stavanger, Göteborg, Aalborg, Copenhagen, Malmö
N, SW, DENMARK, DA

United Netherlands — Amsterdam, Antwerp, Brussels, FL, DU

HOLSTEIN, Hamburg, MECKLENBURG, OLDENBURG, Bremen, HANOVER, BRUNSWICK, ANHALT, Berlin, PRUSSIA, Leipzig, SAXONY, Dresden, SO, g, Prague, Bohemia, C

Cologne, Aix-la-Chapelle, 1818, LUXEMBURG, NASSAU, Frankfurt, HESSE, THURINGIAN STATES, RHENISH BAVARIA, LORRAINE, Strasbourg, ALSACE, BADEN, WÜRTTEMBERG, Stuttgart, Nuremberg, BAVARIA, Munich, Salzburg, Danube, Inn, AUSTRIA, Innsbruck, Tyrol, Neuchâtel, Berne X Gislikon 1847, SWITZ, SONDERBUND (1845-7), The Alps, SAVOY, RR, RR, RR, RR, Laibach, Illyria, SG, G

Lombardy-Venetia, Milan, Novara 1849 X, Brescia, Custozza 1848 X, Peschiera, Verona, Venice, Turin, Mantua, Legnago, Piedmont (K. OF SARDINIA), PARMA, Genoa, Modena, MODENA, Bologna, MASSA LUCCA, Florence, Leghorn, Siena, TUSCANY, PAPAL STATES, SAN MARINO, Macerata, Rome, Appenines, 1821, 1822

KINGDOM OF THE TWO SICILIES, Naples, Salerno, Palermo, Sicily, M

Mediterranean Sea

of the French Bourbons, the archreactionary Charles X, was overthrown in the 'July Revolution' and replaced by the Orleanist dynasty of Louis Philippe. Shortly afterwards a liberal revolution in Belgium dissolved the union with Holland, and the new state received guarantees of its independence and neutrality by the Treaty of London (1839). The success of the July Revolution gave rise to further revolts, but these were crushed by conservative governments. A Polish attempt to regain independence was extinguished by the Russians. Under the July Monarchy, France pursued a guardedly liberal course in home politics, a *rapprochement* with Britain abroad, a policy of imperial expansion in Algeria (where a vicious colonial war was waged to subdue local resistance which endured until 1847), and an economic policy which, while it enriched sections of the bourgeoisie, left France lagging further behind Britain in industrial development (*compare Maps 56 and 57*). The Orleanist regime was increasingly criticized for its corruption, and a severe economic crisis in 1846-7 sounded its death-knell.

The year 1848, the year of revolutions throughout Europe, was the supreme crisis of conservatism (*Map 60*). Beginning in Sicily in January, a wave of revolutions swept through the continent, throwing nearly all conservative governments off balance, and giving a fresh impetus to democratic and nationalist ideals. In France the July Monarchy was replaced by the short-lived Second Republic, which, after the suppression of radical left-wing elements in June 1848, elected Louis Napoleon (nephew of the first Emperor) as President. By 1852 he had transformed the regime into the Second Empire, styling himself Napoleon III, and maintaining a firm grip on power, by a mixture of populism, authoritarianism, and opportunism, until 1870. In Prussia popular disturbances led King Frederick William IV to agree to 'merge Prussia into Germany' and to reign as a constitutional monarch. Similar movements were sparked off in the smaller German states, and a Constituent National Assembly met at Frankfurt from May 1848 to April 1849. Meanwhile the revolutionary surge had reached the Austrian empire where an uprising in Vienna in March 1848 led to the fall of Metternich. A Constituent Assembly in Vienna emancipated the peasantry from surviving feudal burdens. In June 1848 a Slav Congress in Prague demanded national rights for the subject peoples of the empire. However, resolute military action by the Austrian general Windischgraetz crushed the revolution in Prague and later in Vienna. Under the leadership of Schwarzenberg, Hapsburg power was restored. In Hungary a nationalist revolution led by Kossuth was repressed by 1849 after the Hungarians had been defeated by Austrian, Croat, and Russian forces. Revolution against Austrian rule in Italy, supported by King Charles Albert of

Piedmont, was defeated, though the Venetian republic held out until August 1849. By then the revolutionary surge had subsided, and conservative governments nearly everywhere had reasserted control. But 1848 had demonstrated the vulnerability of reactionary regimes, and the year of revolutions marked a decisive stage on the road to nationhood of several peoples, most notably those of Italy and Germany.

The *Risorgimento*, the movement for Italian unification, was a diversified and at times incoherent movement, whose supporters often differed over both means and ends, even over the practicability and desirability of the complete unification of the peninsula. The liberal constitutionalists, among whom the Piedmontese statesman Cavour was outstanding, proved to be the dominant group, but they were challenged by the republicans, whose leaders Mazzini and Garibaldi inspired revolutionaries everywhere, the former by his speeches and writings, the latter by his romantic heroism. A third group, the 'neo-Guelphs', believed that the Papacy was the natural head of a united Italy, and this notion was given some stimulus by the early actions of Pope Pius IX, elected in 1846. However, in the revolution of 1848 Pius fled from Rome, and returned only after Garibaldi's Roman Republic had been destroyed by French troops. The political unification of Italy took place in several stages (*Map 62*). The first, and most important, took place in 1859-60 when France, in alliance with Piedmont, defeated Austria in war, and secured the liberation of Lombardy and its union with Piedmont. In return Napoleon exacted his '*pourboire*' ('tip') in the form of the cession of Savoy and Nice to France by Piedmont. The independent northern duchies decided to join the union. Cavour was inclined to call a halt at this stage, but his hand was forced by Garibaldi who sailed for Sicily with his 'thousand', and, in a brilliant campaign, conquered Sicily and moved up through Naples towards Rome. In order to forestall an attack by Garibaldi on Rome (which, it was feared, would bring about outside intervention), the Piedmontese king Victor Emmanuel II moved south to block the way against Garibaldi. Rome and Venetia remained outside the kingdom of Italy proclaimed in 1861. Further attempts by Garibaldi in 1862 and 1867 to seize Rome were thwarted. In 1866 Venetia fell into Italian hands as a result of the defeat of Austria by Prussia, but it was not until 1870, after the French defeat by Prussia, that Rome was at last captured and the *Risorgimento* appeared complete.

The *Risorgimento* was the foremost example of the union of liberalism and nationalism. By contrast the process of German unification (*Map 61*) was marked by the gradual divorce of the two movements, particularly after 1848, as nationalism came to be increasingly aligned with conservative elements. Italian unification, it was sometimes said, was merely a mask for Piedmontese expansion. There was some truth in this (as was shown by the failure of the new Italy to prevent the ever-widening divergence between the developed north and the primitive south); but in the case of Germany there could be no doubt that the country was united primarily in the form of conquest by Prussia. The dominant genius of German unification was Bismarck (Prussian minister-president

1862-7 and federal chancellor 1867-90) who towered over international politics in the later part of the century even more effectively than had Metternich earlier. Bismarck proceeded, like Cavour, by a deft mixture of diplomacy and war. Unlike Cavour he had, in the Prussian army, a military machine which could win decisive victories without heavy reliance on allies. Prussian victories in three wars within seven years secured German unification. The war with Denmark in 1864 secured Austro-Prussian occupation of the duchies of Schleswig and Holstein. The war with Austria in 1866 saw the decisive defeat of Austria at Sadowa-Königgrätz, the formation of the North German Confederation of German states under Prussian leadership, and the eclipse of Hapsburg aspirations to German leadership. Henceforth it was certain that Prussia would dominate Germany and that Austria would be excluded from the new national state. The final stage came in 1870-1 with the victory over France at Sedan which brought the collapse of the Second French Empire, and the birth of the new German Empire which incorporated not only the south German states but also the annexed French provinces of Alsace and Lorraine, with their substantial German-speaking populations. In January 1871 the Prussian king William I was proclaimed German Emperor in a ceremony held at Versailles. The dream of the romantic German nationalists of the early part of the century seemed fulfilled. But the methods by which German unification had been brought about, and the type of state which was now established, socially conservative and politically authoritarian, hardly fulfilled the hopes of the German liberals. Henceforth nationalism was increasingly to be the handmaiden not of liberalism but of reactionary forces, notably imperialism.

Above left: The 1848 revolution in Italy.

61 The unification of Germany
Under the leadership and, after the defeat of Austria in 1866, the domination of Prussia, Germany was unified to form a highly centralized and authoritarian state, and the leading military and industrial power of continental Europe.

62 The unification of Italy
Despite the brilliance and international fame of the republican heroes Mazzini and Garibaldi, the traditional leadership of Piedmont retained effective control of the Italian *Risorgimento*. After 1870 the benefits of political unity were limited by deep and persistent economic and social divisions.

63 The Balkans in the nineteenth century
As the Ottoman empire retreated, the rise of nationality in the Balkans led through provincial autonomy and war to independence. The political and strategic interests of the great powers ensured their constant, often dangerous, and eventually fatal intervention.

Further reading: Owen Chadwick, *The Secularization of the European Mind in the Nineteenth Century* (Cambridge U.P. 1975); J.H. Lynch, *The Spanish American Revolutions* (Weidenfeld & Nicolson 1973; Norton); P.N. Stearns, *The Revolutions of 1848* (Weidenfeld & Nicolson 1974; Norton); James J. Sheehan, *German History, 1770-1866* (Oxford U.P. 1990); D. Mack Smith, *The Making of Italy, 1796-1870* (Michigan U.P. 1959); Ernest Gellner, *Nations and Nationalism* (Basil Blackwell 1983).

MAP 61 THE UNIFICATION OF GERMANY

Border of German Confederation 1815
Border of North German Confederation 1867
Border of German Empire 1871
Prussia 1815
Prussian gains by 1867
German States still independent 1867-71
X Battle

0   150 km
0   100 miles

A   Anhalt   MS Mecklenburg-Strelitz
B   Brunswick   O   Oldenburg
Ha Hamburg   P   Prussia
H   Hanover   TS Thuringian States

SWEDEN

Baltic Sea

North Sea

DENMARK

Copenhagen

Memel
Tilsit
Königsberg
East Prussia
A

SCHLESWIG
Flensburg
Schleswig
Kiel
Heligoland (Br. to 1890)
Cuxhaven

HOLSTEIN
LÜBECK
Lübeck
MS
MECKLENBURG-SCHWERIN
P
Rostock
Stettin
MECKLENBURG-STRELITZ

Pomerania
Danzig
S   I
West Prussia
Posen
Posen

RUSSIAN EMPIRE
Poland
Warsaw
Vistula

Frisian Is.
Wilhelmshaven
Hamburg
HAMBURG
Ha
OLDENBURG
BREMEN
Bremen
Oldenburg
Weser
Elbe
Wittenberg
Brandenburg
Berlin
Brandenburg
U
S

HANOVER
Hanover
SCHAUMBURG-LIPPE
Osnabrück
LIPPE-DETMOLD
Detmold
Brunswick
BRUNSWICK
B
Magdeburg
Dessau
ANHALT
Halle
A
Leipzig
Saxony
Breslau
Silesia

Amsterdam
NETHERLANDS
The Hague
Münster
Westphalia
Dortmund
Essen
Düsseldorf
WALDECK
Kassel
Göttingen
H
TS
B
H
A
TS
Saxony
Dresden
SAXONY
Erfurt
THURINGIAN STATES
P
Elbe
REP. OF CRACOW (to Austria 1846)
Cracow
50°

Antwerp
Brussels
BELGIUM
Cologne
P
Marburg
EL te. OF HESSE
Fulda
Karlsbad
Prague
Bohemia
Olmütz
Galicia

RHENISH PRUSSIA
Coblenz
NASSAU
FRANKFURT-AM-MAIN
Frankfurt
Mainz
GR. D. OF HESSE
P
GR. D. OF HESSE
Würzburg
Pilsen
Moravia
Brünn

LUXEMBURG
(to Belgium 1839)
Sedan 1870
Luxemburg
Trier
LICHTENBERG
Ludwigshafen
RHENISH BAVARIA
Mannheim
Heidelberg
Fürth
Nuremberg
Regensburg
Danube
AUSTRIAN
Lower Austria
Pressburg
50°

Metz
Saarbrücken
Lorraine
Karlsruhe
Stuttgart
WÜRTTEMBERG
Ulm
BAVARIA
Augsburg
Munich
Inn
Linz
Vienna

Nancy
Strasbourg
(From Fr. 1871)
Alsace
BADEN
HOHENZOLLERN
Upper Austria
EMPIRE
Budapest
Hungary
Danube

FRANCE
Mulhouse
Belfort
Freiburg
Basel
Rhine
Lake of Constance
Constance
Zurich
Salzburg
Innsbruck
Graz
Styria
Drava

Neuchâtel (Pr. 1815-57)
Bern
LIECHTENSTEIN
SWITZERLAND
Lausanne
L. Geneva
Tyrol
The Alps
Carinthia
Laibach
Carniola

Lyon
Grenoble
Turin
Milan
Po
Venice
Trieste
Fiume
Adriatic Sea
Croatia

Sadowa-Königgrätz 1866

MAP 62 THE UNIFICATION OF ITALY

SWITZERLAND

SOUTH
Bolzano
TYROL

Drava

AUSTRIAN EMPIRE

Geneva

SAVOY
(to France 1860)

Chambery

Rhône

THE ALPS

Trento

Udine

Trieste

ISTRIA

Fiume

LOMBARDY
(to Austria 1815-59)

VENETIA
(to Austria 1815-66)

Novara
1849

Milan

Magenta
1859

Custozza
1848
1866

Verona

Peschiera
1848
1866

Solferino
1859

Villafranca

Padua

Legnano

Venice

Turin

PIEDMONT

Mantua

Po

Parma

Zara

Po

Ferrara

PARMA

MODENA

Genoa

Pontremoli
(to Parma 1847)

PAPAL

Bologna

Ravenna

ROMAGNA

Rimini

NICE
(to France 1860)

La Spezia

Fivizzano
(to Modena 1847)

MASSA
(to Modena 1829)

LUCCA
(to Tuscany 1847)

San Marino
(Italian Prot. from 1861)

THE MARCHES

Urbino

Ancona

Adriatic Sea

MONACO
Nice

(Sardinian Prot. 1815-60
French Prot from 1861)

*Ligurian
Sea*

Pisa

Lucca
Florence

Arno

Leghorn

TUSCANY

Siena

Castelfidardo
1860

STATES

Perugia
Assisi

UMBRIA

Apennines

KINGDOM OF SARDINIA

Elba

Talamone

Elba

Tiber

PATRIMONY OF ST PETER

Mentana
1867

Rome

CORSICA
(to France 1768)

Ajaccio

Pescara

Lagosta

NAPLES

Bari

Pontecorvo

Gaeta

Volturno
1860

Benevento

Brindisi

Naples

Salerno

Taranto

Otra

SARDINIA

40°

*Tyrrhenian

Sea*

Gulf of Taranto

KINGDOM OF THE TWO SICILIES

Cagliari

Lipari Is.

Straits of
Messina

Messina

Aspromonte
1862

Reggio

Milazzo
1860

Palermo

Marsala

Calatafimi
1860

SICILY

Catania

Mediterranean

Syracuse

Pantelleria

Sea

Malta
(British 1814)

10°

15°

Legend:

→ Route of Garibaldi's Thousand 1860

→ Route of Victor Emmanuel II 1860

◇ Austrian quadrilateral fortresses

— Italian border 1866-1919

▨ Boundary of Papal States

☐ Kingdom of Sardinia 1815

☐ Territory gained 1859-60

☐ Territory gained 1866

☐ Territory gained 1870

☐ Territory gained 1919

0   200 km

0   150 miles

MAP 63 THE BALKANS IN THE NINETEENTH CENTURY

Budapest
20°
Danube
Klausenburg (Cluj)
Carpathians
Moldavia
RUSSIA
Odessa
25°
Transylvania
Bessarabia
AUSTRIA-HUNGARY
Agram (Zagreb)
Drava
Temesvar
Banat
45°
Transylvanian Alps
Sereth
Galatz
Moldavian, 1856-1878
Croatia-Slavonia
Sava
ROUMANIA
(Autonomous 1829, independent 1878)
Wallachia
Bosna
BOSNIA
(Austrian Prot. 1878, annexed 1908)
Belgrade
Dobrudja
(a. 1878)
Constanta
HERZEGOVINA
Sarajevo
Duna
SERBIA
(Autonomous 1817, independent 1878)
Kragujevac
Morava
Bucharest
Krajova
Danube
(a. 1913)
Dalmatia
Kragujevac
Aleksinac 1876
Plevna 1877
BULGARIA
(Autonomous 1878, independent 1908)
Varna
(a. 1913)
Novibazar
Nish
(a. 1878)
Balkan Mts.
Black Sea
Ragusa
Sanjak of Novibazar
(a. 1913)
MONTENEGRO
Sofia
Stara Zagora
Burgas
Cattaro
(a. 1913)
(a. 1913)
Eastern Roumelia
(Autonomous 1878, to Bulgaria 1885)
(a. 1913)
Scutari
Üsküb (Skopje)
Kumanovo 1912
Vardar
Struma
Philippopolis (Plovdiv)
Maritza
Kirk Kilisse 1912
Adrianople
Luleburgaz 1912
Bosphorus
Adriatic Sea
(a. 1913)
(a. 1913)
Thrace
(a. 1913)
Constantinople
San Stefano
Scutari
Durazzo
Monastir (Bitola)
Macedonia
Kavalla
Sea of Marmara
Marmara
ALBANIA
(Independent 1913)
Salonika
Thasos
Gallipoli
(a. 1913)
Samothrace
Imbros
40°
40°
Lemnos
Dardanelles
OTTOMAN
Janina
Larissa
Aegean
EMPIRE
Corfu
Epirus
Pindus Mts.
Thessaly (a. 1881)
Northern Sporades
(a. 1913)
Mitilini (Lesbos)
Ionian Sea
Ionian Is. (a. 1863)
Santa Maura
Skiros
Sea
Chios
Smyrna
Cephalonia
Missolonghi 1826
Livadia (Independent 1830)
Euboea
Zakynthos (Zante)
Patras
Gulf of Corinth
GREECE
Andros
Samos
Corinth
Piraeus
Athens
Nikaria
Peloponnese
Tripolis (Morea)
Cyclades
Naxos
Dodecanese Is. (Italian occupation 1912)
Cos
Rhodes
Navarino 1827
Milos
Karpathos
Cerigo (Kythira)
Sea of Crete
CRETE
(Autonomous 1898, to Greece 1908)
(to Egypt 1824-40)
35°
25°
Mediterranean Sea

Legend:
- - - - Borders proposed by Treaty of San Stefano, March 1878
—— Borders established by Congress of Berlin, June-July 1878
—— Borders, 1914   a. Acquired

0 — 200 km
0 — 150 miles

The age of European supremacy 9

Above: Pu Yi (on the right), the last emperor of China, ascended to the throne at the age of two.

THE AGE OF IMPERIALISM

The late nineteenth and early twentieth centuries witnessed an unprecedented extension of European power over non-Europeans. Hence the frequent characterization of the period as an 'age of imperialism'. This was, however, as much a time of imperial decline as of imperial expansion. Indeed, the debilitation of the older imperial systems – most notably those of Austria, Ottoman Turkey, and China – and the ensuing diplomatic rivalries, were two of the primary causes of the imperial expansion of countries such as Britain and France.

64 European penetration of the Far East
The 'Opium War' of 1839-42 demonstrated the inability of the Manchu (Ch'ing) empire to withstand the expansion of the European powers. Their domination of the Far East was established as much by exacting commercial privileges as by territorial occupation.

The vulnerability of the old empires became steadily more apparent in the course of the nineteenth century. Austria, bludgeoned into submission by Prussia, not only lost most of its lands in Italy and its position as the leading German power (*Maps 61 and 62*) but was compelled by resurgent Hungarian nationalism to acquiesce in 1867 to the *Ausgleich* ('compromise') whereby the empire was transformed into a 'Dual Monarchy' based on the joint domination of Germans and Hungarians over Slavs. Although unity under Austro-Hungarian rule made considerable economic sense (as was proved when the area broke up into several states after 1918 – *Map 77*) Austro-Hungarian output and industrialization lagged far behind that of Germany. While the Hapsburg regime continued to command impressive reserves of institutional and ideological strength, the nationalist Revolutions of 1848-9 and 1866-7 had demonstrated its essential frailty. The spread of the ideas of romantic nationalism and the rise of Pan-Slav feeling championed by Russia rendered the Austro-Hungarian system increasingly unstable.

Slav opposition to the Hapsburgs was heightened by the success of Slav and other subject nationalities in south-east Europe in gaining independence from the Turks (*see Map 63*). The long territorial retreat of the Ottoman Empire, which had begun in 1699, greatly accelerated in the nineteenth century. The Empire made repeated attempts to recover its strength by internal reforms and modernization, and it enjoyed strong support from other powers (especially Britain, which sought to maintain Ottoman integrity for fear of Russian encroachment on Constantinople and the Dardenelles). Nevertheless one after another of the European subject nationalities wrested autonomy and eventually independence from the Turks. In 1830, after a bitter struggle, Greece won its independence, and by 1878 Serbia and Romania were independent and Bulgaria virtually so.

Meanwhile Ottoman power on the southern shore of the Mediterranean was also disappearing. France conquered Algeria between 1830 and 1848, annexed Tunis in 1881, and harboured ambitions in Morocco (which, however, preserved a precarious independence until 1912) – *see Maps 66 and 74*. Egypt had asserted its autonomy under Muhammad Ali in the early nineteenth century, but his successors drove the country into bankruptcy and financial submission to Britain and France. With the construction of the Suez Canal (opened in 1869) the British began to fear that control of the area by a hostile power might endanger the security of their communications with India. The outbreak of an Egyptian nationalist revolution in 1881 was the occasion for the occupation of the country by British forces the following year. Although successive British governments affirmed their intention to withdraw, a 'veiled protectorate', in which Egypt became in all but name a British possession, endured for nearly three-quarters of a century.

It was, as Gallagher and Robinson point out, 'more than any other cause, the danger of a general Ottoman collapse [which] set off the partition of Africa and brought on the rise of new European empires in north and tropical Africa'. The 'scramble for Africa' (*see Map 74*) in the 1880s and 1890s saw nearly the whole continent subjected to European rule. Britain secured the lion's share of the territorial spoils as she expanded up the Nile valley into east Africa and inland from the west African coast. In southern Africa the discovery of gold and diamonds led to a vast influx of European capital and labour and laid the foundations of the greatest economic power on the continent. An elaborate railway system was constructed, and British rule was extended northward beyond the Zambeze to the shores of Lakes Nyasa and Tanganyika. The French too moved into the hinterland from their

north and west African coastal footholds and established their suzerainty over most of the Sahara and as far south as the Congo basin. Other European powers nibbled at more modest morsels. Bismarck, although sceptical of the value of imperial possessions, gained the German annexation of Tanganyika, Togoland, Kamerun and South-West Africa. Portugal, deprived of her former vast dominion in Brazil (*Map 59*), consoled her national pride by consolidating her position in Portuguese West Africa (Angola) and Mozambique, rebuffing the rapacious advances of acquisitive European rivals. Italy too, disillusioned with the failure of the post-*Risorgimento* regime to recreate Italian greatness, tried her hand at empire-building, only to encounter humiliating disaster when her army was defeated at Adowa by the army of Abyssinia, the one indigenous imperial system in Africa to survive into the twentieth century.

In East Asia (*see Map 64*) the decline of the Ch'ing (Manchu) empire in China afforded the opportunity for rapid European expansion into the area as the decline of the Mughal empire had already done in India (*see Map 65*). In 1839 an attempt by the Chinese Government to enforce a prohibition on the importation of opium led to war with Britain. By the Treaty of Nanking in 1842 China was obliged to cede Hong Kong to Britain and to make a series of commercial concessions, including the opening of several ports to British traders. The T'ai P'ing Rebellion (1850-64), a popular upheaval which convulsed sixteen of China's eighteen provinces, provided the pretext for further European intervention. Anglo-French victories between 1856 and 1860 led to further 'unequal treaties' which extended European commercial and cultural penetration of China. The decrepitude of the Ch'ing Empire made possible the expansion of French sovereignty from its base at Saigon to the whole of Indo-China. Defeated by

MAP 64 EUROPEAN PENETRATION OF THE FAR EAST

RUSSIA

SAKHALIN

MANCHURIA

OUTER
MONGOLIA

Gobi

INNER
MONGOLIA

Amur

Vladivostock

Hakodate

SINKIANG

Newchwang

Peking ⊙

T'ien-chin

Wonsan

Sea
of
Japan

Niigata

THE

Yen-tai

Seoul

KOREA

Edo

Hwang-ho

Inchon

Yokohama

MANCHU EMPIRE

Pusan

Kyoto

Hyoge

J

Osaka

A

TIBET

Shimonoseki

P

Yangtze

Nanking

Chen-chiang

Nagasaki

A

Shang-hai

Kagoshima

Ichang

Han-k'ou

Wu-hu

Ning-po

East
China
Sea

N

Pacific
Ocean

Chiu-chiang

Wen-chou

Hsi-chiang

Meng-tzu

Fu-chou

Ryukyu Is.

BURMA

Canton

T'an-sui

Amoy

Swatow

Tai-wan

Tai-nan

TONKIN

Lung-chou

Hongkong (Br.)

LAOS

Hanoi

Macao
(Port.)

SIA

Rangoon

Chiung-chou

Hai-nan

ANNAN

SIAM

Bangkok

PHILIPPINES

CAMBODIA

Manila

Saigon

COCHIN
CHINA

South
China
Sea

Penang
(Br. 1786)

MALAYA

BRUNEI

NORTH
BORNEO

Halmahera

Malacca
(Br. 1824)

Singapore
(Br. 1819)

SARAWAK

SUMATRA

BORNEO

CELEBES

Moluccas

Seram

NEW GUINEA

Batavia

JAVA

TIMOR

Arafura Sea

Indian
Ocean

Port Essington
(1838-49)

Legend:

■ Ports open to restricted foreign trade before 1840

⊞ Ports opened to foreign trade after the First Opium
War (1839-42)

⊞ Ports open to foreign trade after the Arrow War
(1856-60)

⊞ Other ports opened between 1855 and 1890

Russian territory in 1850

Russian territory gained in 1858

Russian territory gained in 1860

Russian territory gained in 1875

Tributary states of the Manchu Empire

British territory in 1826

British territory in 1856

British territory in 1890

French territory in 1863

French territory gained in 1867

French territory gained in 1884-5

Spanish territory

Netherlands Indies-territory in 1850

Netherlands Indies-territory in 1890

Portugese territory in 1840

German territory gained in 1884

Independent states

0   1000 km
0   600 miles

Japan in 1894-5, China was compelled to yield up her suzerainty over the tributary state of Korea. The Sino-Japanese war was the signal for a 'scramble for China' in the late 1890s, in which the imperial powers vied for railway and other concessions and occupied Chinese ports (*see Map 73*). Chinese resentment of European encroachments found expression in the so-called 'Boxer Rebellion'. This eruption of anti-foreign feeling, spearheaded by a secret society of 'Righteous and Harmonious Fists', enjoyed the support of a fac-

tion of the imperial government. In 1900 a multinational military expedition relieved a siege of the foreign legations in Peking. The vindictive terms subsequently imposed by the imperial powers appeared to spell the doom of the Ch'ing dynasty.

Although formal European rule had not been extended to the greater part of the country, and in spite of American attempts to preserve Chinese integrity by the enunciation of the 'open door' principle in 1899, the Chinese government had by the end of the century effectively been deprived of

mastery in its own house. China was thus an outstanding example of 'informal imperialism', the process whereby imperial powers secured commercial, legal, or diplomatic privileges which gave them influence, in some cases a predominant voice, in the internal affairs of nominally independent states. Another such case was Persia where Britain and Russia carved out spheres of influence in the declining Qajar empire.

The weakening of the old empires, and the consequent power vacuums in much of Asia and

MAP 65 SOUTH ASIA AROUND 1900

BRITISH INTERESTS IN INDIA, 1914

Exports, profits on 10% of British exports, mainly in cotton goods.
Investment, interest on £365m, or 10% of British investment overseas.
'Home Charges', about £25m p.a. sent to Britain to pay for pensions of retired personnel and the costs of Indian government in Britain.
Army, 80,000 British and 230,000 Indian troops, and non-combatants, paid for by Indians' taxes and used for imperial purposes throughout the world.

Legend:
- Boundary of the British Empire until 1947
- Provincial boundaries
- Boundaries of Indian states under provincial jurisdiction
- One meeting of the Indian National Congress 1885-1922
- One meeting of the All-India Muslim League 1906-1922
- Proportions of Hindus, Muslims, Sikhs and others in the provinces of British India (1922)
- British territory before 1858
- British territory acquired after 1858
- British sphere of influence
- Dependent Indian states by 1858
- Indian states newly dependent since 1858
- N.E.F.A. North East Frontier Agency
- Railways (various gauges) in 1909

600 km
300 miles

Africa, cannot alone explain the phenomenal growth of European imperialism in the late nineteenth century. A number of further explanations have been advanced. Imperialism, it is suggested, was the result of a search for outlets for 'surplus capital'. Was it rather a necessary consequence of heightened trade rivalries and moves towards protectionism in Europe? Or did it derive from the need of manufacturing economies for assured sources of supply of cheap raw materials? Or from the need of rapidly expanding populations to find outlets for emigration and settlement? Some historians tend to discount economic motives and stress rather the more purely political origins of the imperial urge. It is thus portrayed as a stepchild of frustrated nationalisms, as a plaything of diplomatic rivalries, or as an attempt by ruling élites to siphon off internal social unrest by the stimulation of 'jingoist' imperial enthusiasms. Although there are grains of truth in several of these suggested causes the search for a 'general theory' of imperialism has been unsuccessful – perhaps not surprisingly in the case of such a far-flung and variegated phenomenon.

Just as there is no historical consensus as to the causes of imperialism, so views diverge as to its nature and effects. Some emphasize its negative aspects: the use of force and repression to establish and maintain imperial rule; the barbarities perpetrated in some colonies by imperialist agents and officials (as in the Congo, governed for a time as the private estate of the King of the Belgians); the distortion of colonial economies to meet the needs of metropolitan countries; the subordination of the interests of indigenous peoples to those of European settlers; the racialism of most imperial powers; the extinction of some non-European cultures; the alienation and psychological dislocation arising from the sudden imposition of westernization. Against all this it is argued that imperialism did not rely only on brute force but in many cases constructed sophisticated governmental systems incorporating indigenous institutions and co-opting local élites. Moreover, it was the imperial powers, led by Britain, that sought (with considerable success) to eliminate the African slave trade in the course of the nineteenth century (compare Map 51). Also on the positive side are often added the development of modern economic infrastructures, the spread of education and literacy, the application of modern medical techniques to the battle against disease (compare Map 66), the unification of large areas containing diverse religions, tribes, and ethnic groups into single units, and the establishment of the rule of law.

Resistance to imperialism reflected its ambivalent impact, for opposition to colonial incursions tended to be more effective the more it borrowed from the ideas and techniques of imperial societies themselves. The British victories over the Indian mutiny (1857-9), the Ashanti of the Gold Coast (1874), the Zulus of South Africa (1879), and the Mahdist forces in the Sudan (1885) showed that technologically inferior anti-imperialist forces might win occasional battles but could not expect enduring success against imperial armies in straightforward military confrontations. By contrast, the Indian National Congress (founded in 1885), based on a marriage of western with Indian techniques of political mobilization, and profoundly influenced by British liberalism, succeeded in compelling the Government of India (which had replaced the East India Company after the mutiny as the agency of British rule) to concede a growing share of political power to Indians (Map 65). In this respect the Indian experience served as a model for some other anti-imperial movements and some other (particularly British) colonial administrations. A similarly ambiguous response to European penetration may be detected in the declining old empires: the constitutional revolution in Persia in 1905, the Young Turk revolution in the Ottoman Empire in 1908, and the republican revolution in China led by Sun Yat-Sen in 1911, were at once against western imperial domination and in themselves evidence of the impact of western political and social ideas.

Among all the imperial powers, one held for a while almost undisputed predominance. Britain indeed attained in the third quarter of the nineteenth century a position more nearly approaching world mastery than perhaps has ever been achieved by any other power in history. It was not merely that Britain had amassed what was territorially the largest empire ever known (see Map 67). Britain maintained its long lead over competitors in industrial innovation and production almost until the end of the century. Until the 1870s she produced more coal than all other countries put together. She was similarly dominant in the production of iron. Britain produced one-third of the world's industrial output in 1870. Britain's foreign trade (in which Lancashire cotton was the largest single element) was greater than that of any two other countries until the 1890s. The pound sterling remained the basis of the international payments system until well into the twentieth century. Britain was the world's largest foreign investor until the First World War (most of the exported capital flowing to the Americas, India, and South Africa, rather than to the new empire). Britain dominated the world's system of transport and communications: herself possessed of the world's best network of roads and railways, she supplied the capital and the technology for the construction of railways in five continents; she owned the majority of the world's submarine cables. Above all, she dominated world shipping: until almost the eve of the First World War the British merchant fleet comprised a larger tonnage than that of all other countries put together. Shielding this massive aggregation of economic might was the Royal Navy, the world's most powerful seaborne force. The age of imperialism was, truly, the British era.

Nevertheless, by the turn of the century Britain's overwhelming predominance was beginning to be eroded. By 1890 the USA had overtaken Britain in the production of iron, and by 1900 in the production of coal and steel (Map 69). Germany too had outstripped Britain in industrial production by the turn of the century (Map 57). By 1913 the USA was producing more than one-third of the world's manufactured goods, whereas Britain's share of world output had slipped below one-tenth. By 1900 Britain was the only major nation which still adhered to free trade, and although Britain still dominated world trade some voices began to be raised in favour of protectionism. Nor was it only economically that Britain now began to appear vulnerable. Britain, alone among the European

65 South Asia around 1900
India became a British Crown Colony after the suppression of the mutiny of 1857-59. Territorial consolidation, the importation of British administrative and educational institutions and economic development (which, however, destroyed the self-sufficiency of the village economies and opened the way to chronic rural over-population) had created by 1900 Britain's greatest imperial possession and a growing independence movement.

123

MAP 66 AFRICA ON THE EVE OF THE SCRAMBLE

Vegetation types:

Desert and dry steppe

Savanna

Upland grassland with occasional forest

Dry forest

Mediterranean

Tropical and subtropical rain forest

Areas infested by tse-tse fly

(ORO) African states c.1880

European settlements and states c.1880:

Afrikaner

British

French

Portuguese

States under Ottoman suzerainty

Areas of missionary activity in 1880

0   1500 kms
0   1000 miles

Right: For many Cecil Rhodes, a key British player in the scramble for Africa embodied the spirit of imperialism.

66 Africa on the eve of the scramble
Before 1880 most of the African continent was unknown to Europeans, and very little of it ruled by them. They were confined to the coast by disease (also the greatest obstacle to African development), the hostility generated by the slave trade and the fact that comparable profits from other sources seemed unlikely.

powers, had no system of conscription and no large standing army. Between 1899 and 1902 she suffered a shattering blow to her prestige in the Boer War: although she was ultimately victorious her difficulties in crushing the Dutch colonists in South Africa cruelly exposed her military weakness and her diplomatic isolation. British policy-makers now began to wonder whether the vast territorial acquisitions of the late nineteenth century had not extended the empire beyond Britain's capacity to sustain or defend it. In 1905 the head of the British Foreign Office suggested that the British Empire might give the appearance 'of some huge giant sprawling over the globe, with gouty fingers and toes stretched in every direction, which cannot be approached without eliciting a scream'.

British paramountcy was further challenged by the development of European alliance systems. In 1879 Bismarck had formed a 'Dual Alliance' between Germany and Austria-Hungary. In 1882 this was expanded to a 'Triple Alliance' by the addition of Italy. Meanwhile Bismarck sought to contain Russia by drawing her into a *Dreikaiserbund* (League of Three Emperors) in company with Austria-Hungary. The heightening of Balkan rivalries between Russia and Austria-Hungary made this impossible to preserve intact, and in 1887 Bismarck replaced it with the so-called 'Re-insurance Treaty', a bipartite arrangement between Germany and Russia. However, in 1890 Bismarck was dismissed by the new German Emperor, William II. The delicate balance of Bismarck's alliance system collapsed with him: Germany now jettisoned Russia and threw in her lot wholeheartedly with Austria-Hungary. This led between 1891 and 1894 to what Bismarck had always feared most and what his entire diplomacy had been concerned to prevent – the crystallization of a Russo-French alliance which presented Germany with the danger of a war on two fronts.

Although the phrase 'splendid isolation', as sometimes applied to British foreign policy in the late nineteenth century, is misleading if taken literally, it is true that Britain in the 1890s held aloof from either camp. The traditions of her foreign policy earlier in the century had been anti-Russian rather than anti-German. It was against Russia that Britain had combined with France, Turkey, and Sardinia to fight in the Crimean War (1854-6). At the Congress of Berlin in 1878 the British prime minister, Disraeli, had helped to deprive Russia of the fruits of her victory in the Russo-Turkish war, and had secured a reversal of the Treaty of San Stefano which Russia had sought to impose on Turkey (*see Map 63*). Throughout the period Britain had been concerned by the apparent threat to her Indian empire posed by Russian advances in central Asia (*Map 70*) – which stimulated Britain too to advance her frontiers in northern India (*see Map 65*). Britain was further inhibited from identifying herself with the Russo-French alliance

by colonial disputes with France, particularly over North Africa. In 1898 a minor Anglo-French confrontation at Fashoda (*see Map 74*) blew up into a serious crisis which seemed to bring Britain and France to the brink of war.

Nevertheless, by the end of the century it was the German empire, with its dynamic economy, its thrusting foreign policy, its assertive demand for a 'place in the sun', and its expanding naval programme which seemed to represent the chief threat to Britain's international hegemony. Although Anglo-German discussions about a possible alliance continued until 1901, it became apparent that the fundamental interests and sympathies of the two powers were diverging. It is the Anglo-Japanese alliance, concluded in 1902, which is traditionally held to mark the end of Britain's 'isolation', but this did not commit Britain to either of the main European power blocs. Even the '*ententes*' signed with France in 1904 and with Russia in 1907 were ostensibly concerned merely with the settlement of outstanding colonial disputes. But they were followed by naval and military conversations which, although short of an alliance, insensibly drew Britain closer to France and Russia. In the diplomatic crises of 1905 and 1911 over

Morocco and of 1908 and 1912-13 over the Balkans the lines hardened between the 'Triple Entente' and the 'central powers'. In the years before 1914 all the European powers greatly increased their expenditure on armaments. Meanwhile, as the struggle for mastery in Europe intensified, the rise of new powers on the periphery of the international system foreshadowed the sudden collapse, at the moment of its greatest imperial extension, of Europe's mastery of the world.

67 Foundations of a world economy
European colonial expansion created a world economy united not only by the establishment of regular communications (telegraph cables joined most parts of the civilized world by 1900) and the exchange of goods and people, but by financial ties through capital investment even more widespread than territorial dominion.

Further reading A. J. P. Taylor, *The Struggle for Mastery in Europe* (Oxford University Press, 1954); John Gallagher and Ronald Robinson, *Africa and the Victorians,* (Macmillan, 1961); J. Berque, *Egypt Imperialism and Revolution* (Faber 1972);John K. Fairbank, *The Great Chinese Revolution, 1800-1985* (Harper & Row 1986, Picador); C. A. Bayly, *Indian Society and the Making of the British Empire* (Cambridge U. P. 1988); Eric Hobsbawm, *The Age of Empire* (Weidenfeld & Nicolson 1987; Random House); D. K. Fieldhouse *Economics and Empire* (2nd ed Macmillan1984). *China and the West* (Hutchinson, 1979).

MAP 67 FOUNDATIONS OF A WORLD ECONOMY

GREENLAND

ICELAND

Faroes Shetland Is.

Orkney Is. Scapa Flow

Aleutian Is.
Dutch Harbour

7000

G
Sitka

Vancouver
Gr Fi
Ti
Seattle

Portland

2250

D F G
San Francisco

San Diego

CANADA

Chicago
UNITED STATES Pittsburg
Baltimore
St. Louis

Bermuda

Boston
New York
Philadelphia

Newfoundland
St. John

Halifax

Cu Gr I
Fi Ti O

1150   900
500
150   150
n.a.
N. America

C
To

To
C
F

Tampa

Bahamas

Crooked
and Acklin I. Caicos and Turks Is.
Inagua Is.
Cayman Is. Te Su
F To
I
BR.
HONDURAS Guantanamo San Juan
Jamaica Nevis and
Kingston PUERTO St. Kitts
RICO
Guadeloupe
Dominica
Martinique
Curaçao Grenada Barbados
Port of Spain Trinidad
and Tobago

Panama
Canal Colon
1914
PANAMA
CANAL
ZONE

to Eastern U.S.A. and Europe

BR.
GUIANA
DUTCH GUIANA
FR. GUIANA

3700

1350 1600
500
800 1200
250
n.a.
Latin America

to N. America

Rio de Janeiro

Coff
Su

Ft
Cu Buenos Aires
Ti
Mt

Falkland Is. Stanley

S. Georgia

Azores

Madeira

Canary Is.

Cape Verde Is.

RIO DE ORO

St. Helena

to Africa, Middle
and Far East

Glasgow Newcastle Kiel
Liverpool M Leeds Canal Kiel
Birmingham M Amst. 1895 Bremerhav
London Brussels Berli
Plymouth Paris Cologne Leipzi
Brest Munich Vienr
Lyon Budapest
Marseille Milan
Barcelona Toulon Ror
Madrid Balearic Naples
Is. Taranto
Cadiz Gibraltar P F Tunis
SPANISH Valetta Ma
MOROCCO ALGERIA
TUNIS
MOROCCO TRIPO
IFNI

FRENCH
WEST AFRICA
2400
1900
900
700 500
n.a. n. n.
Africa

Co
P G
Bathurst GAMBIA NIGERIA
PORT.
GUINEA GOLD TOGOLAND
Freetown SIERRA COAST KAMERU
LEONE
LIBERIA Co Ti P Co P
Accra
Fernando Po
SP. GUINEA

FR
CONGC

KABINDA Ti

Ti
R
Di
ANG

GERMAN
S. W. AFRIC
WALVIS
BAY

Copenhag

Empires in 1914:

British	Portuguese
French	Turkish
German	Japanese
Russian	American
Dutch	Belgian
Italian	Danish
Spanish	

Foreign investment in 1900 and 1914:
(in millions of U.S. dollars)

British investment 1914 German investment 1914
1900 1900

French investment 1914 American investment 1914
1900 1900

n.a. not available   n. negligible

Major shipping routes

Major trade flows

Aden Major bases and coaling stations in 1914
with appropriate imperial colour

Major canals with date of construction

Cities of over 500,000 population

Independent states

The emergence of the modern world 1

Opposite page top: Immigrants on the move in Nebraska, 1886.

Opposite page below: A native American Indian photographed on a reservation in Idaho.

68 The westward growth of the USA.
Systematic extension of its territory by diplomacy, purchase and conquest both within and beyond its frontiers transformed the United States from a small agrarian community into a major continental civilization. The arid high plains beyond the Mississippi constituted the principal barrier to the settlement of the newly acquired lands.

RIVALS TO EUROPEAN SUPREMACY

The sudden eclipse of European world power in the mid-twentieth century was foreshadowed by the emergence as potential 'super-powers' of the USA, Russia, and Japan. Although each of them followed a very different path of development, they shared certain general characteristics. All three underwent vast expansion in population, territory and production.

They industrialized on a massive scale, transforming themselves in the process from overwhelmingly rural to predominantly urban societies. In each the rapid pace of economic and social change led to acute strains between traditional and modernizing institutions and ideologies. And all three alternated between periods of expansionist involvement in international politics and periods of self-absorption and isolationism.

No nation in modern history can match the phenomenal growth of the USA within a few generations from the small agrarian community of the thirteen colonies (*Map 53*) to a continental civilization commanding the world's greatest concentration of economic and military power. The territorial expansion of the USA westwards to the Pacific (see *Map 68*) proceeded in three broad stages. By 1819 all of the region between the old seaboard states and the Mississippi had been admitted to the Union except Michigan (admitted in 1837) and Wisconsin (admitted in 1848). By 1858 five states had been carved out of the vast hinterland of the Louisiana Purchase obtained by Jefferson from France in 1803 for approximately $15,000,000 and admitted to the Union. In addition, Florida, purchased from Spain in 1819, attained statehood in 1845. The third stage was the settlement of the south-western lands detached from Mexico. Texas revolted against Mexico in 1836 and constituted an independent state until it was admitted to the Union in 1845; American

MAP 68 THE WESTWARD GROWTH OF THE USA

✗	Major battles
~~	Navigable rivers
▨	Main trails
▨	Cattle trails to railheads
➤	Railroads for cattle
1844 ↗	Mining strikes
▨	Main Indian reservations in 1875
▨	Significant numbers of non-industrial foreign-born immigrants by 1900
▨	Areas settled by 1830
▨	Areas settled by 1870
▨	Areas settled by 1910

victory in war against Mexico (1846-8) added the present states of Arizona, Nevada, California, and Utah, plus other areas; and the Gadsden Purchase of 1853 acquired a further small strip (now the southern parts of Arizona and New Mexico). Meanwhile a dispute with Britain over the Oregon Territory was settled in 1846 by the concession to the USA of the mainland as far north as the 49th Parallel. Finally, in 1867 Alaska was purchased from Russia for $7,200,000.

Territorial expansion depended on settlement, which proceeded against formidable physical and

West of this line to the Rockies annual average rainfall below 20"

1	Thirteen colonies
2	Acquired by Treaty of Versailles (1783)
3	Louisiana Purchase (1803)
4	From Spain (1810)
5	From Spain (1813)
6	Ceded by Britain (1818)
7	Acquired by Adams-Onis Treaty (1819)
8	Ceded by Britain (1842)
9	Texas annexed (originally Spanish then Mexican) in 1845
10	Oregon Territory (1846). Previously jointly occupied with Great Britain
11	From Mexico by Treaty of Guadalupe Hidalgo (1848)
12	Gadsden Purchase (1853) from Mexico
13	Alaskan Purchase from Russia (1867)

human obstacles. The fast-flowing, navigable rivers eastwards from the Mississippi Valley were vital in locating ports and creating subject economic hinterlands. In the more arid and gently sloping high plains of the trans-Mississippi west, trails rather than rivers marked the lines of movement and settlement. *Map 68* shows how aridity delayed agricultural settlement on the high plains; the wave of migrants leapt across to the west (often encouraged by gold and silver strikes), leaving the interstices to be filled in from the 1870s onwards. Settlement was encouraged by the sale of federal land for as little as $1.25 an acre. After the Homestead Act of 1862 lots of up to 160 acres could be acquired for nothing after 5 years of continuous residence. The human obstacle of the indigenous Amerindian population was overcome by ruthless expropriation and mass murder. By 1838 most of the remaining Indians from the east had been moved to the Indian territory of Oklahoma. In a series of wars (1861-68 and 1875-90) the

Left: Immigrants waiting for the ferry from Ellis Island to New York.

Below left: An Italian family arriving at Ellis Island, New York.

69 The industrial growth of the USA

Abundant mineral resources, a limitless supply of labour from the surplus populations of the Old World and great agricultural wealth, brought together by a transcontinental railway system completed in its essentials in the 1890s, made the United States the greatest industrial power in the world by the early twentieth century .

western tribes were subjugated and confined to reservations.

The growth of the USA's population was no less spectacular. The population was 3,929,000 in 1790; by 1830 it was 12,866,000; by 1880 it was 50,155,000; and 105,710,000 by 1920. Immigration rose to an annual average of over a million by the peak decade before 1914 (*see Map 57*). After 1881 the massive flow of 'new immigration' came from southern and eastern Europe. Within the country there was huge internal migration from east to west and from south to north. The overwhelming majority of the migrants settled in towns, so that the urban population of the USA, which was only 3.3% of the total in 1790, increased to 16% by 1860 and to 33% by 1900. By 1920 the majority of Americans lived in towns .

The transition from an agrarian to an urban vision of society was perhaps the most revolutionary change in the American consciousness. The

—— Main railroads by 1920	●	Automobiles and ancillary industries
▨ Iron ore fields	▲	Oil and gas
Main coal deposits	✳	Industrial conflicts
■ Centres of iron and steel production	→	Immigrant industrial workers from central, southern and south-eastern Europe
Textiles		

0   600 km
0   400 miles

Civil War of 1861-65, in which eleven southern states attempted to secede from the Union and form a separate 'Confederacy', was in essence a conflict between a traditional agrarian society and a dynamic industrial community. Slavery was not really the issue: emancipation was more a consequence than a cause of the war. At first President Abraham Lincoln, the leader of the northern states, stressed that he did not seek to abolish slavery in the south. But he insisted that he was under solemn oath to 'preserve, protect, and defend' the Union. Only in January 1863 did he issue the Proclamation of Emancipation. The defeat of the Confederacy in April 1865 came five days before the assassination of Lincoln. The Civil War was the costliest in American history, leaving over 600,000 dead, but it welded the nation together indissolubly and helped to determine the direction of American social and economic development. The abolition of slavery, confirmed by the northern victory, brought new forms of economic exploitation and misery to the freed slaves from which their descendants began to escape only after the 1930s when large-scale negro migration to the north began. But the war destroyed the power of 'King Cotton'. As Arthur M. Schlesinger Sr. wrote: 'The collapse of plantation capitalism signalized the rise of industrial capitalism.'

The industrialization of the USA (*see Map 69*) was based on a perpetually replenished pool of immigrant labour, on the discovery and exploitation of the continent's tremendous concentration of natural resources, on the development of a sophisticated system of communications, and on the rapid application to industry of technological innovations by dynamic and ruthless entrepre-

MAP 69 THE INDUSTRIAL GROWTH OF THE USA

United States production as percentage of that of the European powers (Great Britain, France, Germany and Austria-Hungary)

neurs. Between 1860 and 1890 coal production increased more than tenfold and iron production nearly elevenfold. By 1910 US production of iron and steel exceeded that of Britain, France, Germany, and Austria-Hungary put together and by the 1920s the USA produced (and consumed) about three-quarters of the world's oil. New industries rose in the early twentieth century, most notably automobile manufacture. The mass production of motor cars, pioneered by Henry Ford, transformed American (and eventually world) society as well as the economy: the 'assembly line' became the characteristic form of factory organization. The stream of immigrant labour for long hampered the growth of effective labour unions in the USA. Resentment of the activities of the 'robber barons' (magnates of railroads, oil, steel, meat-packing and high finance) and fear of the trend towards economic concentration in 'trusts' and combines led to sporadic industrial unrest, sometimes violent. But labour union membership and power remained much weaker than in many other industrial countries. Nevertheless, an inchoate but widespread desire to tame 'big business' and to humanize untrammelled capitalism helped give rise to the Progressive movement which dominated American politics in the early twentieth century. As the USA emerged as the world's greatest economic power she took a more outward-looking and expansive role in world affairs. As a result of victory in the Spanish-American War (1898), she acquired Cuba, Hawaii, and the Philippines (see Map 85). Having thus joined the ranks of imperial powers the USA became, particularly under Presidents Theodore Roosevelt (1901-9) and Woodrow Wilson (1913-21), a major actor in international diplomacy.

Although Russia, unlike the USA, was already a major power in the early nineteenth century, her development lagged far behind that of America. Indeed, a sense of 'backwardness' and of social and cultural inferiority haunted many Russian thinkers and politicians in the nineteenth century, and contrasted markedly with the thrusting self-confidence of maturing American capitalism. From the 1840s onwards Russian social thought was dominated by the debate between the 'Slavophiles', who believed that Russia's salvation lay in a return to her Orthodox religious traditions, and 'Westernizers', such

as Belinsky and Herzen, who attacked religion and adopted many of the liberal and radical ideas of western Europe. The absence in Russia of a substantial mercantile and industrial bourgeoisie, however, prevented liberalism from becoming a major force in Russian politics. The autocracy, until its demise in 1917, consequently played a much more central and directing role in social and economic development than did governments in most other major countries (see Map 71).

More than anything else it was the overwhelming agrarian problem which dominated economic and political discussion in Russia. In 1861 the 'Tsar-Liberator', Alexander II, promulgated the emancipation of the serfs. But Alexander's emancipation decree, as much a symbolic watershed as Lincoln's, proved as much a disappointment. The peasants remained burdened by the large redemption payments which they were compelled to make for their lands. The communal system of tenure tied the peasant to the land and perpetuated primitive techniques of cultivation. By the end of the century the rapid rise in the rural population of European Russia from fifty million in the early 1860s to eighty-two million by 1897 had produced a crisis of rural over-population (see Map 57). The establishment of a Peasant Land Bank in 1882 and the encouragement of emigration to the virgin lands of Siberia (to which some three million peasants had moved by 1914) hardly touched the surface of the problem (Map 70). The legislation inspired by P. A. Stolypin between 1906 and 1911 represented the most serious effort by the tsarist regime to come to grips with the agrarian problem. Stolypin announced that he proposed to back 'the sound and the strong'. His legislation was designed to encourage a shift from communal to private

tenure, the consolidation of land into compact units, the movement of surplus population from the country to the towns, the promotion of more advanced techniques of cultivation, and the creation of a surplus of agrarian income, beyond bare subsistence, to create a market in the country for the manufactured products of the towns. Significant progress had been achieved by 1914 but war, revolution, and civil war led to a collapse of the rural economy (see Map 76). The Bolshevik Revolution of 1917 made the peasants proprietors of the land, but only in the late 1920s did agricultural

Above: Prisoners building a railway near Nertschinsk in Siberia, 1898.

70 Russian expansion into Asia
In the nineteenth century the long expansion of Russia into Asia, in quickening pursuit of land, minerals and icefree ports, brought her into conflict with the Middle Eastern and Asian interests of the European powers, and eventually with Japan. Behind the moving frontier colonization by migrants from European Russia steadily encroached upon the nomadic peoples.

production again reach pre-war levels. Stalin's programme forced collectivization after 1929, accompanied by mass murder of recalcitrants, plunged Russian agriculture once again into chaos. Russian agricultural productivity remained far behind that of western Europe and North America, and Russia, an exporter of grain before the revolution, was compelled in the 1970s to import large quantities of grain from her capitalist rivals, the USA and Canada.

Russian industrial development was far more impressive and was indeed the foundation of her emergence as a 'super-power'. Throughout the nineteenth century, Russian industry remained primitive and expansion slow. Only towards the end of the century was there really significant development and growth. Russian industrialization was characterized by a very high reliance on foreign (particularly French) capital, by a stress on mining and metallurgy, by concentration in large units of production, and by heavy state involvement in industrial development. All of these characteristics except the first endured into the post-revolutionary period (Map 71). The foremost exponent of industrialization under the old regime was S. Y. Witte who presided over economic policy for most of the period between 1892 and 1906. These were years of very swift economic expansion, with an average annual growth rate in the 1890s of 8%. A renewed surge of growth took place between 1906 and 1913. The dislocations of war between 1914 and 1921 were catastrophic for Russian industry. 'War communism' between 1918 and 1921 brought overnight nationalization, attempts to introduce workers' control, and near-total economic collapse. The 'New Economic

MAP 70 RUSSIAN EXPANSION INTO ASIA

The modernization of Japan, like that of Russia, was closely bound up with her relationship with the rest of the world. Until the mid-nineteenth century Japan had kept herself largely insulated from contact with other powers. But in 1853 an American naval squadron under Commodore Perry visited Japan. This marked the start of the opening of Japan to foreign trade and foreign influences (*see Map 64*). In 1858 Russia, Britain, the USA and France imposed 'unequal treaties' on Japan which, although much resented by the Japanese, confirmed foreign influence in the country.

Policy' (NEP) after 1921 permitted a limited return to capitalism, and by 1929 industrial production had surpassed the pre-war level. The 'five-year plan' instituted by Stalin in 1929 marked the beginning of the most intensive period of industrial expansion – particularly striking because it took place against a background of economic depression in the capitalist world (*Map 78*). Although official Soviet figures are dubious there is no question that during this period Russia was ruthlessly propelled into the front ranks of industrial producers. The progress continued after the Second World War, and between 1950 and 1980 the Soviet economy grew from about one-third to more than two-thirds the size of that of the USA. However, much of Soviet industry remained relatively primitive, and it was notable that in the 1960s Russia once again began to rely on large-scale imports of foreign capital and advanced western technology.

The eastward territorial expansion of Russia in the nineteenth century (*see Map 70*) was no less impressive than that of the USA to the west. But Russian imperialism encountered serious internal and external difficulties. The empire contained vast numbers of non-Russian subject nationalities, many (in the east) educationally and socially backward, others (in the west) relatively advanced, most resentful of Russification and highly nation-

alistic. The Jews, confined to the so-called 'Pale of Settlement' (*see Map 60*), were particularly prominent in the revolutionary socialist movement which grew rapidly after the 1890s. Defeat by Japan in 1904-5 (*Map 73*) was the catalyst for revolution in 1905, which came close to toppling the regime. The concession of a Duma (Parliament) in 1905 was soon whittled away by the autocracy which retreated into hidebound conservatism. The liberal-democratic interlude of the February Revolution in 1917 gave way by October to a 'proletarian dictatorship' which by the late 1920s had degenerated into an autocracy far more brutal than that of the tsars.

Top: Forced labour in Siberia.

Above: Widows and orphans at a mass grave following the goldminers' rebellion and ensuing Lena Goldfields Massacres in Siberia (1912).

71 The emergence of modern Russia

After the checks imposed by war and revolution the industrialization of Russia, which had progressed very rapidly from the 1890s to 1914, was resumed with the first five-year plan in 1929. At the same time the beginning of forced collectivization – reversing the movement towards individual peasant proprietorship in the decades immediately before and after the revolution – further depressed the low levels of agricultural productivity which dogged both the old and the new regime.

Isolation from the outside world had not preserved Japan from change. The Tokugawa peace tightly controlled the *daimyo* and their families, and drew the samurai to the courts of their lords. The unintended consequence was the creation of a class of idle and status-conscious consumers which stimulated dramatic urban expansion and a rapid growth of population. By the eighteenth century Edo had more than a million inhabitants, Osaka and Kyoto four hundred thousand each, and four million Japanese, perhaps 15% of the population, lived in cities. Their needs were

supplied by a panoply of trades and crafts, among which textiles, notably silk, and mining and metal work of every kind were particularly thriving. The buying and selling, investing, transporting and brokering which all this demanded nourished effective communications, widespread literacy and numeracy, and a vigorous and sophisticated merchant class. The intensification of agriculture necessary to feed such a rapidly-growing, non-productive population led to substantial gains in efficiency, including the training of much of the work force in disciplines not (it has been argued)

72 The modernization of Japan
The Meiji restoration of 1868 ended the traditional seclusion of Japan and returned power to the imperial government. A deliberate programme of westernization in government and society was accompanied by a state-directed transformation of the economy to make Japan a modern industrial power.

73 The Far East around 1900
After defeating China in the war of 1894-5 Japan competed with the western powers and Russia in a 'scramble for China' which the imperial government, paralysed by corruption and internal dissension, was powerless to resist. Japan confirmed its new status as a world power by overwhelming Russia in the war of 1904-5.

MAP 71 THE EMERGENCE OF MODERN RUSSIA

	Urban population:		
Tundra		Novosi	New town founded before 1917
Coniferous forest	1885 1939	Kemer	New town founded 1917-1940
Mountain forest	• • under 100,000	——	Railways constructed by 1860
Mountain meadow	● ○ over 100,000	——	Railways constructed by 1917
Steppe	■ ◎ over 500,000	- - - -	Major lines added by 1940
Desert and semi-desert	□ over 1,000,000		

Main area of forcible collectivisation 1928-38
▲ Tsarist prisons
Tsarist exile areas
⊙ Labour camps and camp complexes operating in 1930's
White Sea Canal (1931-33)

0 _____ 1000 km
0 _____ 600 miles

MAP 72 THE MODERNIZATION OF JAPAN

National capital
Old imperial capital
Metropolitan prefecture
Prefectural capitals (1890)
Government railways completed by 1907
Private railways completed by 1907
Major factories and mines founded by the government:
Mine: **C** Coal, **G** Gold, **S** Silver
Shipbuilding
Textiles
Other industries

Percentage growth in number of factories employing
more than ten people 1887-1907:

growth of 30% and over
growth of 10-29%
growth of less than 10%

0   300 km
0   200 miles

Sakhalin
(to Japan 1905)

Hokkaido

Sapporo C Horonai

Aomori
Kosaka
Okuzu
Akita Ani Morioka
Kamaishi
Innai
Aburato
Yamagata
Sado Sendai
G Niigata Fukushima

Sea of Japan

Kanazawa Toyama Nagano Utsunomiya
Maebashi
Fukui Tomioka Mito
Shimmachi
Urawa
Matsue Tokyo
Tottori Gifu Chiba
Ikuno Kofu Yokohama
S Qtsu Yokosuka
Kyoto
Okayama Kobe **Nagoya**
Kurashiki Hyogo Nara Aichi Shizuoka
Osaka Tsu
Hiroshima Sakai
Yamaguchi Takamatsu Wakayama
Tokushima

Pacific Ocean

Senju
Fukagawa
Ishikawajima
Shinagawa

Fukuoka Matasuyama
Saga Oita
Mike Kochi
Nagasaki C *Shikoku*
Takashima Kumamoto
C *Kyushu*

Miyazaki
Kagoshima

Continuation southwards

Ryukyu Is.

Naha *Okinawa*

MAP 73 THE FAR EAST AROUND 1900

RUSSIA

OUTER MONGOLIA

Gobi

INNER MONGOLIA

Manchouli —R—

Chinese Eastern Rly

MANCHURIA

Trans-Siberian Rly

Amur

SAKHALIN

Ha-erh-pin

—R— Suifenho

Ch'ang-ch'un
South
Manchurian
Rly.

Chi-lin
Hun-ch'un
Vladivostok

Mukden

Sea of
Japan

Chinwangtao
Peking

Tan-tung

JAPAN

C H I N A

Huang ho

T'ien-chin

Dairen
Port Arthur
(Japanese in 1905)

KOREA

Seoul

Wei-hai-wei
(Lease Britain)
Chaio-chou and
Ch'ing-tao
(Lease-Germany)

Pusan

Tokyo

BE

Chen-chiang
Nanking
Han-k'ou

Su-chou
Shang-hai

Ichang
Sha-shih

Yangtze

Hang-chou

East
China
Sea

Chung-ch'ing

Yo-chou

Ch'ang-sha

San-tu-ao

INDIA

Tengyueh
Kun-ming

Yangtze

Hsi-chiang

Wu-chou

Tai-wan

BURMA
Szemao

Nan-ning
Samshui
Kongmoon

Canton
HONG KONG
Kowloon
New Territories
(New Territories on lease)

Irrawaddy

Hanoi

LAOS

Kuang-chou
(Lease-France)

Rangoon

Mekong

SIAM

ANNAM

Bangkok

CAMBODIA

Saigon

Manila

PHILIPPINES

South
China
Sea

Pacific Ocean

MALAYA

BRUNEI

NORTH
BORNEO

SARAWAK

Singapore

BORNEO

CELEBES

NEW GUINEA

SUMATRA

Batavia

JAVA

TIMOR

Arafura Sea

Indian
Ocean

AUSTRALIA

Legend

	Areas under Russian influence
—R—	Russian administered railway
	Japanese territory gained in 1895
	Japanese territory gained in 1905
	Japanese territory annexed in 1910
	Areas under Japanese influence
—J—	Japanese administered railway
	British territory
	Areas under British influence
—B—	British administered railway
	German territory
	Areas under German influence
—G—	German administered railway
—BE—	Belgian administered railway
	French territory
	Area under French influence
—F—	French administered railway
	U.S. territory annexed 1898
	Netherlands territory
	Portuguese territory
●	Treaty ports opened between 1890 and 1914

0 ___ 1000 km
0 ___ 600 miles

unlike those which would be required by an industrializing economy.

Although the boom in population seems to have levelled off after about 1700 it left a society which was, by current world standards, not only prosperous and firmly governed but highly urbanized and commercialized, with a capable and self-confident managerial élite and a skilled, diverse and well educated work force. On the other hand, since the social values and pretensions of the redundant warrior aristocracy remained intact while their real importance declined along with the value of their incomes, which were fixed in rice, the widening discrepancy between the real and theoretical power and status of different groups in society engendered growing tension and impatience with the political stalemate which the regime so determinedly maintained. Perry's brusque demonstration of modern military power and the diplomatic reverses of the following years pointed irresistably to the conclusion that for Japan the alternative to change was the fate of China.

The modern history of Japan is generally seen as dating from 1868 when the Tokugawa shogunate ended and authority reverted to the young Meiji emperor. The 'Meiji Restoration' began with an explicit statement of receptiveness to foreign ideas pronounced in the emperor's 'Charter Oath': 'Knowledge', he declared, 'shall be sought from all over the world and thus shall be strengthened the foundations of the imperial polity.' There followed soon afterwards the abolition of feudalism, the surrender of fiefs into the hands of the Emperor clearing the way for the establishment of bureaucratic government in the western manner. A centralized system of coinage and taxation was set up. After a short interval local government was placed in the hands of prefects appointed in Tokyo (as Edo had been renamed). Banks and railways, postal and telegraph services, newspapers and printing presses, were rapidly introduced. The early years of modernization bore heavily on the peasantry as rents remained high and the cost of

living rose, and on the many thousands of samurai who could not find a place for themselves in the new world. Widespread revolts, culminating in the savage Satsuma rebellion of 1877, were suppressed, and the government continued a wide-ranging programme of modernizing reforms. In 1885 a cabinet system of government was established, and in 1889 a westward-looking constitution was adopted; this led to the convening of a legislative assembly in 1890. The legal codes were revised, occidental fashions in ideas, clothes, and food spread, and the foundations of a mass education system were laid. By 1905 over 90% of children attended primary schools. Secondary and higher education (particularly technical colleges) developed rapidly after the turn of the century. A modern army and navy were established.

The basis for these reforms was the transformation of the economy of Japan. Industrialization, in which the government played a major role, was concentrated particularly in strategic industries such as munitions and ship-building and in textiles (*see Map 72*). There was a twentyfold expansion in the export of finished goods between 1868 and 1897. The late 1890s and the years after 1895 were boom periods; the outbreak of the First World War led to greatly increased demand for Japanese goods, and the period 1915-20 saw a huge spurt forward. Between 1900 and the late 1930s output of manufactured goods increased more than twelvefold. By 1936 Japan had overtaken Britain as the world's leading exporter of cotton piece goods. By the late 1930s Japan had developed what was in many ways a mature and diversified industrial economy. Industrialization naturally led to rapid urbanization: whereas in 1895 only 12% of the population lived in towns, by the mid-1930s the urban population had increased to 45% of the total. But the Japanese economy had certain weaknesses. On the one hand there were large numbers of small, relatively primitive units of production; on the other, there developed the *zaibatsu*, massive industrial conglomerates, of which the most

important in the 1920s and 1930s were Mitsui and Mitsubishi, which were probably the two largest private economic empires in the world. The zaibatsu, by means of corruption and other forms of covert control, exercised a generally baneful influence over Japanese politics and society. But the most serious weakness of the Japanese economy was her increasing dependence on imported raw materials: by 1930 she was a net importer of coal, and depended on imports for 85% of her iron and steel, 79% of her oil, and a large part of her food. The desire to break out of this apparent stranglehold helped to strengthen imperialist elements in Japan.

Japanese imperialism was in large measure a response to the imperialism of western powers. It began in the 1870s with the incorporation of the Ryuku Islands into Japan and the imposition of an 'unequal treaty' on Korea (*see Map 73*). Rivalry with China in Korea was largely responsible for the outbreak of the Sino-Japanese War in 1895 in which Japan won a stunnng victory. But pressure from Russia, France, and Germany compelled Japan to yield up her claim to have won Port Arthur and the Liaotung Peninsula. The seizure of the peninsula by Russia only three years later aroused strong Japanese animosity, and the conclusion of the alliance with Britain in 1902 placed Japan in a position to confront Russia without fear of intervention. In 1904 she attacked Russia, won another startling victory, and regained the leasehold of the Liaotung Peninsula, and control of south Sakhalin and the Russian-built railways in southern Manchuria. Russia further recognized Japanese paramountcy in Korea, and by 1910 Japan felt strong enough to annex Korea outright.

The emergence of the USA, Russia, and Japan as powers of the first rank was, therefore, already far advanced by 1914 when there began the series of cataclysmic shocks which, within little more than a generation, was to shatter the old European-dominated world order.

Above: The first Japanese diplomatic delegation in Paris, 1862.

74 European imperialism in Africa
The partition of Africa in the 'scramble' ot 1880-1914 was less a development of earlier activity there than an extension of the rivalries of the Great Powers in Europe. The new political geography had little correspondence with African reality; nevertheless it largely survived the decolonization of the 1950s, 60s and 70s.

Further reading: Hugh Brogan, *History of the United States of America* (Longman 1985; Viking Penguin); Richard Hofstader, *The Age of Reform* (Random House 1955; Cape); Hugh Seton-Watson, *The Russian Empire 1801-1917* (Oxford U P); L. Kochan and R. Abraham, *The Making of Modern Russia* (second ed. Penguin 1983); Jack Gray, *Rebellions and Revolutions: China from the 1800s to the 1980s* (Oxford U.P. 1990); Richard Storry, *A History of Modern Japan* (Penguin 1982 edn.).

MAP 74 EUROPEAN IMPERIALISM IN AFRICA

Madeira **1418**
Tangier
SPANISH MOROCCO **1912**
Oran
Algiers
Tunis
Malta **1815** (1964)
TUNISIA (1956)
Tripoli
1881
Benghazi
Mediterranean Sea
Casablanca
Fez
Marrakesh **1912** (1956)
Agadir
MOROCCO
Atlas Mts.
Canary Is. **1496**
IFNI **1860**
SPANISH SAHARA **1912**
RIO DE ORO **1884**
1893 (1960)
MAURETANIA
(1960)
FRENCH SUDAN
Timbuktu
1893/1904
Louis / Senegal
SENEGAL **1637** **1889** (1960)
...BIA **3**
...UGUESE ...INEA **1886** (1958)
SIERRA LEONE **1861** (1961)
Freetown **1787**
LIBERIA
Monrovia (1847)
UPPER VOLTA **1896** (1960)
IVORY COAST **1842/82** (1960)
GOLD COAST **1820/74** (1957)
DAHOMEY **1851/93** TOGOLAND **1894** (1960)
Bingerville
Accra
Lomé Porto Novo (1960)
Lagos
1483 (1975)
Principé
São Tomé
Annobon **1778**
FRENCH WEST AFRICA
1899/1912 (1960)
NIGER
(1960)
CHAD **1884**
Fort Lamy
NIGERIA **1861/1900** (1960)
Benue
KAMERUN **1884** (1960)
Douala
Fernando Póo
RIO MUNI
GABON **1884** (1960)
MIDDLE CONGO
Brazzaville
1843 (1968)
L. Chad
Sahara
FR. EQUATORIAL AFRICA
UBANGI SHARI **1884** (1960)
Ubang...
Congo
Kasai
Leopoldville
Cabinda
Luanda
Atlantic Ocean
BELGIAN CONGO **1885/1908** (1960)
Stanleyville
L. Albert
L. Rudolf
UGANDA **1890/94** (1962)
RUANDA URUNDI (1962) (1962)
L. Victoria
Mwanza
Ujiji
Tabora
GERMAN EAST AFRICA **1890** (1961)
Dar es Salaam
Tanga
Pemba I.
Mombasa
Nairobi
EAST AFRICA **1888** (1963)
Equator
Alexandria
Port Said
Suez Canal (opened 1869)
Cairo
Suez
EGYPT (Br. occ. 1882) (1922)
Libyan Desert
LIBYA **1911**
Marzuk (1951)
(Br. and Fr. administration, 1941-51)
Red Sea
Khartoum
Omdurman **1898**
Blue Nile
White Nile
SUDAN (Anglo-Egyptian Condominium 1899) (1956)
Fashoda
The Sudd
(Br. administration, 1941-52)
Asmara
ERITREA **1889**
Adewa **1896** X
L. Tana Gondar
Addis Ababa
ABYSSINIA (It. occ. 1935-41)
Djibouti (1960)
Berbera
Harar
BR. SOMALILAND **1884**
ITALIAN SOMALILAND **1889** (1960)
Mogadishu
Indian Ocean
Zanzibar **1890** (1963)
Aldabra Is.
Comoro Is. **1841/86** (1975)
MADAGASCAR **1885/1896** (1960)
Tananarive
Diégo Suare...
Fort Dauphin
ANGOLA **1885/1905** (1975)
Benguela
Moçâmedes
1884 SOUTH-WEST AFRICA **1885** (1966)
Windhoek
Walvis Bay (S.A. 1910-1910)
Kalahari Desert
BECHUANALAND
Elisabethville
NORTHERN RHODESIA **1891**
Lusaka
Zambezi
Blantyre
SOUTHERN RHODESIA **1888** (Auton. 1923)
Salisbury
L. Nyasa
NYASALAND (1964)
1891 (1964)
MOZAMBIQUE
Mocambique
Beira
L. Tanganyika
(1980)
1891 (1975)
Capriv Strip
Limpopo
Mafeking **1899 1900**
Pretoria
SWAZILAND **1903** (1968)
Johannesburg
Vereeniging
Vaal
Blood River **1839**
Isandhlwana **1879**
Ulundi **1879**
Rorke's Drift **1879**
Majuba Hill **1881**
Bloemfontein
Kimberley **1899-1900**
Ladysmith **1899/1900**
Pietermaritzburg
BASUTO-LAND
Orange
1868 (1966)
Durban
UNION OF SOUTH AFRICA
Cape Town
1814/1902 (1910)
East London
Port Elizabeth
Lourenço Marques

Legend:
- - - - Borders in 1914
X Battle   ⚔ Siege
〰 Railways c. 1914
1884 Date of imperial acquisition
Belgian territory in 1914
British territory " "
French territory " "
German territory " "
Italian territory " "
Portuguese territory " "
Spanish territory " "
Independent states in 1914
◗ Europeans under 1% of population 1939
◖ Europeans 1%-5% of population 1939
◑ Europeans 5%-10% of population 1939
● Europeans over 10% of population 1939
── Borders in 1987
(1958) Date of independence in colour of last ruling colonial power
0   1500 kms
0   1000 miles

139

The emergence of the modern world 2

The outbreak of the First World War in August 1914 may be explained as first and foremost the product of a German bid for world power.

The immense growth of German industrial and military might since 1871 (*see Map 57*) had nourished the development of dynamic political ambitions for a German-dominated 'Mitteleuropa', a colonial empire including a German 'Mittelafrika' (*see Map 74*), and the permanent subjugation of all Germany's potential European rivals. Underlying all this was hatred of the Slavs, fear of 'encirclement' by the Triple Entente, and resentment of Britain's empire, of her navy, and of her dominance of world trade and of the international capital market (*Map 67*). The German government intended, by means of a war, to establish the Reich as a superpower on a par with Britain. By 1914 the Germans, conscious that they would have to fight in both the east and west, and aware of Russia's programme of military modernization, felt it was 'now or never'. The opportunity came in June with the assassination by Serbs of the Austrian Archduke Franz Ferdinand in Sarajevo. Austria, encouraged by Germany, sent Serbia an ultimatum designed to be so harsh as to ensure rejection. The Serbs, although they were fired by a burning Slav nationalism, and were confident of Russian support, accepted nearly all Austria's demands. But the Austrians, under German influence, nevertheless declared war on Serbia. Russia's immediate decision to mobilize dispelled any prospect of localization of the conflict, and Germany quickly declared war on Russia and France. German violation of Belgian neutrality led Britain to join Russia and France. The Ottoman Empire, fearing partition by the Entente powers, allied itself with Germany. The Entente powers were joined by Japan in August 1914, and by Italy in May 1915, and, after German U-boat (submarine) attacks on merchant shipping, by the USA in April 1917.

The First World War was more catastrophic in its impact on nearly every sphere of human activity

Map legend

Allies	Borders in 1914
Central Powers	Furthest lines of Allied advance
Neutrals	Furthest lines of Central Powers' advance
(1915) Neutrals later joining Allies	Allied convey routes
(1914) Neutrals later joining Central Powers	★ Naval engagements

0   600km
0   400 miles

than any previous war. Although some fighting occurred in Asia and Africa and at sea, the conflict was at its most intense in Europe (*Map 75*). Relying on the pre-war Schlieffen plan, the Germans launched a sweeping thrust through Belgium into France, hoping to knock her out in six weeks, thus enabling Germany to turn her full strength against Russia. However the German army was halted at the River Marne, and the war in the west settled down to static trench warfare for four years, leaving millions of German, French and British dead. In the east the conflict was more mobile but no less bloody. With the issue unresolved on the two central fronts both sides sought alternative strategies. But neither the British landing at Gallipoli in 1915-16 nor the German attempt to starve Britain into surrender by blockade was successful in breaking the impasse.

In its military character (although not its scale) the war was in general fought by traditional means, the key elements being infantry, cavalry, and artillery. But the war boosted technological innovation, and the appearance of tanks and warplanes, although in limited numbers, was a portent of the revolution in warfare of the mid-twentieth century. In most belligerent countries, particularly in Europe, the war had a shattering impact on society, economy, and government. Conscription, food shortages, attacks on civilian populations, war propaganda and hysteria were nothing new in human warfare. But what rendered this perhaps the first 'total war' in history was the vast expansion in the role of government in directing social and economic organization: *laissez-faire* was dead.

By late 1917 Germany had won the war in the east and in March 1918 imposed the draconian Treaty of Brest-Litovsk on Russia (*Map 76*). But although Germany was now free to concentrate on the western front, the entry of the USA to the war, with its huge reservoir of manpower and resources, ensured an eventual Allied victory. By late 1918 a final German push in the west had failed, her allies Austria-Hungary and Turkey had collapsed, and revolution had broken out in Germany. Although no enemy armies were yet on German soil, an armistice took effect on November 11 1918.

The war had convulsive effects on the old empires. In Russia the Tsar abdicated after a liberal revolution in March 1917 (the February Revolution after the Old Style calendar then still used in Russia). The new Provisional Government determined to keep Russia in the war, but it was discredited and demoralized by continuing defeat, desertion, and dislocation, and by a rising demand for peace. The ascent to power of Lenin's Bolsheviks (the extreme left wing of the Russian Social Democratic Party) in November 1917 (the 'October Revolution') was founded on his promise of 'peace, bread, and land.' Although defeated in elections in December 1917, and forced to surrender large areas in the west to the Germans at Brest-Litovsk, the Bolsheviks clung to power and by 1921 had defeated both their internal enemies and interventionist armies of capitalist powers. In the last days of the war the German and Austrian emperors were swept off their thrones by revolution. Short-lived socialist republics in eastern and central Europe soon collapsed, however, leaving Russia for the next quarter-century as the sole exemplar of a communist state. Perhaps the most momentous of the anti-imperial revolutions was that of Mustafa Kemal (later known as Ataturk). From 1919 onwards he drove Greek forces out of Asia Minor, to be followed by the enforced exodus of the ancient Greek communities of the Black Sea and Aegean littorals (*Map 5*). He expelled all occupying forces, reversed the imposed peace treaty, deposed the Sultan, and pronounced the end of the Islamic Caliphate (symbol of Islamic political unity since the death of the Prophet). Ataturk

MAP 75 THE FIRST WORLD WAR

The Western Front 1914-18

- Furthest German advance 1914
- Furthest German advance 1918
- Trench warfare 1914-17
- Siegfried Line March 1917
- Armistice line 11 Nov 1918

0   150km
0   100miles

Opposite page above: The landscapes of Europe, as well as human beings, were devastated by heavy shelling shown in this picture of a woodland battleground in France.

75 The First World War
The supremacy of defensive over offensive techniques made the Great War one of relatively little movement, especially on the Western Front, and enormous casualties, engaging armies many times larger than ever before. The resources of the belligerent powers were deployed and their civilian populations involved to a quite unprecedented degree, making this the first 'total' war.

consolidated Turkey as a national state, and propelled her on a path of modernization which was to inspire a later generation of post-colonial politicians in Asia and Africa.

Allied war aims, as enunciated in the American President Wilson's 'Fourteen Points', had presaged a relatively generous peace. In the event the treaties imposed on the defeated powers after a peace conference at Paris in 1919 humiliated the vanquished without in the long run benefiting the victors. Germany, convicted in the Treaty of Versailles of 'war guilt', was forced to cede territory in the east and the west, to pay massive reparations, and to constrict her armed strength within narrowly defined limits (*Map 77*). East Prussia was divided from the rest of Germany by a narrow strip of land gained by the new Polish state – the 'Polish corridor'. Austria, reduced to a German-speaking rump around Vienna, was barred from uniting with Germany. Hungary too was diminished to a small national state, losing two-thirds of her pre-war territory and population. The old empires were replaced by a patchwork of small 'successor states', formed in ostensible accordance with the principle of 'national self-determination'. But far from resolving national problems the new political structure in Europe aggravated them. All the new states contained substantial national minorities; the defeated powers resented the 'dictated peace' and itched to regain lost territories; the successor states lived in terror of the 'revisionist' ambitions of their former masters. Outside Europe too the peace treaties helped to stimulate local nationalisms. The Anglo French carve-up of the ex-Ottoman Fertile Crescent provoked Arab unrest. The Chinese, who had hoped that the 'Fourteen Points' would lead

MAP 76 REVOLUTION IN EUROPE

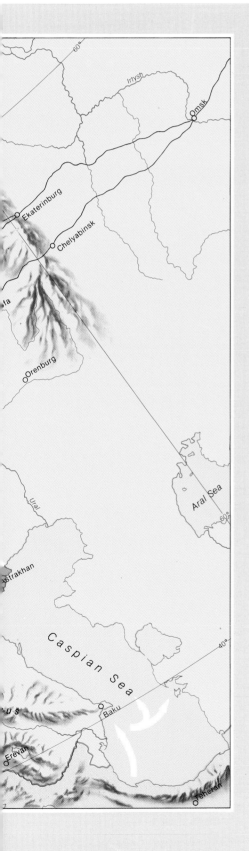

the western powers to treat them on a basis of equality, resented the transfer to Japan of former German territories in China. Wilson, disillusioned by the selfish aggrandizement of his allies, acceded to their demands in order to gain their acquiescence to the Covenant of the League of Nations, the world organization which he hoped would guarantee peace. However the League's prospects were gravely damaged by the US Senate's repudiation of the Charter. The USA remained outside the League and embarked on an 'isolationist' course for the next two decades.

The international economic order, shattered by the war, never fully recovered. Britain's former pre-eminence as a producing, trading, and investing centre was in tatters. In company with others Britain was humiliatingly obliged to 'renegotiate' her war debts to the USA. The victorious powers had hoped to finance their debt payments out of German reparations, but these were not forthcoming, and even the French occupation of the Ruhr in 1923 failed to secure payment on the desired massive scale. Germany, together with most of central and eastern Europe after the war, was gripped by hyperinflation which had profoundly unsettling social effects. During the middle and late 1920s a partial recovery of the international economy occurred. But the crash on the New York Stock Exchange in 1929 was the signal for descent into the most severe economic crisis of the century, by which only Soviet Russia and some undeveloped countries remained unafflicted (*Map 78*). Banks failed, stock markets collapsed, businesses were bankrupted, international trade slumped, demand for all types of goods plummeted, and further millions were thrown out of work. Everywhere confidence in liberal capitalism was shaken, and the general reaction was to resort to protectionist, beggar-my-neighbour policies with competitive devaluations and high tariff walls. The British, American, and French currencies were forced off the gold standard. Even Britain abandoned free trade in 1932. Some measure of recovery was achieved in the later 1930s, but a functioning international economic system was not resurrected. Meanwhile the insecurities induced by the Great Depression had helped to engender political deformations which wrecked the flimsy constructions of the peace treaties.

Economic recession and aggressive nationalism, heightened by frustration with the consequences of the peace treaties, led to the rise of violent authoritarian movements and their seizure of the reins of government. Demagogic militarist dictatorships became the order of the day. Mussolini's fascist movement in Italy, which took power in 1922, formed the prototype for such regimes, with its accent on brute force, national prestige, and imperial expansion, and its contempt for intellectuals and for parliamentary democracy. The insecure Weimar constitution in Germany was by 1933 reeling under the impact of economic collapse (with six million unemployed) and fierce rivalry between communists and socialists. In 1933, after emerging in free elections as the largest party in Germany, Hitler's National Socialists (Nazis) took power with the support of conservatives. A ruthless totalitarian state apparatus replaced the rickety Weimar structure: Jews, socialists, trade unionists and liberal intellectuals were attacked and placed in concentration camps, the *Reichstag* (Parliament)

was burned down, books were thrown on bonfires, and a pagan, racialist, anti-democractic ideology was inculcated by state propaganda. The economy was regenerated by massive expansion of the armaments industries. The bourgeois decencies of imperial and Weimar Germany gave way to the cult of 'blood and soil' and to hysterical mob adulation of the leader. Authoritarian regimes, often with a similar tinge, sprang up in much of Europe, notably in Spain after the bloody civil war of 1936-9 (*see Map 80*). In Soviet Russia too a savage despotism developed, with the usual apparatus of secret police, censorship, torture, prison camps, repression of all opposition, rule through a single party, and stress on economic self-sufficiency (*Map 71*). Stalin, who by the late 1920s had eliminated all potential rivals for power in the USSR, launched the country on a hectic course of heavy industrialization, collectivization of agriculture, and military reinforcement, accompanied by mass murder of kulaks (peasant proprietors), 'purges' of dissidents, and show trials. Japan, severely affected by the Depression, descended into the 'dark valley' of militarism. The efforts of the *Kuomintang* government of China to counter fragmentation into regional warlordism by unifying the country economically and politically evoked fears of a threat to Japanese economic interests and helped to stimulate Japanese expansionism into Manchuria and China (*Map 79*). On the other side of the Pacific also, democracy failed to withstand the impact of economic crisis, with dictators assuming power in Brazil and Argentina after military coups in 1930. Only in the states around the North Atlantic seaboard did liberal democracy survive in the late 1930s as the characteristic form of government, and even here economic enfeeblement, social malaise, and fear of war seemed to portend collapse in the face of totalitarian attack.

77 Central Europe between the wars
The peace treaties divided the old dynastic empires into what purported to be nation-states but in fact contained large national minorities. In consequence they engaged in continuous border disputes while living in perpetual dread that the defeated powers, Germany, Hungary and Bulgaria, would seek to overturn what they regarded as a dictated peace.

78 The Depression
The crash of the New York Stock Exchange in October 1929 was followed by the collapse of businesses and of financial confidence all over the developed world. While new industries developed in many regions the high unemployment and acute depression which followed, especially in areas dependent on traditional industries, imposed additional strains on democratic regimes, many of which failed to survive.

Further reading: B. H. Liddell Hart, *The First World War* (second ed. Cassell 1970); E. H. Carr, *The Russian Revolution from Lenin to Stalin* (Macmillan, 1979); J. K. Galbraith, *The Great Crash* (third edn. Houghton Mifflin 1972; Hamish Hamilton); A.J. Nicholls, *Weimar and the Rise of Hitler* (second edn. Macmillan 1979); A. Polonsky, *The Little Dictators* (Routledge 1975); Anthony Copley, *Ghandhi: Against the Tide* (Basil Blackwell 1987); Edgar Snow, *Red Star over China* (second edn. Gollancz 1968; Grove Weidenfeld).

76 Revolution in Europe
In the civil war which followed the Russian revolution of October 1917 the 'White' (anti-Bolshevik) forces were supported by the western powers, and especially by Poland which, its independence confirmed by the Congress of Versailles, sought territorial expansion. Elsewhere in Europe revolutionary outbreaks were widespread from the last months of the Great War, but were ultimately abortive.

MAP 77 CENTRAL EUROPE BETWEEN THE WARS

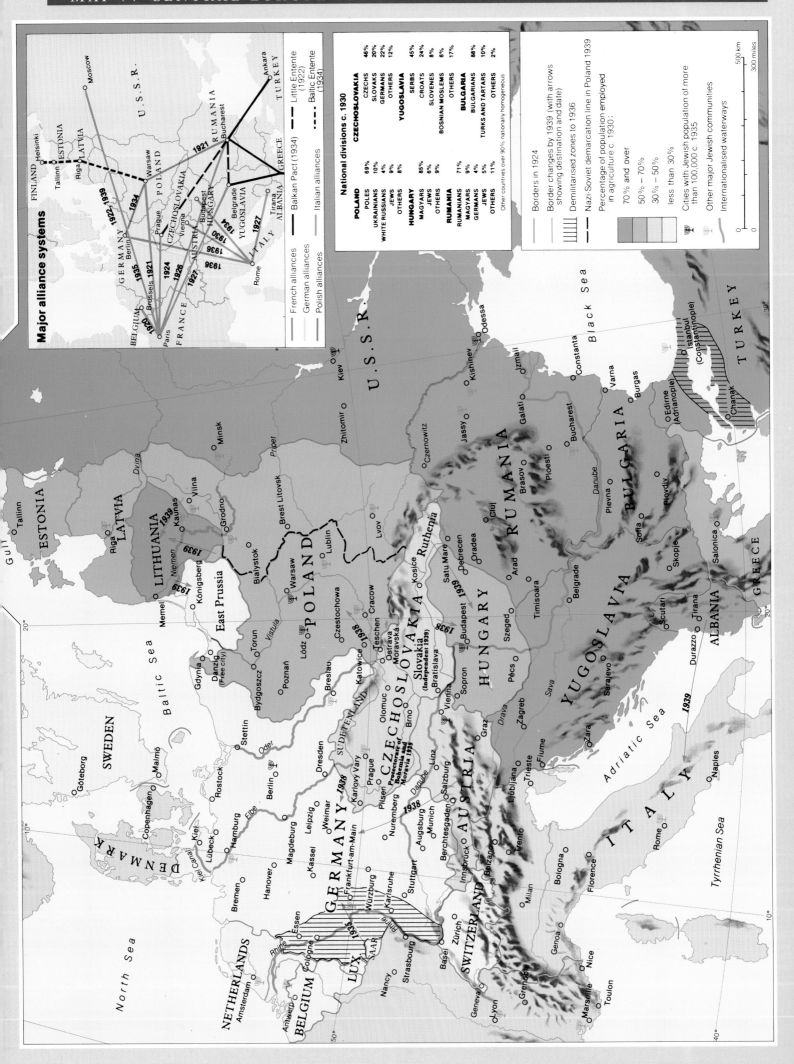

Major alliance systems

Little Entente (1922)
Baltic Entente (1934)
Balkan Pact (1934)
Italian alliances

French alliances
German alliances
Polish alliances

National divisions c. 1930

POLAND		
POLES	69%	
UKRAINIANS	10%	
WHITE RUSSIANS	4%	
JEWS	9%	
OTHERS	8%	

CZECHOSLOVAKIA		
CZECHS	46%	
SLOVAKS	20%	
GERMANS	22%	
OTHERS	12%	

HUNGARY		
MAGYARS	85%	
JEWS	6%	
OTHERS	9%	

YUGOSLAVIA		
SERBS	45%	
CROATS	24%	
SLOVENES	8%	
BOSNIAN MOSLEMS	6%	
OTHERS	17%	

RUMANIA		
RUMANIANS	71%	
MAGYARS	9%	
GERMANS	4%	
JEWS	5%	
OTHERS	11%	

BULGARIA		
BULGARIANS	88%	
TURKS AND TARTARS	10%	
OTHERS	2%	

Other countries over 90% nationally homogeneous

Borders in 1924

Border changes by 1939 (with arrows showing destination and date)

Demilitarised zones to 1936

Nazi-Soviet demarcation line in Poland 1939

Percentage of population employed in agriculture c. 1930:

70% and over
50% – 70%
30% – 50%
less than 30%

Cities with Jewish population of more than 100,000 c. 1935

Other major Jewish communities

Internationalised waterways

0   300 miles
0   500 km

144

MAP 78 THE DEPRESSION

North-Western states

Edmonton

Calgary

Seattle

Canadian Prairies

CANADA
9

Newfoundland

St. John's

Nova Scotia

Quebec

Halifax

Montreal

11904

10697

San Francisco

California

Los Angeles

1900

Kansas City

UNITED STATES
120

The 'Dust Bowl' states

Detroit

Chicago

New England

Boston

New York

Pittsburgh
Pittsburgh
Coalfield

Tennessee
Valley

Atlanta

Old Cotton Belt

Houston

New Orleans

Texas

Florida

Increase in industrial production 1929-32

Decline in industrial production between 1-30%

Decline in industrial production over 30%

Areas of economic revival

Areas of declining economic activity

Major migration routes of workers

1932
1928   1934   Registered unemployed (in thousands)

n.a.   No unemployment figures available

45   Population figures c.1931 (in millions)

Changes in Gross National Production, 1929-32: (1932 figure shown as a percentage of that of 1929)		
Canada	62·4%	
Czechoslovakia	89·6%	
France	89·9%	
Germany	80·8%	
Italy	94·8%	
Sweden	91·1%	
U.K.	94·5%	
U.S.A.	71·6%	

1932   1929

63   23

n.a.

FINLAND
3·5

97

24   22

SWEDEN
6

33   35

23

NORWAY
3

7

3   3

ESTONIA
1

15

5   5

LATVIA
2

126

256

342

2745

1217

2159

Glasgow

Newcastle

104

63

21

Belfast

Manchester

EIRE
3

UNITED
KINGDOM
45

Birmingham

28

Cardiff

London

337

349

271

126

57

97

332

2285

Hamburg

Berlin

Leipzig

Cologne

Lille

DENMARK
3·5

NETHERLANDS
8

BELGIUM
8

LUX.

2462

LITHUANIA
3

Danzig

554

677

POLAND
32

Cracow

Prague

39

66

GERMANY
66

310

288

156

CZECHOSLOVAKIA
14·5

151   57

HUNGARY
8·5

38

10   17

ROMANIA
18

Paris

308

376

15

FRANCE
42

54

8

65

SWITZ.

AUSTRIA
6·5

1006

Turin

324

963

ITALY
40

15

6   15

YUGOSLAVIA
14

22   33

n.a.

BULGARIA
6

ALBANIA
1

Naples

GREECE
6

33

n.a.   n.a.

PORTUGAL
6·5

SPAIN
23·5

The emergence of the modern world 3

The Second World War was more truly a global conflict than the first. In a sense it consisted of three wars, intertwined but distinct.

These centred around: the Japanese attempt to build an East Asian empire which brought her into conflict with China and the western powers which had interests in the area; the German ambition to dominate continental Europe (coupled with the Italian desire to render the Mediterranean an Italian lake) which led to war with Britain and France; and the German attack on the Soviet Union which made Russia the ally of Britain and the USA. The roots of the Far Eastern war lay in the aim of the Japanese militarists to establish a 'New Order in East Asia' – a sphere of Japanese paramountcy in which western interests would be eliminated, and economic resources exploited to Japan's exclusive benefit. The invasion of Manchuria in 1931 marked the beginning of the descent to war (*Map 79*). The League of Nations was a broken reed, unable to compel Japan to withdraw from Manchuria – although Japan withdrew from the League. A puppet state, Manchukuo, was erected under the nominal suzerainty of the last Chinese emperor, in reality under the supervision of Tokyo. Japan's twenty-year alliance with Britain had been permitted to lapse in 1922, and in 1936 Japan's new diplomatic alignment was sealed by the Anti-Comintern Pact with Nazi Germany.

The Japanese invasion of China in 1937 is sometimes held to mark the real beginning of the Second World War. However, the British Empire and the USA were not at this stage engaged, and Japan did not declare war on Britain upon the outbreak of the European war in September 1939, nor on the USSR after Hitler's attack in mid-1941. Nevertheless further Japanese incursions in China and French Indo-China provoked an American, British, and Dutch economic embargo which led to the fatal decision in December 1941 to attack the US naval base at Pearl Harbor (in Hawaii), thus drawing the USA into both the Pacific and the European wars.

The war in Europe also arose out of the bid for imperial aggrandizement of an authoritarian regime. Hitler's Nazi movement had cultivated the myth of the 'stab in the back' (the notion that Germany had not been militarily defeated by the Allies in 1918 but had been the victim of internal conspiracy by socialists and Jews). The Nazis had played on the widespread resentment in Germany of the punitive impositions of the Versailles Treaty. Massive rearmament in breach of the treaty was accompanied by the demand for *lebensraum* ('living-space'), revision of borders, and the inclusion within the fatherland of the substantial German minorities outside the Third Reich (*Map 77*). The remilitarization of the Rhineland (in further breach of the treaty) in March 1936 failed to evoke an effective response from Britain and France. In late 1936 Hitler and Mussolini allied in the so-called 'Rome-Berlin Axis'. Meanwhile Italian forces attacked the ancient and backward empire of Abyssinia (Ethiopia), providing a further demonstration of the ineffectualness of the League. Both Italy and Germany sent forces to aid the fascists in the Spanish Civil War, which was seen as an ideological and military testing-ground between 1936 and 1939. Russia sent some aid to the Spanish Republican government, but France (although ruled by a left-wing 'Popular Front' government) and Britain enunciated the doctrine of 'non-intervention', which effectively ensured a fascist victory.

The 'appeasement' policy of the democracies was the product of a profound horror of war on the part of a generation traumatized by the nightmare of 1914-18, compounded by the isolationism of the USA, the slowness to rearm of Britain, and the deep internal divisions in France. Moreover, the suggestion of an alliance with Bolshevik Russia was anathema to many conservatives. Hitler's annexation of Austria in 1938 (the *Anschluss*), and his demand for territorial concessions from Czechoslovakia brought matters to a head. At the Munich conference in September 1938, Britain and France avoided war by conceding Hitler's demands and permitting the emasculation of Czechoslovakia. Six months later the rump of Czechoslovakia was occupied by Germany, and Hitler turned his attention east towards Poland. Undeterred by a British guarantee to Poland, Hitler demanded the redress of various grievances concerning Danzig and the Polish corridor (Poland's link with the Baltic coast). In August 1939 he scored a diplomatic coup with the surprise conclusion of the Nazi-Soviet pact, under which Germany and Russia secretly agreed to a renewed partition of Poland. This was a *carte blanche* for the German attack on Poland on September 1 1939, which induced the British empire and France to declare war on Germany.

Germany conquered western Poland in a fortnight, and the USSR then occupied the eastern portion and later took the opportunity to attack Finland and swallow the Baltic republics of Latvia, Lithuania, and Estonia (*Map 81*). After September 1939 a period known as the 'phoney war' ensued, in which little fighting occurred and there was even the whisper of a negotiated peace. But in May 1940 Germany attacked the Low Countries and France, and in a spectacular seven-week '*Blitzkrieg*' won a smashing victory which made her the dominant power in Europe, and attracted Italy into the war as a junior ally eager to share the spoils.

Britain now stood alone under the inspiring leadership of Churchill, Prime Minister from May 1940. In the aerial 'Battle of Britain' the Royal Air Force prevented the Luftwaffe from gaining mastery of the skies, and thereby thwarted Hitler's cross-Channel invasion plans. Meanwhile the American President Roosevelt, although conscious of what was still a strongly isolationist mood in Congress and among public opinion, nudged the USA closer to war with the 'Lend-Lease' agreement, by which the USA agreed to 'lend' Britain fifty surplus destroyers in return for long-term 'leases' on bases in the Caribbean and western Atlantic (*Map 85*).

In April 1941 Germany moved into Yugoslavia and Greece in a campaign which, although it inflicted further painful humiliations on Hitler's enemies, delayed (and thereby gravely imperilled) his most ambitious, and ultimately fatal, gamble – the attack on the Soviet Union on June 22 1941. This turned Stalin into the involuntary ally of Churchill and Roosevelt and inaugurated the critical phase of the war.

Even more than the First World War this was 'total war' – more extensive in its scope, more intensive in its impact, producing breathtakingly rapid innovations in military technique, scientific invention, and economic and social organization. Unlike its predecessor the Second World War was

79 The Far East 1931-45
With the invasion of Manchuria in 1931 Japan, increasingly under the domination of its military leaders, and badly affected by the Depression, embarked upon a programme of military expansion designed to secure its domination of Asia and especially to eliminate western economic influence. The Far East consequently became a major theatre of the Second World War.

MAP 79   THE FAR EAST 1931-45

Japanese territory before Sept. 1931
Areas occupied by Japan, 1931-2
Areas occupied by Japan, 1933
Areas occupied by Japan 1937-41
Areas occupied by Japan, 1941-5
Railways under Japanese control before Oct. 1931
Areas of French Indo-China annexed by Thailand, 1940
Chinese People's Republic, 1937-45
Route of the Chinese Communists' Long March, 1934-5
Area under Soviet political influence
British colonial or Commonwealth territory not occupied by Japan
Netherlands colonial territory not occupied by Japan
Areas declared 'independent' under Japanese control
Anglo-American counter attacks   Atomic bombs
Main routes of Allied air attacks
Chinese counter attack
Soviet attacks

0 _____ 1000 kms
0 _____ 600 miles

U.S.S.R.
Sakhalin
8 Aug 1945
Kurile Is.
8 Aug 1945
Nomonhan May 1939
Amur
Empire of
MANCHURIA
8 Aug 1945
Ha-erh-bin
Manchukuo
Ch'ang-ch'un
Hokkaido
Gobi
Changkufeng July 1938
Vladivostok
8 Aug 1945
Pao-t'ou
Jehol
Mukden
J A P A N
Dairen
Port Arthur
Pyongyang
Sea of Japan
Honshu
Marco Polo Bridge July 1937
Peking
T'ien-chin
Huang-ho
Seoul
Tokyo
Hwang-ho
Ch'ing-tao
Hsin-hai-lien
Hiroshima
Yen-an
Hsi-an
Hsu-chou
CHINA
Huang-ho
Nanking
Nagasaki
Kyushu
Shikoku
East China Sea
Chung-ch'ing
Yangtze
Hang-chou
Shang-hai
Ryukyu Is.
Aug. 1945
INDIA
Ledo
Myitkyina
Imphal March July 1944
Burma Road
Kun-ming
Jui-chin
Fu-chou
Okinawa
1 April-22 June 1945
Ogasawara Is. (Japan)
Lashio
Mandalay
(Autonomous region)
TIBET
Hsi-chiang
Amoy
Iwo Jima
29 Feb 1945
BURMA (Br.)
May 1945
Irrawaddy
Canton
Swatow
T'ai-wan
1 Dec 1944
Rangoon
LAOS
Hanoi
Haiphong
Macao (Port.)
Hong Kong (Br.)
Mariana Is. (Japan)
Saipan
THAILAND
FRENCH INDO-CHINA
Hai-nan
South China Sea
9 Jan 1945
Tinian
15 June 1944
Bangkok
VIETNAM
Mekong
CAMBODIA
Phnom Penh
Saigon
Corregidor May 1942
Manila
PHILIPPINES (U.S.)
Pacific Ocean
Guam (U.S.)
21 July 1944
Kota Baharu
15 Dec 1945
Leyte
20 Nov 1944
Yap
Caroline Is. (Japan)
MALAYA (Br.)
Kuala Lumpur
10 June 1945
NORTH BORNEO (Br.)
BRUNEI (Br.)
1 May 1945
Palau Is.
Singapore
SARAWAK (Br.)
15 Sept 1944
Sumatra
Borneo
Morotai
Halmahera
22 April 1944
Celebes
Hollandia
New Guinea
PAPUA
Indian Ocean
Batavia
Java
NETHERLANDS INDIES
Seram
Timor (Port.)
Arafura Sea
Port Moresby
Darwin
AUSTRALIA

147

pre-eminently a war of movement in which the characteristic forms of locomotion were not infantry or cavalry but motorized armour and warplanes. Warfare in East Asia and Africa still provided some scope for human ingenuity in 'guerrilla' campaigns with only limited mechanization, but in general the capability to invent, construct, deploy and operate machines and sophisticated instruments became the determining element in the war. Britain and the USA in particular gained the edge in scientific warfare, most notably with their 'Manhattan Project' for the manufacture of the atomic bomb (in which they were greatly aided by

intellectual emigrants from Nazi Europe).

Remarkably, in spite of their authoritarian regimes, the Axis powers were less successful in gearing their economies to the requirements of total war. Germany sought to exploit the resources of occupied Europe to the full, but her ruthless 'New Order' in Europe did not succeed in creating a coherently integrated continental war economy. Even Germany attained her full productive capacity only in 1944. The Japanese 'Co-Prosperity Sphere' in East Asia (*Map 79*) embittered occupied populations and failed to produce vitally needed goods: by early 1943 Japan was losing ten times as

much shipping sunk as was being replaced by new building. In contrast the Allies not only succeeded in concentrating their productive efforts more intensively and rationally, but also pooled their (potentially far greater) resources in what was, particularly in the case of Britain and the USA, very intimate co-ordination. Indeed, although the Russians stood somewhat apart, the co-operation of the Allies in every sphere – economic, military, and diplomatic – contrasted tellingly with the wary suspiciousness of one another with which the Axis powers fought their separate wars. Beyond the battlefield, the factory, and the laboratory, the

MAP 80 FASCIST EUROPE

arena of conflict extended into men's minds. This was an ideological struggle in which the wireless, the printed word, and the cinema were potent weapons.

If the war stimulated sophisticated technological and scientific advances, it also discredited the outlook, hitherto widespread, which equated the material civilization of the white races with moral superiority. For the war was conducted with a ruthless ferocity and disregard of humane values which dwarfed the horrors of all previous conflicts. Civilian populations were drawn into the struggle as never before. German, Japanese, and Russian

treatment of prisoners-of-war was often brutal. Terror bombing of cities, a tactic initiated by Germany but adopted also by the Allies, left hundreds of thousands of dead. The age-old distinction between combatants and civilians was blurred, especially in those areas of occupied Europe where anti-Nazi resistance movements sought to conduct guerrilla warfare, which in some areas developed into internecine conflict between resistance forces and 'collaborators' or between communists and anti-communists.

Inspired by Hitler's obsessive anti-semitism, the Nazis (often, particularly in eastern Europe, with the active support of local populations) gathered together the Jews of Europe in 'ghettos' or forced-labour concentration camps (*see Map 80*). Hundreds of thousands of Jews were murdered during the early years of the war by special killing squads ('*Einsatzgruppen*') or by other military and paramilitary units. Later special mass murder centres were established in eastern Europe, such as the Auschwitz camp, to which millions of Jews and others were deported, killed in gas chambers, and cremated. Resistance, such as the revolt of the Jews in the Warsaw Ghetto in 1943, was hopeless. Nor did the Allies take effective action to admit significant numbers of refugees from the holocaust or seek to blunt its impact.

In spite of initial German and Japanese successes, the tide of the war had begun to turn by early 1943. In June 1942 American air and naval forces in the central Pacific won an important victory over the Japanese in the Battle of Midway Island, which for the first time threw the Japanese on to the defensive (*Map 79*). In November 1942 British forces defeated a German army at el Alamein in Egypt, thereby preventing German capture of the Suez Canal, vital to British imperial communications (*Map 81*). Still more significant was the dramatic Russian stand in defence of Stalingrad, where in February 1943 large German armies capitulated, decisively halting the German advance into the USSR.

Thenceforth the stubborn resistance of the Axis powers was slowly ground down. The first to collapse was Italy where in mid-1943 Mussolini was overthrown and replaced by a government which surrendered to the Allies. However, before the Allied forces in southern Italy could capitalize fully on this success, the Germans had occupied the northern half of the peninsula whence they were dislodged only after long and gruelling battles in 1944 and 1945. The crucial battles were fought elsewhere. During 1944 the Red Army steadily pressed the Germans back on the eastern front while demanding that the western allies open a 'second front' in north-west Europe. After some delays this was at last secured on 6 June 1944 ('D-Day'), when American and British troops landed in Normandy. By late 1944 nearly the whole of France had been liberated, although even now German resistance was such that in December 1944 a surprise German offensive in the Ardennes achieved temporary success. But this was soon reversed, and by early 1945 the Allies in the west were advancing into Germany on a broad front. In late April they met the Russians at the Elbe, and by May 8 were able to celebrate V-E (Victory in Europe) Day.

Japan now faced certain defeat, but continued to defy her enemies even after Germany's collapse. Japanese surrender on August 14 1945 came only after the USA had dropped atomic bombs on Hiroshima and Nagasaki causing huge, hideous casualties. The world war thus terminated, but the mushroom cloud of Hiroshima cast a shadow over the moral quality of the victory, and darkened the prospects of post-war international harmony, perhaps even of long-term human survival.

---

81 The Second World War in Europe
The second great war of the century was shaped this time by the rapid movement of both land and air forces, with correspondingly widespread devastation. The European powers exhausted one another and domination passed to the USA and Russia, whose intervention had decided the outcome of the war.

Above: The sinking of the *USS California* at Pearl Harbor, December 7 1942. The USS California settling into mud

80 Fascist Europe
The violent authoritarian movements which, assisted by economic recession and resentment of the Versailles settlement, seized power in much of inter-war Europe, shared an aggressive nationalism and brutal hostility to minorities. These reached a peak in Nazi Germany.

Further reading: Akira Iriye, *The Origins of the Second World War in Asia and the Pacific* (Longman 1987); A. Bullock, *Hitler and Stalin* (Collins 1991); Ian Kershaw, *The Hitler Myth* (Oxford U. P. 1987); G. Wright, *The Ordeal of Total War* (Harper & Row, 1968); W.L.S. Churchill, *The Second World War* (Cassell, 1945-54); Martin Gilbert, *The Holocaust* (Collins 1986).

MAP 81 THE SECOND WORLD WAR IN EUROPE

Legend:

- German invasions with dates
- Axis advance by date shown
- Allied invasions with dates
- Allied advance by date shown
- Allied convoy routes
- Major German air raids
- Major Allied air raids
- Oil wells
- Oil pipelines
- Neutral states

| 0 | 300 kms |
| 0 | 200 miles |

FINLAND

Helsinki

Gulf of Finland

Tallinn

Estonia

Riga

Latvia

Dec. 1944

Memel

Lithuania

Königsberg

Kovno

Suwalki

Danzig

Warsaw

22-6-41

Lodz

Bialystok

P O L A N D

Katowice

Cracow

Lublin

December 1944

VAKIA

Budapest

Dec. 1944

H U N G A R Y

Szeged

Arad

Temesvar

Belgrade

Cetinje

A V I A

Durazzo

Tirana

6-4-41

Larisa

17-4-41

G R E E C E

Athens

20-5-41

Heraklion

Crete

Ladoga

Dec. 1944

Nov. 1942

Leningrad

Dec. 1941

June 1944

Pskov

December 1941

Minsk

White

Russia

Pinsk

Pripet Marshes

Kovel

Lutsk

December 1943

Brody

Lvov

late June 1944

Tarnopol

Vinnitsa

Czernowitz

Carpathians

Kolozsvar

R O U M A N I A

Ploiesti

Bucharest

Danube

B U L G A R I A

Sofia

Plovdiv

Skopje

Edirne

Varna

Burgas

Yaroslavl

Gorki

Kazan

40°

50°

Moscow

Volga

Smolensk

Mogilev

Gomel

Kursk

U. S. S. R.

Kharkov

Kiev

Zhitomir

Berdichev

U k r a i n e

Kirovograd

Dnieper

Dnestr

Bug

Odessa

Galati

Constanta

Saratov

December 1941

November 1942

Stalingrad

Stalino

Rostov

Azov

Volga

Astrakhan

Caspian Sea

Caucasus

Tbilisi

Batum

Yerevan

Erzerum

25-8-41

Ba

IRAN

Crimea

Yalta

Sebastopol

B l a c k   S e a

Zonguldak

Samsun

Istanbul

Bursa

Ankara

T U R K E Y

Izmir

Aegean Sea

Taurus Mts.

Antalya

Rhodes

Nicosia

Cyprus

M e d i t e r r a n e a n   S e a

Iskenderun

Aleppo

S Y R I A
(France)

Tripoli

Beirut

Damascus

Haifa

8-6-41

Jerusalem

P A L E S T I N E
(Br. mandate)

T R A N S - J O R D A N

10.5.41

Mosul

Kirkuk

Habbaniyah

Baghdad

I R A Q

30°

Benghazi

Tobruk

April 1941

Sidi Barrani

Mersa Matruh

Alexandria

El Alamein

22-6-41

Nov. 1942

C y r e n a i c a

Quttara Depression

E G Y P T

Cairo

Nile

Suez Canal

Port Said

Suez

40°

Sea

The emergence of the modern world 4

82 Europe since the Second World War
After 1945 the areas of Europe which had been controlled by the armed forces of the USSR and by those of the western democracies confronted one another in parallel political, economic and military blocs. By 1990 the nations of the west had secured prosperity and considerable political and economic integration, while the Communist regimes of the east collapsed in poverty and chaos.

THE POST-WAR WORLD

Even before the end of the Second World War the new pattern of international relations was beginning to emerge. Of the five 'great powers' in the victorious wartime coalition, three had been disastrously weakened and two immeasurably strengthened by the years of struggle.

Britain was economically exhausted by the war, and its post-war Labour government, preoccupied with social reform at home, was compelled to cut a much-reduced figure on the diplomatic stage. The claim of France to 'great power' status was barely conceded by her allies, and accorded ill with France's impoverished condition after the trauma of Nazi occupation. China's 'great power' status was thrown into question as the *Kuomintang* government's grip on power became ever more tenuous (*see Map 85*). By contrast the USA and the USSR had emerged by 1945 as the unquestioned 'super-powers' of the post-war era. Of the two the USA was by far the more powerful. Her prodigious wartime economic growth rendered her by 1945 the producer of over half the world's manufactured goods. Moreover she possessed nuclear weapons, whereas the USSR detonated its first atomic bomb only in 1949.

Mutual suspicions as to post-war ambitions had been evident at the 'big three' wartime conferences at Tehran in 1943, Yalta in February 1945, and Potsdam in July 1945. The severe strains between the USSR and the western allies had surfaced in mid-1944, particularly over the Russian refusal to allow adequate aid to be given to the anti-Nazi rising of the (anti-communist) Polish underground movement in Warsaw. At the end of the war communist and western forces confronted one another in a great arc stretching from central Europe through the middle east to east Asia (*Map 84*). The United Nations, successor to the now-defunct League of Nations, was established at the San Francisco Conference in mid-1945, with the primary aim of preserving world peace. Although the UN succeeded, unlike the League, in securing the

MAP 82   EUROPE SINCE THE SECOND WORLD WAR

European Community
from 1958
from 1973
from 1981
from 1986
from 1990

COMECON 1949-1990
USSR
Other members

Areas of secessionist activity

Democracies
Communist
Dictatorship/military government

171 GNP GDP real growth 1965-c.1989 (1965=100)

adhesion of nearly all independent states, it soon became apparent that world politics would henceforth be dominated by the east-west rivalry for power, influence, and prestige, a contest dubbed after 1947 the 'cold war'.

The 'iron curtain' which descended across Europe generally followed the lines secured by Russian and western forces at the end of the war (*Map 81*). Determined to establish firm buffers against any possible threat to the USSR, Stalin annexed large territories from Finland, East Prussia, Poland, Czechoslovakia, and Romania. In Poland, Romania, Bulgaria, and Hungary non-

communist elements were squeezed out and communist-dominated 'puppet' regimes took office under Russian supervision. In Czechoslovakia in February 1948 democratic politicians were eliminated and a communist-directed 'coalition' government installed. Only in Yugoslavia, where the resistance forces headed by Josip Broz (Tito) assumed power, was a communist government successful in maintaining independence from Moscow. In Greece a bitter civil war broke out late in 1944. British troops supported the anti-communists, while Stalin, as he had promised in October 1944, refrained from intervention. After renewed fighting in 1947-9 the pro-western groups achieved victory.

In the immediate aftermath of the war the democratic governments of western Europe were heavily dependent on American military protection and

---

83 Population and movements of people after 1945
Economic opportunity, poverty, war and persecution have made the second half of the twentieth century an age of mass migration on a scale quite unknown in any previous epoch, both reflecting and reinforcing the national and international tensions from which it has arisen.

84 Great power conflicts since 1945
The mutual distrust of the USA and USSR divided much of the post-war world into opposing camps in a series of occupations and military alliances, and produced a succession of confrontations when war seemed imminent. A period of relaxation after the Cuba crisis of 1962 was followed in the early 1980s by a massive arms race, before political and economic crisis in the USSR effectively brought the cold war to an end.

MAP 83 POPULATION AND MOVEMENTS OF PEOPLE AFTER 1945

Indonesia 0·5

Italy
Yugoslavia
Turkey
(total 3·0)

E. Germany 3·0

Poland
U.S.S.R.
Romania
Czech.
Hungary
Yugoslavia
(total 14·0)

0.1

0.2

W. Germany

4.0

8.2

Bangladesh
E. Africa
Ireland
W. Indies
Pakistan
India
(total 2·0)

Portugal
Spain
Italy
Morocco
Tunisia
Algeria
(total 2·0)

Oslo

Stockholm

Glasgow
Belfast
Dublin
Liverpool
Birmingham
London

Leeds
Man.

Copenhagen

5.1

Amst.
13.4
61.8
Brussels
Munich

56.0
16.9
Prague
Vienn

Hambu
Be

U.K.

France

Paris

52.9

6.4

Lyon

7.5

Milan

55.8

Turin

Ro

Vancouver

Seattle

Portland

Edmonton

Winnipeg

22.8

Bordeaux

Madrid

35.5

Marseille

Naples

San Francisco

Denver

213.6

Montreal

Ottawa

Toronto
Buffalo

Boston

Detroit

Minneapolis-
Saint Paul

Milwaukee
Chicago

Cle.
Pitt.

Indianapolis

Cincinnati

New York
Philadelphia
Baltimore
Washington D.C.

Canada

Greece
Germany
France
U.S.A.
Italy
Britain
(total 2·0)

Lisbon

8.8

Yugoslavia 0·4

Italy

Algiers

16.8

Casablanca

5.8

Barcelona

17.3

Los Angeles

Phoenix

Kansas City

St Louis

Memphis

Dallas

Atlanta

Germany 0·75
Italy 0·5
Poland 0·3
U.K. 0·5
Mexico 1·1
Canada 0·5
W. Indies 1·1
Puerto Rico
Cuba 0·4

illegal
immigrants
5·0

U.S.A.

Houston

New Orleans

60.1

Monterrey

Guadalajara

Mexico City

Miami

Havana

0.2

9.1

4.6

4.7

3.1

1.3

5.7

4.6

0.1

2.0

Santo Domingo

5.3

3.0

4.0

2.2

4.1

0.9

6.0

3.1

0.5

2,0

11.7

2.8

4.4

9.9

2.2

Accra

1.7

6.7

Ibadan

Lagos

69.2

6.4

Maracaibo

Caracas

Chad 0·1

Cameroon

0.3

12.0

0.8

0.4

0.1

Medellin

29.7

Bogotá

Cali

Quito

6.7

15.8

Lima

Belém

Fortaleza

Recife

Salvador

107.1

Brasilia

0.5

1.

Angola
Uganda
Rwanda
Burundi
(total 0·3)

Zaire

Kinshasa

Zaire
Namibia
(total 0·6)

Angola

La Paz

5.6

Belo Horizonte

Rio de Janeiro

São Paulo

2.6

10.3

Valparaiso

Santiago

25·4

Cordoba

Montevideo

Buenos Aires

3.1

Porto Alegre

Cape Tow

Percentage population growth, 1945-75

under 25%

25-50%

50-100%

over 100%

Density of population, 1975:
(persons per sq. km.)

0-10

10-50

50-100

over 100

Population of selected cities

1945 1975

under ½ million

½-1 million

over 1 million

15.9 Population 1975 (millions)

Volume of Migration:
(showing origin and destination of migrants)

17 million

17·1

Estimated numbers
(in millions) from
selected sources

1 million

Arctic Circle

4.7
Helsinki
Leningrad
Riga
Moscow
Perm
Sverdlovsk
Minsk
Gorky
Chelyabinsk
Omsk
Novosibirsk
Warsaw
254.4
Kuibyshev
Kiev
Kharkov
Lvov
Dnepropetrovsk
Donetsk
Volgograd
0.3
Budapest
trade
21.2
Odessa
Rostov-on-Don
Sofia
Bucharest
8.7
Tbilisi
Istanbul
9.0
Ankara
39.2
Baku
Athens
Aleppo
Afghanistan 1·0
Tashkent
Alma-Ata
1.4
Harbin
0.6
7.4
11.1
Tehran
Pakistan
Mukden
Beirut
Baghdad
Kabul
15.9
Seoul
110.9
2.9
Damascus
19.3
Peking
Tientsin
Nagoya
Tokyo
Alexandria
Amman
4.4 Tel Aviv-Jaffa
1.0
Lahore
33.9
Kyoto
Yokohama
Cairo
1.9
70.3
Delhi
12.6
1.2
838.8
Pusan
Osaka
— 37.2
Middle East
Israel 1·0
0.3
Nanking
0.1
0.2
Shanghai
Riyadh
Karachi
598.1
Chungking
5.5
0.8
Ahmadabad
Dacca
Canton
14.8
Asia and Africa
C. and E. Europe
(total 1·4)
Bombay
Hyderabad
76.8
Calcutta
31.2
Hong Kong
Vietnam 0·26
1.7
E. Pakistan
Rangoon
3.3
17.8
6.7
W. Pakistan
India 1·3
42.3
Bangkok
44.0
Manila
42.5
27.9
0.1
India 7·2
Bangalore
Madras
Thailand
8.1
Saigon
Addis Ababa
2.7
3.2
India
14.0
Cambodia
Vietnam
Laos
(total 0·3)
Vietnam
Cambodia
Philippines
(total 0·1)
Saudi Arabia
11.5
13.3
Yemen 1
Egypt 0·5
12.1
Singapore
2.3
4.2
Somalia
Ethiopia 1·5
0.1
2.7
3.8
Sudan
Ethiopia 0·4
Uganda
Chad
Zaire
130.0
0.9
24.9
15.2
E. Pakistan 12
W. Pakistan 5·1
2.8
Dar es Salaam
Uganda
Rwanda
Zaire
(total 0·1)
Djakarta
4.9
5.0
Tanzania
9.2
Salisbury
7.6
0.7
6.4
Johannesburg
0.5
Rwanda
Burundi
(total 0·15)
Durban
25.5
1.0

N. Korea 3·0
S. Korea
Vladivostok
Japan
China 2·9
S.E. Asia 0·7
Korea 0·9
Philippines
U.S.S.R. 0·5
Australia
Taiwan
China 2·0
China
Malaysia (total 0·1)

Tropic of Cancer

Equator

Tropic of Capricorn

Perth
Brisbane
13.5
Adelaide
Sydney
Auckland
G.B.
Italy
Yugoslavia
Greece
(total 2·0)
Australia
Melbourne
Wellington
3·1

155

MAP 84 GREAT POWER CONFLICTS SINCE 1945

GREENLAND

CANADA
(83)

Thule

ICELAND
Keflavik
Reykjavik 1986

NORWAY
SWEDEN (65)

1969 * U.K. (323)
Holy Loch
Upper Heyford
West Berlin
1948
E. GER.
W. GER. (486)
CZE

UNITED STATES
(2,144)

Glassboro 1967 †
Camp David 1959 † Washington 1987, 1990

Paris 1960 †
Geneva 1985
Vienna 1961
AUST.
SWIT. (1,100)
SLA
ITALY (207)

1974 *
PORTUGAL
FRANCE (557)
SPAIN (320)

Azores

Bermuda

Torrejón
Gaeta Naples
Rota • Gibraltar
Bizerte (to 1968)
Sigonella
Malta 1989 Malta (to 19
(to 1968)
TUNISIA

MOROCCO
Wheel (to 1970

MEXICO
(139)

1961
1965
1954

1962

CUBA
(162)
Guantánamo
HAITI *
1986
DOM!NICAN REP.

1983

WESTERN SAHARA
ALGERIA (169)
* 1976-90
* 1954-62
LIBY (71)
* 196

• *Belize*
GUATAMALA
(19)
HONDURAS
(19)
EL SALVADOR *1979
1979
1989
NICARAGUA
* 1979
(72)

COSTA RICA
* 1948
Panama

1979 * GRENADA

MAURITANIA
* 1978
MALI
* 1968
1991

NIGER
* 1974

VENEZUELA
(71)
* 1948
* 1990
SURINAM
GUYANA
FR. GUIANA

GUINEA-BISSAU
* 1959-74, 1980
GUINEA
* 1984
BURKINA FASO *1980
IVORY COAST
GHANA
TOGO
BENIN
* 1966
1979
1966,1967-70
NIGERIA
(94)

PANAMA

COLOMBIA
(66)

ECUADOR
(42)

LIBERIA
1980,1990

CAMEROON

EQUATORIAL GUINEA * 1979
GABON

Ascension Island

1977

BRAZIL
(283)

PERU
(127)
* 1968

BOLIVIA
(20)
* 1965
1980

1960

ANGO (50)

1975

* 1961-

PARAGUAY
(16)

NAMIBI
* 1966-8

CHILE (101)
* 1973

ARGENTINA
(73)
* 1955, 1976
* 1973
URUGUAY
(32)

1982

• *Falkland Is.* (from 1982)

Soviet-American Nuclear Balance		
	USA	U.S.S.R.
1986 Nuclear warheads deployed	12,846	10,716
1991 START treaty ceilings	10,360	8,040

FINLAND
(35)
Porkkala (to 1955)

† Moscow 1972, 1988, 1991

U.S.S.R.
(5,130)

1969

LAND
1968
1956
NG
956 ✳1989
ROMANIA
BULGARIA

† Vladivostok 1974

JAPAN
(243)

MONGOLIA
(25)

1945-6

1979

1969

1969

1950

NORTH KOREA
[1,340]

Midway Is.

Yokosuka

Pearl Harbor

TURKEY ✳
(654) 1960, 1980
Kabul
CYPRUS ✳1961
Akrotiri LEB
SYRIA
GREECE
1975-91 (392)
964
ISRAEL
1958
IRAQ
1958
[704] JORDAN (800)
56
(70)
1958
✳1978
AFGHANISTAN
(50)
✳1977

IRAN
(705)

TIBET
1950

CHINA
(2,950)

✳1945-9

SOUTH KOREA
(601)

Port Arthur (to 1955)

1950

Okinawa

PAKISTAN
(481)

KUWEIT
1961
1991
*Daharan
(to 1962)* ● *Bahrain (to 1971)*
SUDAN
EGYPT
(445)
✳1952
SAUDI ARABIA
(67) *Sharjah (to 1971)*
UN. ARAB
EMIRATES
OMAN

NEPAL

INDIA
(1,260)

✳1971

-1979

BANGLADESH

1962
✳1988

Hong Kong

TAIWAN
(424)

BURMA
(MYANMAR)
(186)

1953-75

✳1945-75

Suez (to 1956)

MAD
4)
SUDAN
(57)
Dahlak Is.
68-
SOUTH YEMEN
OMAN
✳1965-75
1985
✳1962
Aden (to 1967) ● *Socotra*
DHBOUTI

VIETNAM

Clark (to 1991)

THAILAND
(256)
✳1991
CAMBODIA
✳1970-
1970
1964

PHILIPPINES
(113)
✳1986

Subic Bay

Da Nang (to 1972)
Cam Ranh Bay

Guam

ETHIOPIA
(227)
✳1974,1991

1965,
1979
AFRICAN
REP

SOMALIA
(43)

SRI LANKA
(38)
✳1983-

MALAYSIA
(110)
✳1948-60

AIRE (CONGO)
(50)
✳1971
UGANDA
(6)
KENYA
(14)
1960-3
RWANDA
BURUNDI
✳1966
TANZANIA
(40)

Diego Garcia

Singapore (to 1976)

ZAMBIA
(16)
✳1964-

MADAGASCAR
(21) ✳1973

✳1965

INDONESIA
(281)

PAPUA
NEW GUINEA

✳1976-9
ZIMBABWE
(RHODESIA)
(42)
MOZAMBIQUE
(28)

BOTSWANA

North West Cape

onstown (to 1957)

OUTH AFRICA
(106)

AUSTRALIA
(70)

New Caledonia

Bases/Military Action

● ——→	*U.S.S.R.*	†	Major powers' summit conferences	
● ——→	*US*	✳	Revolutions and civil wars	
● ━━▶	*UK*	◜◞	'Iron Curtain'	
● ——→	*France*		US blockade	
○	*USSR/US/UK/Fr*		USSR blockade	
● ┅┅▶	*UN*		Declared nuclear powers by 1987	
● ┄┄→	*Other communist countries*	(67) [1100] × 10³	Total armed forces Rapidly mobilised reserves	

———— Borders in 1987

Power Blocs in 1987

Warsaw Pact 1955-1991
Other Communist States
N. Atlantic Treaty Organisation
U.S. Allies
Organisation of American States
Organisation of African Unity
Arab League
Other States

NEW ZEALAND
(13)

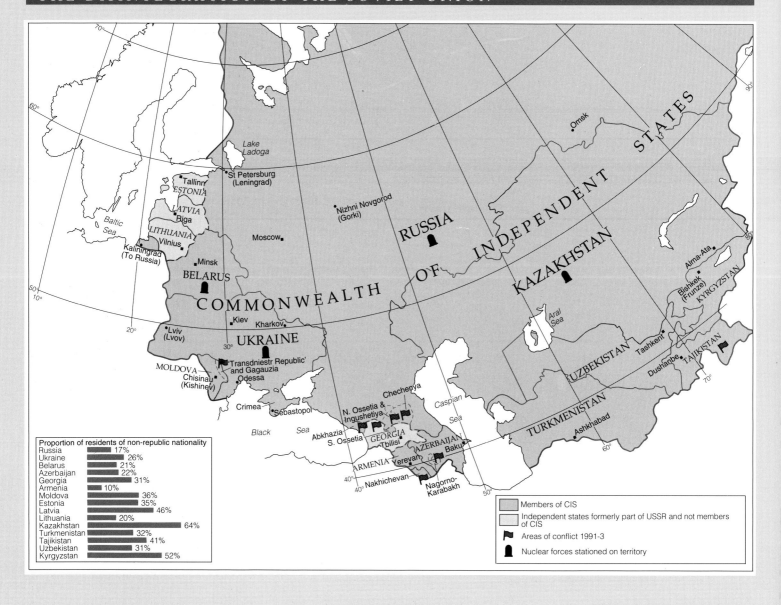

Proportion of residents of non-republic nationality

Russia	17%
Ukraine	26%
Belarus	21%
Azerbaijan	22%
Georgia	31%
Armenia	10%
Moldova	36%
Estonia	35%
Latvia	46%
Lithuania	20%
Kazakhstan	64%
Turkmenistan	32%
Tajikistan	41%
Uzbekistan	31%
Kyrgyzstan	52%

Members of CIS

Independent states formerly part of USSR and not members of CIS

Areas of conflict 1991-3

Nuclear forces stationed on territory

economic aid. The Marshall Plan, inaugurated by the US Secretary of State George Marshall in June 1947, provided their war-ravaged economies with assistance worth $17,000 million, stimulating their rapid recovery. Under Russian influence, however, the east European states rejected American aid. In 1949 most west European states joined the USA in the North Atlantic Treaty Organization (NATO) with the aim of 'containing' the Soviet Union. The Warsaw Pact of 1955 formalized the military alliance of the USSR with its east European satellites, whose economies were subordinated to Russian interests.

The focus of the cold war in Europe was on Berlin and the fate of Germany. In its old form the German problem was solved after the war. Over thirteen million Germans were expelled from eastern Europe (*see Map 83*), the majority moving to western Germany in the greatest European population movement of the century. Poland shifted west, being compensated for her eastern losses to the USSR by western gains at the expense of Germany (*see Map 82*). Germany, shorn of these lands and of East Prussia, was divided into four occupation zones. In 1949 the American, British, and French zones united to form the Federal Republic of Germany which was granted full independence in

1955. The communist German Democratic Republic (GDR) was established in the Russian-occupied zone. The position of West Berlin, as an enclave within East Germany, gave rise to three major international crises. In 1948-9 a western airlift defeated a Russian land blockade of West Berlin. Ten years later a Russian ultimatum (rejected by the western powers) demanded that western forces leave West Berlin. In August 1961 the East German government, alarmed at the huge exodus of its citizens to the west, erected a wall separating East from West Berlin. After severe economic tribulations in the late 1940s both German states made dramatic recoveries from the 1950s onwards to emerge among the industrial leaders of their respective blocks, the GDR being absorbed into the Soviet orbit while the Federal Republic, led by Chancellor Konrad Adenauer, pursued a pro-western course.

Although the Russo-American rivalry in East Asia never produced direct fighting between the superpowers, the cold war in this area was punctuated by a series of bitter localized wars. The Chinese civil war ended in 1949 in total victory for the communist forces headed by Mao Tse-tung (*Map 85*). The rump of the anti-communist armies withdrew to the island of Formosa (Taiwan) where they

remained under American protection. In 1950 North American forces, joined by small contingents from their allies, intervened to resist the invasion of South Korea by communist North Korea, itself aided by Chinese troops. The war ground to a halt along the original partition line of the 38th parallel in 1953. The 'loss of China', as it was seen in the USA, helped to engender a profound anti-communist reaction among Americans, culminating in the hysteria of 'McCarthyism' (after the anti-communist demagogue, Senator Joseph McCarthy) in the early 1950s. However, the USA remained determined to maintain its influence in East Asia, and in 1954 formed the South-East Asia Treaty Organization (SEATO) with Britain, France, and several Asian states.

The cold war reached its climax in the late 1950s and early 1960s as both super-powers developed hydrogen bombs and inter-continental missile delivery systems. The poisoning of the atmosphere by above-ground nuclear tests, the building-up of vast arsenals of hydrogen bombs capable of destroying nearly all human beings, and the danger of nuclear 'proliferation' to smaller powers cast over the world a shadow of prospective self-immolation. For one week in late October 1962 it seemed to shudder on the brink of catastrophe as a result of a

Russo-American conflict over Cuba. The USSR had sought to install offensive missiles armed with nuclear warheads on Cuba, where a revolutionary movement headed by Fidel Castro had in 1959 ousted a pro-American dictatorship. The American President, John F. Kennedy, blockaded the island and demanded the removal of the missiles. The crisis ended when the Russian leader, Nikita Khrushchev, yielded to the American demands.

With the resolution of the Cuban crisis the cold war gradually eased, giving way to a period of 'détente', while new powers challenged and steadily eroded the predominance of the super-powers, heralding the end of the 'bi-polar' era.

In western Europe renewed economic strength and moves towards economic integration provided a basis for foreign policies more independent of the USA. In 1951 France, Germany, Italy and the Benelux countries formed the European Coal and Steel Community, and by the Treaty of Rome in 1957 created a European Economic Community (EEC) involving an unprecedented measure of economic integration between major sovereign states (*Map 82*). The EEC enjoyed spectacular growth in production and trade in the 1960s. Britain joined, after two unsuccessful attempts, in 1972, at the same time as Ireland and Denmark, and by 1986 Greece, Portugal and Spain, having rid themselves of dictatorships, had become members. Agreement to abolish internal tariffs by 1992 heralded a further large step towards European economic and political integration.

In the communist world too the overwhelming dominance of the super-power diminished. From 1960 onwards China engaged in a virulent ideological conflict with the USSR, whose leaders were denounced by Mao Tse-tung as 'revisionists'. Ideological warfare intensified between 1966 and 1969 during the internal upheaval in China known as the 'cultural revolution'. That the conflict was a serious threat to world peace became clear with the development of armed skirmishes along the disputed Russo-Chinese border and with the emergence of China as a nuclear power in the late 1960s.

As the Sino-Soviet conflict deepened the USSR and later China moved into a period of cautious 'détente' with the western powers. In 1963 the USA, USSR, and UK (but not France or China) signed a partial nuclear test ban treaty. The persistent irritant of the German question was eased after 1969 by the conciliatory '*Ostpolitik*' of the socialist West German Chancellor, Willy Brandt. In 1972 and 1979 the two super-powers signed agreements on the limitation of strategic weapons. From the early 1970s China too moderated her hostility to the western powers, re-opening relations with the USA and seeking closer links with western Europe. The Soviet invasion of Afghanistan in 1979 and the installation of a new 'hard-line' American administration in 1981 was

reflected in a massive super-power arms race in the 1980s which threatened to upset the delicate equilibrium of the 'balance of terror' that had kept a tenuous peace for more than three decades.

The death of Stalin in 1953 had excited hopes of democratization in eastern Europe, but his successors sought to maintain a firm grip on power over other communist states. In November 1956 Russian troops crushed a brief attempt by Hungary to withdraw from the Warsaw Pact. In August 1968 the USSR again used armed strength to destroy the democratic reforms which had been introduced by the Czechoslovak communists headed by Alexander Dubcek. Nevertheless there was an easing of the atmosphere in eastern Europe as the grim Stalin years gave way to a period of relative economic prosperity. Yugoslavia maintained its independence of Moscow, and Soviet power was further challenged in the ideological domain by the increased tendency of west European communist parties (most notably the Italian) to defy directives from Moscow.

In March 1985 Mikhail Gorbachev took over as leader of a Soviet Union whose economy and political institutions betrayed signs of serious weakness. Gorbachev instituted a far-reaching programme of internal political and economic reforms, under the slogan of *perestroika* (reconstruction). He withdrew Soviet troops from Afghanistan by 1989. He opened the door to the collapse of the Soviet-imposed communist regimes in eastern Europe before the new 'springtime of the peoples' in 1989. The decisive moment came with the peaceful breach of the Berlin Wall in November 1989. This was followed in rapid succession by the collapse of communist regimes throughout eastern Europe and the reunification of Germany in October 1990.

Across most of eastern Europe democratic elections produced anti-communist governments that proceeded to dismantle the centralized command economy. Ethnic tensions, long suppressed under Communism, bubbled once again to the surface. In

Czechoslovakia these were resolved peacefully but at the price of the separation of Slovakia from the Czech lands in 1993. In Yugoslavia a bitter civil war broke out in 1991, first between Serbs and Croats, then pitting both against Bosnian Muslims. The war produced tens of thousands of dead and millions of refugees.

Within the Soviet Union too nationalist tensions led to secessionist demands. The Baltic states of Lithuania, Latvia, and Estonia, occupied by the USSR since 1940, successfully asserted their independence by 1991. Conflict between the central government and nationalist movements led to violence in the Baltic states and the Caucasus. Meanwhile deteriorating economic conditions discredited the Gorbachev regime, providing the cue in August 1991 for a botched coup attempt by the Communist rearguard. By the end of the year the near-collapse of the Soviet economy had reduced the power of the central government to such an extent that Gorbachev was compelled to resign and the Soviet Union dissolved. In Russia reformist elements headed by Boris Yeltsin took power. Together with ten other former Soviet republics Russia formed the Commonwealth of Independent States. But continuing economic difficulties and heightened ethnic tensions between and within several of the new states darkened their prospects.

Further reading: Daniel Yergin, *Shattered Peace* (Houghton Mifflin 1977; Penguin); Derek W. Urwin *Western Europe since 1945* (4th ed. Longman 1989); Geoffrey Hosking, *The First Socialist Society* (2nd ed., Harvard U.P. 1990); William Shawcross, *Alexander Dubcek* (2nd edn. Hogarth 1990; Simon & Schuster); Misha Glenny, *The Fall of Yugoslavia* (Penguin, 1992)

The emergence of the modern world 5

At the close of the Second World War China was a victorious ally of the United States, and Japan a defeated enemy.

But within four years China had fallen to a Communist revolution (*Map 85*) and Japan had become essential to America's anti-Communist strategy. Japan's former colony, Korea, had been divided into American and Soviet zones, while Formosa and Okinawa became bases for United States forces.

Initially America's occupation of Japan sought to weaken and pacify a potential enemy. However, her desire for trade and fear of Communism soon produced policies to stimulate Japan's economic recovery. In contrast, the founding of the People's Republic of China in October 1949 created a

government which criticized American 'imperialism', occupied Tibet, and looked to the Soviet Union for political and military support. In June 1950 pro-Soviet North Korean forces invaded the pro-American South, and United States and Chinese forces soon intervened. Tension between Washington and Peking was heightened and their embittered relations further increased Japan's military importance. America encouraged the beginnings of Japanese re-armament and in September 1951 forty-eight non-Communist powers signed a peace treaty with Japan. In April 1952 Japan's

political independence was formally restored.

Japan's economic recovery continued throughout the 1950s and by 1956 her standard of living surpassed that of the pre-war years. Some Japanese resented their country's dependence on the United States and others feared that their country might be drawn into a war between the super-powers, but government and industry believed that only the United States could provide the markets and protection necessary for continued prosperity.

For China problems of reconstruction, modernization and agricultural improvement were

Opposite page above: Car factory in Pusan, South Korea, 1987.

Opposite page below: Tokyo Stock Exchange, where more than one million shares – five times the volume of the New York Stock Exchange – are traded daily.

Below: Vietnamese government troops on an anti-Communist mission in August 1962.

85 The retreat of imperialism in Asia
The Japanese victories of the Second World War destroyed the prestige of the European powers in Asia and opened the way to rapid decolonization in the post-war years, but continuing Great-Power intervention prolonged the bitter struggles between the successor states and exacerbated political and social instability, most tragically in South-East Asia.

Further reading: Jonathan D. Spence, *The Search for Modern China* (Norton 1990; Century Hutchinson); John Gittings, *China Changes Face: the Road from Revolution, 1949-1989* (Oxford U.P. 1990); Anthony Short, *The Origins of the Vietnam War* (Longman 1989); Roger Buckley, *Japan Today* (Cambridge U. P. 1990); R. Drifte, *Japan's Foreign Policy* (Routledge/RIIA 1989).

immense but the Communist government secured a greater degree of order and unity than had existed for more than a century. The Soviet Union assisted the new regime in many industrial and agricultural projects, but by 1960 China's more revolutionary ideology and her militant foreign policy led to worsening relations with the Soviet Union.

In China domestic policies often underwent drastic changes of style and direction as leaders sought to combine economic progress with revolutionary enthusiasm. These dramatic fluctuations reached their peak in the 'Cultural Revolution', which began in 1966. This nationwide movement combined social turmoil and revolutionary ardour. In these same years America's involvement in the Vietnam War stimulated Russian and Chinese help for Hanoi and temporarily concealed the depth of hostility between Moscow and Peking.

By 1972 the Cultural Revolution and the Vietnam War had diminished in intensity, while China's fear of Moscow led to policies based on anti-Soviet strategy rather than Communist ideology. China now formally forgave Japan for her aggression in the 1930s (*Map 79*), and mutual trade increased rapidly. This improvement in Sino-Japanese relations soon received further stimulus from decisions in America and the Middle East. America's failure in Vietnam led her to reduce her military presence in East Asia, and in 1971 the success of Japanese goods in the American market led to President Nixon's measures to restrict the entry of Japanese products. The return of Okinawa to Japanese administration in 1972 was less important than Japan's doubts regarding the future openness of the American market and the dependability of American military protection. In 1973 the high price and restricted supply of oil which followed the Arab-Israeli war further threatened Japan's economy, and led her to seek alternative oil supplies and markets in China and South-East Asia.

In these years China felt increasingly insecure in her relations with the Soviet Union, while the death of Mao Tse-tung, in 1976, and the removal of the radical 'gang of four', in 1977, made it easier for China's leaders to replace policies based upon ideology by the 'Four Modernizations'. These new policies aimed to increase China's economic well-being and her ability to defend herself against the Soviet Union. By 1978 Japan's need for markets and China's need for modern technology had produced a mutual agreement which provided for large increases in trade and Japanese help in the development of China's industry and natural resources. Perhaps surprisingly, Soviet policy in East Asia showed little sign of major changes. The USSR, like China, attempted to secure Japanese help in the exploitation of her underdeveloped territories (*see Map 71*), but Japanese officials and businessmen doubted the reliability of Soviet undertakings and feared that Moscow might draw them into its dispute with Peking. Indeed, while Japan's relations with China underwent rapid improvement, those with the Soviet Union appeared frozen in the patterns of the cold war. Not only did the Soviet Union take a particularly severe attitude in fishery negotiations, but she still refused to return four small islands – Habomai, Shikotan, Kunashiri and Etorufu – which Japan claimed were part of her national territory.

During the 1980s the shared interests of China and Japan produced a cordiality in their relations that was almost without precedent in the twentieth century. Japan feared the growing power of the Soviet navy and China resented the growth of Russian influence in Vietnam; as a result, both criticized Russia's intervention in Afghanistan and her support for Hanoi's occupation of Kampuchea. In 1989 Sino-Japanese relations deteriorated somewhat temporarily following the massacre of students in Tienanmen Square but economic imperatives soon dictated the restoration of good relations between Peking and Tokyo.

By 1990 the effective ending of the cold war between the United States and the USSR finally removed the perceived Soviet threat to northern Japan, although Gorbachev's visit to Tokyo in 1991 failed to resolve the long-standing territorial dispute which continued to plague Soviet-Japanese relations. In the Korean peninsula friction between North and South continued, but South Korea's prestige rose rapidly. Seoul's remarkable economic growth led Moscow to seek closer ties with the South, leaving North Korea increasingly isolated from her previous ally and patron.

MAP 85 THE RETREAT OF IMPERIALISM IN ASIA

Caspian Sea

Aral Sea

U.S.S.R.

Ulan Bator

MONGOLIA

Tashkent

Herat

AFGHANISTAN

Hindu Kush

IRAN

Kabul

Peshawar

Kandahar

Islamabad

KASHMIR

Quetta

Lahore

Amritsar

TIBET
1951

Lhasa

PAKISTAN

1947

Indus

Delhi

Himalaya

NEPAL

Kathmandu

Thimbu BHUTAN

Karachi

Lucknow

Ganges

Patna

Brahmaputra

Rann of Kutch

Allahabad

Dacca

INDIA

Chandernagore
(1950)

BANGLADESH
(E. PAKISTAN
until 1971)

BURMA

Dien Bi
Ph

1947

Nagpur

Calcutta

Irrawaddy

Mandalay

1954

Diu
(1961)

Daman
(1961)

Salween

LAOS

Bombay

Vientiane

Arabian Sea

Hyderabad

Bay of Bengal

1948

Rangoon

THAILAND

Goa
(1961)

Yanam
(1954)

Andaman Is.
(India)

Bangkok

Madras

CA

195

Laccadive Is.
(India)

Pondicherry
(1954)

Mahé
(1954)

Karikal
(1954)

Nicobar Is.
(India)

M

SRI LANKA
(Ceylon)

MALAYA

Colombo

1948

1957

Maldive Is.

Kuala Lumpur

1965

Malé

Indian Ocean

Singapore

1963

Sumatra

MANCHURIA
1946
(Russian occ. 1945-6)

Vladivostok

Mukden
1-11-48

Chinchow
15-10-48

Peking
⊙ 31-1-49

Port Arthur
(Russian base 1945-55)

24-4-49
○ Taiyuan

Yen-an ○

Hsi-an ○
20-5-49

Kai-feng ○
19-6-48

Huang-ho

CHINA

Nanking
23-4-49

Shanghai
27-5-49

23-5-49
○ Nanchang

17-5-49
Wuhan ○

Chungking ○

Yangtze

Sea of Japan

JAPAN

'U.S.S.R. admin.
1945-8)
DEMOCRATIC
PEOPLES REPUBLIC
OF KOREA

Pyongyang ⊙

1945

⊙ Seoul

REPUBLIC
OF KOREA
(U.S. admin. 1945-8)

⊙ Tokyo

East China
Sea

Ryukyu I.S.
(Returned to Japan 1972)

Taipei ⊙

TAIWAN
(FORMOSA)

**(Remains under
Nationalist control)**

1945

Bonin Is.
(Returned to Japan 1968)

Canton ○

Macao   Hong Kong
(Port. admin.)   (Br.)
**(Transfer to   (1984: agreement to
China in 1999) transfer to China in 1997)**

Hanoi ○
Haiphong ○
Gulf of Tonkin

NORTH
VIETNAM

1954

Hué ○
○ Da Nang

South China
Sea

Mekong

…ODIA   SOUTH
VIETNAM

Pnom Penh ○ ○ Da Lat

⊙ Saigon
Ho Chi Minh City
(re-named 1975)

Pacific Ocean

Manila ⊙

PHILIPPINES

1946

Mindanao

Mariana Is.

Guam
(U.S.)

…LAYSIA   Kota Kinabaru SABAH
1963

(Indep. 1984) BRUNEI
(Br.)

SARAWAK
1963

Kuching ○

Borneo
(Kalimantan)

Celebes
(Sulawesi)

Moluccas

Palau Is.

Caroline Is.

WEST IRIAN
1963

New
Guinea

PAPUA NEW GUINEA
1975

I N D O N E S I A

Djakarta ○

Soerabaya ○

Java

1949

1976

Timor

Port Moresby ⊙

Legend

- ⬤ ex-French colonies
- ⬤ ex-British and Australian colonies
- ◯ ex-Dutch colonies
- ◯ ex-Portuguese colonies
- ⬤ ex-Japanese colonies
- ⬤ ex-U.S. colonies
- ◯ Areas under U.S. administration before 1945
- ╌╌ Areas under U.S. administration after 1945 (previously Japanese)
- (1954) Date indicating establishment of Indian administration
- **1954** Dates of independence
- States independent in 1945
- Colonies made independent 1946-50
- Colonies made independent 1951-60
- Colonies made independent 1961-70
- Colonies made independent after 1970
- *1951* Territories restored to Chinese Central control with date
- 23-4-49 Urban centres taken by Communist forces in the Chinese Civil War with dates
- ╱╱╱ Japanese colony restored to China 1945
- Russian gains from Japan 1945
- ⊙ Capital city

0   1000 kms
0   600 miles

The emergence of the modern world 6

*C*ontemporary history is dominated by the heightened competition of a rapidly growing population for control of the Earth's territory and resources.

A series of local and regional power struggles erupted in the aftermath of the collapse of European imperialism. The inability of many post-colonial societies to conquer endemic poverty, famine and over-population exacerbated ethnic, religious and economic divisions within and between new states. In decolonized Asia and Africa (as in interwar Europe) independence seemed to increase rather than diminish human aggression, giving rise to vast refugee movements (*see Map 83*), mass murder of civilians, and relapse to authoritarian forms of government. The obstinately persistent gap between wealthy societies (mainly in the northern hemisphere) and the 'Third World' was visible not only in figures for per capita national income but also by such measures as life expectancy at birth (*see Map 87*).

The Second World War shattered the prestige of many of the imperial powers, helping to stimulate anti-colonial nationalisms and force the pace of European withdrawal from Asia and Africa. In 1947 Britain accorded independence to India. The sub-continent split into two sovereign states. The smaller, Muslim state of Pakistan was formed out of north-western India and east Bengal, the two portions of the new country being separated by a thousand miles of territory belonging to the larger, secular state of India (*Map 85*). Partition was accompanied by massive bloodshed and huge movements in population. Pakistan initially pursued a pro-American foreign policy, while India, under the leadership of Gandhi's disciple, Jawaharlal Nehru, followed a 'neutralist' course. A military government took power in Pakistan by 1958, whereas India was one of the few post-colonial states to preserve parliamentary democracy. Relations between India and Pakistan remained sour, embittered in particular by a dispute over Kashmir. In 1965 they fought an inconclusive war. A fierce civil war in Pakistan in 1971 broadened into another Indo-Pakistani conflict in which India won a decisive victory. East Pakistan, under Indian protection, became the new, independent state of Bangladesh.

The British withdrawal from India marked the start of a general European evacuation of South Asia (*see Map 83*). The most humiliating colonial ejection from the region was that of France from Indo-China after defeat at Dien Bien Phu in 1954. Independent states were formed in Laos, Cambodia, and Vietnam, which was partitioned at the 17th Parallel between a communist north and a non-communist south. American efforts in the 1960s to shore up the South Vietnamese regime

against communist revolution aided by attack from the north gave rise to a murderous war involving, at its peak in 1968, more than half a million American troops. Strong opposition to the war in the USA helped bring about a gradual American military withdrawal, completed by 1973. By 1975 communist forces had ousted the South Vietnamese regime and had taken power in Laos and Cambodia as well. In Cambodia the victorious revolutionaries perpetrated a ruthless 'pastoralization' of the cities, resulting in millions of deaths and the destruction of the country's economy and social organization. In 1977 Vietnam invaded

Cambodia, eventually occupying most of the country and installing a government of its own choosing. But guerrilla warfare between rival factions, often backed by outside powers, continued in the 1980s.

During the decade after 1957 most of the British and French colonies in Africa achieved independence. France had already recognized the independence of Morocco and Tunisia in 1956, but she clung doggedly to Algeria in the face of an increasingly bloody nationalist revolution there. The Algerian war culminated in 1958 in the collapse of the Fourth French Republic and the return to power of General De Gaulle as President. He consolidated the institutions of the Fifth Republic in a presidential regime, and in 1962 granted independence to Algeria. In west and east Africa colonial rule was shaken off with little or no bloodshed (*Map 74*). In the Belgian Congo, however, chaos followed the sudden Belgian withdrawal in 1960. Powerful western economic interests sponsored the formation of an independent state in the mineral-rich southern province of Katanga. Order was eventually restored by an international force dispatched by the United Nations. A civil war broke out also in Nigeria in 1966, ending in 1970 with victory for the central government over the army of the secessionist eastern region, 'Biafra'.

White rule in southern Africa held out a little longer. Portugal, which had held coastal areas of Angola and Mozambique for more than three centuries (*compare Map 36*), engaged in an increasingly costly struggle during the 1960s and early 1970s to repress nationalist guerrillas. As in France in 1958, colonial warfare led to political upheaval at home: in 1974 a military junta carried out a peaceful 'revolution of flowers'. The new democratic government speedily conceded independence to nearly all Portugal's colonies. But the anti-colonial struggle in Angola was transformed into a fierce civil war between rival factions, drawing the intervention on opposing sides of Cuban and South African forces. Meanwhile Rhodesia (formerly Southern Rhodesia), ruled by a small white minority, had issued a 'unilateral declaration of independence' in November 1965. With South African support the Rhodesian whites succeeded for a time in defying United Nations economic sanctions and maintained their oligarchic society intact. But by 1980 they too were compelled to accept black majority rule.

Opposite page: Celebrating independence, Algiers July 6 1962.

86 The Middle East since 1945
With the decline of British power, especially after the abortive Anglo-French invasion of Egypt in 1956 and the growing dependence of the developed world on imported oil, the USA and USSR became the main external forces in the Middle East, where the creation of Israel in 1948 had led to four Arab-Israeli wars by 1973.

87 Foundations of a post-imperial world
By the later twentieth century the growth of population, especially in the poorest regions, presented the world with acute difficulties. They were heightened by the decline of the traditional industrial powers and the high political and economic costs of energy, control of which seemed certain to be a decisive factor in any new international order.

MAP 86 THE MIDDLE EAST SINCE SINCE 1945

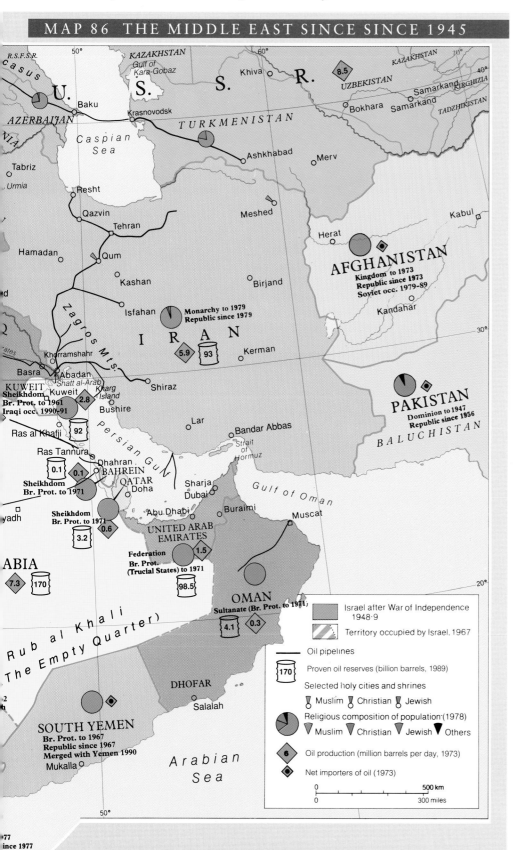

Legend:
- Israel after War of Independence 1948-9
- Territory occupied by Israel, 1967
- Oil pipelines
- 170 Proven oil reserves (billion barrels, 1989)
- Selected holy cities and shrines
  - Muslim   Christian   Jewish
- Religious composition of population (1978)
  - Muslim   Christian   Jewish   Others
- 6 Oil production (million barrels per day, 1973)
- Net importers of oil (1973)

0   500 km
0   300 miles

MAP 87 FOUNDATIONS OF A POST-IMPERIAL WORLD

GREENLAND

CANADA
438

UNITED STATES
4,864

BERMUDA
1.4

MEXICO
152

CUBA
27
0.3
BELIZE
HONDURAS
JAMAICA
4.1
2.6
NICARAGUA
2.9
7.6 GUATAMALA
EL SALVADOR
PANAMA
4.8
COSTA
RICA
4.7
5.1

HAITI 2.2
DOMINICAN REP. 4.7
PUERTO
RICO

VENEZUELA
59
COLOMBIA
37

TRINIDAD
4.2

GUYANA
0.3 SURINAM
1.1
FR. GUIANA

ECUADOR 11

BRAZIL
329

PERU
29

BOLIVIA
3.9

4.8
PARAGUAY

CHILE 19

ARGENTINA
83

URUGUAY 7.4

ICELAND 5

NORWAY 84

SWEDEN 160

DENMARK 95

EIRE 27
U.K.
730
NETH
144
BELG.
LUX
FRANCE
899
SWIT
178
765
117
GERMANY
1,290
CZE
AUST
YUC
SLAV
ITALY

PORTUGAL
37
SPAIN
302

MOROCCO
18
ALGERIA
58
TUNISI
69

WESTERN
SAHARA

MAURITANIA
MALI 1.8
NIGER
2.2

SENEGAL
0.2 GAMBIA
4.5
GUINEA-BISSAU
2.3 GUINEA
BURKINA
FASO
2
SIERRA LEONE
LIBERIA
8.6
IVORY
COAST
GHANA
5.6
TOGO
BENIN
1.5
NIGERIA
32
CAMEROON
11

EQUATORIAL
GUINEA
0.1
GABON
CONGO
3.2

ANGOLA
6.9

1.5
NAMIBIA

Life expectancy at birth, c.1983
(by country)

- 45 years or less
- 46-64 years
- 65 years or more
- Not available

Gross National Product per capita, c.1984
(dollars)

- Less than 400
- 401 - 1000
- 1001 - 5000
- Over 5000

Gross National Product c.1988
(billions of dollars)

328 **BRAZIL**

FINLAND 92

U.S.S.R. 2,500

AND 3

NGARY 65

ROMANIA 79

BULGARIA 51

GREECE 48

TURKEY 52

CYPRUS 38

LEB.

ISRAEL 4.4

SYRIA 20

IRAQ 41

JORDAN

IRAN 94

AFGHANISTAN 3.1

KUWEIT 26

PAKISTAN 37

UN. ARAB EMIRATES 24

7.1

SAUDI ARABIA 87

OMAN 1

YEMEN 5.7

SOUTH YEMEN

LBYA 23

EGYPT 33

HAD .8

SUDAN 8.1

ETHIOPIA 5.8

CEN FRICAN REP. 1.1

SOMALIA 1

UGANDA 4.5

KENYA 8.3

RWANDA

BURUNDI

ZAIRE 5.7

TANZANIA 3.8

ZAMBIA 2.2

MALAWI

ZIMBABWE 1.2

MOZAMBIQUE 6.1

BOTSWANA 1.6

SOUTH AFRICA 78

SWAZILAND

LESOTHO

MADAGASCAR 2.1

MONGOLIA 3.6

NORTH KOREA 20

SOUTH KOREA 150

JAPAN 2,757

CHINA 357

NEPAL

BHUTAN

TAIWAN 125

HONG KONG 55

INDIA 271

BANGLADESH 18

BURMA (MYANMAR) 7.4

LAOS

THAILAND 55

VIETNAM 13

CAMBODIA 0.6

PHILIPPINES 38

SRI LANKA 7

BRUNEI 3.1

MALAYSIA 32

SINGAPORE 24

INDONESIA 76

PAPUA NEW GUINEA 2.9

AUSTRALIA 204

NEW ZEALAND 32

After 1980 only South Africa (and its appendage of South-West Africa or Namibia) remained under white domination. By far the richest country on the continent, South Africa was ruled after 1948 by the Nationalist Party which pursued the policy of *apartheid* or 'separate development'. This sought to maintain white supremacy by the enforcement of discriminatory laws directed against the black majority and by racial segregation. Scattered undeveloped tracts of land were set aside as 'Bantustans' and granted nominal independence. But these secured neither international recognition nor internal acquiescence. Bloodshed in 1960 and again in 1976 heightened international criticism. From 1984 onwards severe internal violence convulsed the country and evoked fierce government countermeasures. The white minority regime, bolstered by powerful armed forces and by the country's rich mineral resources and highly developed economy, remained entrenched in power. Nevertheless, international isolation and domestic unrest eventually drove the regime, under President F. W. de Klerk, to seek an accommodation with the African National Congress, whose de-facto leader Nelson Mandela was released from prison in February 1990 and immediately assumed a leading political role.

Latin America in the post-war period remained closely tied, politically and economically, to the United States. In this region in particular, the refusal of the Roman Catholic church to sanction artificial methods of birth control contributed to the rapid population growth rate which overwhelmed the social and economic resources of many countries. Nearly all countries on the South American mainland succumbed to military rule at some stage in the post-war period. In 1973 the left-wing government of Salvador Allende in Chile was deposed by an American-inspired coup and replaced by a brutal military dictatorship. Argentina returned to democratic rule when a similar regime collapsed after its attempt to buttress its position by occupying the Falkland Islands (Malvinas) in 1982 ended in defeat by British expeditionary forces. By the mid-1980s military regimes in Latin America and the Caribbean had, with few exceptions, given way to elected civilian governments. But these confronted almost insuperable problems of massive inflation, towering foreign debt, and deep cleavages between wealthy elites and poverty-stricken masses. The exploitation of natural resources such as oil brought a modicum of prosperity to some countries like Venezuela, but even oil failed to lift Mexico (or little Trinidad) out of the mire of economic backwardness and social misery. American interventions in Guatemala in 1954, the Dominican Republic in 1965, Grenada in 1983 and Panama in 1989 ensured that those countries remained in the pro-American camp. For long Cuba was the only state in the region openly to defy the United States. But in 1979 the pro-American Somoza dictatorship in Nicaragua was overthrown by leftist revolutionaries who succeeded in maintaining power in spite of raids by American surrogates operating from Honduras, until they surrendered it voluntarily, following electoral defeat, in February 1990.

In the Middle East, as elsewhere after the Second World War, British and French imperialism collapsed, although not without severe withdrawal pains. France withdrew from Syria and Lebanon at the end of the war. In 1948 Britain abandoned Palestine where a bitter civil war had broken out between Arabs and Jews. The latter established the State of Israel and defeated repeated attacks by neighbouring Arab states. In 1956 Israel joined Britain and France in invading Egypt. Israel scored a swift victory, but Britain and France suffered a humiliating political defeat, abandoned even by their chief ally, the USA. The Suez affair was held to be definite proof that the age of European imperialism was past. Further Arab-Israeli wars in 1967 and 1973 led to renewed Israeli victories. For three decades the Arab states refused to accept the existence of Israel, but in 1977, in a startling *volte-face*, President Sadat of Egypt visited Israel and started a process which led to the signature of an Egyptian-Israeli peace treaty in 1979. Other Arab states, however, denounced the treaty as a betrayal. In 1982 Israel intervened in Lebanon, where a bloody civil war had raged since 1975. Israel withdrew most of her forces by 1985, but the Lebanese civil war continued until 1991, horrifying the world with the spectacle of a society in a Hobbesian state of disintegration. From 1987 onwards serious civil unrest, known as the *intifada*, disrupted the Israeli-occupied territories on the West Bank of the Jordan and the Gaza strip. Peace talks between Israel and its Arab neighbours, including the Palestinians, opened in Madrid in 1991 but were slow to produce results.

International attention was focused on the Middle East in the 1970s and 1980s above all because of the heightened importance of the region's oil reserves, by far the largest in the world. In 1960 the major oil-producing states had formed a cartel known as the Organization of Petroleum Exporting Countries (OPEC). The economic boom of the late 1960s and early 1970s, and the loss of self-sufficiency in oil by the world's largest consumer, the USA, created a great increase in demand which enabled OPEC to demand vast price increases, particularly after 1973. Another steep increase took place in 1979 following the revolution in Iran, in which the pro-American Shah was ousted by Islamic nationalists.

Greed for the oilfields at the head of the Persian Gulf twice tempted the Iraqi dictator Saddam Hussein, to invade his neighbours. In 1980 he precipitated eight years of desperately bloody but ultimately profitless war with Iran. Six weeks were sufficient for a United Nations force under American leadership to dislodge him from Kuwait, which he had occupied in August 1990. Iraq suffered total and devastating military defeat, but Saddam survived to wreak savage vengeance against his Kurdish and Shi'ite subjects.

The dramatic oil price rises of the 1970s were one of the major causes of the world-wide recession after 1974. This, the worst 'slump' since the 1930s, produced widespread unemployment, high levels of inflation, rocketing interest rates, wildly fluctuating currency values, and a halt to the rapid economic growth of the post-war period. The poorest countries were often the hardest hit. Although some economies (notably the United States) had recovered by the mid-1980s, and in spite of the dramatic collapse of the oil cartel after 1985, there was no return to the more settled economic conditions of the pre-1973 era. The recession of the early 1990s even affected the hitherto impregnable German and Japanese economies. Among the ex-Communist states only Poland, Hungary and the Czech Republic showed signs of making an effective transition to a market economy. In much of Africa millions hovered on the verge of starvation. Pressures everywhere towards economic nationalism represented perhaps the gravest threat to international order. In what was now a global market, if not yet in any real sense an international community, man faced anew, though with no great certainty of solution, the fundamental questions of survival and social organization with which he had grappled since the dawn of civilized life on earth.

Above: Burning oil wells in Kuwait two months after the end of the Gulf War, as trouble continued.

Further reading: Geoffrey Barraclough, *An Introduction to Contemporary History* (second edn. Viking Penguin 1968); M.E. Yapp, *The Near East since the First World War* (Longman 1990); Judith M. Brown, *Modern India: Origins of an Asian Democracy* (Oxford U. P. 1985); Alistair Horne, *A Savage War of Peace: Algeria, 1954-62* (Macmillan 1977; Viking Penguin); R.B. Smith, *An International History of the Vietnam War: 1, Revolution versus Containment, 1955-61; 2, The Struggle for Southeast Asia, 1961-65* (Macmillan, 1983, 1985; St Martin's Press); Shjaul Bakhash, *The Reign of the Ayatollahs* (second edn. Basic Books 1986; Unwin).

United States historical maps

INTRODUCTION

The search for adventure, wealth, and freedom has inspired those coming to America since the discovery of the New World.

The Spaniard Cortez, confessing to a "sickness of the soul only gold could cure," exemplified the early explorer who set out to claim land and gold for his king and riches for himself. But Great Britain soon discovered that true wealth lay in the land itself, and in North America chose colonization as the road to political and economic power. The maps that follow chronicle the remarkable development of Britain's one-time colony – the United States. Covering eight historical periods, the maps illustrate the country's foundation and expansion westward, its richly varied population, and three major conflicts – the Revolutionary and Civil wars and World War II. The maps portray these developments in a vivid, colorful style, depicting often overlapping events, such as the construction of transcontinental railways and the rise and fall of the great cattle empires. Short summaries accompanying each map provide more detailed information of each historical period. A series of tables at the end of this section list the entry of the states into the union, the flow of immigrants by nationality, and recent shifts in regional population.

From the beginning, the vastness of the continent challenged the imaginations of early settlers. The new land offered not only abundant natural resources but the opportunity to experiment with various social, religious, and political ideals. Freed from traditional European constraints, Americans rapidly created an economy and industry that outstripped the combined production of Europe. These successes built into the national character expectations for a continually rising standard of living and unlimited opportunity.

But the nation's growth was not always a steady progress forward. Native Americans and other racial minorities have long struggled for an equal place in American society. And as far back as the early 1800s, some people felt the nation's emphasis on commercial development meant neglecting the long-term consequences of uncontrolled growth. Finally, the legacy of World War II – that America would enjoy continued political and economic expansion – left the country somewhat unprepared for the problems that emerged only decades later. Conflicts abroad, increasing international economic competition, as well as domestic concerns affecting the well-being of all its citizens are major issues that challenge the United States.

Yet the maps show the development of a confident and energetic people. Perhaps the national experience of taming a continent, creating a vast industry, and absorbing millions of newcomers into the culture may prove to be adequate preparation for meeting the problems of today. It has seemed, in the past, that the nation is never more resourceful than when facing a difficult challenge.

THE AMERICAN COLONIES, 1700

The fabulous wealth discovered by Spain in Central and South America touched off a race among other nations – chiefly France and England – to share in the riches of the New World.

By the early 1600s, French holdings in North America reached from the Appalachian Mountains to the western plains and north beyond the Great Lakes; while Spain claimed the south and southwest regions. As the map on the following page shows, Great Britain possessed only a narrow strip along the Atlantic seaboard and a small area in the northwest.

Dreams of finding easy treasure faded; England and France began to realize the commercial and military value of colonizing these lands. Except for the settlements at Québec, Trois-Rivières, and Montréal, however, few people immigrated to the French regions. In contrast, America fired the imaginations of the English people. Even so, the early settlers of Jamestown and similar camps barely survived the "starving times," when disease and lack of food decimated the small population. The settlements slowly began to prosper as more immigrants arrived, bringing with them a complex array of religious, social, and political beliefs.

Most of the settlements were clustered near waterways and along the sea coast, leaving large inland areas virtually uninhabited. Provincetown, Plymouth, Philadelphia, and the Chesapeake settlements – founded as religious communities – became thriving commercial centers by the late 1600s. Boston and New York prospered as port cities, and towns scattered along the coast benefited from a growing fishing industry. The rich farmlands of Maryland, Virginia, and the Carolinas proved ideal for valuable cash crops such as cotton and tobacco. As the transplanted European population grew, native Indian tribes were forced out of coastal areas and pushed further west. By 1700, the colonies were loosely organized into eleven provinces. The population, with its unusual social, political, and religious makeup, was already markedly different from any society in Europe.

England was clearly winning the race to settle and develop its colonies. With the eventual defeat of France in the French and Indian War (1754-63), Great Britain became the dominant power in North America.

INDEPENDENCE, 1775-1783

To many historians, the Revolutionary War remains the single most important event in American history, instilling in the people a sense of their nation's special destiny. The war arose from conflicts between a diverse, fiercely independent colonial population and a British government determined to tighten its control over King George's colonies. Americans viewed the revenue acts passed to subsidize Britain's colonial army as a threat to their political and economic freedoms. Mounting hostility finally erupted in the Boston Massacre of 1770. By 1775, colonial resistance had become armed rebellion. The map on page 169 depicts the major battles and strategies of the war.

Expecting easy victories at Lexington, Concord and Bunker Hill, the British, instead, suffered heavy losses defeating the Yankee militia. Action in the western regions remained indecisive for both sides. By July, 1776, Britain was mounting a full-scale military effort to end the rebellion. Though well equipped and trained, the British army often had to deal with a largely hostile population and fight in wilderness terrain. In contrast, the Americans, outnumbered and poorly equipped, were fighting for their own land. The British sought to divide the colonies by isolating New England. They defeated George Washington's Continental Army at Long Island and New York; but at the end of 1776, Continental troops had captured Princeton and Trenton. The American victory at Saratoga in October, 1777, dealt a final blow to Britain's northern strategy. And by the following year, France had allied itself with the American cause.

From 1778 onward, Britain concentrated on the South and the sea coast. British Commander Cornwallis captured Savannah, Charleston, and Camden, but could not secure the countryside. American irregular forces continually harassed the British army until it withdrew to the coast. Finally, in October, 1781, Cornwallis surrendered his entire command to Washington and Rochambeau, Commander of the French forces dispatched to aid Americans, at Yorktown.

The peace treaty of 1783 recognized American independence and more than doubled the size of the former territory. The victorious Americans believed that their emerging nation was destined to lead the world toward liberty.

MAP
LEGEND

- Settled area: each dot represents 500 rural population.
- More than 5,000 people
- Less than 5,000 people

Huron Indian Tribe

(1634) Founding Date

SCALE

miles 0   50   100   150

kilometers 0   50   100   150   200

Québec
Dec. 1775

Montréal
Nov. 1775

MASS.
(District of Maine)

Fort Ticonderoga
May 1775

Falmouth

NEW
HAMPSHIRE

Fort Stanwix
Aug. 1777

Fort Oswego
July 1777

Saratoga
Oct. 1777

Manchester

Fort Niagara

Oriskany
Aug. 1777

Fort Herkimer

Bennington
Aug. 1777

Loyalists & Brant

Herkimer & Arnold

Lexington
& Concord
April 1775

Bunker Hill
June 1775

Geneseo

Cherry Valley
Nov. 1778
Loyalists & Brant

Albany

NEW YORK

MASS.

Boston
Mar. 1776

Fort Pontchartrain

Johnson & Indians

Newtown
Aug. 1779

CONN.

Providence

R.I.

Fort Sandusky

Loyalist & Indian raid

Sullivan

New Haven

Wyoming Valley
July 1778

White Plains
Oct. 1776

PENNSYLVANIA

Easton

Fort Lee
Nov. 1776

Long Island
Aug. 1776

New York
Sept. 1776

Howe from Halifax July 1776

Fort Pitt

Princeton
Jan. 1777

Monmouth
June 1778

Germantown
Oct. 1777

Valley Forge

Trenton
Dec. 1776

Brandywine
Sept. 1777

Wilmington

Philadelphia
Nov. 1777

Forts Mercer & Mifflin
Nov. 1777

Howe from Halifax July 1776

Clark to Fort Vincennes Feb. 1778

MD.

Baltimore

NEW JERSEY

Boonesborough

VIRGINIA

DEL.

Proclamation Line 1763

APPALACHIAN MOUNTAINS

Charlottesville

Tarleton June 1781

Lafayette June-Sept. 1781

Washington & Rochambeau (Fr.) Aug.-Sept. 1781

Washington & Rochambeau (Fr.) July-Aug. 1777

Howe from New York July-Aug. 1777

Graves from New York

Richmond

Petersburg

Yorktown
Aug.-Oct. 1781

Off the Chesapeake Capes
Sept. 1781

Norfolk

De Grasse (Fr.) from West Indies Sept. 1779

Cornwallis May 1781

Guilford
Courthouse
Mar. 1781

Salem

Cornwallis Jan. 1781

Cornwallis April 1781

Cornwallis Aug. 1780

N.C.

Frontier Settlers

King's Mountain
Oct. 1780

Ferguson

Charlotte

Morgan Dec. 1780

Cowpens
Jan. 1781

S.C.

Tarleton Jan. 1781

Moore's Creek
Bridge
Feb. 1776

Fort Ninety Six
June 1781

Winnsboro

Gates

Greene Mar. 1781

Camden
Aug. 1780

Ft. Augusta
Feb. 1779

Rawdon

Eutaw Springs
Sept. 1781

Georgetown

Briar Creek
Feb. 1779

Asche Feb. 1779

Charles Town
May 1780

Clinton & Cornwallis from New York Jan. 1780

Campbell from New York Dec. 1778

Campbell Feb. 1779

Prevost May 1779

Lincoln Oct. 1779

GEORGIA

Savannah
Dec. 1778
Oct. 1779

Prevost Jan. 1779

D'Estaing (Fr.) from West Indies Sept. 1779

Wilmington

MAP
LEGEND

American
Colonies

Indian
Reserve

British
Occupied
City

American
Occupied
City

British
Held Fort

American
Held Fort

British
Victory

American
Victory

British
Forces

American
Forces

SCALE

miles 0   50   100   150

kilometers 0   50   100   150   200

The rallying cry of "Manifest destiny!" reflected the American belief that providence itself had granted the United States exclusive right to settle North America.

The country's rapidly expanding population and commercial development, the flood of European immigrants, and a growing transportation system all played a part in the first great western migration.

In 1803, Thomas Jefferson, deeply concerned about European influence on the continent, made the bold step of purchasing the Louisiana Territory from France – in one stroke doubling the nation's size. Early explorers such as Zebulon Pike and Meriwether Lewis and William Clark brought back glowing reports of the territory's rich land and abundant fur trade. In 1819, Spain ceded the remainder of Florida to the Republic. For many people in the crowded eastern states, including hundreds of Irish and German immigrants, the new lands represented opportunities for a better life. Soon a complex network of turnpikes, canal and river systems, and railroads carried settlers into the Mississippi Valley and parts of Texas, and opened the lands to eastern markets.

As the Louisiana Territory became more densely settled, pioneers began to push beyond the formal borders of the country. By the early 1840s, the St. Joseph, Missouri rail line served as a starting point for wagon trains heading west over the Oregon, Santa Fe, Fremont, and California trails. Mexico, attempting to stop the flow of settlers into its lands, soon found itself at war with the Americans, losing Texas in 1836 and its vast southwestern territories in 1848. The Gadsden Purchase of 1853 completed America's southernmost border. In the Pacific Northwest, early explorers and settlers had strengthened American claims to the Oregon Territory, held jointly with Great Britain. The two countries agreed in 1848 to divide the land at the 49th Parallel. As more settlers poured into these territories, native Indian tribes were forced off their lands and eventually moved to reservations.

In little over half a century, America had fulfilled its manifest destiny on the continent. Seventeen new states had joined the Republic, eight of them west of the Mississippi. Only the deepening conflict over slavery seemed to dim the nation's brilliant future.

MAP LEGEND

Canals

Railroads

▲ Port Cities

● Other Cities

☐ States as of 1803

Roads

Width of flow lines are proportional to actual numbers of immigrants entering the United States through the ports indicated during the period 1840-1855.

SCALE

miles 0   100   200   300   400

kilometers 0   200   400   600

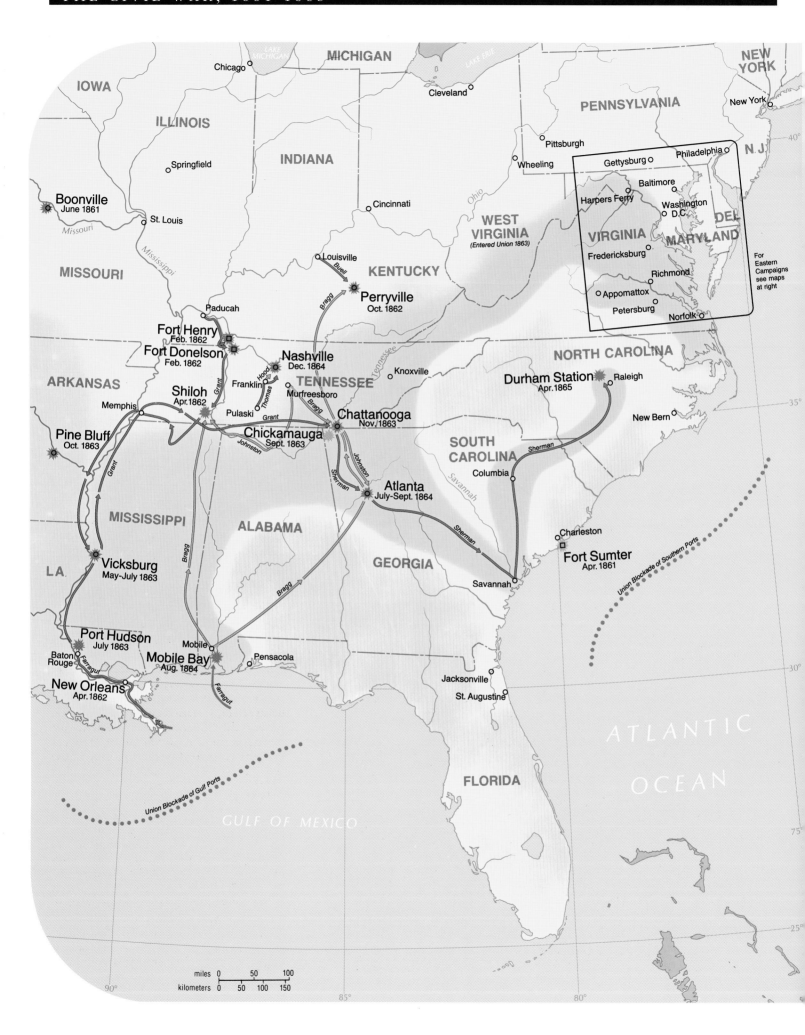

NEW YORK

New York

PENNSYLVANIA

IOWA

Chicago

LAKE MICHIGAN

MICHIGAN

LAKE ERIE

Cleveland

ILLINOIS

INDIANA

Pittsburgh

Wheeling

Gettysburg

Philadelphia

N. J.

Springfield

Cincinnati

WEST VIRGINIA
(Entered Union 1863)

Baltimore

Harpers Ferry

Washington
D.C.

DEL

Boonville
June 1861

St. Louis

Ohio

VIRGINIA

MARYLAND

Missouri

Louisville

KENTUCKY

Buell

Fredericksburg

Richmond

For Eastern
Campaigns
see maps
at right

MISSOURI

Mississippi

Appomattox

Perryville
Oct. 1862

Petersburg

Norfolk

ARKANSAS

Paducah

Bragg

Fort Henry
Feb. 1862

Fort Donelson
Feb. 1862

Nashville
Dec. 1864

Tennessee

Knoxville

NORTH CAROLINA

Durham Station
Apr. 1865

Raleigh

Hood

Shiloh
Apr. 1862

Franklin

Thomas

Grant

Murfreesboro

Memphis

Pulaski

Grant

Bragg

Chattanooga
Nov. 1863

Pine Bluff
Oct. 1863

Chickamauga
Sept. 1863

New Bern

Johnston

SOUTH
CAROLINA

Sherman

Grant

Johnston

Columbia

Savannah

MISSISSIPPI

ALABAMA

Sherman

Atlanta
July-Sept. 1864

LA.

Vicksburg
May-July 1863

Bragg

Sherman

Charleston

Union Blockade of Southern Ports

GEORGIA

Fort Sumter
Apr. 1861

Savannah

Port Hudson
July 1863

Mobile

Baton
Rouge

Farragut

Mobile Bay
Aug. 1864

Pensacola

New Orleans
Apr. 1862

Farragut

Jacksonville

St. Augustine

ATLANTIC

OCEAN

FLORIDA

Union Blockade of Gulf Ports

GULF OF MEXICO

miles   0   50   100
kilometers 0   50   100   150

1861-1863

1864-1865

By the 1860 presidential election, it was clear that compromise on the issue of slavery could no longer hold the nation together.

While the North vehemently denounced slave holding, the South as passionately defended its way of life against a "despotic" federal authority. Soon after Abraham Lincoln was elected president, the South seceded from the union and chose Jefferson Davis to head a new government in Richmond, Virginia. By May, 1861, the United States and the Confederacy were at war.

Both sides expected a quick end to the conflict. But after the decisive Confederate victory at Bull Run in July, the war bogged down. Not until early 1862 did the Union army, under George Brinton McClellen and Ulysses S. Grant, take the offensive, winning in the west at Fort Henry, Fort Donelson, and Shiloh. McClellen's subsequent move against Richmond, though supported by the Navy, was stopped by Confederate forces under the command of Robert E. Lee in the Seven Days battle. With the Union offensive stalled, Lee and Pope launched a Confederate invasion of the North, reaching Antietam before being pushed back into Virginia. But the Union losses at Fredericksburg and Chancellorsville encouraged Lee to attempt a second invasion. In July, 1863, he was defeated at Gettysburg in the most decisive battle of the war. That same month, Grant captured Vicksburg, and joining William Tecumseh Sherman, Commander of the Tennessee troops, went on to win at Chattanooga, driving the Confederate troops back into Georgia.

By 1864, the North's economic superiority and the Union naval blockade had become critical factors in the war. In May of that year, Grant and George Meade, Commander of the Army of the Potomac, made the final march on Richmond. Although defeated by Lee in the battle of the Wilderness, and again at Spotsylvania and Cold Harbor, Grant's well-supplied troops continued to press toward Richmond and Petersburg. In a coordinated effort, Sherman began his march to the sea, capturing Atlanta, Savannah, and Columbia before turning north to Raleigh. On April 9, 1865, Lee finally surrendered to Grant at Appomattox Court House: The Union had been preserved.

When the war ended, the nation had undergone profound changes. The Emancipation Proclamation had abolished slavery; the South's agricultural economy lay in ruins. But the conflict had awakened the industrial might of the North. If one way of life had been lost, another was already rising to take its place.

MAP LEGEND

Union

Union Penetration of Confederate Area 1862-1865

Confederate

Union Victory

Confederate Victory

Battle Indecisive

Union Forces

Confederate Forces

The final settlement of the West involved the greatest movement of people in the nation's history. In only thirty years – one generation after the Civil War – the "Great American Desert" had been transformed into the mineral and agricultural empire of the Republic.

The railroad boom of this era soon opened the plains and mountain-desert regions to settlement. Between 1869 and 1884, four transcontinental railways were built; along with the overland stage, they linked the industrial East to the West. In a few years, the railroads were shipping cattle and grain east, carrying mail and payrolls, helping to supply the frontier army, and bringing settlers, many of them immigrants, into western territories.

The first wave of settlers were miners. In the 1860s and '70s, gold and silver strikes in the Black Hills, Nevada, Colorado, Arizona, and Montana brought thousands of prospectors swarming into Indian lands. Inevitably, war broke out with tribes in the north and southwest. Although the Indians won isolated battles – the most famous at Little Big Horn – they could not prevail against the army's superior weapons. By 1887, the Indians and buffalo were gone from the open range.

Ranchers and farmers soon followed in the miners' wake. From the mid-1860s to the late 1880s, a vast cattle empire dominated Texas, Wyoming, and Montana. Cattle drives up the Chisholm and Sedalia trails helped inspire the romance of the cowboy, a figure that, like the notorious western outlaw, quickly passed into American legend. But the open range was short-lived. Sheepherders soon challenged the ranchers, and farmers began fencing off grazing land and planting crops in the semi-arid soil. In the end, windmills and barbed wire tamed the West as effectively as the railroads and Colt repeating revolver.

By 1890, an almost continuous line of settlement stretched from the Midwest to the Pacific, and population in the territories had soared. The "frontier" had all but disappeared. Ten new states joined the Union, bringing with them the regional flavor of the West. Only the great waves of immigration in the early 1900s would compare with the extensive migration of this era.

MAP
LEGEND

Settled by 1890

Indian Reservations 1880

Railroads

Trails West

Buffalo Herds 1870

Cattle Trails

Mining

Indian Battle

Incident of Violence

1867 Dates of Admission

SCALE

miles 0 50 100 150 200 250
kilometers 0 100 200 300 400

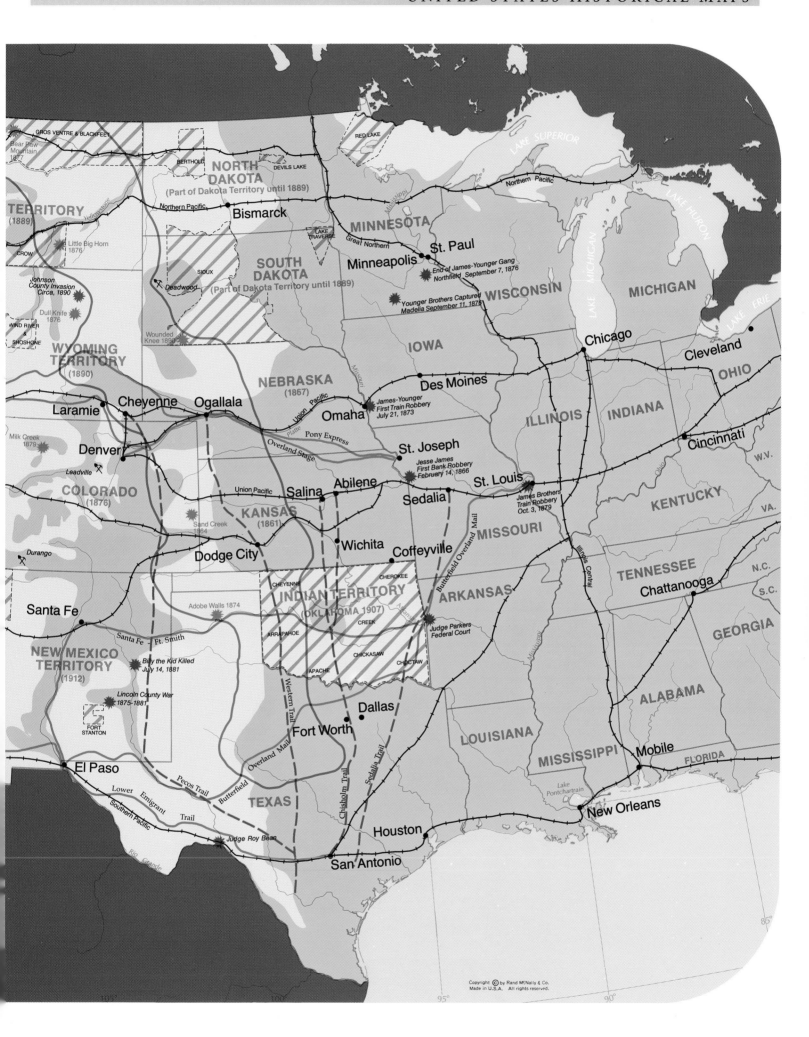

GROS VENTRE & BLACKFEET

Bear Paw
Mountain
1877

TERRITORY
(1889)

Little Big Horn
1876

CROW

Johnson
County Invasion
Circa, 1890

Dull Knife
1876

WIND RIVER
&
SHOSHONE

Milk Creek
1879

WYOMING
TERRITORY
(1890)

Laramie

Cheyenne

Denver

Leadville

COLORADO
(1876)

Durango

Santa Fe

NEW MEXICO
TERRITORY
(1912)

El Paso

Lower   Emigrant   Trail

Southern Pacific

RIO Grande

BERTHOLD

NORTH
DAKOTA
(Part of Dakota Territory until 1889)

DEVILS LAKE

Northern Pacific

Bismarck

Yellowstone

LAKE
TRAVERSE

Northern Pacific

RED LAKE

LAKE SUPERIOR

LAKE HURON

MINNESOTA

Great Northern

St. Paul

Minneapolis

End of James-Younger Gang
Northfield   September 7, 1876

SOUTH
DAKOTA
(Part of Dakota Territory until 1889)

Deadwood

SIOUX

Younger Brothers Captured
Madelia September 11, 1876

WISCONSIN

LAKE MICHIGAN

MICHIGAN

LAKE ERIE

Wounded
Knee 1890

IOWA

Chicago

Cleveland

NEBRASKA
(1867)

Des Moines

ILLINOIS

INDIANA

OHIO

W.V.

Ogallala

Union Pacific

Omaha

James-Younger
First Train Robbery
July 21, 1873

Platte

Pony Express

Cincinnati

Overland Stage

St. Joseph

Jesse James
First Bank Robbery
February 14, 1866

St. Louis

KENTUCKY

VA.

Union Pacific

Salina

Abilene

Sedalia

James Brothers
Train Robbery
Oct. 3, 1879

Dodge City

KANSAS
(1861)

Sand Creek
1864

Wichita

Coffeyville

MISSOURI

Butterfield Overland Mail

TENNESSEE

Chattanooga

N.C.

S.C.

Adobe Walls 1874

CHEYENNE

CHEROKEE

INDIAN TERRITORY
(OKLAHOMA 1907)

ARKANSAS

Santa Fe – Ft. Smith

Billy the Kid Killed
July 14, 1881

ARRAPAHOE

CREEK

Judge Parkers
Federal Court

GEORGIA

Lincoln County War
1875-1881

CHICKASAW

CHOCTAW

Arkansas

FORT
STANTON

APACHE

Western Trail

ALABAMA

Dallas

Fort Worth

Overland Mail

Chisholm Trail

Sedalia Trail

LOUISIANA

MISSISSIPPI

Mobile

FLORIDA

Pecos Trail

Butterfield

TEXAS

Lake
Pontchartrain

New Orleans

Judge Roy Bean

Houston

San Antonio

Copyright © by Rand McNally & Co.
Made in U.S.A.   All rights reserved.

105°

100°

95°

90°

85°

For the first one hundred years of its history, the United States opened its doors to all nationalities. Often war, famine, or oppression drove millions of people from their homelands to American shores.

The accompanying map depicts where these immigrants and the children of mixed or foreign parentage had settled by 1910.

European immigrants who arrived before, and two decades after, the Civil War, came primarily from England and Ireland, Scandinavia, and Germany. While the Irish tended to remain in the eastern cities, other immigrants seized the chance to journey westward to Oregon, then later to the northern plains states and parts of Texas and California. Many were skilled farmers and artisans, and blended quickly into the mainstream of American life. By the early 1900s, however, the character of immigration had changed considerably. Conditions in eastern and southern Europe led over eight million people to make the arduous journey across the Atlantic. Most of these immigrants, illiterate and unskilled, crowded into the poorer sections of industrial cities such as New York, Boston, and Chicago, creating ethnic communities that insulated them from the language and customs of their new country. Yet they answered industry's insatiable demand for labor, and filled the factories, mines, textile and steel mills, stockyards and railroads, helping to build the industrial might of the nation.

On the West Coast, the Chinese and Japanese did not fare as well. Their numbers alarmed American workers, and in 1882, the first in a series of immigration laws was passed, restricting the entry of Asians into the United States. Mexicans and Latin Americans entering California and the southwestern states often encountered the same resistance and hostility.

In contrast, since the South lacked both heavy industry and available land, immigrants tended to bypass this region in favor of the North and West. Also, restrictive state immigration laws made it difficult for the foreign-born to settle in the South.

The constant stream of newcomers helped create a rich and varied culture in America, making it truly a "nation of nations." Immigrants, and the children of immigrants, contributed immeasurably to the country's industry, science, and arts, and in two world wars, served their new country with distinction.

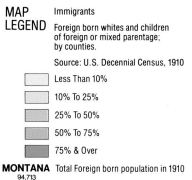

MAP LEGEND

Immigrants

Foreign born whites and children of foreign or mixed parentage; by counties.

Source: U.S. Decennial Census, 1910

Less Than 10%
10% To 25%
25% To 50%
50% To 75%
75% & Over

MONTANA
94,713
Total Foreign born population in 1910

SCALE

miles 0 100 200 300 400
kilometers 0 200 400 600

NORTH DAKOTA
156,654

MINNESOTA
543,595

Minneapolis

SOUTH DAKOTA
100,790

LAKE SUPERIOR

MICHIGAN
597,650

LAKE HURON

MAINE
110,562

VT.
49,921

N.H.
96,667

WISCONSIN
512,865

Milwaukee

LAKE ONTARIO

NEW YORK
2,748,011

Buffalo

MASS.
1,059,245

Boston

CONN.
329,574

R.I.
179,141

NEBRASKA
176,662

IOWA
273,765

Chicago

LAKE ERIE

Cleveland

PENNSYLVANIA
1,442,374

Pittsburgh

Newark

N.J.
650,788

New York

Detroit

ILLINOIS
1,205,314

INDIANA
159,663

OHIO
598,374

Philadelphia

Baltimore

DEL.
17,492

Kansas
City

Cincinnati

WEST
VIRGINIA
57,218

Washington
D.C.
24,902

MARYLAND
104,944

KANSAS
135,450

St. Louis

Missouri

MISSOURI
229,779

KENTUCKY
40,162

Ohio

VIRGINIA
27,057

Nashville

NORTH CAROLINA
6,092

OKLAHOMA
40,442

TENNESSEE
18,607

ARKANSAS
17,046

SOUTH
CAROLINA
6,179

Atlanta

MISSISSIPPI
9,770

ALABAMA
19,286

GEORGIA
15,477

ATLANTIC

TEXAS
241,938

LOUISIANA
52,766

Jacksonville

FLORIDA
40,633

OCEAN

San Antonio

New Orleans

GULF OF MEXICO

Tropic of Cancer

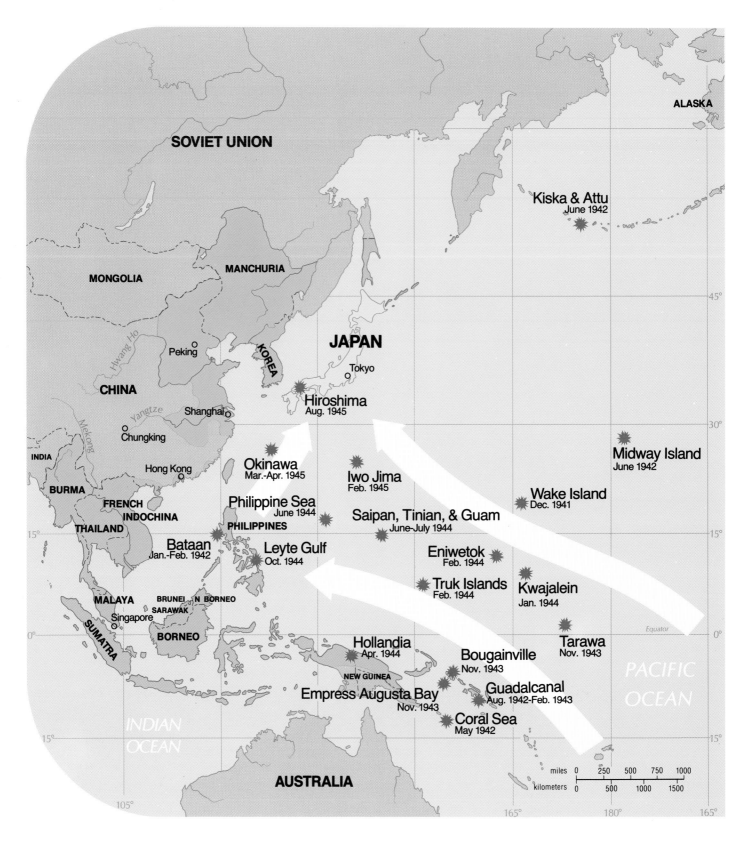

ALASKA

SOVIET UNION

Kiska & Attu
June 1942

MONGOLIA

MANCHURIA

45°

KOREA

JAPAN

Peking

Tokyo

CHINA

Hiroshima
Aug. 1945

Midway Island
June 1942

30°

Shanghai

Chungking

INDIA

Okinawa
Mar.-Apr. 1945

Iwo Jima
Feb. 1945

Wake Island
Dec. 1941

Hong Kong

BURMA

Philippine Sea
June 1944

Saipan, Tinian, & Guam
June-July 1944

FRENCH
INDOCHINA

PHILIPPINES

THAILAND

15°

Bataan
Jan.-Feb. 1942

Leyte Gulf
Oct. 1944

Eniwetok
Feb. 1944

15°

Truk Islands
Feb. 1944

Kwajalein
Jan. 1944

MALAYA

BRUNEI N BORNEO

SARAWAK

Singapore

SUMATRA

BORNEO

Equator

Tarawa
Nov. 1943

0°

Hollandia
Apr. 1944

Bougainville
Nov. 1943

PACIFIC
OCEAN

NEW GUINEA

Empress Augusta Bay
Nov. 1943

Guadalcanal
Aug. 1942-Feb. 1943

INDIAN
OCEAN

15°

Coral Sea
May 1942

15°

AUSTRALIA

miles 0   250   500   750 1000
kilometers 0   500   1000   1500

105°   165°   180°   165°

Hwang Ho
Yangtze
Mekong

T he United States entered World War II almost totally
unprepared to fight on the two fronts of Europe and the
Pacific. Yet its vast industrial capacity proved to be a decisive
factor in the Allied victory, and eventually thrust America into a
position of world leadership.

Early in the war, however, the Axis alliance seemed
invincible. By 1942, Germany had swept through
most of Europe, isolated Great Britain, and launched an invasion of Russia. In North Africa, Rom-
mel, Commander of German forces, threatened the
vital Suez Canal. Russian leader, Joseph Stalin des-

parately called for a "second front" in Europe to
relieve his hard-pressed troops, but the Allies were
unprepared to invade the continent. Instead, in
November, 1942, Dwight D. Eisenhower, U.S.
General and Allied Supreme commander in North
Africa, led a coordinated attack on Morocco and
Algeria, and by May of the next year had driven
the Axis powers out of North Africa. Bolstered by
American material, Soviet troops regained the offensive in the 1942-43 winter war and began forc-
ing the Germans back toward Berlin. Finally, after

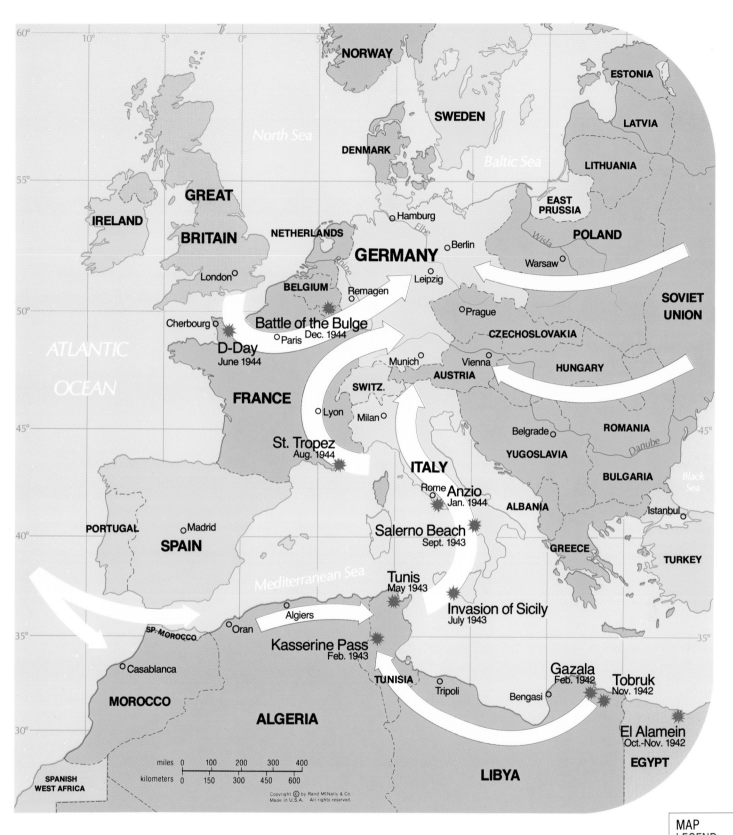

an ill-advised invasion of Sicily, the Allies landed on the beaches of Normandy and southern France in June, 1944. Caught between advancing Russian and Allied troops, Germany surrendered on May 7, 1945.

In the early months of the Pacific war, Japan had quickly overrun Manchuria, Southeast Asia, Singapore, and Indonesia and gained control of the seas. But by 1942, Allied forces had defeated the Japanese navy at Coral Sea, Midway, and Solomon Islands, and in 1944, destroyed the remaining fleet

at Leyte Gulf. Douglas MacArthur, Commander of the U.S. Forces in the Far East, liberated the Philippines in October of that year and, with Chester Nimitz, Commander of the U.S. Pacific Fleet, launched a two-pronged attack toward Japan. Capturing one island after another, American forces were soon poised to invade the Japanese mainland. Instead, in early August, 1945, the first atomic bombs were exploded over Hiroshima and Nagasaki. Japan surrendered on August 14.

The war had profoundly changed the world. The

United States and Russia now faced one another as rival superpowers over a divided Europe, and the spectre of the atom bomb haunted the world. As people returned to peacetime, it was hoped that the newly chartered United Nations would provide a forum for all nations to seek peaceful solutions to world problems and to begin to build a more lasting peace throughout the world.

MAP
LEGEND

▨	Allied Powers
▨	Axis Powers
▨	Axis Controlled Areas
▨	Neutral Nations
✸	Battles
⬅	Allied Advances

181

Over 250 million people lived in the United States in 1990. *Metropolitan areas were home to 77 % of those Americans.*

Through most of the twentieth century, metropolitan areas have been centers of population growth. Though rates of growth have slowed, these areas continue to attract people in search of greater economic opportunities. The accompanying map shows the distribution of population and the dense concentration of Americans in major urbanized areas.

Until the late 1950s, the Industrial belt – stretching from the Northeast to St. Louis – continued to attract businesses and labor. Thousands of blacks from the South and whites from Appalachia migrated North to the great cities, while inner-city whites moved to the rapidly growing suburbs. By the late 1950s and early 1960s, many light industries were also leaving the inner city not only for the suburbs but for the Sunbelt of the West and South where labor and energy costs were lower and tax incentives more attractive. In addition, a growing aerospace and electronics industry drew a large, highly skilled work force to Florida, Texas, and California.

Changing American lifestyles also contributed to the exodus to warmer climates. The ecology movement of the 1960s that carried into the 1990s encouraged people to escape from crowded industrial areas to less developed sections in the Southwest and Pacific states. In contrast, rural areas – particularly the drier western states – were losing population as people sought employment in cities and the new industrial regions. More retired people looked to the Sunbelt as a place to enjoy their later years. The retirement and leisure communities that grew up in Florida, Arizona, and California continue to attract people at a greater rate than cities in the North.

The latter decades of the century have witnessed a wave of immigrants from Asia and Latin America that has contributed to the ethnic variety as well as to the growth of the nation.

This growing nation, aided by a well-developed communication and transportation system and a substantial resource base, continued to move, settle, and redefine the American society of the 1990s.

MAP LEGEND

Population density per square mile (kilometer) by counties, 1990.

- Over 1,000 (over 400)
- 250 to 1,000 (100 to 400)
- 100 to 250 (40 to 100)
- 50 to 100 (20 to 40)
- 25 to 50 (10 to 20)
- 10 to 25 (4 to 10)
- 0 to 10 (0 to 4)

Source: 1990 U.S. Census

SCALE

miles   0   100   200   300   400

kilometers   0   100   200   300

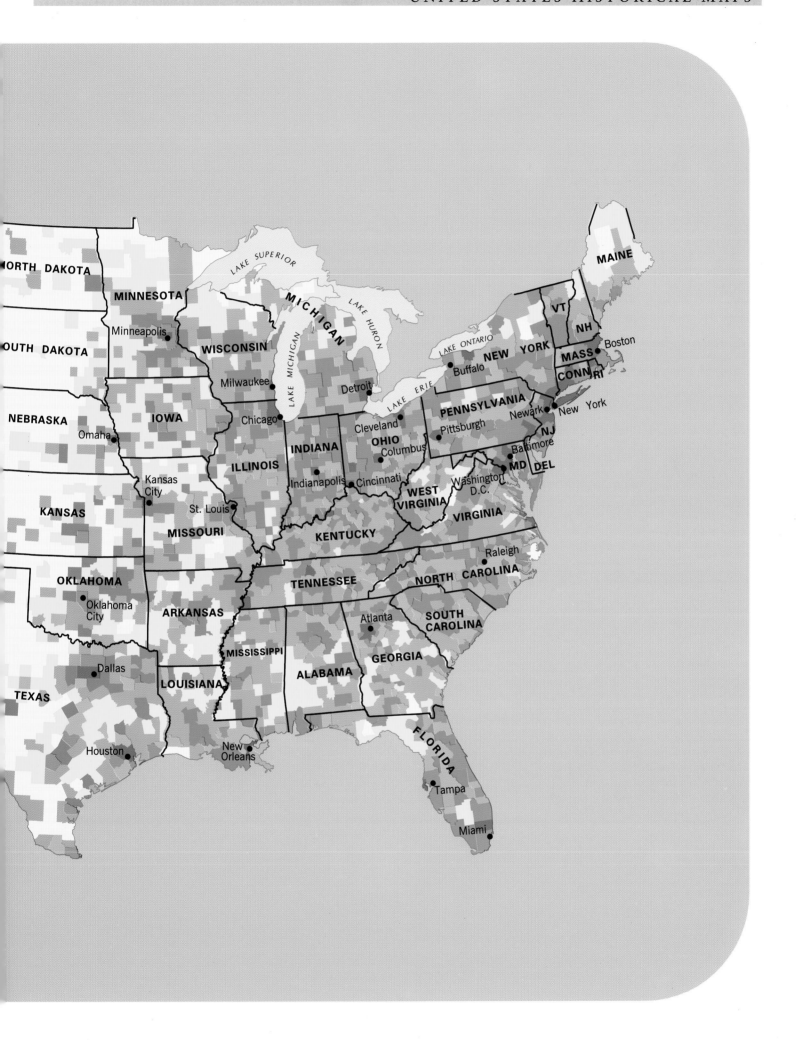

The tables below reflect three major movements im American History – the filling out of the nation's boundaries, the flow of immigrants entering the United States, and the latest trends in population shifts. These figures depict a nation in a state of constant change and development.

THE EXPANDING NATION

State	Date Admitted	No.	State	Date Admitted	No.	State	Date Admitted	No.
Alabama	Dec. 14, 1819	22	Louisiana	April 30, 1812	18	Ohio	March 1, 1803	17
Alaska	Jan 3, 1959	49	Maine	March 15, 1820	23	Oklahoma	Nov. 16, 1907	46
Arizona	Feb. 24, 1912	48	Maryland	April 28, 1788	7	Oregon	Feb. 14, 1859	33
Arkansas	June 15, 1836	25	Massachusetts	Feb. 6, 1788	6	Pennsylvania	Dec. 12, 1787	2
California	Sept. 9, 1850	31	Michigan	Jan. 26, 1837	26	Rhode Island	May 29, 1790	13
Colorado	Aug. 1, 1876	38	Minnesota	May 11, 1858	32	South Carolina	May 23, 1788	8
Connecticut	Jan. 9, 1788	5	Mississippi	Dec. 10, 1817	20	South Dakota	Nov. 2, 1889	40
Delaware	Dec. 7, 1787	1	Missouri	Aug. 10, 1821	24	Tennessee	June 1, 1796	16
Florida	March 3, 1845	27	Montana	Nov. 8, 1889	41	Texas	Dec. 29, 1845	28
Georgia	Jan. 2, 1788	4	Nebraska	March 1, 1867	37	Utah	Jan. 4, 1896	45
Hawaii	Aug. 21, 1959	50	Nevada	Oct. 31, 1864	36	Vermont	March 4, 1791	14
Idaho	July 3, 1890	43	New Hampshire	June 21, 1788	9	Virginia	June 25, 1788	10
Illinois	Dec. 3, 1818	21	New Jersey	Dec. 18, 1787	3	Washington	Nov. 11, 1889	42
Indiana	Dec. 11, 1816	19	New Mexico	Jan. 6, 1912	47	West Virginia	June 20, 1863	35
Iowa	Dec. 28, 1846	29	New York	July 26, 1788	11	Wisconsin	May 29, 1848	30
Kansas	Jan. 29, 1861	34	North Carolina	Nov. 21, 1789	12	Wyoming	July 10, 1890	44
Kentucky	June 1, 1792	15	North Dakota	Nov. 2, 1889	39			

A NATION OF IMMIGRANTS: 1851-1988

Region	1851-70	1871-90	1891-1910	1911-30	1931-50	1951-70	1971-88
Europe—Northern and Western Belgium, England, Denmark, Finland, France, Germany, Ireland, Netherlands, Norway, Scotland, Sweden, Switzerland	4,463,000	5,849,000	3,553,500	2,298,200	693,900	1,498,800	469,100
Europe—Southern and Eastern Austria, Bulgaria, Czechoslovakia, Greece, Hungary, Italy, Poland, Portugal , Romania, Spain, Turkey, U.S.S.R., Yugoslavia	54,900	1,158,600	8,140,700	4,525,100	261,100	983,300	790,200
Asia China, India, Iran, Japan, Korea, Laos, Philippines, Vietnam	106,000	187,800	195,900	172,500	32,700	398,300	3,029,200
America Canada, Latin America, Mexico, West Indies	241,300	831,000	400,900	2,660,400	514,800	2,576,300	3,800,600
Other Countries African countries, Australia, New Zealand, Pacific Islands	47,700	26,300	72,300	38,300	31,500	121,900	291,300

REGIONAL TRENDS IN POPULATION: 1970-2000

Region	1970	1980	1990	2000	Per Cent Change		
					1970-1980	1980-1990	(Projected) 1990-2000
Northeast Connecticut, Maine, Massachusetts, New Hampshire, New Jersey, New York, Pennsylvania, Rhode Island, Vermont	49,061,000	49,137,000	50,809,000	51,810,000	0.2%	3.4%	2.0%
North Central Illinois, Indiana, Iowa, Kansas, Michigan, Minnesota, Missouri, Nebraska, North Dakota, Ohio, South Dakota, Wisconsin	56,590,000	58,854,000	59,669,000	59,596,000	4.0	1.4	-0.1
South Alabama, Arkansas, Delaware, District of Columbia, Florida, Georgia, Kentucky, Louisiana, Maryland, Mississippi, North Carolina, Oklahoma, South Carolina, Tennessee, Texas, Virginia, West Virginia	62,813,000	75,349,000	85,446,000	96,919,000	20.0	13.4	13.4
West Alaska, Arizona, California, Colorado, Hawaii, Idaho, Montana, Nevada, New Mexico, Oregon, Utah, Washington, Wyoming	34,838,000	43,165,000	52,786,000	59,422,000	23.9	22.3	12.6

There has been no attempt to standardize the spelling of place names in this Atlas. Many places have changed their names in the course of history; many different forms of transcription or romanization have been used for oriental names; and many places, especially the best-known ones, are more familiar to English-speaking readers in their modern, Anglicized form than in the vernacular which may be more common for their less-well-known neighbours. The maps in this Atlas reflect this diversity. Rather than attempt to impose any rule of thumb such as modern internationally-accepted spellings the editor has asked the contributors to use the spellings and forms which students in their particular fields are most likely to encounter in their reading on the subject. Thus two maps of the same area, separated in date by two or three hundred years, may show minor differences. Sometimes, also, local forms are shown, sometimes Anglicized ones. It is hoped that these differences will be aids to general clarity rather than confusion.

The list that follows is intended to be a guide to the major places that have changed their names significantly over the centuries. Minor variations, modernizations or Anglicizations have been ignored; but where cultural, political or linguistic developments have given rise to entirely new names, these are listed below. The modern forms, given in bold type, are those usually to be found in The Times Atlas of The World (6th ed., 1980);the variants are mostly to be found on the maps in the present volume. The main entry for each place is listed under its modern spelling with its variants in roughly chronological order; a major (though not necessarily the only) map reference has also been given.

Only town names, sites of battles, archaeological sites and some rivers have been included in this list. The names of regions and countries, which have changed in both name and area too much to be included in a list of this kind, are to be found in the main index.

INDEX OF ALTERNATIVE PLACE NAMES

ACKNOWLEDGEMENTS

It would be quite impossible to list all the sources which have been consulted in the preparation of these maps. Among general works of reference, those much used include:

Atlas zur Geschichte (2 vols., Leipzig 1976).

C.M Cipolla, ed., *The Fontana Economic History of Europe* (6 vols., London 1972-)

H.C Darby and H Fullard, eds., *The New Cambridge Modern History Vol. XIV, Atlas* (Cambridge, 1970).

M.Gilbert, *Atlas of American History* (London, Weidenfeld and Nicolson, 1968).

Grosser Historischer Weltatlas, ed. J.Engel (3 vols., Munich 1953-70).

A.Herrmann, *An Historical Atlas of China* (Edinburgh, 1966). *The International Atlas* (New York, Rand MacNally, 1974).

H.Jedin, K.S Latourette and J. Martin, *Atlas zur Kirchengeschihte* (Freiburg, 1970).

H.Kinder and W.Hilgemann, *The Penguin Atlas of World History* (2 vols., London, 1974, 1978)

C.McEvedy and R.Jones, *Atlas of World Population History* (London, Penguin Books 1978).

W.H McNeill, *The Rise of the West* (Chicago, Chicago U.P., 1968)

B.R Mitchell, *European Historical Statistics, 1750-1970* (London, 1975).

W.G Moore, *The Penguin Encyclopedia of Places* (London, 1971).

Ramsey Muir, *Historical Atlas*, ed. R.F Treharne and H Fullard (London, Philip, 1966).

D.E Pitcher, *An Historical Geography of the Ottoman Empire* (Leiden, 1973).

The New Oxford Atlas (Oxford, 1975).

J.M Roberts, *The Hutchinson History of the World* (London, 1976).

The Statesman's Yearbook.

The Times Atlas of the World, comprehensive edition (London, 1976).

The United Nations Yearbook.

G Westermann, *Grosser Atlas zur Weltgeschichte* (Brunswick, 1976).

The Editor and contributors are also grateful to acknowledge specific obligations in respect of the following:

Map 17: 'Frontier of literacy' – P Riché, *Education and Culture in the Barbarian West* (Engl. trans.), Columbia, South Carolina U.P., 1976), pp 177-183.

Map 21: states of Kievan Russsia – G Vernadsky, *A History of Russia* 2 (New Haven, Yale U.P., 1948), endpaper; spread of Glagolitic rite – A.P Vlasto, *The Entry of the Slavs into Christendom* (Cambridge, Cambridge U.P., 1970), p 204.

Map 22, 24: itineraries – Carlrichard Bruhl, *Fodfum, Gistum, Servitium Regis* (Köhn, Böhlau, 1968), vol. II.

Map 23: Viking graves – D.M Wilson, 'Scandinavian Settlement in the North and West of the British Isles',

Transactions of the Royal Historical Society 5th series 26 (1976), pp 108-9.

Map 26: Latin sees in Frankish Greece – P Fedelto, *La chiesa Latina in Oriente* (Verona, 1973-76), II: *Hierarchia Latina Orientis, Studi Religiosi,* 3.

Map 28: Pegolotti – J.K Hyde, *Society and Politics in Medieval Italy* (London, Macmillan, 1973), Map 6.

Map 31: Mongol strategy – O Lattimore, 'The Geography of Chingis Khan', *Geographical Journal* CXXIX, 1963, 1-7.

Map 36: distribution of peoples – G.W Hewes, *A Conspectus of the World's Cultures in 1500 A.D.*

Map 38: economic regions – G William Skinner, ed., *The City in Late Imperial China*, (Stanford, Stanford U.P., 1977), pp 214-15; couriers – Y.W Cheng, *Postal Communication in China and its modernisation, 1860-96* (Cambridge, Mass., Harvard U.P. for East Asian Research Center, 1970), pp 11,22.

Map 40: Mughal service élite – M Athar Ali, 'Towards an interpretation of the Mughal Empire', *Journal of the Royal Asiatic Society,* 1976, No.1, p45.

Map 42: Origins of Hapsburg infantry – G Parker, *The Army of Flanders and the Spanish Road,* (Cambridge, Cambridge U.P., 1972), p28 Fig. iv.

Map 43: population figures – P Channu, *Amérique et les Amériques* (Paris, 1964), p22. More estimates differ widely.

Map 45: imports of slaves – P Curtin, *The Atlantique Slave Trade* (Madison, Milwaukee and London, 1969), p268.

Map 47: currency – F Braudel and L Spooner, 'Movements of Prices, 1450-1650' in *Cambridge Economic History of Europe*IV, ed.E.E Rich and C.H Wilson (Cambridge, Cambridge U.P., 1967), p463; Dutch engineers – J van Deem, *Dredge, Drain, Reclaim* (The Hague, Nijhoff, 1962).

Map 48: iconoclastic riots in Netherlands – G Parker, *The Dutch Revolt* (London, Allen Lane, 1977), p77; dissemination of printing – L Febvre and H.J Martin, *L'apparition du livre* (Paris, Albin Michel,1958), map opposite p272.

Map 52: T Bestermann, ed. *The complete Works of Voltaire* (Geneva, 57 vols., 1968-); P.M Scholes, ed., *Dr. Charles Burney's Musical Tours in Europe* (London, Oxford U.P., 1969); C.B Oldham ed., *The Letters of Mozart and his Family* (London, 1938).

Map 54: Great Fear – G.Lefebvre, *The Great Fear of 1789 – Rural Panic in Revolutionary France* (Engl. trans. London, New Left Books, 1970), p4; town councils – L.A Hunt, *Revolution and Urban Politics in Provincial France, Troyes and Reims 1786-1790* (Stanford, Stanford U.P., 1978), p136; federalist revolts – original material supplied by Paul Hansen (University of California at Berkeley) from his thesis in progress, *The Federalist Revolt of 1793: a Comparative Study of Caen and Limoges.*

Map 55: departmental government – J Godechot, *Les institutions de la France sous la révolution et l'empire* (Paris, 1968), p112.

Map 57: railways in 1848 – J Jouffroy, 'Aperçu du développement du réseau ferré en Europe', *Annales de Géographie xl* (1931), pp 504-18.

Picture Acknowledgments

The publishers wish to thank the following organisations and individuals for their kind permission to reproduce the photographs in this book:
● ET Archive: 25, 48, 101, 149 / British Museum: 58, / Museum of Fine Art, Boston: 34 ● Mary Evans Picture Library: 93, 116 ● French Picture Library / Barrie Smith: 32 ● Hirmer Fotoarchiv: 15 ● Michael Holford: 16 ● Hulton Picture Library: 2, 12, 14, 120, 129 top, 130 bottom, 138, 163 / Bettman: 130 top ● Imperial War Museum: 140 ● David King Collection: 134 top, 134 bottom ● Magnum Photos Ltd / René Burri: 161 top, 161 bottom / Salgado: 166 ● Mansell Collection: 102, 108, 112 ● National Maritime Museum: 71 ● Oxford Picture Library / Chris Andrews: 60 ● Peter Newark's Pictures: 132 ● Christine Osborne Pictures: 44 top ● Paul Popper: 84 ● Tony Stone Associates: 44 bottom ● Topham Picture Library: 79, 159, 160 ● Werner Forman Archive: 74 ● Zefa Picture Library: 129 bottom.

Editors: Frances Adlington, Jackie Hoy, Caz Philcox, Carolyn Pyrah Art editor: James Hughes Picture researchers: Jenny Faithfull, Christine Rista